SEX IN CONSUMER CULTURE

The Erotic Content
of Media and Marketing

LEA's COMMUNICATION SERIES

Jennings Bryant and Dolf Zillmann, General Editors

For a complete list of titles in LEA's Communication Series, please contact Lawrence Erlbaum Associates, Publishers, at www.erlbaum.com.

SEX IN CONSUMER CULTURE

The Erotic Content
of Media and Marketing

Edited by

Tom Reichert
University of Georgia

Jacqueline Lambiase
Texas Tech University

LEA LAWRENCE ERLBAUM ASSOCIATES, PUBLISHERS
2006 Mahwah, New Jersey   London

Senior Acquisitions Editor:	Linda Bathgate
Assistant Editor:	Karin Wittig Bates
Cover Design:	Kathryn Houghtaling Lacey
Textbook Production Manager:	Paul Smolenski
Full-Service Compositor:	TechBooks
Text and Cover Printer:	Hamilton Printing Company

This book was typeset in 10/12 pt. Palatino, Italic, Bold.
The titles were typeset in Franklin Gothic, Bold and heads in Palatino, Bold, Bold Italic.

Lawrence Erlbaum Associates, Inc., Publishers
10 Industrial Avenue
Mahwah, New Jersey 07430
www.erlbaum.com

Library of Congress Cataloging-in-Publication Data

Sex in consumer culture : the erotic content of media and marketing / edited
  by Tom Reichert, Jacqueline Lambiase.
    p.   cm.—(LEA's communication series)
    Includes bibliographical references and indexes.
    ISBN 0-8058-5090-2 (casebound : alk. paper)—ISBN 0-8058-5091-0 (pbk. : alk. paper)
    1. Sex in advertising.   2. Sex in mass media.   I. Reichert, Tom.
  II. Lambiase, Jacqueline.   III. Title.   IV. Series.

  HF5827.85.S496   2006
  659.1—dc22

                                                              2005016938

Printed in the United States of America
10 9 8 7 6 5 4 3 2 1

Contents

Part II: Sexualizing Products

Part III: Sexualizing People

Foreword

Please allow me to begin by being subjective and waxing nostalgic. More specifically, I would like to compare and contrast the erotic environment of my childhood with that which prevails as my children reach maturity.

MY YOUTH

I grew up on a farm, so for me sex—real sex, not erotica—was an everyday part of reality. When a cow "came in" (i.e., reached estrus), we made sure a bull was available to "service her," and we sat on the fence to watch and make sure the job was done right. We boarded a fine stallion on our farm, so the triumphant whinny that accompanied the successful mounting of a receptive filly was a regular part of my farm music. My beautiful Collie, Duchess, had more than a hundred puppies, and we never owned a male dog; so, promiscuity was a common occurrence, the primary ramification of which was that I had to find homes for more squirming fur balls than I ever want to remember. Some of our neighboring farm families had from six to 10 children. So yes, sex was rampant and birth control was largely absent; but I do not remember sex ever being "an issue."

This was also the case for my personal sexual socialization. My mother was a school librarian who often used her first-born as a test reader for potentially controversial novels, so we read together and discussed with candor Betty Smith's *A Tree Grows in Brooklyn*, Henry Miller's *Tropic of Cancer*, and many other novels with sexual thema. When it came time for "that" talk when I was 8, my father pulled out the sex education materials he had used with military personnel preparing to go on leave in Paris after WWII, complete with audio-visual aids and canned jokes. I'll never forget his ice-breaking joke about how to use a condom: "You take the rubber out of its wrapper, put it on the head of your penis, and unroll it—until you run out of penis or run out of rubber." Envision this complete with an accompanying diagram, and you'll get an accurate sense of my first "birds and bees" discussion.

Throughout my coming of age, "real world" sex was natural (which I later learned was not necessarily typical). In contrast, the symbolic media environment of that period was largely sanitized of either sex or sensuality. Consider television programming: Lucy's pregnancy (Lucille Ball, *I Love Lucy*, CBS, 1951–1957) was a delicate subject, and Rob and Laurie Petrie (Dick Van Dyke and Mary Tyler Moore, *The Dick Van Dyke Show*, CBS, 1961–1967) still slept apart in twin beds although married. The top-rated films of the 1950s were *Lady and the Tramp* (1955), *Peter Pan* (1953), *Cinderella* (1950), and *The Ten Commandments* (1956); for the 1960s, *101 Dalmatians* (1961), *The Jungle Book* (1967), and *The Sound of Music* (1965) were the top draws; and for the 1970s, the top-rated movies included *Star Wars* (1977) and *Jaws* (1975). None of these movies was sexually adventurous. Books were certainly tip-toeing into the realm of erotica during this period, with James Jones's *From Here to Eternity* (1951) and Henry Miller's *Tropic of Cancer* (1961) as examples, but for the most part, the best-seller list was dominated by Daphne du Maurier, James A. Michener, Frances Parkinson Keyes, and the like. In advertising, sexuality was making some breakthroughs, such as with the Maidenform Bra campaign featuring attractive models in brassieres who "dreamed they were (fill in fantasy here) in their Maidenform Bras," and Noxzema's spokeswoman with the "come hither" voice telling men to "take it off; take it all off." Normative advertising, however, was still relatively chaste.

MY CHILDREN'S YOUTH

The sexual environment in the late 20th and early 21st centuries, when my children are reaching maturity, contrasts dramatically for the most part with my own earlier experiences in coming of age. In terms of their early exposure to real sex, we still own a farm so barnyard breeding helped provide insight into the mechanical aspects of sex. But when it came time prior to middle school for Mom and Dad to explain human sexual behavior, the media and their peers had already filled our children's minds with so many false images that our lessons were less in the service of education than in correcting misinformation. For once I found myself agreeing with Neil Postman, who proclaimed that the media were largely responsible for *The Disappearance of Childhood* (New York: Delacorte Press, 1982). What had happened to my children's generation is that sex had thoroughly permeated consumer culture, was so readily accessible to anyone at any age, and was so distorted by ulterior commercial motives, that commercial pandering and an incredible hypersexuality had mangled and perverted that which is natural and beautiful about sexual behavior.

The media have to take much of the credit or blame for creating the contemporary sexual environment. Consider television. The transition from the innocence of Rob and Laurie Petrie to the coarse and blatant sexuality of today's sitcoms in less than three decades is truly remarkable and leaves one to ponder what the future can possibly bring. Regarding motion pictures, although many of today's major blockbusters are PG-rated, it is R-rated films that are the staple of most adolescents' movie viewing; moreover, consumption of pornography of all sorts has become a rite of passage for adolescents in many circles. Two media that were not even around in my own childhood—electronic games and the Internet—provide access to some of the most extreme and explicit examples of commercially mangled erotica imaginable.

Moreover, ready access to sexual messages is not the only issue. Today's agents of socialization (e.g., family, school, church) have not seriously come to grips with what these drastic changes in our social ecology and dominant symbolic environment mean for current and future generations of our youngsters. It is important for thoughtful and rigorous scholars to chronicle the evolution in the erotic content of today's media messages, for this is the very air that young people breathe today.

SEX IN CONSUMER CULTURE: THE EROTIC CONTENT OF MEDIA AND MARKETING

Fortunately, Tom Reichert and Jacqueline Lambiase have accepted the challenge of pulling together, organizing, and editing the work of many of the academy's finest scholars of the erotic content of media and marketing. In the current volume, these contributors not only describe the sexual content of contemporary media, they describe and explain how sex and sensuality are used to brand and sell all sorts of products and services in today's marketplace. This is an extremely important effort, and the talented contributors obviously have accepted the editors' challenge with conviction.

That challenge is now passed on to those readers who are the beneficiaries of this rich repository of scholarship. Within these pages you will find an authoritative profile of the erotic content of today's media and marketing mix. The question becomes: What can and should we do with this information? One of the great challenges of contemporary educators is to create critical consumers, to encourage critical reception and decision-making among those we are charged with educating and socializing. One dimension of consumer education today is to enable youth to recognize that their symbolic environment typically is filled with stylized images of sexuality, many of which are inaccurate, and to consider the ramifications of consuming a steady diet of such a sensationalized media message system. The concomitant scholarship on the *impact* of such images of unrealistic hypersexuality in media and marketing has lagged far behind that of *description*. However, to the extent we can draw upon the research on the perceptual, attitudinal, and dispositional impact of regular and prolonged exposure to hardcore pornography, we must come to grips with the possibility that such sensationalized erotic content has the potential to distort the perceptual reality of consumers, especially those young consumers who lack the primary experiences and critical literacy to place such unrealistic narratives in context. Hopefully this awareness will constitute a clarion call for a new generation of research into the social, psychological, and cultural impacts of the erotic content of modern media and marketing.

—Jennings Bryant
University of Alabama

Preface

Sex sells. It always has, beyond that cliché's inevitable appearance in media and marketing conversations. Obvious sexual availability serves as both attention-getter and deal-maker, and it is as old as our species.

Humans carry sexual content upon their own bodies—content that has been coded after millennia of sexual relationships. Shapes of buttocks, breasts, and broad shoulders have been hard-wired into our brains and then onto our minds, as an evolving grammar of both survival and pleasure. Mass media endlessly replicate these pleasurable images in advertising and in entertainment programming, to attract attention, to spark controversy in order to attract attention, to offer pleasure, and, ultimately, to sell media products and consumer goods that may be connected to aforementioned pleasure.

This sexual grammar, codified by scholars in this volume through qualitative and quantitative means, deserves our scrutiny because it is not only about content (buttocks, breasts, and broad shoulders), but also about form in much of our mass communication. Those cherubs of the baroque era and those angels of the Victorian age have matured into suggestively clad young women adorning our culture's most public spaces. Erotic advertising decorates New York's Times Square, London's underground stations, boutiques at international airports, and banner ads on the Web. Sex-tinged programming appears in video games, on talk radio, in movie houses, and within television content distributed worldwide to huge audiences.

Along with content and form, context matters a lot when sex happens publicly. Gendered magazines such as *Maxim* and *Cosmopolitan* are accepted repositories of erotic images, available at grocery stores and newsstands to people of all ages. Sex is safe in these magazines and their many clones. Baby Phat advertises its tennis shoes using the body of a nude woman plastered in Times Square, and Calvin Klein uses a woman kissing a man's buttocks on an urban billboard to sell jeans. Both images flew under the radar of censorship squads in 2004. Yet, when a classically styled Eve appeared in a mural on the public square of Pilot Point, Texas (population 3,800), the image's nudity and sexuality were contested and ultimately partially concealed in 2003. Janet Jackson's breast needs no mention, but it was an exposure too far, appearing as it did in a mainstream event covered internationally on television in 2004. Sexual games in St. Patrick's Cathedral in New York for the amusement of a Boston radio audience was too much, as well, in 2002.

In the intersection of content, form, and context, then, this volume's scholars meet to discuss sexual information as it is used in mass media to sell products and programs: What happens when sexual content created for adults reaches children? What meaning do sexual words and images have within the contexts of sporting events, trade shows, video games, personal ads, or clothing catalogs? How might erotic content created for 21st-century audiences evoke racial or gender stereotypes of ages past, and how do these stereotypes affect human relationships? What effects might sex-tinged images have on audiences, and where should the focus be for new effects research? Where are the current boundaries between pornography and mainstream sexual depictions?

These questions and related queries serve as heuristics for this collection, whose scholars seek vocabularies, codes, and schema for ways that sexual appeals are used in mass media for commercial purposes. In consideration of contextual boundaries, commercial forms, and erotic content, these researchers derive rich interpretations of sexually oriented imagery as it appears in Western media culture. Their ideas will matter to culture, gender, media, and marketing scholars—as well as to observers of popular culture in general—because these images convey important information about sexuality, selling, and programming strategies in a free-market economy that mixes boudoir with business.

ACKNOWLEDGMENTS

This volume is our second book with Erlbaum. We sincerely appreciate the opportunity to contribute to this area of research, and we are grateful for the commitment of those at LEA who see the value and need for contributions about sex in the media.

Once again, we appreciate the efforts of our tireless editor at LEA, Linda Bathgate. We appreciate not only Linda's insight and commitment, but also that of the series editor, Jennings Bryant. Especially, we appreciate Jennings' willingness to frame this collection by writing a foreword with his insights on the topic. Overall, Linda and Jennings, along with three anonymous reviewers, gave us valuable suggestions that increased the volume's scope and worth. We also wish to thank Karin Bates at LEA for all of her diligent assistance.

We want to acknowledge the extraordinary work of scholars who have worked in many disciplines to establish a precedent for this research. Their groundbreaking and continuing work, along with the studies included in this collection, continues to enhance the ethos of this important area of study.

Much gratitude goes to our wonderful contributors for their diligent and brilliant work: Julie Andsager, Jason Chambers, Kathy Forde, Jami Fullerton, Stephen Gould, Diane Grimes, Sri Kalyanaraman, Alice Kendrick, Tray LaCaze, Larry Lance, Dana Mastro, Pierre McDonagh, Debra Merskin, Emily Moyer-Gusé, Mary Beth Oliver, Carol Pardun, Art Ramirez, Jonathan Schroeder, Jamie Skerski, Stacy Smith, Gary Soldow, and Susannah Stern. We sincerely appreciate both your patience and perseverance as you often worked with tight deadlines and long delays between correspondence. We enjoyed the process and hope you did as well.

We express appreciation to colleagues in the Department of Journalism at the University of North Texas and in the Departments of Advertising and Public Relations at both the University of Alabama and University of Georgia. Librarians Cynthia Eagan and Stacy Anderson deserve much thanks, too.

To Jill, Beverly, and Christimae for their unflagging support for the value of this and related pursuits. And to Repp, a new arrival on the scene.

To Tom, Tacy, and Emma, as always.

List of Contributors

Julie Andsager (Ph.D., University of Tennessee) is an Associate Professor in the School of Journalism and Mass Communication at the University of Iowa. Her research centers on gender and the media, particularly regarding health issues and public opinion.

Jason Chambers (Ph.D., Ohio State University) is an Assistant Professor in the Department of Advertising at the University of Illinois at Urbana-Champaign. His research focuses on the history of African Americans in the advertising industry. In particular, he is interested in how African Americans and other minorities first entered the advertising industry and how their experiences have differed from that of their White counterparts. He is also interested in the role minorities have played in the development of consumer culture and in the impact of advertising on cognition among minority groups.

Kathy Roberts Forde (Ph.D., University of North Carolina at Chapel Hill) is an Assistant Professor in the School of Journalism and Mass Communication at the University of Minnesota. Her research focuses on the history, craft, and legal/ethical implications of narrative journalism as well as media literacy.

Jami Fullerton (Ph.D., University of North Texas) is an Associate Professor in the School of Journalism and Broadcasting at Oklahoma State University, where she teaches advertising and mass communication. Her research interests include the portrayal of gender in advertising and cross-cultural communication. Prior to entering academe, Dr. Fullerton worked in the advertising industry in Dallas, Texas.

Stephen J. Gould (Ph.D., City University of New York) is Professor of Marketing at Baruch College, CUNY. He has previously published in *Psychological Review, Journal of Consumer Research, Journal of Business Research, Journal of Advertising*, and *Journal of Advertising Research*, among others. His research, consulting, and teaching interests span consumer behavior and the self, technology, consumer sexuality, integrated marketing communications, product placement, ethics and corporate responsibility, qualitative methods, cultural trends and thought, and cross-cultural research.

Diane Susan Grimes (Ph.D., Purdue University) is Associate Professor of communication and rhetorical studies at Syracuse University. Research interests include critical organizational communication, diversity issues, whiteness, feminist theory (especially black and postmodern feminism), and (auto)ethnography. Outlets for her recent work include *Management Communication Quarterly, Journal of Business Communication, TAMARA: The Journal of Critical Postmodern Organization Science,* and *Journal of Organizational Change Management.*

Sriram "Sri" Kalyanaraman (Ph.D., Penn State University) is an Assistant Professor in the School of Journalism and Mass Communication at the University of North Carolina at Chapel Hill. His primary research interests pertain to examining the psychosocial aspects of new media and communication technologies. His secondary interests examine social and marketing effects of sexual and violent content in audiovisual media. His research has appeared in *Journal of Broadcasting & Electronic Media, Journal of Advertising,* and *Communication Research.*

Alice Kendrick (Ph.D., University of Tennessee) is a Professor in the Temerlin Advertising Institute in the Meadows School of the Arts at Southern Methodist University. In addition to serving in the American Advertising Federation and the National Advertising Review Board, her research has been published in *Journalism Quarterly, Journal of Advertising Research,* and *Journal of Service Marketing,* and she coauthored *Successful Advertising Research Methods.*

Tray LaCaze (M.A., University of North Texas) is an advertising professional and artist in Dallas, Texas. His research interests include gender representation in advertising. Work from his thesis was published in the proceedings of the American Academy of Advertising.

Jacqueline Lambiase (Ph.D., University of Texas at Arlington) teaches public relations at Texas Tech University. Her research interests include media images of women and men as well as computer-mediated communication. She co-edited and contributed to *Sex in Advertising: Perspectives on the Erotic Appeal* (Lawrence Erlbaum Associates, 2003), and her work has been published in *Journalism & Mass Communication Quarterly, Sexuality and Culture,* and in seven edited collections on gender, rhetoric, electronic media, and communication ethics.

Larry Lance (Ph.D., Purdue University) is an Associate Professor of Sociology at the University of North Carolina at Charlotte. He has conducted research and taught classes in human sexuality and sport. Dr. Lance has edited three books and authored about 40 articles in various journals and books. He has also presented some 70 papers at professional meetings and conferences.

Dana Mastro (Ph.D., Michigan State University) is an Assistant Professor in the Department of Communication at the University of Arizona. Her research examines the role of the media in the process of stereotype formation and application. More specifically, her work focuses on the impact of exposure to media stereotypes on perceptions of racial/ethnic minorities, the influence of media images on self-esteem among minorities, and the effects of television portrayals on interracial contact.

Pierre McDonagh (Ph.D., Cardiff University, Wales) is Lecturer in Marketing at Dublin City University. He teaches and researches in the area of marketing communication and social responsibility. He has published widely on social issues in marketing, including editing *Green Management: A Reader* (ITBP, 1997) and a special issue of the *European Journal of Marketing* on societal marketing.

Debra Merskin (Ph.D., Syracuse University) is a former advertising media director and currently teaches communication studies in the School of Journalism and Communication at the University of Oregon. Her research in cultural studies focuses on media representations of race, ethnicity, and gender, specifically on sexual portrayals in the media. Her publications appear in journals such as *Mass Communication & Society, American Behavioral Scientist, Sex Roles, Journalism & Mass Communication Quarterly,* and *Journal of Current Issues in Advertising Research* and in books such as *Growing Up Girls* (Peter Lang, 1999), *Sexual Rhetoric* (Peter Lang, 1999), and *Girl Wide Web* (Peter Lang, forthcoming).

Emily Moyer-Gusé (M.A., Michigan State University) is a doctoral student in the Department of Communication at the University of California, Santa Barbara. Her area of inquiry focuses on adolescents' sexual learning from media content.

Mary Beth Oliver (Ph.D., University of Wisconsin-Madison) is a Professor in the Department of Film-Video & Media Studies at Penn State. Her research focuses on the social and psychological effects of media on viewers. In particular, she is interested in viewers' selection of and responses to media entertainment and in media and stereotyping. Her research has appeared in *Journal of Communication, Journal of Broadcasting & Electronic*

Media, Media Psychology, Human Communication Research, and *Communication Research.*

Carol J. Pardun (Ph.D., University of Georgia) is Professor and Director of the School of Journalism at Middle Tennessee State University. Her research focuses on the impact of the media on adolescent sexual health. She is the former journal editor of *Mass Communication and Society* and her research has appeared in *Journal of Broadcasting & Electronic Media, Journal of Advertising Research, Youth & Society, Public Relations Review,* and elsewhere.

Artemio Ramirez, Jr. (Ph.D., University of Arizona) is an Assistant Professor in the School of Communication at the Ohio State University. His research focuses on computer-mediated communication, interactivity, and information-seeking behavior online. His research has appeared in national publications including *Communication Monographs, Human Communication Research, Journal of Social and Personal Relationships,* and *Journal of Communication.*

Tom Reichert (Ph.D., University of Arizona) is Associate Professor in the Department of Advertising and Public Relations at the University of Georgia. His research interests include media and politics, social marketing, and the content and effects of sex in the media. His research has appeared in *Journal of Advertising, Journal of Communication,* and *Journalism Quarterly.* He authored *The Erotic History of Advertising* (Prometheus, 2003) and co-edited and contributed to *Sex in Advertising: Perspectives on the Erotic Appeal* (Lawrence Erlbaum Associates, 2003).

Jonathan E. Schroeder (Ph.D., University of California, Berkeley) is a Professor in the School of Business and Economics at the University of Exeter, UK, and Visiting Professor in Marketing Semiotics at Bocconi University, Milan. His research focuses on the production and consumption of images, with specific attention to photography as information technology. His book *Visual Consumption* (Routledge, 2002) introduced a theory of visual consumption to the consumer research literature. He is editor of the forthcoming book, *Brand Culture* (Routledge).

Jamie Skerski is a Ph.D. candidate in the Department of Communication & Culture at Indiana University, Bloomington. Her research emphasizes the intersection of rhetorical theory, media, and critical cultural studies. Specifically, she considers the ways in which female subjectivities are discursively constituted and circulated throughout popular culture.

Stacy L. Smith (Ph.D., University of California, Santa Barbara) is an Assistant Professor of Entertainment at the Annenberg School for Communication at the University of Southern California. Her research interests involve the effects of television, film, and video game violence on children's cognitive and affective responding.

Gary Soldow (Ph.D., University of Minnesota-Twin Cities) is a Professor and Chair of the Department of Marketing at Baruch College/CUNY. His research has been in the area of interpersonal communication and persuasive outcomes in contexts such as personal selling. In addition, he has done research in advertising regarding effects of conflicting messages. His articles have appeared in *Journal of Advertising, Journal of Advertising Research, Journal of Marketing,* and *Journal of Public Policy and Marketing,* among others. He has also written a textbook dealing with personal selling from an interpersonal communication perspective.

Susannah Stern (Ph.D., University of North Carolina at Chapel Hill) is an Assistant Professor of Mass Communication at the University of San Diego. Her research is situated at the intersection of electronic media and youth culture. She is particularly interested in how adolescents experience and participate in the mediated world. Issues of gender and sexuality are commonly examined in her work, which has been published in various refereed journals and edited collections.

SEX IN CONSUMER CULTURE

The Erotic Content
of Media and Marketing

Chapter 1

Peddling Desire: Sex and the Marketing of Media and Consumer Goods

Tom Reichert
University of Georgia

Jacqueline Lambiase
Texas Tech University

Today, we live in a more conservative political environment that emphasizes family and religious values. Parents, pressure groups, and lawmakers soundly criticize the media for their portrayals of sex. Yet the outlets for and diversity of sexual fare continue to grow along with the toleration of sexual imagery. We love our media sex, and we hate it, too. (Sapolsky, 2003, p. 296).

Media scholar Barry Sapolsky's observation about our culture's love for media sex could not be truer. Young men's magazines such as *Maxim, Blender, Stuff,* and *FHM* collect huge profits but are little more than scaled-down versions of *Playboy* and *Penthouse*. Similarly, network and cable programs continue to push the boundaries of provocation and decency. For example, one writer described a scene from the prime-time FX Network dramatic comedy *Nip/Tuck* as follows: The "episode features a woman, down on all fours, having rough and verbally graphic sex with a man" (Friedman, 2003, p. 19). According to the writer, there were few complaints as advertisers hopped on board to capitalize on the program's success. So, on the one hand, it appears that marketers are giving us the sex we want and that our appetite for titillation is insatiable.

But the other half of Sapolsky's observation is evident as well, as many Americans seem to have had enough. In 2003, for instance, the Federal Communications Commission (FCC) received 240,342 complaints regarding television and radio programs (Peyser, 2004). The increase was exponential compared to the 111 such complaints received in 2000 or even the 13,922 complaints in 2002. In addition to complaining to the FCC, parents and other citizens are also targeting marketers that use sex to appeal to teenagers and young adults (e.g., Abercrombie & Fitch) with boycotts and letter-writing campaigns. Combined with policymakers who have upped the fines for shock jocks and music superstars—think of Bono's use of the "f-word," Britney and Madonna's French kiss, and Janet Jackson's right breast—it appears that at least for some Americans the line has been crossed.

Sex may thrive in popular culture and in promotional activities precisely because it has been sanitized from many political, educational, and religious discourses. Negation of sexual content in some spheres of life probably ensures that it will remain an active presence in others, and in our own time, this content is carried by mass media in its many forms. The collection of chapters in this book weighs in on the cultural duplicity noted by Sapolsky, by documenting and describing the nature of sexual content in America's public media and promotional spaces. That sex is present is no surprise. Far from heralding the obvious, however, the media and marketing scholars whose essays and research reports comprise this book paint an intriguing and eroticized vision of the mediated landscape. In so doing, they review pertinent research and break new ground in their analyses of sexualized media, advertising content, and promotional culture.

SEX AND PROMOTIONAL MARKETING

Most social science work that studies mediated sexuality in mainstream America falls within two related but distinct literatures. One area may be characterized as traditional content and effects investigations conducted by mass communication scholars. Typical fare includes content analyses of television programming (e.g., prime time, soaps), music videos, magazines (e.g., editorial content, covers), books, film, and video games. As a result of this work, we know that sexual information is quite common in mainstream media but that its presence varies between and among media. For example, Farrar et al. (2003) reported that 71% of prime-time television programming contains sexual language, behavior, and images. This comprehensive multiyear study, funded by the Kaiser Family Foundation, provides solid findings useful to journalists, policymakers, and those in the industry. Other mass communication scholars focus on effects research, generally characterized as microlevel investigations such as those that examine the influence of sex or beauty ideals on consumers' body images (see Bissell & Zhou, 2004; Harrison, 2000).

The second research area is commonly referred to as sex in advertising research. Research in this domain is concerned with the use of sex for promotional uses—to sell products and to influence how consumers think and feel about certain products or brands. As with media research, sexual content in ads also varies between and among media (Reichert, 2002). Academic researchers in this vein may be affiliated with mass media departments but are just as likely to reside in marketing programs.

As a metaphorical boundary exists between editorial content and advertising/marketing within these academic programs and within the professions, so too does a boundary exist between these two research areas. In an editorial-versus-advertising world, these separated fields rarely cite literature in the other area when reviewing or describing the content and effects of sexual information (for example, see Brown, 2002). The assumption is that both phenomena are distinct, although both are concerned with similar sexual content and, more importantly, both have similar goals with relation to consumers. Sex is added to programming to attract viewers, just as sexual appeals are added to advertising to attract consumers.

For example, in the media literature there is little discussion of how sex operates or functions in mainstream media beyond the implicit assumption that sex is used to attract the attention of certain audiences—those people who find sexual information pleasurable and arousing. In this sense, network promos or movie trailers can sprinkle in quick cuts of passionate kisses, erotic encounters, or disrobing as an implicit promise that more is in store. The same is true of magazine covers featuring partially clad women. As one writer put it: "The cover of any successful magazine is a shrewd advertisement for what lies inside" (Handy, 1999, p. 75). And, once inside a gendered magazine such as *Cosmopolitan* or *Maxim*, readers make little distinction between sex-tinged editorial content and the sexually oriented advertising that pays for content—these magazines, instead, become a seamless feast of eroticized eye candy.

Aside from simply attracting viewers, sex can influence audiences in other ways as well. For example, the hedonic value of sex can make the viewing experience more pleasurable, meaning that viewers will stay tuned longer either in anticipation of the erotic scene(s) or because what they are viewing is pleasurable. Consider the placement of cheerleaders and female sportscasters within sports coverage. The result is higher ratings and, subsequently, higher rates that networks may charge advertisers to reach those audiences. Similarly, music videos represent promotion for performers much like going on tour. Not only do videos represent programming content for consumer goods when aired on MTV or VH1, but they are also essentially ads for the artist and record company.

Simply, we believe that sexual content in media and advertising is used for similar purposes and that dialogue between these two should be increased instead of separated by a hollow dichotomy between advertising and editorial separations. Indeed, media content can certainly be considered a "product" as it is either bought and paid for directly (i.e., consumers who buy magazines, films, music) or indirectly (i.e., firms that pay networks for access to viewers; advertising).

Although it is easy, within the covers of one book, to include discussions of both promotional products and mass media products that have been sexualized, it is difficult to construct a single definition that fits this global approach. Courtney and Whipple (1983) defined sex in advertising as "sexuality in the form of nudity, sexual imagery, innuendo, and double entendre ... employed as an advertising tool for a wide variety of products" (p. 103). For the purposes of this volume, we expand on Courtney and Whipple's definition to mean sexual information that is employed by marketing culture or by mass media programming in order to sell goods or to sell media products themselves.

SCOPE OF THE COLLECTION

In addition to combining scholarly research that addresses both promotional and editorial products, this collection seeks to document these sexualized representations and to offer multiple perspectives from scholars working across several disciplines.

The first goal, that of documenting representation, meant that authors in this collection would fully describe, more than in any previous single source, the depictions and meanings of sexual content across the media landscape. Central questions that formed the foundation of each chapter include the following: What does sexual information look like? What forms does it take? What cultural work is done by these sexualized images? Who is consuming these erotic representations? And, who is sexualized? Not to give away the answers, but there is probably little surprise that much sexual content still consists of heterosexist images of women fitting the Western beauty ideal: slender, tall, curvaceous, and young. In many instances, this body type is displayed through revealing clothing as a woman strikes a provocative pose—either by herself, with a man, or in some cases another woman—in advertising, in live promotional activities, and in entertainment programming. Yet, other sexualized portrayals are evident as well, and some include men and homoerotic images of men.

Researchers in this collection not only describe these representations, but often, they also problematize sexualized depictions that target adolescent audiences or that rely on pornographic conventions. Another strength of this collection is its discussions of racial variance and racist ideology as it pertains to sexualized images of women. Four chapters specifically review and advance the literature on sexualized racial representations, and other chapters provide evidence of when these depictions are lacking or merely present in broadest stereotype.

The second goal of this collection works to cultivate an interdisciplinary approach, in a similar way to our previous Erlbaum volume in Jennings Bryant's communication series, *Sex in Advertising: Perspectives on the Erotic Appeal*. Like that collection, this volume brings together scholars who write from multiple viewpoints and methodologies in their explorations of the nature of erotic content. Sex can be conceptualized, operationalized, and quantified as much previous social science research demonstrates, but lenses that capture the qualitative essence of sexual information are just as necessary and relevant when describing sex in media. Although much research in this present volume comprises rigorous content analyses conducted by mass communication scholars, other studies utilize historical analysis, narrative interviewing, semiotic analysis, and other interpretive methodologies. The inclusion of both quantitative and qualitative methods strengthens the field of research covering sexualized media content, both by charting the patterns of sex-tinged media and by testing theories and developing interpretive codes that will inform future research into eroticized media and marketing.

Sexualizing Media

Exploring how sex is used to eroticize media, chapters in this first section of the collection describe the nature of sexual content in mainstream media forms, including film, music videos, video games, magazines, sports programming, and Spanish-language network programming. For example, Mary Beth Oliver and Sri Kalyanaraman report the results of a content analysis of sexual content in movie trailers. In addition to public relations efforts and the creation of "buzz," trailers are a primary form of movie promotion that is closely akin to product advertising. The authors report that sexual content is present in a sizeable portion of trailers, although findings are moderated by movie genre.

In a related sense, music videos represent a form of entertainment programming and serve to promote an artist's recordings. Julie Andsager not only provides a concise review of sex in music video research, but also builds on her past research by articulating a typology of the uses of sex by female artists in their videos. Andsager argues that women such as Britney Spears and Christina Aguilera, as well as Madonna and Shania Twain, sexually brand themselves—and often rebrand themselves—depending on the status and goals of their music careers.

Sex also finds expression in video game culture. Lara Croft, the animated and freakishly curvaceous heroine of the popular Tomb Raider video game, not only stimulated incalculable sales for the game, but the character also produced a lucrative cult following. To capitalize on this fandom, the Lara Croft franchise released two feature movies featuring Angelina Jolie, whose overt sexuality stimulated more fantasies among the games' demographic, that of adolescent boys. Beyond Lara Croft and Tomb Raider, characters and situations in video games are becoming increasingly sexualized. Some of these conclusions are presented by Stacy Smith and Emily Moyer-Gusé in a review and summary of their work relating to analysis of mainstream video game content. Among Smith's and Moyer-Gusé's findings is that character hypersexuality is much more common than instances of sexual behavior and sexualized violence.

Sexual branding works across other media, too. Certain gendered magazines for men and women have long included sexual information on covers and within articles to garner audiences for such content, and a new breed of men's magazines has capitalized on this formula with much financial success. One of these, *Maxim*, started publication in the United States in 1997, and it shook the existing men's magazine market by quickly claiming a circulation that reached 2.5 million readers in just 3 years. Popular press reports focused on the response of *Maxim*'s competitors—longtime magazines such as *GQ* and *Esquire*—claiming that their cover formulas had changed radically by becoming more sexualized to meet *Maxim*'s challenge. Although editors at other men's magazines denied *Maxim*'s influence on their own branding and competitive strategies, a content analysis by Jacqueline Lambiase and Tom Reichert suggests otherwise.

The introduction of female sideline reporters for sports entertainment is another way that sexuality and gender are used to promote and enhance media for male audiences. While the use of such reporters may seem to herald advances for women in sports broadcasting, Jamie Skerski reminds us that increased representation does not always mean a change in values. Rather, she asserts, women are sidelined as usual within an unchanged context of hypermasculinity and violent competition. She traces not only the creation of sexualized female images in sports programming, but also the circulation of these objectified images in men's magazines and on Web sites. Her study provides evidence of "extreme multiplicity," when multiplicity means not diversity, but more of the same (Fiske, 1996, p. 239).

Perhaps the highest rates of sexual promotional content exist in network promos—the ads networks produce and air to promote their own programming (see Walker, 2000). Jami Fullerton and Alice Kendrick extend previous work by comparing promos aired on Univision, a Spanish-language network, and NBC. Not only do the authors report that sexual content exists in 40% of Univision promos, but the authors also situate their findings within the context of sex and sex roles in Americanized Latino culture.

Sexualizing Products

That sex is used to sell products is no surprise. What "constitutes" sex in advertising is explored in greater detail in the following chapters, especially the types of sexual content advertisers place in their messages to appeal to consumers. The first two chapters provide valuable overviews of the types and levels of sexual content directed toward two audiences: adolescents and Internet users. Other chapters in this section examine erotic advertising content in specific product categories such as fashion, digital cameras, and beer.

An area of great concern to many activists and policymakers is the exposure of children and adolescents to sexual content. In their chapter, Carol Pardun and Kathy Forde report findings from their multiyear grant that examines the influence of mediated sex on teenage girls and boys. The researchers examined advertising in programs most watched by Black and White adolescents and found that sexual content in ads varies by audience race and gender. In addition to this information, the chapter contains descriptions of the nature of sexual content directed to these vulnerable audiences. For example, one disturbing finding is that most sexual interactions in ads occur between unmarried, and potentially uncommitted, characters.

Moving from traditional media to new media, in one of the very few systematic analyses of "mainstream" sexual content on the Internet, Art Ramirez describes a thorough content analysis of the prevalence of sex in ads appearing on popular news, sports, and entertainment sites. For example, Ramirez found that 17% of ads on news sites (e.g., CNN.com, FoxNews.com, MSNBC.com) and 23% on entertainment sites (e.g., BET.com, Eonline.com) contained sexually oriented content (i.e., physically attractive models posed in seductive ways). As important, Ramirez's sampling technique, involving randomized capturing of screen grabs, provides an excellent example of sampling Web content so it can be subject to traditional content analysis methods.

Moving from the aggregate to the specific, the next chapter explores how alcoholic beverages and sexual themes are intimately entwined in American advertising, despite corporate brewers' occasional abstinence from these themes. Although Jason Chambers is a historian, the three beer campaigns he describes in his chapter are rather contemporary, all occurring since 1990. More important, he answers the question: What do beer commercials featuring a "Swedish Bikini Team," a "catfight," and "twins" have in common? Chambers situates the three controversial beer campaigns as ways in which marketers attempt to sexually brand their products while appealing to young males, and he provides interpretation and context about why two of these campaigns were more effective than the third.

Tom Reichert and Tray LaCaze explore the use of sex for a product category in which sex is a common element: fashion. In their report, the authors examine how the images in Polo brand magazine ads have transitioned from preppy and wholesome to urban and erotic. Couching their discussion in terms of brand-concept management, the authors speculate as to how and why a successful fashion brand such as Polo/Ralph Lauren can successfully sexualize its image.

Fashion advertising also serves as the subject of Debra Merskin's work on pornographic conventions used by women's clothing makers in advertising. She uses film, communication, and fashion theories to weave together sexually oriented narratives that emerge from fashion advertising. While these pornographic codes may serve as subtext within such advertising, they work to normalize objectification of women and girls as sexually available, sometimes with violence as the next logical step in these narratives. Because female viewers of all ages are the intended consumers of such advertising from fashion magazines, women's conditioning by these pornographic conventions deserves our attention.

Theorizing about the "logic of pornography," Jonathan Schroeder and Pierre McDonagh scrutinize digital camera advertising in order to demonstrate the ways that pornography infiltrates mainstream marketing of information technology and the branding of products for largely male audiences. This logic works by creating desire both for products and for flesh through a kind of sanctioned voyeurism. These circulating images of eroticized women in digital camera advertising, found in print and on the Web, trivialize sexuality, place female "objects" under surveillance, and again normalize pornographic conventions in mainstream culture.

Sexualizing People

While the first two sections of this collection focus on the types of media and media products using sexual content for marketing, this final section focuses on people themselves, as participants in erotic branding, as stereotypes, and as consumers of eroticized media. As the ultimate expression of people participating in sexual marketing, the last chapter in this section analyzes the ways that people market themselves through sexy personal ads.

Corporate America often uses female workers to sexually brand products and services in live promotional activities—think of the Dallas Cowboys cheerleaders, "booth babes" at trade shows, or the Miller Lite girls with free beer giveaways at your local bar. Using in-depth narrative interviewing of female employees, Jacqueline Lambiase chronicles and interprets these activities through semiotic analysis. Expected by their employers to generate cocktail-party and call-girl vibes, these female employees use physical attractiveness, eroticized clothing, and well-known sexual scripts to sell products and attract attention. The study's findings confirm sexual-scripting theory as well as document implicit employer demands for sexual-behavior patterns well beyond the boundaries of explicit marketing policies.

How types of people become sexualized is at the heart of Stephen Gould's chapter. In it, he extends his theory of advertising lovemaps to explain how people and their contexts may become fetishized within fashion photography. According to Gould, no longer should stilettos, leather, and feet represent the full range of objects commonly referenced in discussions of paraphilic phenomenon. Using examples of people featured in the "Style" section of the *New York Times Magazine*, Gould makes it clear that future discussions of what people find attractive in others should be considered in any discussion of mediated sexual displays.

Audience research on effects and preferences is also encouraged by Dana Mastro and Susannah Stern, who study race and gender as critical factors regarding sexualized images in prime-time television advertising. In their study of minority representation in network commercials, these scholars discover an absence of minority portrayals in ads aired during prime time, but broad use of stereotyped sex roles and appearance when minorities are depicted. Indeed, one strength of this chapter is its summation of racial erotocization.

Dovetailing with this study of racial depictions, Diane Grimes undertakes a different methodology to describe sex and minority representation. Armed with a critical–cultural interpretivist framework, she reveals interactions present in a series of Planned Parenthood ads that appeared in a campus newspaper. Drawing on rich cultural sex stereotypes for Black and Asian women, Grimes argues that the ads—intentionally or not—reinforce certain perceptions when paired with images of White men in a sexual-health context.

Gary Soldow uses historical methods to demonstrate the wily way that marketers target gay audiences with homoerotic imagery that not only does not offend heterosexual audiences, but appeals to them as well. Through these images, sexuality—whether gay or straight—resides in the eye of the beholder, from ancient Greece to fascist Germany, and on to the contemporary androgynous marketing of Abercrombie & Fitch.

As the ultimate embodiment of "sexualizing people," a study by Larry Lance explores how people sell themselves when looking for romantic partners in personal ads. Lance reviews the personals literature, including his own work, as it relates to mate attraction and related concepts. As interesting, Lance reports an informal analysis of sex-relevant personal ads—those placed by singles and couples "in search of" sexual partners and a range of sexual experiences. His analysis convincingly demonstrates that product manufacturers and media promoters are not the only ones who use sex to attract audiences, brand products, and sell goods.

REFERENCES

Bissell, K., & Zhou, P. (2004). Must see TV or ESPN: Entertainment and sports media exposure and body image distortion in college women. *Journal of Communication, 54*, 5–21.

Brown, J. D. (2002). Mass media influences on sexuality. *Journal of Sex Research, 39*, 42–45.

Courtney, A. E., & Whipple, T. W. (1983). *Sex, stereotyping and advertising*. Lexington, MA: Heath.

Farrar, K., Kunkel, D., Biely, E., Eyal, K., Donnerstein, E., & Fandrich, R. (2003). Sexual messages during prime-time programming. *Sexuality & Culture, 7*, 7–37.

Fiske, J. (1996). *Media matters: Race and gender in U.S. politics*. Minneapolis: University of Minnesota Press.

Friedman, W. (2003, August 25). Edgy "Nip/Tuck" draws advertisers. *Advertising Age*, 19.

Handy, B. (1999, February 15). Bosom buddies. *Time*, 75.

Harrison, K. (2000). The body electric: Thin–ideal media and eating disorders in adolescents. *Journal of Communication, 50*, 119–143.

Peyser, M. (2004, February 23). Family TV goes down the tube. *Newsweek*, 52–54.

Reichert, T. (2002). Sex in advertising research: A review of content, effects, and functions of sexual information in consumer advertising. *Annual Review of Sex Research, 13*, 241–273.

Sapolsky, B. S. (2003). The attraction and repulsion of media sex. *Journal of Broadcasting & Electronic Media, 47*(2), 296–302.

Walker, J. (2000). Sex and violence in program promotion. In S. T. Eastman (Ed.), *Research in media promotion* (pp. 101–126). Mahwah, NJ: Lawrence Erlbaum Associates.

PART I

Sexualizing Media

$$\boxed{\text{Chapter 2}}$$

Using Sex to Sell Movies: A Content Analysis of Movie Trailers

Mary Beth Oliver
Pennsylvania State University

Sriram Kalyanaraman
University of North Carolina, Chapel Hill

The quick pacing of film cuts abounds with seduction: a close-up of three women's pelvises in bikinis and fishnet hose rocking their hips from side to side, two women surfers at the shore alluringly moving toward one another in an apparent kiss, a woman explaining to a male surfer that when his stick is "big" she "likes to ride it rough and hard." While it may seem that these images are part of a typical adult video, they are instead but a few of the scenes featured on a trailer, approved for all viewing audiences, for the movie *Charlie's Angels: Full Throttle*.

As with most trailers, this example is a fast-paced jumble of images and sound. However, with the motion picture industry now spending approximately $1.4 million for movie trailers per film (MPA Worldwide Market Research, 2001), the images and sound featured in trailers are far from haphazard. Rather, movie trailers are carefully crafted productions intentionally designed to attract the largest possible audience. Ideally, within a few minutes, a successful movie trailer should provide viewers with glimpses of the advertised film that are interesting, memorable, and enticing enough to encourage viewer selection over the hundreds of other possible entertainment choices (including other trailers) that are in competition for the viewers' attention.

Obviously, the formats employed and the portrayals featured in movie trailers take many forms and presumably reflect the content of the film being advertised. It is also important to note that most trailers are brief—ranging from approximately 30 seconds to 3 minutes in length. Consequently, producers of movie trailers exercise a great deal of leeway in

FIG. 2.1. *Charlie's Angles: Full Throttle.* Columbia Pictures. 2003 (not in analysis).

selecting the types of images that will be featured. This leads to some important questions: What sorts of images "make the cut"? What types of portrayals do previews "sell" as a way of enticing viewers to the theater? This chapter focuses specifically on depictions of sexuality and reports the results of a content analysis examining the patterns of the use of sexuality as part of that montage of images and sound characteristic of the movie-trailer genre.

ENTERTAINMENT PROMOTION AND VIEWERS' ENTERTAINMENT CHOICES

The importance of entertainment marketing is evidenced, in part, in terms of the sheer amount of money devoted to promotion. For example, recent estimates suggest that the four major networks spend as much as $4 billion a year in television promos (Eastman, 2000). Similarly, the average total marketing costs for MPAA films released in 2001 was $31 million, up from $12 million in 1990 (MPA Worldwide Market Research, 2001).

Is media promotion effective in increasing viewers' interest? In terms of interest in motion pictures, research generally suggests that promotion and trailers specifically are significant predictors. For example, Faber and O'Guinn (1984) examined the relative perceived importance of a variety of different types of information on college students' selection of motion pictures. Among all the sources examined, respondents rated previews as providing the most useful and important information and as having the most influence on their decision making. The authors interpreted these results by suggesting that previews are particularly influential because they provide viewers with a glimpse of what they can expect to see in the actual full-length feature.

De Silva's (1998) telephone survey of Michigan residents revealed similar evidence for the importance of movie advertising in predicting viewers' selection decisions. In that survey, respondents reported the importance of a variety of different factors that affected their entertainment decisions, including the presence of stars in the movie, the director, awards, advertising, and previews seen in theaters, among others. Although the story type of the movie, word-of-mouth interactions, and the presence of stars were rated as the most important predictors of movie attendance, previews, reviews, and advertising were rated as the next most important factors in affecting attendance. In addition, almost 20% of the sample mentioned that previews were the primary factor that attracted them to the last movie they had seen or rented.

In addition to descriptive and correlational data, experimental evidence also provides support for the idea that movie marketing affects viewers' expectations concerning what the previewed films will offer. Eastman, Bradbury, and Nemes' (1985) field experiment examined how promotional materials for a crime–adventure movie affected moviegoers' expectations about the movie prior to viewing it, and how those expectations were confirmed or not confirmed after the film had been seen. In their study, participants about to view the opening show for the action movie *Thief* were shown either a 126-second trailer for the movie, a 90-second "teaser" for the movie, or no promotional materials. The results showed that viewing the promotion materials significantly increased viewers' expectations concerning how much the movie would contain suspense, suffering, violence, and romance. Given other research suggesting increased effectiveness of promotional materials that imply the entertainment will be exciting, memorable, and "not boring" (Eastman & Bolls, 2000), viewers' increased expectations of suspense, suffering, violence, and romance may be indicative of a "successful" promotion.

SEXUALITY AND PROMOTION

Although Eastman et al. (1985) did not find that the promotional materials for *Thief* increased perceptions that the film would contain sexual content per se, this finding may simply reflect that the portrayals in the promotion did not feature images of sexuality. However, content analyses of television and motion picture content suggest that sexuality is a common portrayal. For example, Kunkel, Cope-Farrar, Biely, Farinola, and Donnerstein (2001) reported that almost 70% of all prime-time television sitcoms contained at least some type of sexual content. Similarly, Greenberg et al. (1993) reported that the R-rated films in their sample contained an average of 17.5 sexual behaviors and 9.8 instances of nudity, with sexuality particularly focused on the female characters. Given the prevalence of sexual content in television and motion picture entertainment, it follows that content analyses tend to report that sexual imagery is prevalent in media promotion as well.

Most research on sexuality in media promotion has focused on television promotion specifically. For example, Soley and Reid (1985) reported that 20.8% of the advertisements appearing in *TV Guide* during the 1982–1983 season contained references to sexuality. More recently, Sapolsky, Tabarlet, and Kaye (1996) content analyzed the number of visual and verbal references to sexuality on network television promotions appearing during prime time. These authors reported that approximately 20% of the promotions contained sexual behaviors or references, with an average of approximately three incidents per hour. Similarly, Walker's (2000) content analyses of television promos reported that 21.5% of the promos appearing in 1998 featured sexual behaviors (up from 13.3% in 1994), and 23.4% of the 1998 promos featured sexual language (up from 11.3% in 1994).

Given the increase in sexual content in television promotion, it seems reasonable to assume that the audience is perceived as being more accepting of and enthusiastic about such content. However, the idea that sexual portrayals serve as effective selling devices in entertainment marketing has received equivocal empirical support. For example, Williams (1989) examined the association of Nielsen ratings with the amount of sexuality and violence appearing in *TV Guide* advertisements. This study concluded that sex and violence in media marketing lead to greater program ratings, though this conclusion was based on the observation that five out of the nine television series that used sexual and violent images evidenced higher Nielsen ratings during the advertised period. Similarly, Shidler and Lowry's (1995) analysis of sexual portrayals in network promos found that the rate of sexual behaviors increased by 5.04 acts per hour during sweeps periods. However, these authors also reported that such increases in sexual behaviors were not predictive of greater viewer ratings.

Although the aforementioned studies offer mixed support for the idea that "sex sells," it is important to recognize that these studies employed aggregate data. Consequently, the specific effects of sexual content on viewers' perceptions, interests, and anticipated enjoyment are speculative. In contrast, research that has examined individual-level data has tended to report stronger effects of sexual portrayals, suggesting that sexual content and viewers' anticipation of sexual content are generally associated with higher levels of interest. For example, Ingold (1997) asked respondents in his mail survey to describe what their reactions would be to television programs in which the characters began to behave in an intimate fashion.

While over half of the respondents (58%) reported that such portrayals would make no difference in their responses, among the male respondents, 16% reported that they would enjoy the portrayals and 26% reported that it would make them more interested in the program.

Additional studies have reported similar findings in terms of how advisory ratings indicating sexual content affect viewers' perceptions. For example, Bahk (2000) asked male and female college students if they would be more or less likely to view television programs and movies that were associated with advisory ratings indicating the presence of mature subject matter, sexuality, violence, or adult language. The results showed that advisories for sexuality were associated with reports of significantly greater likelihood of viewing among both males and females, but that advisories for violence were associated with greater likelihood of viewing among male participants only (see also Bahk, 1998; Ingold, 1999).

Finally, the importance of sexual content in influencing media behaviors has been demonstrated through the use of film descriptions that imply different types of sexual portrayals. Specifically, Bogaert (2001) presented male college students with 14 different promotional descriptions of motion pictures. Among the 14 descriptions were 2 descriptions of films featuring erotic sex, 2 featuring women with insatiable sexual appetites, 2 featuring violent sex, 2 featuring child sex, and 2 featuring novel sex. Additionally, two descriptions featured violent but nonsexual themes, and two featured neither violence nor sexuality. Participants first indicated their likelihood of viewing each of the described films and subsequently selected two films that they would like to view in a subsequent study. Although participants reported the greatest likelihood of viewing those films devoid of sex and violence, they were most likely to choose to see the films featuring insatiable sexual women for the subsequent study.

RATIONALE FOR PRESENT RESEARCH

To summarize, content analyses of television and motion picture entertainment suggest that sexual portrayals are common, and particularly so in terms of sexual portrayals of females. Similarly, research on television media promotion suggests that sexual content is prevalent, with variations in prevalence (e.g., during sweeps periods) implying that entertainment marketers may believe that viewers will be attracted to media entertainment featuring sexualized portrayals. Consistent with this reasoning, self-report measures of viewers' television and movie preferences generally suggest that indications of sexual content are unlikely to inhibit viewers' interests and may, in fact, increase their enthusiasm for viewing.

As such, the present chapter reports the results of a content analysis of sexual portrayals in movie previews featured on video rentals. This content analysis is part of a larger study designed to examine both sexual and violent images (see Oliver & Kalyanaraman, 2002), though the results reported here focus explicitly on sexuality and the gender of the characters who are depicted in sexual scenes. Specifically, the purpose of this chapter is to explore two related questions:

RQ1: What is the prevalence of sexuality in movie previews, and how does prevalence vary as a function of MPAA ratings and genre?

RQ2: How is sexuality in previews portrayed in terms of the gender of the characters who are depicted in sexual ways?

METHOD

Sample

The sample of previews analyzed in this study consisted of previews appearing on 47 randomly selected titles of films released during 1996 or appearing in Billboard's top-20 rental charts during 1996. Duplicate movie previews were excluded from the sample ($N = 19$), resulting in a total sample size of 107 movie previews and 325 characters appearing in the previews.

Units of Analysis

The first unit of analysis was the movie preview itself. Some promotion materials were excluded, such as materials concerning audiences' reactions to the film, materials pertaining to how the film was produced, or rereleases of older films. The resulting sample consisted of movie previews for films with release dates spanning the years 1992 through 1997. The previews ranged in length from 23 seconds to 185 seconds ($M = 93.66$, $SD = 42.84$). The second unit of analysis was the character. Only individuals who were shown using dialogue or who appeared in three or more separate incidents during the course of the preview were coded as characters. Although both animated and nonanimated characters were included in the analysis, almost all characters coded (98.2%) were actual, human actors.

Coding Scheme

Sexuality. Within the previews, sexual scenes were defined as scenes in which characters were (a) shown engaging in sexual behaviors (e.g., kissing, petting, initiating or suggesting sexual contact, engaging in intercourse); (b) shown as nude or undressing; (c) shown in revealing or provocative clothing designed to increase sexual appeal; or (d) shown as the object of sexual gaze. Clearly nonsexual behaviors (e.g., a nude baby on a bearskin rug) were not counted as sexual scenes in this study. It is important to note that this definition meant that it was possible for sexual scenes to feature only one individual. Consequently, sexual scenes were coded as featuring only female characters (one or more female characters), featuring only male characters, or featuring male and female characters together. The total number of sexual scenes in the previews was calculated by summing these three categories. Analyses employing the character as the unit of analysis coded only whether or not the character was ever shown as involved in a sexual scene.

Demographic Characteristics of Characters. Several demographic characteristics were coded for each character, including age and gender. In terms of age, coding categories included child (15 years of age or younger), young adult (16 to 29 years of age), adult (30 to 65 years of age), older adult (older than 65 years), "aged with time" (i.e., the character was shown "aging" throughout the course of the trailer such that more than one age category was depicted), and "other" (i.e., it was impossible to determine the age of the character because the character took a nontraditional form such as an animal, a Martian, etc.).

MPAA Ratings and Genres.   In addition to coding sexuality in the previews, the MPAA ratings for each of the previewed films were also coded. In addition, the genre or genres for each previewed film as listed on the Internet Movie Database (www.imdb.com) were coded. Because most films were associated with multiple genres, all genres were included as separate variables and these variables were coded as "mentioned" or "not mentioned" for each film. The genres included Action Adventure, Animation, Comedy, Crime, Documentary, Drama, Family, Fantasy, Film Noir, Horror, Musical, Mystery, Romance, Sci-Fi, Short, Thriller, War, and Western.

Coding Reliability

All of the movie previews were coded by a graduate student who had been trained in the coding scheme and coding procedures. To examine the reliability of the coding decisions, a second graduate student independently coded a random sample of 25 previews. Pearson correlations between coders' ratings were used as the reliability indicator for ratio-level data (e.g., number of sexual scenes; Riffe, Lacy, & Fico, 1998), and a modification of Scott's Pi suggested by Potter and Levine-Donnerstein (1999) was used as the reliability indicator for categorical data (e.g., gender of characters). These indicators showed acceptable reliabilities for all of the variables coded in the movie previews: sexual scenes involving only female characters (.78), sexual scenes involving only male characters (1.0), sexual scenes involving both male and female characters (.96), gender of characters (1.0), age of characters (.77), dialogue of characters (.97), and character appearance in a sexual scene (.81).

RESULTS

Sexuality Within Trailers

Presence and Prevalence of Sexual Scenes. The first set of analyses was conducted to examine the presence and prevalence of sexuality contained within the previews themselves (see also Oliver & Kalyanaraman, 2002). A total of 249 sexual scenes were counted across the previews included in the sample, with slightly over half (56.1%) of the previews containing at least one sexual scene. On average, the previews contained 1.51 sexual scenes per minute ($SD = 2.31$), though this measure was strongly positively skewed (skewness $= 2.10$), largely due to a small number of films with a very large number of sexual scenes. For example, the preview for the film *Man in the Attic* contained 19 sexual scenes, the preview for *Flirting with Disaster* contained 12 sexual scenes, and the preview for *Fear* contained 10 sexual scenes. Because of problems associated with skewness, subsequent

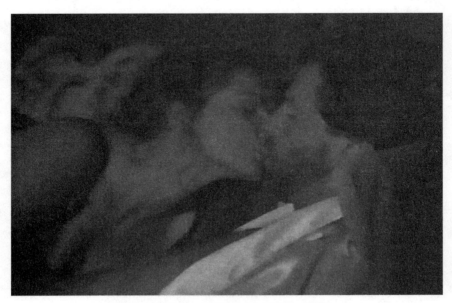

FIG. 2.2. *Desperado.* Columbia Pictures. 1995.

FIG. 2.3. *Desperado*. Columbia Pictures. 1995.

analyses of sexual prevalence either employed nonparametric procedures or examined only the presence (present/absent) of sexual scenes.

Gender Composition in Sexual Scenes. The majority of sexual scenes (63.5%) featured both male and female characters. Many of these scenes simply showed characters kissing, though a substantial number of scenes featured apparently nude characters in bed together in such a way that sexual intercourse was strongly implied. Sexual scenes featuring only female characters were the next most common type of portrayal (31.7%), with many scenes featuring women looking longingly into the camera, undressing, flashing their cleavage, or admiring their own reflections in mirrors. Scenes featuring only male characters were portrayed infrequently (12.0%), $\chi^2(2, N = 249) = 128.70, p < .001$, with most of these scenes featuring males going shirtless or approaching a character who was not included in the frame.

Sexual Scenes and MPAA Ratings. To examine the presence of sexual scenes as a function of MPAA rating, movies were first categorized as either R-rated or "less than R-rated" (G, PG, and PG-13). This categorization was necessary because the majority of films in the sample (57%) were R-rated, with PG-13-rated films accounting for 19.6% of the sample,

PG-rated for 18.7%, and G-rated films for only 3.7%. An examination of the rate of sexual scenes per minute revealed significantly higher rates for previews of R-rated films ($M = 1.73, SD = 2.46$) than for previews of films rated lower than R ($M = 1.24, SD = 2.11$), Mann-Whitney $U = 1059.50$, $z = -2.09$, $p < .05$. Similarly, an examination of the presence of sexual scenes revealed that a significantly larger percentage of previews for R-rated films (67.2%) than for lower-rated films (42.2%) contained at least one sexual scene, $\chi^2(1, N = 106) = 6.58$, $p < .05$. It is important to note, however, that the presence of sexual scenes in previews for films rated lower than R was almost entirely accounted for in terms of the PG-13-rated films. None of the four previews for G-rated films and only 4 of the 20 PG-rated previews featured any sexual scenes.

Sexual Scenes and Genres. Finally, to explore the presence of sexual scenes as a function of the genre of the previewed film, five different analyses were conducted for the genres action/adventure, comedy, thriller/horror, drama, and romance. Because films were often categorized as representing more than one genre, these analyses were not independent. Consequently, a more conservative confidence level ($p < .01$) was utilized to protect the familywise alpha. Table 2.1 reports the analyses of the rates per minute of sexual scenes as a function of genre. Action adventures tended to have lower rates of sexual scenes than did other genres, dramas and romances higher rates. However, these differences were significant for romances only. Table 2.2 reports similar results for the analyses of the presence of sexual scenes. Only romance genres differed significantly from other genres, with all of the previews within this genre featuring at least one sexual scene. Despite the fact that only romances showed a clearly higher rate and prevalence of sexual scenes compared to other genres, it is important to note that romances accounted for only 14 of the 107 previews in the sample.

Character Gender and Sexual Scenes

A total of 325 characters appeared in the trailers included in the sample. There were almost twice as many males (62.77%) as females (37.23%), and the vast majority of the characters were either adults (68.62%) or young adults (20.62%), with children (2.77%) and older adults (1.85%) representing a very small proportion of the sample.

The analysis of sexual scenes in terms of the character's gender revealed that a significantly larger percentage of females (48.76%) than males (29.90%) were portrayed as sexual, $\chi^2(1, N = 325) = 11.60$, $p < .001$. Because of the large disparity in sexual portrayals as a function of gender, additional analyses were conducted to further examine the nature of this disparity. The first analysis examined gender differences among characters who were

TABLE 2.1
Rate per Minute of Sexual Scenes in Each Genre by All
Other Genres

	Genre		U	z
	Action Adventure	Other Genres		
M	1.01	1.75	954.50	−2.00
SD	1.67	2.53		
N	34	73		
	Drama	Other Genres		
M	2.23	1.12	1000.50	−2.11
SD	3.16	1.57		
N	38	69		
	Thriller/Horror	Other Genres		
M	1.22	1.63	1085.50	−0.67
SD	1.78	2.50		
N	31	76		
	Comedy	Other Genres		
M	1.54	1.50	1216.00	−0.65
SD	1.91	1.59		
N	38	69		
	Romance	Other Genres		
M	4.09	1.12	190.50	−4.45*
SD	3.87	1.70		
N	14	93		

Note. Across all genres, $M = 1.51$, $SD = 2.31$ ($N = 107$).
*$p < .001$

young adults and among characters who were adults. Although gender differences were evident in both age categories, the differences were more pronounced among young adults than adults. Among adults, 29.53% of the males versus 44.59% of the females were shown as involved in sexual scenes, $\chi^2(1, N = 223) = 4.96$, $p < .05$. In contrast, among young adults, 41.18% of the males and 75.76% of the females were portrayed in sexual ways, $\chi^2(1, N = 67) = 8.23$, $p < .01$.

Whereas the previous analysis compared gender differences within age group, an interesting alternative way of examining these data is in terms of age differences within gender. That is, these data also illustrate that while the percentage of male characters who were sexual did not differ significantly among young adults (41.18%) versus adults (29.53%), $\chi^2(1, N = 183) = 1.73$, $p = .19$, females were significantly less likely to be shown in sexual ways as they aged (young adults: 75.76%, adults: 44.59%), $\chi^2(1, N = 107) = 8.93$, $p < .01$.

The second set of analyses examined the presence and rate of sexuality in the trailers as a function of the presence of female characters. Among the 103 trailers in the sample that featured at least one character, 29 of the trailers

TABLE 2.2

Percent of Trailers in Each Genre Featuring at Least One Sexual Scene by All Other Genres

	Genre		χ^2
	Action Adventure	Other Genres	
	41.18%	63.01%	4.50
N	34	73	
	Drama	Other Genres	
	68.4%	49.28%	3.65
N	38	69	
	Thriller/Horror	Other Genres	
	54.8%	56.58%	0.03
N	31	76	
	Comedy	Other Genres	
	60.5%	53.62%	0.47
N	38	69	
	Romance	Other Genres	
	100.00%	49.46%	12.62*
N	14	93	

Note. Across all genres, 56.07% ($N = 107$).
*$p < .001$

(28.16%) featured only male characters, 70 (67.96%) featured both male and female characters, and only 4 (3.88%) featured only female characters. A chi-square analysis was employed to examine differences in the presence of sexual scenes between all-male and mixed-gender trailers. This analysis revealed that while 34.48% of the all-male trailers contained at least one sexual scene, this proportion jumped to 67.14% when the trailers featured at least one female character, $\chi^2(1, N = 99) = 8.96$, $p < .01$. Furthermore, it is important to note that among the all-male trailers that featured sexual portrayals, none of the sexual portrayals focused on male characters only. That is, all of the sexual scenes in these trailers featured both genders or featured females only, though these female appearances were not coded as characters because they either never spoke during the trailer or were shown in fewer than three scenes. Finally, although all-female trailers were excluded from this analysis due to their infrequency in the sample, it is worth noting that among the four all-female trailers examined, only one was devoid of any sexual scenes.

The final analysis conducted also examined the prevalence of sexuality, though this time as a function of the *number* of female characters in the trailer. Consistent with previous results, this analysis showed that the number of females appearing in a given trailer was significantly associated with a higher rate of sexual scenes per minute (Spearman's $r = .39$,

FIG. 2.4. *Diabolique*. Warner Bros. 1996.

$p < .001$), whereas the number of males in the trailer was unrelated to the rate of sexual scenes (Spearman's $r = .12$, $p = .23$).

DISCUSSION

Findings from this content analysis offer empirical insights into the idea that "sex sells," a commonly accepted principle among producers of motion picture marketing. On average, the previews in this sample featured slightly more than one sexual scene per minute, though it is important to keep in mind that this average was inflated due to a few films featuring a very large number of scenes. With this said, over half of the previews in this sample contained at least one sexual scene, with over two thirds of trailers for R-rated films featuring one or more portrayals of sexuality.

What genres of films are most likely to feature sexual scenes in their marketing? The analysis of sexual scenes by genre showed that the only significant predictor was romance, with films in this genre containing a higher prevalence and rate of sexual scenes compared to films outside this genre. However, the fact that romance genres represented only a small number of films in the sample suggests that sexual portrayals are commonly employed in the marketing of a wide assortment of entertainment.

Perhaps the most consistent findings obtained in these results were the patterns associated with gender. First, these analyses showed that while the majority of sexual scenes featured both male and female characters together, portrayals focused on females only accounted for almost one third of the sexual scenes. For example, in the trailer for *Empire Records*, the camera focuses exclusively on a young woman in an extremely short skirt as she dances provocatively in front of a mirror. In contrast, portrayals focused on male characters only were very rare. In addition to featuring more scenes focused on female sexuality specifically, it is striking to note that approximately three fourths of all young adult females were portrayed as sexual. Finally, analyses of the prevalence and rate of sexuality in the trailers as a function of the gender of the characters present showed that trailers containing female characters were significantly more likely than trailers featuring no female characters to feature at least one sexual portrayal. Furthermore, these analyses showed that as the number of female characters in the trailers increased, so too did the rate of sexual scenes.

The patterns in portrayals associated with gender are consistent with studies that have examined sexual portrayals in a variety of other media offerings, including both advertising and entertainment. For example, Signorielli, McLeod, and Healy's (1994) content analysis of commercials on MTV reported that females in these advertisements were significantly more likely than males to be shown as very physically fit, very attractive, and as the object of gaze. In addition, only females in the sample were portrayed as wearing "skimpy" or "sexy" clothing. Coltrane and Messineo (2000) reported similar findings in their analysis of commercials that aired during heavily viewed shows in the mid-1990s. These authors reported that females in these commercials were significantly more likely than males to be portrayed as "sex objects," defined by such characteristics as being the object of sexual gaze, demonstrating "alluring behaviors," and wearing provocative clothing. Lin (1998) also found that female models in prime-time television commercials were significantly more likely than male models to be attractive, in good physical shape, as wearing provocative clothing, and as younger, among other attributes. Based on these results, Lin (1998) concluded that "women are in the vanguard of primetime television's attempt to use sex for selling products in the U.S." (p. 472).

The idea that images of sexuality would focus more on females than males is not surprising in many respects. Sexuality taking the female form has a very long history and is demonstrated in almost all forms of artistic and cultural expression—painting, sculpture, poetry, entertainment. What is somewhat surprising, however, is that movie trailers' attempts to lure viewers into the theater via the use of sexual imagery appear to emphasize a presumably heterosexual, male viewing audience. Of course, this interpretation is merely speculative at this point, as the present content analysis did not make distinctions between types of sexuality (e.g., implied intercourse versus romantic interactions). However, targeting younger male moviegoers appears to be an important function of trailers, and as such likely results in a preponderance of some types of images over others. As one

FIG. 2.5. *Just Married*. 20th Century Fox. 2003 (not in analysis).

movie marketer explained, "The objective of nearly every trailer is to get teenage boys' butts into seats. . . . And that means going for as much violence and sex as you can jam into $2\frac{1}{2}$ minutes" (Streisand, 1999, p. 56).

Whether or not the inclusion of sexual imagery in motion picture promotion is *successful* in capturing viewers' attention and influencing their entertainment choices awaits future exploration. On the one hand, research on the effects of sexual advisories on viewers' reported media interests suggests that sexual imagery may be an effective marketing ploy (e.g., Bahk, 1998, 2000; Ingold, 1999). On the other hand, research exploring males' and females' responses to sexually explicit entertainment suggests that sexual imagery may run the risk of offending or alienating female viewers, especially if the imagery is devoid of portrayals suggesting intimacy or romance (Mosher & MacIan, 1994; Murnen & Stockton, 1997; Quackenbush, Strassberg, & Turner, 1995). The idea that the *nature* or *context* of sexual portrayals likely plays a role in viewers' responses should not be understated here, as it is important to keep in mind that trailers featuring sexual imagery contain a host of other portrayals, including images of adventure, violence, and suspense, among others. Ultimately, future research employing experimental methods would likely benefit from examining how each of these types of variables alone and in combination affects viewers' interest and anticipated enjoyment (e.g., Zillmann & Mundorf, 1987).

Moreover, it is likely that movie producers create several different versions of a preview and ultimately select one that is assumed to appeal to their intended audience. While the differences between different versions of a preview, especially in terms of sexuality and violence, may be of particular interest to experimental researchers, future research may also employ both qualitative and quantitative methodology to examine the relationship between the amount of sexuality in the preview versus the amount of sexuality in the actual movie.

In addition to employing experimental procedures to examine the effects of movie trailers, future research in this area should also attempt to account for several limitations present in this study. For example, this research examined trailers that appeared on somewhat older movies (most from 1996). Certainly, future research should employ a more recent sample of films and may consider including a larger range of years to allow for examinations of changes over time. In addition, the films included in this study were predominantly R-rated. Although this distribution reflects the distribution of films released during the time period examined, future research should consider including a larger percentage of films with PG and PG-13 ratings so that a more thorough examination could be conducted on the types of sexual portrayals most likely to be viewed by younger audiences. Finally, the coding scheme employed in the present research did not distinguish between different *types* of sexual behaviors (e.g., kissing, nudity, etc.). Certainly, future research would benefit from employing a more detailed coding scheme that would provide a clearer picture of the nature of sexual behaviors that are typical in motion picture promotion.

With these limitations in mind, one clear interpretation of the data obtained in this analysis is that sexuality is a common marketing tool for motion picture entertainment. However, movie trailers do not appear to sell sexuality in a general sense, but rather to sell female sexuality specifically. Not only did female characters appear to be largely necessary for sexuality to be featured, femaleness, in and of itself, appeared to be sufficient to warrant a sexual portrayal. This further implies that when viewers are "sold" movie entertainment featuring female characters (and particularly young adult characters), what they are largely sold is movie entertainment featuring *sexual* female characters. The "success" of this practice and, more importantly, the *ethics* of this type of marketing are issues worthy of our attention and our future research.

REFERENCES

Bahk, C. M. (1998). Descriptions of sexual content and ratings of movie preferences. *Psychological Reports, 82*, 367–370.

Bahk, C. M. (2000). College students' responses to content specific advisories regarding television and movies. *Psychological Reports, 87*, 111–114.

Bogaert, A. F. (2001). Personality, individual differences, and preferences for sexual media. *Archives of Sexual Behavior, 30*, 29–53.

Coltrane, S., & Messineo, M. (2000). The perpetuation of subtle prejudice: Race and gender imagery in 1990s television advertising. *Sex Roles, 42*, 363–389.

De Silva, I. (1998). Consumer selection of movies. In B. R. Litman (Ed.), *The motion picture industry* (pp. 144–171). Boston: Allyn & Bacon.

Eastman, S. T. (2000). Orientation to promotion and research. In S. T. Eastman (Ed.), *Research in media promotion* (pp. 3–18). Mahwah, NJ: Lawrence Erlbaum Associates.

Eastman, S. T., & Bolls, P. D. (2000). Structure and content in promotion research. In S. T. Eastman (Ed.), *Research in media promotion* (pp. 55–100). Mahwah, NJ: Lawrence Erlbaum Associates.

Eastman, S. T., Bradbury, D. E., & Nemes, R. S. (1985). Influences of previews on movie viewers' expectations. In B. A. Austin (Ed.), *Current research in film: Audiences, economics and law* (pp. 51–57). Norwood, NJ: Ablex.

Faber, R. J., & O'Guinn, T. C. (1984). Effect of media advertising and other sources on movie selection. *Journalism Quarterly, 61*, 371–377.

Greenberg, B. S., Siemicki, M., Dorfman, S., Heeter, C., Stanley, C., Soderman, A., & Linsangan, R. (1993). Sex content in R-rated films viewed by adolescents. In B. S. Greenberg, J. D. Brown, & N. Buerkel-Rothfuss (Eds.), *Media, sex, and the adolescent* (pp. 45–58). Cresskill, NJ: Hampton Press.

Ingold, C. H. (1997). Responses to televised depictions of intimacy. *Psychological Reports, 80*, 97–98.

Ingold, C. H. (1999). Television audience's response to "mature subject matter" advisories. *Psychological Reports, 85*, 243–245.

Kunkel, D., Cope-Farrar, K. M., Biely, E., Farinola, W. J. M., & Donnerstein, E. (2001). *Sex on TV: A biennial report to the Kaiser Family Foundation*. Santa Barbara: University of California, Santa Barbara. Retrieved May 10, 2003, from the World Wide Web: http://www.kff.org/.

Lin, C. A. (1998). Use of sex appeals in prime-time television commercials. *Sex Roles, 38*, 461–475.

Mosher, D. L., & MacIan, P. (1994). College men and women respond to X-rated videos intended for male or female audiences: Gender and sexual scripts. *Journal of Sex Research, 31*, 99–113.

MPA Worldwide Market Research. (2001). *2001 US economic review*. Motion Picture Association of America. Retrieved May 1, 2002, from the World Wide Web: http://www.mpaa.org/useconomicreview/.

Murnen, S. K., & Stockton, M. (1997). Gender and self-reported sexual arousal in response to sexual stimuli: A meta-analytic review. *Sex Roles, 37*, 135–153.

Oliver, M. B., & Kalyanaraman, S. (2002). Appropriate for all viewing audiences? An examination of violent and sexual portrayals in movie previews featured on video rentals. *Journal of Broadcasting & Electronic Media, 46*, 283–299.

Potter, W. J., & Levine-Donnerstein, D. (1999). Rethinking validity and reliability in content analysis. *Journal of Applied Communication Research, 27*, 258–284.

Quackenbush, D. M., Strassberg, D. S., & Turner, C. W. (1995). Gender effects of romantic themes in erotica. *Archives of Sexual Behavior, 24*, 21–35.

Riffe, D., Lacy, S., & Fico, F. G. (1998). *Analyzing media messages: Using quantitative content analysis in research.* Mahwah, NJ: Lawrence Erlbaum Associates.

Sapolsky, B. S., Tabarlet, J. O., & Kaye, B. K. (1996). Sexual behavior and references in program promotions aired during sweeps and nonsweeps periods. *Journal of Promotion Management, 3,* 95–106.

Shidler, J. A., & Lowry, D. T. (1995). Network TV sex as a counterprogramming strategy during a sweeps period: An analysis of content and ratings. *Journalism & Mass Communication Quarterly, 72,* 147–157.

Signorielli, N., McLeod, D., & Healy, E. (1994). Gender stereotypes in MTV commercials: The beat goes on. *Journal of Broadcasting & Electronic Media, 38,* 91–101.

Soley, L. C., & Reid, L. N. (1985). Baiting viewers: Violence and sex in television program advertisements. *Journalism Quarterly, 62,* 105–110, 113.

Streisand, B. (1999, June 14). Lawyers, guns, money. *U.S. News & World Report,* 56–57.

Walker, J. R. (2000). Sex and violence in program promotion. In S. T. Eastman (Ed.), *Research in media promotion* (pp. 101–126). Mahwah, NJ: Lawrence Erlbaum Associates.

Williams, G. A. (1989). Enticing viewers: Sex and violence in TV Guide program advertisements. *Journalism Quarterly, 66,* 970–973.

Zillmann, D., & Mundorf, N. (1987). Image effects in the appreciation of video rock. *Communication Research, 14,* 316–334.

Chapter 3

Seduction, Shock, and Sales: Research and Functions of Sex in Music Video

Julie Andsager
University of Iowa

Popular music has long been the fulcrum of a symbiotic relationship between the fans and corporate media interests, using the artist as conduit. In fact, artists are often referred to as *product* in internal corporate communications. By creating public recognition of artists' faces and images beyond the music, music videos have enhanced the identification fans feel for certain artists. Videos are so integral to artist promotion that some critics argue they have become more important to the industry than the quality and innovation of music itself (Aufderheide, 1986). Through video, "the artist is also subtly selling a lifestyle, not just the music" (Chang, 2003, p. 18).

Interestingly, music video further offers the artist a means of "communicating an attitude toward the process of promoting one's self" (Gow, 1996, p. 66). If this assumption is accurate, the images that artists construct through video often appear either to embrace or denounce this promotional medium. Physical attractiveness and the ability to convey sex appeal have proven the making of many artists. In other words, to paraphrase The Buggles—from their prophetic video inaugurating MTV in 1981 ("Video Killed the Radio Star"; Segal, 2001)—video can kill a radio star, but it has the ability to give life to a television star.

Producers of music video exploit its visual power to emphasize sexuality in general as well as exploiting the sexual personae of musical artists, just like producers of advertising, television, and film. It is no surprise that sex is a seemingly omnipresent feature of music video. After all, sex has long been a focus of rock and popular music (Carey, 1969) as well as soul and country music (Singletary, 1983). Sexual content in video assumes a

31

variety of forms—from touching one's self or others to simulated sexual acts. Recent content studies have not recorded the increasing frequency and degree of sexual imagery in music video over time, but the anecdotal evidence of this phenomenon is unmistakable as clothing, language, and innuendo continue to become more provocative.

Music videos present somewhat of a challenge for comprehensive study. At the most basic level, their purpose is to serve as a form of advertising for an artist (Chang, 2003). Thus, in some characteristics—length and focus on product—music videos may resemble television advertising. Indeed, Pettegrew (1995) noted that MTV in particular is "a perfectly integrated text for commercial appeals to consumers' senses" (p. 491) because the videos and advertising look remarkably similar. Unlike TV ads, however, the music and lyrics are integral to the composite of the medium. This "unique and complex mix of visual and aural elements makes music videos difficult to examine" (Cummins, 2003, p. 1). Still, in content analyses, scholars have been able to apply operational definitions fairly consistently across genres and over time.

This chapter reviews findings of scholarly research conducted on sexual content in music videos since the 1981 inception of MTV. Specifically, I examine the ways in which researchers have attempted to capture sexuality, which may be omnipresent but is difficult to measure. The chapter expands on a typology previously introduced regarding how artists' images are sexualized through music video in order to shape their careers and target their intended fan base (Andsager & Roe, 2003).

SEXUAL CONTENT IN MUSIC VIDEO

Sex has been a mainstay of music video since the early days of MTV. Of course, videos were also presented on television in late-night programs such as *Friday Night Videos*, which aired on the NBC network, but economic pressures from broader audiences served by broadcast networks likely forced videos to remain somewhat family-friendly in order to garner airplay. In fact, a study that compared sexual portrayals on MTV to *Friday Night Videos* and WTBS's *Night Tracks* found significantly more sexual content on MTV than the other two (Sherman & Dominick, 1986). Because of its commercial function, music video must attract the audience's attention and convey a message quickly inside a truncated story line. Sexual stereotypes provide a means of both attracting attention and conveying a message quickly. Furthermore, Aufderheide (1986) argued that "music video's lack of a clear subject carries into its constant play with the outward trappings of sex roles" (p. 69).

The nature of sexual activity in music video has evolved over time in more or less the same manner that television—both cable and

FIG. 3.1. Britney Spears performed "I'm a Slave 4 U" at the 2001 MTV Video Awards clad in a python and little else in an attempt to top the striptease she did the previous year in her metamorphosis.

network—has, moving from a fairly traditional context to more overtly sexual portrayals. Early studies of music video noted that sexual content was often implied rather than blatant, focusing on flirtation among characters or innuendo such as strategically placed microphones or camera angles (Baxter, De Riemer, Landini, Leslie, & Singletary, 1985; Sherman & Dominick, 1986). Studies employing the same definitions of sexual reference have found that roughly two thirds of music videos contained sexual imagery (McKee & Pardun, 1999; Pardun & McKee, 1995; Sherman & Dominick, 1986). Jhally (1995), however, noted that when female characters in videos are not participating in such activities, they appear either to be preparing for sex—taking a sensuous bath, for example—or scheming to obtain it.

The comparatively traditional sexual content that these studies analyzed usually included kisses, hugs, light touches, and suggestiveness. As the 1980s progressed and competition for airplay became fierce, artists became more provocative. Prominent artists led by Madonna, Prince, George Michael, and Duran Duran toyed with sexuality and nudity and expanded the boundaries of sexual representations and societal trends (according to MTV, at least; see McNair, 2002). In 1990, suggestive sexual activity, such as pelvic thrusts, long lip licking, or stroking, was present in 89% of MTV videos (Sommers-Flanagan, Sommers-Flanagan, & Davis, 1993). Obviously sexual scenes of bondage, exhibitionism, and voyeurism appeared in less than 2% of videos, however (Sherman & Dominick, 1986). Suggestions of homosexuality, which would become more blatant in the late 1990s as lesbian chic pervaded advertising (Reichert, Maly, & Zavoina, 1999), were present in about one fourth of videos (Sherman & Dominick, 1986). Sexual or erotic content based on a more holistic definition comprised a moderate to significant role in less than 20% of music videos aired in 1994, though the percentage varied by genre (19.1% on Black Entertainment Television, 18.1% on VH-1, 9.8% on MTV, and 5.9% on CMT; DuRant et al., 1997). It is important to note that race plays a role in depictions of sexuality in music video just as it does throughout the mainstream media. African American men and women were more often engaged in sexual behaviors than their White counterparts on both MTV and BET in the mid-1980s (Brown & Campbell, 1986).

Although music videos vary across genre in terms of settings, character roles, story lines, and incidence of sexual activity, videos are remarkably consistent in systematically representing females as objects and males as subjects (Jhally, 1995). Producers of music video are frequently male (Andsager & Roe, 1999; Jhally; Lewis, 1995), suggesting that the vision and stories presented in the videos are largely grounded in male perspectives and fantasy.

Although Lewis (1995) rightly contended that music videos can offer "a unique space for the articulation of gender politics by female artists and audiences" (p. 504), content analyses certainly demonstrate that men dominate the world of music video in terms of sheer numbers. Since the inception of MTV and its counterparts, males tend to appear more often than females in music videos, at roughly a 2:1 ratio. Table 3.1 presents a summary of the gender disparities reported in a number of studies over time and across musical genres. These findings reinforce the notion that male producers and artists strongly influence video content. Target audiences do not appear to play a major role in this unbalanced ratio, because a study of MTV commercials found them to be much more representative

TABLE 3.1

Ratios of Females to Males—Artists and Characters—in Music Videos

Study	Year Videos Aired	Networks Sampled	Female Artists and/or Characters	Male Artists and/or Characters
Brown and Campbell (1986)	1984	BET, MTV	15%	78%
Sherman & Dominick (1986)	1984	MTV, NBC, WTBS	24%	76%
Greeson & Williams (1986)*	1985	MTV	11%	89%
Vincent, Davis, & Boruszkowski (1987)**	1985	MTV	21%	79%
Vincent (1989)**	1986–1987	MTV	25%	75%
Seidman (1992)	1987	MTV	36%	64%
Sommers-Flanagan, Sommers-Flanagan, & Davis (1993)	1990	MTV	32%	59%
Gow (1996)	1990–1992	MTV	17%	80%
Seidman (1999)	1993	MTV	37%	63%
Andsager & Roe (1999)	1997	CMT	28%	71%

Note. Percentages in some studies do not add to 100 because individuals may have been coded as androgynous.

*Greeson and Williams did not randomly sample videos, so their findings may not be representative of MTV in 1985 as a whole.

**These studies combined bands and duos of mixed gender with female artists, thus over-representing female artists.

of gender, with males comprising 54% of characters and females 46% (Signorielli, McLeod, & Healy, 1994). This more balanced portrayal was likely due to the fact that girls watch more music video on average than boys (Strouse, Buerkel-Rothfuss, & Long, 1995); thus, products advertised on MTV may have been aimed at girls more frequently than boys. Music videos seem to present male-oriented stories most often to young females, perpetuating age-old ideas about gender roles and fantasies.

Physical appearance is inherent in the way that the media construct sexuality and attractiveness. For female artists, physical appearance and sexuality tend to be emphasized more than musical abilities, as close-ups and revealing clothing are required components of their roles in videos (Gow, 1996). Two variables that researchers have attempted to use to investigate the importance of female appearance in videos are body fitness and the types of clothing worn by the artists and characters. A content study of these variables in MTV commercials found that female characters were significantly more likely to be coded as very attractive than men (55% of females to 2% of males), to be coded as very fit (56% of females to 14% of males), and to wear skimpier or sexier clothing (see Table 2; Signorielli,

TABLE 3.2
Clothing Worn by Females and Males in Music Video

Study	Year Videos Aired	Networks Sampled	Females in Alluring/ Sexy Clothing	Males in Alluring/ Sexy Clothing
Sherman & Dominick (1986)	1984	MTV, NBC, WTBS	50%	10%
Seidman (1992)	1987	MTV	36%	4%
Signorielli, McLeod, & Healy (1994)*	1991	MTV	55%	7%
Seidman (1999)	1993	MTV	33%	7%
Andsager & Roe (1999)	1997	CMT	41%	5%

*Study examined clothing worn by characters in MTV commercials, not music videos.

McLeod, & Healy, 1994). Table 3.2 provides a summary of previous studies' findings on use of sexy, alluring, skimpy, or provocative clothing in music videos by gender.

Early female characters in videos were portrayed in a narrow range of roles. Not surprisingly, these female roles were often based in sexuality, as "prostitutes, nightclub performers, goddesses, temptresses, and servants" (Aufderheide, 1986, p. 69). Supporting characters in top MTV videos of the early 1990s were overwhelmingly models or companions if they were female, but male supporting characters were more often workers (Gow, 1996). Seidman (1992) found that males on MTV videos in 1987 were most likely to be identified with male stereotypical occupations and females with traditionally female occupations, although males played more "neutral" roles than women. Seidman's (1999) replication of his early work using videos aired in 1993 found, however, that the characters in the neutral roles were female almost as often as male—and the incidence of gender-neutral roles increased. Perhaps more important, the proportion of people of color included on MTV videos rose by 26% (to 37% of all characters).

The range and levels of activity granted to characters and artists in music video vary by gender. Although gender stereotypes do not inherently convey messages about sex, they can help shape attitudes about how men and women should behave with regard to sexuality. For example, women may be portrayed in subservient roles or men may be portrayed as sexual aggressors. Most studies have found females in video to be passive or victimized (Rich, Woods, Goodman, Emans, & DuRant, 1998; Sommers-Flanagan, Sommers-Flanagan, & Davis, 1993). In one analysis, 80% of aggressors in video were the main characters, and about the same number were male (Rich et al., 1998). It is important to note that Black characters, especially males, were most likely to be coded as aggressors—25% of videos—but they were also most likely to be the victims of violence in music videos (41% of victims). Similarly, MTV males were more aggressive, domineering, and adventuresome than their female counterparts in the late 1980s (Seidman, 1992). Several of these characteristics changed over time, as—6 years later—the only significant differences between the sexes were that females were more affectionate and nurturing than males, and male characters were more adventuresome and violent (Seidman, 1999).

Traditional gender roles in music video have been examined in several studies through a media sexism scale (Pingree, Hawkins, Butler, & Paisley, 1976). The sexism scale consists of four points, in ascending order ranging from "condescending" to "fully equal." More than half of MTV videos by male artists portrayed women at the lowest level during the mid-1980s. Female artists at the time presented women in a variety of levels, leaning toward "fully equal" (Vincent, 1989; Vincent, Davis, & Boruszkowski, 1987). A decade later, female country artists' videos frequently portrayed women as fully equal to men, while more than two thirds of female characters' portrayals in male artists' videos were coded as condescending or traditional (Andsager & Roe, 1999). As shown in Table 3.1, however, male artists' videos were far more likely to appear on CMT than those of female artists.

DOES VIDEO CONTENT MATTER?

As is evident throughout this volume, sexual and erotic content in media is pervasive in Western culture and becoming more brazen as time progresses. Research on the content of music video indicates that these trends are readily apparent in music video. At the same time, however, music video airplay has decreased on television, as formerly all-video networks such as MTV, VH-1, and CMT have moved toward other original entertainment programming. Although MTV2, VH-1 Classic, and GAC (Great American Country) remain devoted to video, they are not widely available to consumers. Music video today is primarily distributed over the Internet, where videos are accessible on these networks' Web sites, artists' Web sites, and other media venues.

The obvious question, then, is why music video merits attention from media scholars and consumers. The answer is twofold. First, music video is a vital component of the complete musical artist package; it creates face recognition and an initial image, and, as I discuss in the following section, it is often designed to cement or expand an artist's fan base. Second, the primary target audience of music videos is adolescents to young adults (Sun & Lull, 1986). MTV, for example, has long been the primary network targeting and obtaining adolescent to college-age viewership (Burgi, 2001).

Music videos do appear to influence adolescents' sexual attitudes, and the gender of the adolescent can affect his or her interpretation of music (e.g., Wells & Hakanen, 1991) or a video (Toney & Weaver, 1994). The relevant research on music video effects was summarized in more detail elsewhere (Andsager & Roe, 2003), but I present a brief overview here. Much like the emotions associated with male and female characters in music video, high school males have been found more likely to associate confidence, anger, and pride with music than females, who tended to associate music with emotions such as hope, excitement, and happiness (Wells & Hakanen, 1991). This disparity is reflected in music video as well, where studies consistently indicate that males prefer videos that disturb them, and females find disturbing videos less enjoyable (Toney & Weaver, 1994). Toney and Weaver noted that college-aged males tended to like heavy metal videos and their female counterparts preferred soft-rock videos that the entire sample rated as romantic; it is no accident that these genres are clearly targeted at young men and women, respectively.

Several studies that have experimentally examined the effects of as few as one music video on adolescents' attitudes toward sexual behaviors have produced reliable and intuitive results. Overall, viewing of sexually charged music videos can increase the acceptability of premarital sex, with some variation of their influence due to gender, age, and family interaction (Calfin, Carroll, & Shmidt, 1993; Greeson & Williams, 1986; Strouse, Buerkel-Rothfuss, & Long, 1995). Unfortunately, because music videos sometimes link sex and violence (see Jhally, 1995), they can also increase acceptability of violence against women, again with some slight variation by viewer race and gender (Hansen & Hansen, 1988, 1990; Johnson, Adams, Ashburn, & Reed, 1995; Kalof, 1999).

A TYPOLOGY OF ARTIST SEXUALITY IN MUSIC VIDEO

If the purpose of music video is to initially introduce an artist to an intended audience, create his or her image, and then perhaps to alter that image, it is useful to attempt to understand the ways in which artists' sexuality is utilized in such endeavors. Clearly, a music video can contain sexual content that does not directly involve the artist, "but the association of sexuality via imagery in a video or the audience's reaction to the artist/song connotes sexual feelings that naturally transfer to an artist. It is often impossible to disentangle these components" (Andsager & Roe, 2003, p. 88). Although imagery and plots involving characters other than the artist may be based on the decisions of producers far removed from the artist's original vision, the sexual imagery that the artist is willing to engage in is of particular interest. The extent to which an artist will go to create a sexualized persona may reveal a great deal about the purpose of such sexual imagery in music video.

TABLE 3.3
Typology of Artist Sexuality in Music Video

	Strategy		
	Metamorphosis	Fantasy Fulfillment	Power
Purpose	Presents artist in a more mature or "edgier" light	Offers a variety of sexual stereotypes of the artist	Provides strong, self-confident image of the artist
Target Audience	New; expands to older and male audience, crosses genres	New and current; seeks to maintain base and add new (male) fans	Current fans; taps mature, though not necessarily older, female audience
Examples	Britney Spears, "I'm a Slave 4 U"	Britney Spears, "Toxic"	Missy Elliott, "I'm Really Hot"
	Christina Aguilera, "Dirrty"	Beyonce Knowles, "Crazy in Love"	Trisha Yearwood, "Everybody Knows"
	Faith Hill, "This Kiss"	Faith Hill, "The Way You Love Me"	

Because male artists have been granted wider-ranging roles and images in music video than female artists (Aufderheide, 1986; Gow, 1996; Lewis, 1995; Seidman, 1992, 1999), the production of female artists' sexuality is of particular interest. If women are portrayed in a fairly narrow scope, what messages might they be conveying about female sexuality? What purpose does sexuality serve for female artists' music videos?

According to a typology outlined previously (Andsager & Roe, 2003), sexuality performs three functions in music video. Sex may be used as: (a) metamorphosis for an artist in some kind of transition, (b) fantasy fulfillment, or (c) a form of power. The typology is displayed in Table 3.3 with selected music videos as exemplars; these videos are fully described elsewhere (Andsager, 1999; Andsager & Roe). In this discussion, I illustrate how these uses of an artist's sexuality are purposefully introduced (by producers, directors, managers, or, occasionally, by the artists themselves) in order to tap a predefined target market.

Sexuality as Metamorphosis

Like any metamorphosis, a musical artist's use of sexuality in this manner is intended to convey "the illusion that an artist has evolved into a different being, generally a more mature and edgier version of his or her former self" (Andsager & Roe, 2003, p. 88). The metamorphosis, similar to that of a butterfly, presents an entirely new version of the artist imbued with full-blown sexuality. For teen artists, the transition into adulthood often proves unmanageable, resulting in the end of their pop music careers, as in the cases of Tiffany, Marie Osmond, and Debbie Gibson. These young women did not attempt to employ their sexuality but remained true to their original, innocent images and fans. In the country music genre as well, female artists who burst onto the scene in their early teens have faltered in the transition from innocent girl to knowing woman; Tanya Tucker in the 1970s and LeAnn Rimes in the 1990s each experienced a decline in their fortunes, followed by successful reemergence after a hiatus. Country fans, however, tend to be a bit older on average than pop music audiences, which may make the metamorphosis slightly problematic.

More successful have been recent young female pop artists who have attempted to use their sexuality to redefine themselves. Britney Spears and Christina Aguilera, both of whom got their show business breaks as stars of *The New Mickey Mouse Club* when they were adolescents, scored their first major solo hits when they were 17. For Spears, the ". . . Baby One More Time" video featured her as a high school girl with a ponytail, a short skirt, and a bit of bare midriff. Aguilera's "Genie in a Bottle" showed her in loose harem pants and cut-off T-shirt. Both teenagers attracted a great deal of press, platinum album sales, and a huge fan base of girls ages 8–18. The timing of their breakthroughs also allowed the media to play up a competitive feud between the two—Aguilera as the more talented, slightly sexier; Spears as the cute girl next door.

But the late-teen years are a time of rapid growth, perhaps accelerated by fame and success. Spears and Aguilera both made bold sexual statements in the first videos released from their later albums. By the age of 20, both were thin and muscular, blonde and pierced, often appearing at public events in skimpy clothes. Each released a controversial video in which, barely clad, she writhed against male and female dancers in steamy scenes seemingly out of an orgy, with hands and tongues liberally applied to the singers ("I'm a Slave 4 U" for Spears, "Dirrty" for Aguilera; see Figs. 3.1 and 3.2). Their newly crafted images led marketers to note that there is "a nod to porn chic in the makeup, styling and fashion" (Stanley, 2004, p. 4) of Spears and Aguilera. Not too surprisingly, both videos drew a furor of criticism from the media—and the parents of the singers' young fans. The commentary notably focused not on the music, though even the titles suggest a racier streak than the previous hits, but on the women's sexuality.

Why did Spears and Aguilera risk the possible alienation of their established fan base with these music videos? While both explicitly stated that their intention was to attract new audiences, at least in Spears's case, her album sales subsequently declined dramatically (Hall, 2003). As with any drastic change in marketing messages, however, the sex-as-metamorphosis strategy gambles the loss of the primary fans. After all, while the physical changes occur within their idols over many months, the young girls who comprise the fan base for female artists like Spears and Aguilera see only

FIG. 3.2. Christina Aguilera's *Maxim* cover shot to promote the album *Dirrty* was cleaner than the video for the song. Although Aguilera wore slightly more clothing in the *Dirrty* video, the choreography was provocative.

the results in rapid-fire, easily comparable succession. Much of the identification these girls have for the stars—and, thus, much of the attraction—may be lost, because "young girls do not see themselves in such a rapid metamorphosis" (Andsager & Roe, 2003, p. 90).

It is instructive to note at this point music video's supporting role in the perpetuation of the sexual double standard. Sexuality as metamorphosis for female artists, as we have seen, garners criticism and, in some cases, decreased sales, suggesting the alienation of their fans. On the other hand, many young male artists, usually in their late teens or early 20s, have successfully separated themselves from the "boy bands" in which they began their careers, often by metamorphosis into sexually mature images presented in their solo videos. Examples range across genres, from Bobby

Brown, formerly of New Edition, who used metamorphosis in "My Pre-rogative," to Justin Timberlake of 'N Sync in "Cry Me a River" to Ricky Martin of Menudo in "La Vida Loca."

If sex as metamorphosis is a strategy for expanding or changing audience segments, it may also be effective for artists who have an established image. Chronically mature male artists have occasionally employed the metamorphosis strategy to launch solo careers distinctive from their previous work with groups. George Michael's break from the duo Wham! was obvious when he released "I Want Your Sex" in 1987, a video that was so sexually explicit for the time as to garner restricted airplay on MTV. Mature female artists have tended not to use the strategy; however, few female artists break out successfully from groups.[1] Female country music artists such as Shania Twain and Faith Hill garnered substantial crossover success in the pop arena after sexualizing their images ("You Win My Love" and "This Kiss," respectively).[2] Thus, it seems that the use of sexuality as a marketing tool may well pay off for many artists, albeit occasionally at the sacrifice of (a portion of) an established fan base. For youthful artists such as Britney Spears and Christina Aguilera who seek to mature from one album to the next, it remains to be seen whether the metamorphosis is worth the gamble.

Sexuality as Fantasy Fulfillment

Because sexuality and music video are nearly inextricably entwined, it could be argued that video serves to fulfill sexual fantasies. As articulated in this category, however, fantasy fulfillment refers to "the chameleon-like nature of artists who engage different stereotypes" (Andsager & Roe, 2003, p. 91). The use of sexualized stereotypes may occur across a variety of videos, as in the case of Shania Twain, who has assumed a different sexual persona in each of her videos, or within one video, as Faith Hill did when she portrayed a waitress, a dominatrix, and a nurse ("The Way You Love Me"). This strategy can be simply stated: "If you don't care for me *that* way, try this."

For the purpose of continuity, Britney Spears again provides an unam-biguous example. Having transitioned from a teenage girl to a sexual being before our eyes from the videos supporting her first album to her third, the

---

[1]Diana Ross from The Supremes and Belinda Carlisle from The Go-Gos are notable exceptions.

[2]As I have discussed elsewhere, male country artists tend to establish one image and retain it (Andsager & Roe, 1999, 2003). Male artists in the country genre are not imbued with the range of roles that females appear to be allowed in music video, nor do they alter their physical appearances for on-stage appearances over time. This discrepancy may be an artifact of the traditional nature of the genre.

music videos from Spears's fourth album presented yet another Britney. For the fourth album, the 22-year-old Spears and her marketing team attempted to attract "a slightly new audience this time. . . . She's growing up, and we want to make sure that the fans are changing too," said Laura Bartlett, senior vice president of Jive Records International (Hall, 2003, p. 1). Interestingly, though Bartlett noted that the music itself on the "In the Zone" album intended to target the gay market, the videos were clearly designed for heterosexual men.

"Toxic," released in 2004, features Spears in three roles, and each one allows her to assume a different hair color (blonde, red, black) as well as a different stereotype. First, she plays a sexually insatiable, blonde flight attendant in a skimpy uniform who cannot control her urges, to the point of seducing a balding, overweight male passenger in the plane's lavatory. Then, as a redhead, she is a futuristic passenger on a man's motorcycle; this sequence is inexplicably interspersed with sexually charged girl-on-girl scenes.[3] Finally, Spears appears as (apparently) a homicidal cat burglar, climbing the side of a tall building in a skintight suit to seduce yet another man, this time dropping poison in his mouth as she straddles him.

In her latest videos, Spears takes cues for her sexuality more directly from fantasies such as those that might be seen in soft-core pornography. Lesbian chic, or the use of sanitized images of two attractive young women posed in sexual ways, serves two audiences (Reichert, 2001). Primarily, it seeks to fulfill heterosexual male fantasies, but, as a secondary function, it may also serve young women as a source of instruction in attracting males. Thus, from a marketing perspective, the fantasy-fulfillment purpose for this album and the continuing evolution of Britney were apparent not only in its videos, but also in the explicit kiss that Spears and Madonna shared onstage at the 2003 Video Music Awards. "Clearly, the kiss at the MTV Awards segued into the Madonna single and the video in a big way," said Jive president Barry Weiss (Hall, 2003, p. 1). What is important to note about Spears's use of the fantasy-fulfillment video strategy is that she has, perhaps, taken her sexuality to its extreme—for network television, at least—at the age of 22.

A more typical example of sexuality as fantasy fulfillment can be found in Beyonce Knowles (see Fig. 3.3). The same age as Spears, Knowles made her career breakthrough in the girl group Destiny's Child, then released her first solo album in 2003. In the "Crazy in Love" video released from that album, Beyonce (as she is commonly known) appears as a girl of the "hood" in satin hot pants, baseball jacket, and cap and as a model

---

[3]The first video released from "In the Zone" was "Me Against the Music," in which Spears and Madonna hinted at a same-sex relationship, though Madonna vanished before they could kiss.

FIG. 3.3. Though Beyonce Knowles portrays a slightly more wholesome image than many of her peers, she is not above grinding against male dancers at her concerts, as in this 2004 performance with an unnamed dancer.

wearing a dress with plunging neckline on the catwalk, among other roles. Her subsequent video, "Me, Myself and I," alternates imagery of Knowles with black hair, nude in a bath, with imagery of her as a blonde lounging about in a slinky black gown. Despite the hint of nudity in the latter video, Knowles never appears in the extreme costumes nor engages in the exaggerated sexuality of Spears (or Aguilera). Her sexuality is suggestive, not blatant.

Why the difference in marketing? Outside of music, Knowles emphasizes her family life and the importance of church in her life, projecting a more stable image than Spears. Thus, the focus of media attention is her talent rather than her sexuality. Further, the age-old stereotype of African American women as being overly sexual may also influence Knowles and her producers to avoid associating her image with such tried-and-untrue notions.

Sexuality as Power

Perhaps the least frequent use of sexuality in music videos is that of the third category of this typology. For female artists, the use of their sexuality as *power to* control their own fate (French, 1987) is relatively rare. *Power to* means that the artists "are very clearly in charge of a situation, and if their sexuality figures in the video, they seem to have wanted it that way" (Andsager & Roe, 2003, p. 93). In other words, the artist presents herself as the subject, rather than the object, of the viewer's gaze; she tends to look directly into the camera and frequently appears to be amused by or dismissive of the viewer's interest in her sexuality (Andsager, 1999). Unlike the previous two categories, which seem unlimited by genre, sexuality as power seldom occurs in pop music, but is a frequent strategy in rap by female artists (Roberts, 1991) as well as some country music (Andsager, 1999).

Among the artists who have demonstrated sexuality as power within their music videos are Madonna, country artists Trisha Yearwood and Terri Clark, and hip-hop star Missy Elliott. Though the messages emanating from Madonna may be mixed at times—most notably in "Express Yourself," in which she is clearly powerful as an executive, to the point of using the macho crotch-grabbing gesture first employed by Michael Jackson, then is shown chained to a bed and bruised—she always implies by her gaze that she is in control of the situation. In "Material Girl," Madonna's tribute to Marilyn Monroe, she holds a group of male dancers entranced, obviously toying with them while winking at the audience.

Elliott, who underwent a shift in image when she lost a significant amount of weight, did not use her slimmer figure to move to a more sexualized image. Rather, she continues to rely on close-ups of her face interspersed with some choreography. That these women are confident about themselves is evident by their facial expressions. Lewis (1995) suggests that this type of female perspective portrays "female fantasies of the overthrow of male domination and the forming of alliances among women" (p. 504).

It is important to note the difference between *power to* and *power over* (French, 1987). If *power to* refers to the ability to control one's own fate, then *power over* means the ability to control another person's choices. This is the

FIG. 3.4. In the video-within-a-video sequences of "Jenny From the Block," Jennifer Lopez frequently pulled her shirt up while pushing the waistband of her pants down, as if to inject more sexuality into the "video." Ironically, the supposed video shoot featured Lopez in more clothing than she has worn in any of her real videos.

type of power that male artists are frequently granted within music video. As Jhally (1995) argued, female characters in male artists' videos appear to be in states of suspension, merely waiting for their men to return for sex. Often, female characters appear in groups to service a male artist, rather than individually seeking his full attention. This scenario is illustrated in many rap videos, perhaps most notably Snoop Doggy Dogg's 1994 "Gin and Juice" video, in which he enters a bedroom with several young women as his friend hands him a roll of condoms.

The distinction between *power to* and *power over* may be largely an artifact of traditional gender roles. That is, females are taught to use their sexual charms in an attempt to get what they need or want; males are socialized to believe that sex is something at their disposal. The sometimes subtle portrayal of these relationships within music video may be impossible outside the lens of gender through which we, as viewers, perceive the world.

This typology of sexuality in music video is, at most, a framework for understanding how (female) artists are marketed for audience consumption. It is not intended to be exhaustive; indeed, the majority of music videos produced for female artists do not fall within these three categories. The bulk tend to feature a woman or girl as the object of gaze, whether that of the viewer or a male character, in some kind of romantic story line. These videos tend not to be overly sexual in nature, though obviously the artist is depicted as a sexual being, but are intended as traditional videos to garner airtime and please—but not risk offending—the audience. Examples include many of Jennifer Lopez's videos; for instance, in "Jenny from the Block," the story line is that of tabloid reporters following Lopez as she shoots a music video, with scenes from her "personal life" interspersed (see Fig. 3.4). Here, Lopez is pictured in a bikini, in jeans and T-shirt, and a variety of other costumes; she kisses her boyfriend; she dances; but there is none of the blatant, often gratuitous sexual imagery depicted in the sexuality as fantasy fulfillment or sexuality as metamorphosis categories of the typology. Because Lopez is the object of the viewers' gaze for the entire video, however, this cannot be classified as sexuality as power. Moreover, her strategy in the music video being filmed within the music video is to dance in a slightly sexually provocative way, but it is clear that she is being directed to do so.

WHAT IS THE FUTURE OF SEXUALITY IN MUSIC VIDEO?

Music videos were developed as marketing tools to construct an artist's image and, in so doing, to tap specific audiences of fans. The early music videos of the 1980s may have been titillating at times, but the music video of the 21st century is another breed altogether. Sexuality is a much more prominent feature, with videos continually pushing the boundaries of what is acceptable. Near nudity, lesbian chic, and (compared to network television) more-than-suggestive depictions of sexual activity abound. Thus, many artists attempt to compete for airplay, media attention, and record sales by exploiting their sexuality to greater degrees.

For female artists, who have never enjoyed as much video airtime as their male counterparts, the challenge of competing on the sexual playing field is particularly daunting. Unlike male artists, they rarely use nearly nude female models and dancers as props that simultaneously express sexual desire for the artist. Female artists must toe a fine but apparently blurry line between maintaining parentally approved images (at least for the youngest artists) and generating enough sales to retain their professional contracts and status. These competing goals present many female artists with a quandary: If a female artist does not rely on her sexuality to develop a comparatively small but devoted audience, can she hold onto a recording contract?

The question may already be moot. At the same time as MTV and other music video-based networks have decreased the amount of hours devoted to playing videos, the Internet has allowed audiences to go directly to artists' own Web sites to view their music videos. For artists and their producers, the problem becomes one of attracting media attention so that audiences will be drawn to seek product from new or fading artists. Thus, over the past months, television viewers have been subjected to a new kind of marketing strategy—the sexual stunt on live programs. In 2003, Britney Spears and Madonna performed that extensive, open-mouthed kiss on the music awards show, igniting a frenzy of media attention. Not to be outdone, Janet Jackson followed 6 months later with a Super Bowl halftime performance in which Justin Timberlake ripped the breastplate off her suit, exposing her breast. The latter incident sparked an investigation by the Federal Communications Commission. In both cases, the singers had new albums to promote.

Music video may be on its way to obsolescence, but the sexual strategies included in the typology discussed in this chapter may be here to stay. Only time will tell whether audiences will continue to notice and evaluate female artists for their sexuality, and where the boundaries of such strategies lie.

REFERENCES

Andsager, J. L. (1999). Contradictions in the country: Rituals of sexual subordination and strength in music video. In M. G. Carstarphen and S. C. Zavoina (Eds.), *Sexual rhetoric: Media perspectives on sexuality, gender, and identity* (pp. 224–237). Westport, CT: Greenwood.

Andsager, J. L., & Roe, K. (1999). Country music video in country's year of the woman. *Journal of Communication, 49*, 69–82.

Andsager, J. L., & Roe, K. (2003). "What's your definition of dirty, baby?": Sex in music video. *Sexuality & Culture, 7*, 79–97.

Aufderheide, P. (1986). Music videos: The look of the sound. *Journal of Communication, 36*, 57–78.

Baxter, R. L., De Riemer, C., Landini, A., Leslie, L., & Singletary, M. W. (1985). A content analysis of music videos. *Journal of Broadcasting & Electronic Media, 29*, 333–340.

Brown, J. D., & Campbell, K. (1986). Race and gender in music videos: The same beat but a different drummer. *Journal of Communication, 36*(1), 94–106.

Burgi, M. (2001, June 11). In-your-face music. *Media Week*, p. SR8.

Calfin, M. S., Carroll, J. L., & Shmidt, Jr., J. (1993). Viewing music-videotapes before taking a test of premarital sexual attitudes. *Psychological Reports, 72*, 475–481.

Carey, J. T. (1969). Changing courtship patterns in the popular song. *American Journal of Sociology, 74*, 720–731.

Chang, S. (2003, November 29). Product placement deals thrive in music videos. *Billboard*, p. 18.

Cummins, G. (2003). *Sex in music videos: A review of the content and effects.* Unpublished manuscript. University of Alabama.

DuRant, R. H., Rome, E. S., Rich, M., Allred, E., Emans, S. J., & Woods, E. R. (1997). Tobacco and alcohol use behaviors portrayed in music videos: A content analysis. *American Journal of Public Health, 87*, 1131–1135.

French, M. (1987). *Beyond power: On women, men, and morals.* New York: Ballantine.

Gow, J. (1996). Reconsidering gender roles on MTV: Depictions in the most popular music videos of the early 1990s. *Communication Reports, 9*, 151–162.

Greeson, L. E., & Williams, R. A. (1986). Social implications of music videos for youth: An analysis of the content and effects of MTV. *Youth & Society, 18*, 177–189.

Hall, R. (2003, November 22). Britney sexes up the music. *Billboard*, p. 1.

Hansen, C. H., & Hansen, R. D. (1988). How rock music videos can change what is seen when boy meets girl: Priming stereotypic appraisal of social interactions. *Sex Roles, 19*, 287–316.

Hansen, C. H., & Hansen, R. D. (1990). The influence of sex and violence on the appeal of rock videos. *Communication Research, 17*, 212–234.

Jhally, S. (1995). *Dreamworlds II: Desire, sex, and power in music video.* Northampton, MA: Media Education Foundation.

Johnson, J. D., Adams, M. S., Ashburn, L., & Reed, W. (1995). Differential gender effects of exposure to rap music on African American adolescents' acceptance of teen dating violence. *Sex Roles, 33*, 597–605.

Kalof, L. (1999). The effects of gender and music video imagery on sexual attitudes. *Journal of Social Psychology, 139*, 378–385.

Lewis, L. A. (1995). Form and female authorship in music video. In G. Dines & J. M. Humez, *Gender, race and class in media* (pp. 499–507). Thousand Oaks, CA: Sage.

McKee, K. B., & Pardun, C. J. (1999). Reading the video: A qualitative study of religious images in music videos. *Journal of Broadcasting & Electronic Media, 43*, 110–122.

McNair, B. (2002). *Striptease culture: Sex, media and the democratisation of desire.* London: Routledge.

Pardun, C. J., & McKee, K. B. (1995). Strange bedfellows: Symbols of religion and sexuality on MTV. *Youth & Society, 26*, 438–449.

Pardun, C. J., & McKee, K. B. (1996). Mixed messages: The relationship between sexual and religious imagery in rock, country, and Christian videos. *Communication Reports, 9*, 163–172.

Pettegrew, J. (1995). A post-modernist moment: 1980s commercial culture and the founding of MTV. In G. Dines & J. M. Humez (Eds.), *Gender, race and class in media* (pp. 488–498). Thousand Oaks, CA: Sage.

Pingree, S., Hawkins, R. P., Butler, M., & Paisley, W. (1976). A scale for sexism. *Journal of Communication, 26*(4), 193–200.

Reichert, T. (2001). "Lesbian chic" imagery in advertising: Interpretations and insights of female same-sex eroticism. *Journal of Current Issues and Research in Advertising, 23*, 9–22.

Reichert, T., Maly, K. R., & Zavoina, S. C. (1999). Designed for (male) pleasure: The myth of lesbian chic in mainstream advertising. In M. Carstarphen & S. C. Zavoina (Eds.), *Sexual rhetoric: Media perspectives on sexuality, gender, and identity* (pp. 123–134). Westport, CT: Greenwood.

Rich, M., Woods, E. R., Goodman, E., Emans, S. J., & DuRant, R. H. (1998). Aggressors or victims: Gender and race in music video violence. *Pediatrics, 101*, 669–674.

Roberts, R. (1991). Music videos, performance and resistance: Feminist rappers. *Journal of Popular Culture, 25*, 141–152.

Segal, D. (2001, August 1). Arrested development: At 20, the music channel refuses to grow up. *Washington Post*, p. C1.

Seidman, S. A. (1992). An investigation of sex-role stereotyping in music videos. *Journal of Broadcasting & Electronic Media, 36*, 209–216.

Seidman, S. A. (1999). Revisiting sex-role stereotyping in MTV videos. *International Journal of Instructional Media, 26*, 11–23.

Sherman, B. L., & Dominick, J. R. (1986). Violence and sex in music videos: TV and rock 'n' roll. *Journal of Communication, 36*(1), 79–93.

Signorielli, N., McLeod, D., & Healy, E. (1994). Gender stereotypes in MTV commercials: The beat goes on. *Journal of Broadcasting & Electronic Media, 37*, 91–101.

Singletary, M. W. (1983). Some perceptions of the lyrics of three types of recorded music: Rock, country and soul. *Popular Music and Society, 9*, 51–63.

Sommers-Flanagan, R., Sommers-Flanagan, J., & Davis, B. (1993). What's happening on Music Television? A gender role content analysis. *Sex Roles, 28*, 745–753.

Stanley, T. L. (2004, January 26). Porn crosses over to media mainstream. *Advertising Age*, p. 4.

Strouse, J. S., Buerkel-Rothfuss, N., & Long, E. C. J. (1995). Gender and family as moderators of the relationship between music video exposure and adolescent sexual permissiveness. *Adolescence, 30*, 505–517.

Sun, S., & Lull, J. (1986). The adolescent audience for music videos and why they watch. *Journal of Communication, 36*, 115–125.

Toney, G. T., & Weaver, III, J. B. (1994). Effects of gender and gender role self-perceptions on affective reactions to rock music videos. *Sex Roles, 30*, 567–583.

Vincent, R. C. (1989). Clio's consciousness raised? Portrayal of women in rock videos, re-examined. *Journalism Quarterly, 66*, 155–160.

Vincent, R. C., Davis, D. K., & Boruszkowski, L. A. (1987). Sexism on MTV: The portrayal of women in rock videos. *Journalism Quarterly, 64*, 750–755, 941.

Wells, A., & Hakanen, E. A. (1991). The emotional use of popular music by adolescents. *Journalism Quarterly, 68*, 445–454.

Chapter 4

Voluptuous Vixens and Macho Males: A Look at the Portrayal of Gender and Sexuality in Video Games

Stacy L. Smith

University of Southern California

Emily Moyer-Gusé

University of California, Santa Barbara

Several politicians have been clamoring for a congressional cure to objectionable video game content (Pereira, 2003a). These concerned voices are arguing that some games feature too much sex and violence, which could be dangerous content features for children and adolescents to witness. For instance, *Duke Nukem* introduces gamers to naked and bound women begging to be murdered and *Grand Theft Auto 3* (*GTA3*) rewards players for killing prostitutes after sex (Voice Male, 2003, p. 7).

Parents and advocacy groups are also alarmed at the sexual content in games (Pereira, 2003b; Walsh, Gentile, VanOverbeke, & Chasco, 2002). In response to *GTA3*, the executive directors of the Men's Resource Center of Western Massachusetts and the Everywoman's Center at the University of Massachusetts stated, "The manufacturer...is making enormous profits from a video game that promotes a culture of disrespect and violence toward women. This is insulting and harmful to girls and women and boys and men everywhere. Rewarding players for killing women in a sexualized context should never be a source of entertainment" (Voice Male, 2003, p. 7). Interestingly, an online Gallup poll of 517 adolescents recently showed that nearly three fourths (71%) of teenage boys reported playing games in the *Grand Theft Auto* series (National Institute on Media and Family, 2003).

Given these societal concerns, it becomes important to examine just how much sexual content is actually featured *across* the entire landscape of video games—not just in a particular game or series. In addition, we define sexual content loosely in this chapter to include gender roles, hypersexuality (e.g., sexually revealing clothing, nudity, unrealistic body types), and implicit and explicit sexual behavior and language. A broad approach is taken because the representation of gender and attributes of sexuality in video game content may subtly or blatantly teach and reinforce antisocial effects such as gender role stereotypes and body image disturbance.

This chapter is divided into four major sections. The first examines the prevalence of video games in the lives of children and adolescents. Assessing how much time children spend with this medium will illuminate their potential patterns of exposure to objectionable depictions. The second section reviews the content analyses of characters in video games. In particular, we focus on the distribution of gender as well as the way in which characters are presented in this interactive medium. The third section looks at the portrayal of sexual content in video games. What little that is known about hypersexuality, sexual content, and sexualized violence in games will be reviewed. The final section examines the use of sexual appeals in advertising content for video games. Specifically, the frequency of sexual content on the jacket covers of games will be delineated.

It is important to note that this chapter addresses *content patterns* in games, not theory or effects. To date, there has been very little—if any—research on the impact of video game play on children and adolescents' sexual attitudes, beliefs, and behaviors despite related research on the effects of exposure to sexualized depictions using other media (for review, see Donnerstein & Smith, 2001; Malamuth & Impett, 2001; Signorelli, 2001; Ward, 2002), evoking mechanisms such as social cognitive theory, priming, and cultivation theory. Because the aim of this chapter is to substantiate the presence of sexual content in games, this literature base will be referenced but not reviewed.

VIDEO GAME USE

Video game technology is wildly popular in the lives of some Americans. According to the Entertainment Software Association (n.d.), the average player is a 29-year-old male. While these gamers are important to consider in terms of purchasing power as well as the potential reason sexual content may be embedded in games, the real concern is children's and adolescents' exposure to objectionable material. Indeed, at least one piece of anti-video game legislation has been crafted so that it is a federal crime to sell or rent games to children with violence and/or explicit sexual content (Pereira, 2003a, ¶1). Consequently, it is important to examine just how much time children and adolescents spend with this interactive technology.

Commissioned by the Kaiser Family Foundation, a recent nationwide survey revealed that 82% of homes with 8- to 18-year-olds feature a video game player such as a Sony PlayStation, Nintendo GameCube, or Microsoft Xbox (Roberts, Foehr, Rideout, & Brodie, 1999). The same study also shows that 25% of American households with children in this age range have three or more game consoles. Almost half (45%) of 8- to 18-year-olds have a console in their own room.

Given that so many children have access, the next question to address is how much time they spend playing video games. On average, 2- to 18-year-olds spend roughly 20 minutes per day with video games (see Roberts et al., 1999). Yet, there seem to be distinct individual differences in this point estimate. For age, 2- to 7-year-olds spend substantially less time playing video games per day (8 minutes) than do 8- to 18-year-olds (27 minutes). Further distinctions can be made within this last age grouping: 8- to 13-year-olds spend 32 minutes per day playing whereas 14- to 18-year-olds spend 20 minutes. Gender differences are also notable. Among 8- to 18-year-olds (Roberts et al., 1999), boys spend substantially more time playing games per day (41 minutes) than do girls (12 minutes).

What types of games are children most likely to play during this time frame? The Roberts et al. (1999) study shows that the top three genres of video games among 2- to 18-year-olds are action (i.e., *Duke Nukem*), sports (i.e., *NBA Street*), and adventure (i.e., *Lara Croft Tomb Raider*). It is also important to consider data on top-selling games, as almost half (45%) of purchasing decisions for the home are made by children *and* their parents conjointly (Federal Trade Commission, 2000, p. 53). According to market trends collected by NPD Funworld for the first half of 2003, 7 out of the 10 best-selling games were rated "T" (Teen) or "M" (Mature) by the Entertainment Software Rating Board (ESRB). Those games were: *Enter the Matrix (T)*, *Grand Theft Auto: Vice City (M)*, *The Getaway (M)*, *The Sims (T)*, *Socom: Navy Seals (M)*, *Def Jam Vendetta (T)*, and *Tom Clancy's Splinter Cell (T)*. A few of these games have content descriptors that specify the themes may be suggestive and the content may contain mature sexual material.

Children are playing video games but this leisure-time activity is really influenced by age and gender. Although time spent playing video games is less than the amount of time spent watching television (Roberts et al., 1999), research reveals that parents are less likely to supervise children's game-playing experience (Woodward & Gridina, 2000). Without such mediation, exposure to gender stereotypical and sexualized portrayals in video games may have a more pronounced effect than such depictions on television programming.

REPRESENTATION OF GENDER IN VIDEO GAMES

Two issues are important to examine in terms of gender portrayals: prevalence and role. Prevalence refers to the sheer number of characters in games that are male or female. Role refers to whether a character is stereotyped in some specific sex-linked way. Both of these issues are important when examining media content and may influence children's perceptions of, beliefs about, and attitudes toward their own as well as the opposite sex (see Signorielli, 2001).

In terms of prevalence, the portrayal of gender is quite imbalanced. Braun and Giroux (1989) assessed the portrayal of males and females in 21 popular games at coin-operated arcades. The results showed that almost 60% of the games featured males whereas less than 5% featured females. A disparity was also found with male and female voices in games (~20% vs. 2%, respectively).

Whereas these early data refer to trends in arcade games, more recent efforts have been conducted on portrayals of gender and sexuality in console-based games (Beasley & Standley, 2002; Children Now, 2000; Children Now, 2001; Downs & Smith, 2004). Examining 24 of the most popular games for Sony PlayStation, Sega Dreamcast, and Nintendo 64, Children Now (2000, p. 4) found that 92% had male lead characters whereas only 54% had female lead characters. Expanding their sample to 70 top-selling games for 6 different platforms and personal computers, Children Now's (2001) follow-up study showed a similar gender-based chasm. Of the 1,716 characters identified, 64% were male, 17% were female, and 19% were non-human. The gender disproportion only increased when player-controlled characters were examined (73% males, 12% females, 15% nonhuman).

Beasley and Standley (2002) assessed characters in a random sample of 47 games on Nintendo 64 and Sony PlayStation. Of the 597 characters assessed, 71.5% were male and 14% were female. A total of 15% of the characters had a gender that was not ascertainable. Similar findings were recently obtained by Downs and Smith (2004), examining gender portrayals in 60 popular Microsoft Xbox, Nintendo GameCube, and Sony PlayStation 2 games. Across all three studies, asexual characters such as robots or machines were more likely than women to be portrayed in games.

In addition to sheer prevalence, scholars also have also examined the roles or functions of male and female video game characters. Dietz (1998) assessed the roles of female characters in 33 Nintendo and Sega Genesis games. In 21% of the games, females were portrayed as the "damsel in distress" (p. 434). As Dietz (1998, p. 435) describes one of these games: *The Adventures of Bayou Billy* ... shows a woman in a low-cut, red dress. The woman has large, well-rounded breasts. A man is holding her and has a knife placed at her throat. Apparently, this man has kidnapped Annabelle and Billy's mission is to save her." Other games featuring similar roles for females include *Teenage Mutant Ninja Turtles* and *Double Dragon*. Dietz (1998) added that even games targeting younger audiences often depict this theme. Commenting on the game *Tiny Toon*, Dietz stated, "Babs the Bunny has been kidnapped and needs to be rescued. Babs has large lips and seductive, droopy eye lids" (1998, p. 434). Outside of the victim role, 15% of the games showed females as bystanders or in secondary roles designed to help or facilitate male characters' behaviors.

Children Now (2001) also examined the types of roles characters fill in video games. Among the 70 games in their sample, a full 50% of the female characters were portrayed as a prop or bystander to the action (p. 12). The most frequent role for males, in contrast, was that of the competitor (47%). Looking specifically at those characters players can control, 70% of male main characters were competitors compared to only 37% of females. Participants, or those characters which follow the instructions of the game player, were more likely to be females than males at a ratio of 7 to 1 (Children Now, 2001, p. 13).

Character actions also fell along stereotypical lines in the Children Now (2001) study. Males were more likely than females to be involved in physical aggression (52% vs. 32%), whereas the opposite was true for verbal aggression (5% vs. 9%). Females were more likely than their male counterparts to help/share (32% vs. 15%) and be nurturing (8% vs. 2%). Females were also more likely than males to scream (18% vs. 5%) in video games, which makes sense given their frequent role of victim or bystander. At least one study has examined how sex influences involvement with violence, a traditional "male" activity. Smith, Lachlan, and Tamborini (2003) examined the perpetrators of violence in 60 popular games for Sega Dreamcast, Sony PlayStation, and Nintendo 64. Not surprisingly, the researchers found the males were more than three times as likely as females to be the initiator of violence (79% vs. 21%, respectively).

Overall, the frequency and types of roles for males and females in games seem clear. Males outnumber females by roughly four to one. This gender discrepancy almost mirrors the differences in time spent playing games by boys and girls, as previously noted (Brody, 2000; Funk & Buchman, 1996; Roberts et al., 1999). Such underrepresentation may not only communicate powerful messages about the importance of males and females in society, but it may also shape youngsters' attitudes and interest in other types of technology such as computers. Research has shown that in schools, girls tend to lag behind boys in terms of computer use and they often see computers as belonging to males more than females (Cassell & Jenkins, 1998, p. 12). Although it is not entirely clear how console games contribute to computer use, the gender differences found in video game playing may have a role in the differential computer and other technological habits of boys and girls. Future research should explore this link. Outside of the gender imbalance, the research indicates that females are more likely to be shown in secondary roles in video games compared to males and that both genders perform traditional stereotypical behaviors. As such, games may be perpetuating the very gender-based stereotypes that many parents and advocacy groups have been fighting for years.

SEXUAL CONTENT IN VIDEO GAMES

Consider some of the recent quotes by journalists about sexual content in games: "Nekkid people are coming to a video game near you. Some will be funny. Some will be sexy. And some will be just plain raunchy" (Morris, 2004, ¶2) or "Acclaim Entertainment... is preparing to introduce BMX XXX, a game centered on the extreme sport of BMX biking that includes scenes of prostitutes, strippers, and other seamy stuff" (Tran, 2002, ¶2). Such headlines, in combination with the press attention surrounding *GTA3*, may suggest to some that sexual content is rampant in games.

Or is it? At first glance, the most blatant type of material in most games seems to be hypersexuality as several digital divas are portrayed on-screen with unrealistic body images. For instance, Lara Croft in *Tomb Raider*, Libya in *State of Emergency*, and Tina in *Dead or Alive: Xtreme Beach Volleyball* are shown with uncharacteristically large breasts and unusually small waists. *Dead or Alive* even lists in the game's manual the height and weight of all possible player-controlled characters as well as their bust, waist, and hip measurements. Based on the heights and weights given, 50% of the females shown in the *Dead or Alive* manual would be classified as underweight according to a standard Body Mass Index (BMI) scale (Centers for Disease Control, 2004).

A few studies have looked rigorously into hypersexuality in games (Beasley & Standley, 2002; Children Now, 2000; Downs & Smith, 2004). Typically, hypersexuality is not defined in these studies but rather refers to sexually revealing clothing, amount of exposed skin, and/or body type. Sexually revealing clothing appears to be plentiful in popular video games (Children Now, 2000). As one reporter aptly stated about female attire in games, "Play the video game 'Dead or Alive' long enough and you'll start believing that the toughest female martial artists prefer to wear skirts that barely cover their panties and bustiers that runneth over with cleavage" (Benedetti, 2001, ¶2).

Examining 1,716 characters across 70 top-selling games, Children Now (2001) found that females often wore clothing that exposed their skin. Among the females' outfits, 21% partially brandished their breasts (7% fully), 13% partially bared their buttocks (8% fully), and 20% showed their stomachs (Children Now, 2001, p. 14). Of the females in Beasley and

Standley's (2002) study, almost half were sleeveless "wearing clothing such as halter tops, tank tops, or bathing suits" (p. 287). Such seductive clothing was oftentimes fashioned on vixens with archetypelike figures. Of those games with a minimum of one lead female character, Children Now's (2000, p. 4) findings show that 38% of the females had large breasts and 46% had unusually small waists. Children Now (2001, p. 13) found that just over 1 in 10 females (11%) had voluptuous bodies with uncharacteristically large breasts and small waists. In addition, unhealthy or unrealistic body images were featured on almost 20% of the females in the sample. Among the women showing cleavage in Beasley and Standley's (2002) study, 41% were categorized as having breasts that were "voluptuous" in nature.

Females are not the only ones presented unrealistically, however. Although much less is known about male depictions, many games seem to feature men with hypermusclarized bodies. For example, *Def Jam Vendetta* and *Tao Feng: Fist of the Lotus* are games that feature male characters who possess exaggerated shoulders and abs that are pretentiously perfect. How common are these types of portrayals in video games? Children Now (2001) found that 33% of males ($n = 1,106$) in 70 popular console and PC-based games were shown with excessively buff bodies.

In total, the handful of studies that have been conducted show that there is a fair amount of hypersexuality in games. Such portrayals may function as eye candy to attract the attention of young adolescent males. These types of depictions also may have negative effects on boys' expectations about and treatment of females (Children Now, 2001, p. 14). For young females, these depictions may communicate body image ideals that are difficult, if not impossible, to attain. Studies show that media exposure to thin ideals on television and in magazines has been linked to body dissatisfaction and eating disorder symptomatology in both correlational and experimental studies with undergraduates (Botta, 2003; Harrison & Cantor, 1997; Stice, Schupack-Neuberg, Shaw, & Stein, 1994; Stice & Shaw, 1994), middle and high school students (Botta, 2003; Harrison, 2000a), and even children as young as first grade (Harrison, 2000b). While these studies do not reflect games specifically, the exaggerated portrayal of female characters' bodies suggests that this interactive technology *may* also play a role in body image disturbance among young players.

When considering more blatant forms of sexual content in games, there is much less empirical research. Yet, we know that young viewers learn about sexual topics such as prostitution from entertainment programming (Greenberg, Linsangan, & Soderman, 1993). Applying this finding to video games suggests the possibility that youngsters may learn similar information when playing games like *Grand Theft Auto*, which features prostitutes as a part of the unfolding narrative. Aside from learning, video games featuring sexual content may also influence viewers' attitudes toward intimate behavior. Again, sex on television has been shown to influence attitudes and moral evaluations of sex (Bryant & Rockwell, 1994; Calfin, Carroll, & Schmidt, 1993; Greeson & Williams, 1986; Strouse & Buerkal-Rothfuss, 1993), suggesting that sexual content in video games may have similar effects on players.

Only two studies could be found that have assessed sexual behavior in games. Thompson and her research team have been interested in how the ESRB's age- and content-based ratings influence the portrayal of objectionable content such as violence, sex, profanity, and drug use in games. Examining 55 games rated "E" for everyone, Thompson and Haninger (2001) found only two instances of a suggestive theme. Specifying these depictions, the authors (2001, p. 596) "noted the provocative leather outfit worn by Ai Fukami in *Ridge Racer V*, the screen shot between her thighs, and the phrases 'curb your desire' and 'push it to the limit' in the introduction. We also noted sexual innuendo in *Gex 3: Deep Cover Gecko.*"

More recently, Haninger and Thompson (2004) analyzed a variety of sexual content in video games rated "T" for teen audiences (i.e., 13 and above). The "T" rating suggests that the game may contain violence, mild or strong language, and/or suggestive themes (ESRB, 2001). The age-based rating is also accompanied by content descriptors, indicating whether the game contains violence, blood, sexual themes, profanity, comic mischief, substances, or gambling. Haninger and Thompson sampled 20% of all the "T"-rated games on the market by April 2001. In their study, sexual themes were defined as "behaviors (e.g. provocative touching or moaning) or dialogue related to sex, as well as depictions of exposed breasts, buttocks, or genitals" (Haninger & Thompson, 2004, p. 859). Using this definition, 27% of the games in the sample contained sexual themes. A slightly lower proportion of games (20%) contained an ESRB content descriptor for such material.

Examples of the specific nature of sexual themes found in Xbox and Nintendo GameCube games are provided by the authors in a separate article (see Haninger, Ryan, & Thompson, 2004). In one example, taken from the "T"-rated game *WWF SmackDown!*, the authors note a 20-second film clip where Val Venis, a wrestler, is shown sitting in a hot tub with two women. The scene depicts sexual images and an expression on Venis's face suggestive of oral sex (Haninger et al., 2004, Table 6, ¶3). In another example, the game *The Elder Scrolls III: Morrowind* allows players to enter a brothel named "Desele's House of Earthly Delights," where three women dance on a stage in their underwear. One of these dancers asks the player if he is "looking for a good time" (Haninger et al., 2004, Table 6, ¶2).

When the definition of sexual themes was expanded to include subtler hypersexuality of characters such as pronounced cleavage, large breasts, or provocative clothing, the proportion of games containing sexual themes increased to 46%. In addition to this, the hypersexuality of males and females was examined. Among the games in their sample, Haninger and Thompson (2004) found that females were much more likely to be shown partially nude or engaging in sexual behaviors than were males.

Outside of these studies, only one investigation has looked specifically at the linkage of sex and violence. This is a particularly lethal combination that has been found to increase males' callousness (Bell, Kuriloff, Lottes, & Nathanson, 1992; Linz, Donnerstein, & Penrod, 1984) and decrease their empathy (Linz, Donnerstein, & Penrod, 1988) toward female victims of sexual assault. Smith et al. (2003) examined the degree to which sexual assault was featured in 60 of the most popular video games in 1999. Only six instances of sexual assault appeared across 1,389 violent interactions. These six portrayals were featured in five games (*WWF Attitude, Soul Caliber, Marvel v. Capcom, 007,* and *Virtual Fighter*). Given that these data were collected on antiquated games and platforms, it becomes imperative to see if the prevalence of sexual assault has increased over the last few years. This is particularly important because of the massive popularity of *Grand Theft Auto* games, which are known for their juxtaposition of sex and violence.

PACKAGING OF GAME CONTENT

Whereas the studies reviewed thus far focused on game content, other investigations have assessed point-of-purchase advertising. Creative displays featured on the jacket covers of games may depict attributes of play that magnetize young consumers. Sexual and violent content may be particularly influential promotional strategies, especially for male teenage gamers. The use of violence on jacket covers has already been reviewed elsewhere (see Smith, in press). Consequently, the focus of this section will be to review what is known about the portrayal of gender and sexuality on the box art of games.

Only a few studies have examined the tactics used on the jacket covers (Brand & Knight, 2002) of games. The earliest research was conducted by Provenzo (1991), who was particularly interested in the portrayal of gender. Looking at gender representation on jacket covers of 47 top-selling Nintendo games, Provenzo (1991, p. 108) found that males substantially outnumbered females at a ratio of 13 to 1 (i.e., 115 males vs. 9 females). It is also important to note that figures with no ascertainable gender (e.g., monsters, mythlike creatures, robots) were more likely to be portrayed on jacket covers than were females. This finding mirrors the content patterns previously described. For example, males ($n = 20$) were depicted as dominant figures on the box art whereas females ($n = 3$) were depicted as submissive.

Children Now (2000) also examined the box art of 24 top-selling video games for Sony PlayStation, Sega Dreamcast, and Nintendo 64. Consistent with Provenzo's findings, females appeared infrequently on the covers. Although 54% of the games had lead female characters, only two covers depicted females. And, both games showed female characters in a provocative light (Children Now, 2000, p. 7).

Perhaps the most comprehensive assessment of gender and sexuality on game covers was undertaken recently by Smith, Pieper, and Choueiti (2004). These researchers examined the covers of 74 top-selling games in the United States during the first 6 months of the 2003 calendar year. Of the 74 games, 32% ($n = 24$) were designed for the Nintendo GameCube, 34% ($n = 25$) for Sony PlayStation 2, and 34% ($n = 25$) for Microsoft Xbox. Using ESRB indicators, a total of 38% ($n = 28$) were rated "E" for everyone, 42% ($n = 31$) were rated "T" for teen (i.e., ages 13 and above), and 20% ($n = 15$) were rated "M" for mature (i.e., ages 17 and above). Examining the front and back covers of games, measures captured the distribution of gender, the presence of sexually revealing clothing (i.e., tight garments or

TABLE 4.1
Prevalence of Gender and Sexual Content on Video Game Box Art

Variable Name	E Rated Games	T/M Rated Games	% Overall
Gender-Related Variables			
% of game covers w/1 or more women*	32%	52%	45% ($n = 33$)
range of women on covers	1 to 6	1 to 12	1 to 12
% of game covers w/1 or more men*	82%	93%	89% ($n = 66$)
range of men	3 to 19	2 to 26	2 to 26
Sex-Related Variables			
% of game covers w/partial nudity	36% ($n = 10$)	48% ($n = 22$)	43% ($n = 32$)
Of those game covers w/women ...			
% showing partial female nudity	67% ($n = 6$)	75% ($n = 18$)	73% ($n = 24$)
Of those game covers w/men ...			
% showing partial male nudity	26% ($n = 6$)	21% ($n = 9$)	23% ($n = 15$)
% of game covers w/sexually revealing clothing	39% ($n = 11$)	52% ($n = 24$)	47% ($n = 35$)
Of the game covers w/sexually revealing clothing ...			
% showing women in such attire	56% ($n = 5$)	79% ($n = 19$)	73% ($n = 24$)
Of those game covers w/sexually revealing clothing ...			
% showing men in such attire	35% ($n = 8$)	33% ($n = 14$)	33% ($n = 22$)
% of game covers w/sexual behavior	0%	3% ($n = 2$)	3% ($n = 2$)

Note. Table is adapted from Smith (in press). A total of 74 games were evaluated: 38% ($n = 28$) were rated by the ESRB as E for "everyone" (i.e., 6 and above), 42% ($n = 31$) were rated T for "teens" (i.e., 13 and above), and 20% ($n = 15$) were rated M for "mature" (i.e., 17 and above).
*human or anthropomorphized characters.

those designed to arouse interest), partial nudity (i.e., showing part of a character's chest, stomach, buttocks, or upper thighs), and sexual behavior (i.e., acts which communicate a sense of physical or likely intimacy).

Table 4.1 shows the sample-wide findings as well as breakdowns by game rating. In terms of gender, males (89%) were substantially more likely than females (45%) to be featured on the box art of games. Not only are these prevalence findings of interest, but also the concentration of males and females on the jacket covers varied. Of those games with men on the jacket covers, a range of anywhere from 2 to 26 different human or anthropomorphized male characters were visually portrayed. The range for females was less than half of this amount (1 to 12 characters), however.

When we consider the sexual content on game packaging, there appears to be a great deal of hypersexuality. Of the games featuring women, for example, nearly three fourths (73%) of the covers portray them partially nude and in sexually revealing clothing. Given that there are only 33 games with women on the jackets, these findings suggest that most of the box art presents females in a provocative manner. For men, however, the picture looks different. Less than a quarter of the games with men on the covers depict them partially naked and a third of the games show them in revealing attire. Outside of hypersexuality, only 3% ($n = 2$) of the covers showed sexual behavior which was entirely benign in nature (e.g., man with his arm[s] around a woman).

CONCLUSION

The purpose of this chapter was to review what is known about the prevalence of gender and sexuality in video games. Two major conclusions can be drawn from the research to date on games and their packaging. First, video game content is male-dominated. The prevalence of male characters as well as the roles they occupy communicate strongly that gaming is a man's world. Second, when females are shown, it is often in a secondary and sexualized context.

In all fairness, males are more likely than females to play games. As such, the content patterns may simply reflect strategic marketing decisions to appeal to male consumers. As noted in the first section, many preteen and teenaged males spend time playing video games. These developing youth may be drawing stereotypical conclusions about men and women that affect their psychosocial development. Given that there are no studies assessing the impact of gender-role stereotyping and hypersexuality in games, this assertion is speculative at best. Yet, two meta-analyses reveal that playing violent video games is associated with increases in aggression (Anderson & Bushman, 2001; Sherry, 2001), suggesting that messages found in this medium can have antisocial effects. Thus, exposure to popular console-based game content may be having a negative impact on male and female children's sex-role socialization. Surely, research is needed in this domain.

Outside of gender inequities and issues of hypersexuality, the findings from the content studies suggest that video games contain very little sexual content and even fewer instances of the juxtaposition of sex and violence. While more recent research is needed, this review of literature suggests that objectionable content in games like *Grand Theft Auto* or *Duke Nukem* may be the exception and not the norm. As such, parents, advocacy groups, and congressional leaders may be encouraged that the types of portrayals generating the most societal concern occur infrequently across top-selling games. Yet, it is important to note that over 8 million copies of *Grand Theft Auto: Vice City* sold within 3 months of its release (Workman, 2003). With such diffusion, even a single game featuring potentially problematic content should be cause for concern.

REFERENCES

Anderson, C. A., & Bushman, B. (2001). Effects of violent video games on aggressive behavior, aggressive cognition, aggressive affect, physiological arousal, and prosocial behavior: A meta-analytic review of the scientific literature. *Psychological Science, 12*, 353–359.

Beasley, B., & Standley, T. C. (2002). Shirts vs. skins: Clothing as an indicator of gender role stereotyping in video games. *Mass Communication & Society, 5*, 279–293.

Bell, S. T., Kuriloff, P. J., Lottes, I., & Nathanson, J. (1992). Rape callousness in college freshmen: An empirical investigation of the sociocultural model of aggression towards women. *Journal of College Student Development, 33*(5), 454–461.

Benedetti, W. (2001). Girls and video games: More males play them, but that could be about to change. *Seattle Post-Intelligencer Reporter*. Retrieved June 7, 2004, from http://seattlepi.nwsource.com/lifestyle/46402_gamegap.shtml.

Botta, R. A. (2003). For your health? The relationship between magazine reading and adolescents' body image and eating disturbances. *Sex Roles, 48*(9–10), 389–399.

Brand, J., & Knight, S. J. (2002). *Diverse worlds project*. Retrieved June 12, 2004, from http://www.diverseworlds.bond.edu.au/Default.htm.

Braun, C. M. J., & Giroux, J. (1989). Arcade video games: Proxemic, cognitive, and content analyses. *Journal of Leisure Research, 21*, 92–105.

Brody, M. (2000). Playing with death. *Brown University Child and Adolescent Behavior Letter, 16*(11), 8.

Bryant, J., & Rockwell, S. C. (1994). Effects of massive exposure to sexually oriented prime-time television programming on adolescents' moral judgment. In D. Zillmann, J. Bryant, & A. C. Huston (Eds.), *Media, children, and the family: Social scientific, psychodynamic, and clinical perspectives* (pp. 183–196). Hillsdale, NJ: Lawrence Erlbaum Associates.

Calfin, M. S., Carroll, J. L., & Schmidt, J. (1993). Viewing music videotapes before taking a test of premarital sexual attitudes. *Psychological Reports, 72,* 475–481.

Cassell, J., & Jenkins, H. (1998). Chess for girls? Feminism and computer games. In J. Cassell & H. Jenkins (Eds.), *From Barbie to Mortal Kombat: Gender and computer games* (pp. 2–45). Cambridge, MA: MIT Press.

Centers for Disease Control. (2004). Body mass index calculator. Retrieved October 7, 2004, from http://www.cdc.gov/nccdphp/dnpa/bmi/calc-bmi.htm.

Children Now. (2000). *Girls and gaming: A console video game content analysis.* Oakland, CA: Author. Retrieved May 17, 2004, from http://www.childrennow. org/media/video-games-girls.pdf.

Children Now. (2001). *Fair play? Violence, gender, and race in video games.* Oakland, CA: Author.

Dietz, T. L. (1998). An examination of violence and gender role portrayals in video games: Implications for gender socialization and aggressive behavior. *Sex Roles, 38,* 425–442.

Donnerstein, E., & Smith, S. L. (2001). Sex in the media: Theory, influences, and solutions. In D. G. Singer & J. L. Singer (Eds.), *Handbook of children and the media* (pp. 289–307). Thousand Oaks, CA: Sage.

Downs, E., & Smith, S. L. (2004). *Keeping abreast of hypersexuality: A video game content analysis.* Paper to be submitted to the Mass Communication Division at the International Communication Association, New York, NY.

Entertainment Software Association. (n.d.). Top ten industry facts. Retrieved October 6, 2004, from http://www.theesa.com/pressroom_main.html.

Entertainment Software Rating Board (2001). Retrieved September 26, 2004, from http://www.esrb.org.

Federal Trade Commission. (2000). *Marketing violent entertainment to children: A review of self regulation and industry practices in the motion picture, music recording, and electronic games industries.* Retrieved May 1, 2004, from http://www. ftc.gov/reports/violence/vioreport.pdf.

Funk, J. B., & Buchman, D. D. (1996). Children's perceptions of gender differences in social approval for playing electronic games. *Sex Roles, 35*(3–4), 219–231.

Greenberg, B. S., Linsangan, R., & Soderman, A. (1993). Adolescents' reactions to television sex. In B. S. Greenberg, J. D. Brown, & N. Buerkel-Rothfuss (Eds.), *Media, sex, and the adolescent* (pp. 196–224). Cresskill, NJ: Hampton Press.

Greeson, L. E., & Williams, R. A. (1986). Social implications of music videos for youth: An analysis of the content and effects of MTV. *Youth & Society, 18*(2), 177–189.

Haninger, K., Ryan, S. M., & Thompson, K. M. (2004). Violence in teen-rated video games. *Medscape General Medicine.* Retrieved May 14, 2004, from http://www. medscape.com/viewarticle.

Haninger, K., & Thompson, K. M. (2004). Content and ratings of teen-rated video games. *Journal of the American Medical Association, 291* (7), 856–865.

Harrison, K. (2000a). The body electric: Thin–ideal media and eating disorders in adolescents. *Journal of Communication, 50*(3), 119–143.

Harrison, K. (2000b). Television viewing, fat stereotyping, body shape standards, and eating disorder symptomatology in grade school children. *Communication Research, 27*(5), 617–640.

Harrison, K., & Cantor, J. (1997). The relationship between media consumption and eating disorders. *Journal of Communication, 47,* 40–67.

Linz, D., Donnerstein, E., & Penrod, S. (1984). The effects of multiple exposures to filmed violence against women. *Journal of Communication, 34*(3), 130–147.

Linz, D., Donnerstein, E., & Penrod, S. (1988). Effects of long-term exposure to violent and sexually degrading depictions of women. *Journal of Personality and Social Psychology, 55,* 758–768.

Malamuth, N., & Impett, E. A. (2001). Research on sex in the media: What do we know about effects on children and adolescents? In D. G. Singer & J. L. Singer (Eds.), *Handbook of children and the media* (pp. 269–287). Thousand Oaks, CA: Sage.

Morris, C. (2004, May 12). Video games get raunchy. *CNN/Money.* Retrieved May 12, 2004, from http://money.cnn.com/2004/05/11/technology/e3_nekkidgames/.

National Institute on Media and the Family. (2003, September 23). *Gallup poll: More than 70 percent of teenage boys have played "Grand Theft Auto" video games.* Message sent from MediaWise enews.

Pereira, J. (2003a, January 10). Just how far does First Amendment protection go? Videogame makers use free speech to thwart proposals to keep violent, adult fare from kids. *Wall Street Journal,* B1.

Pereira, J. (2003b, September 25). Games get more explicit—and so do warning labels. *Wall Street Journal,* D1.

Provenzo, E. F. (1991). *Video kids: Making sense of Nintendo.* Cambridge, MA: Harvard University Press.

Roberts, D. F., Foehr, U. G., Rideout, V., & Brodie, M. (1999). *Kids and media at the rate the new millennium.* Menlo Park, CA: Kaiser Family Foundation.

Sherry, J. (2001). The effects of violent video games on aggression: A meta-analysis. *Human Communication Research, 27,* 409–431.

Signorielli, N. (2001). Television's gender role images and contribution to stereotyping: Past, present, future. In D. G. Singer & J. L. Singer (Eds.), *Handbook of children and the media* (pp. 341–358). Thousand Oaks, CA: Sage.

Smith, S. L. (in press). Perps, pimps, and provocative clothing: Examining negative content patterns in video games. In P. Vorderer & J. Bryant (Eds.), *Playing computer games: Motives, responses, and consequences.* Mahwah, NJ: Lawrence Erlbaum Associates.

Smith, S. L., Lachlan, K., & Tamborini, R. (2003). Popular video games: Quantifying the presentation of violence and its context. *Journal of Broadcasting and Electronic Media, 47*(1), 58–76.

Smith, S. L., Pieper, K., & Choueiti, M. (2004). [Video game packaging and ad copy: Are gaming publishers in compliance with the ARC?] Unpublished raw data.

Stice, E., Schupack-Neuberg, E., Shaw, H. E., & Stein, R. I. (1994). Relation of media exposure to eating disorder symptomology: An examination of mediating mechanisms. *Journal of Abnormal Psychology, 103,* 836–840.

Stice, E., & Shaw, H. E. (1994). Adverse effects of the media portrayed thin-ideal on women and linkages to bulimic symptomatology. *Journal of Social & Clinical Psychology, 13*(3), 288–300.

Strouse, J., & Buerkal-Rothfuss, N. (1993). Media exposure and the sexual attitudes and behaviors of college students. In B. Greenberg, J. Brown, & N. Buerkel-Rothfuss (Eds.), *Media, sex and the adolescent* (pp. 277–292). Cresskill, NJ: Hampton Press.

Thompson, K. M., & Haninger, K. (2001). Violence in E-rated video games. *Journal of the American Medical Association, 286*(5), 591–598, 920.

Tran, K. T. L. (2002, October 14). Will sex sell videogames? A racy new title will tell. *Wall Street Journal,* B1.

Voice Male (2003, Summer). *Condemning misogynist video games.* Retrieved September 10, 2004, from Proquest database.

Walsh, D., Gentile, D., VanOverbeke, M., & Chasco, E. (2002). Mediawise video game report card. *National Institute on Media and the Family.* Retrieved October 6, 2004, from http://www.mediafamily.org/research/report_vgrc_2002-2.shtml.

Ward, L. M. (2002). Understanding the role of entertainment media in the sexual socialization of American youth: A review of empirical research. *Developmental Review, 23,* 347–388.

Woodard, E. H., & Gridina, N. (2000). *Media in the home: The fifth annual survey of parents and children.* Philadelphia: Annenberg Public Policy Center.

Workman, R. C. D. C. (2003). GTA: Vice City hits big sales numbers! *Intensity Magazine.* Retrieved October 7, 2004, from http://www.intensity-magazine.com/news/528.

Chapter 5

Sex and the Marketing of Contemporary Consumer Magazines: How Men's Magazines Sexualized Their Covers to Compete With *Maxim*

Jacqueline Lambiase
Texas Tech University

Tom Reichert
University of Georgia

Anyone who has seen even a single issue of *Maxim* magazine could easily describe its typical cover: one part image of a vaguely familiar B-list actress, sexually dressed and posed; and one part text, both sensational and salacious (see Fig. 5.1). This formula has proven to be attention-getting, and not just for the magazine's 2.5 million subscribers who mostly include the coveted demographic of men ages 18–34. Numerous popular press accounts and trade articles have focused on *Maxim* as a catalyst for sexualizing the men's magazine landscape, causing longtime men's lifestyle magazines such as *Esquire* and *GQ* (*Gentlemen's Quarterly*) to try its recipe for "celebrity plus sex equals more readers" (Bounds, 1999; Gremillion, 1997; Handy, 1999; Jacobson, 2002; Turner, 1999). But, has *Maxim*'s success in the United States been accompanied by changes in existing men's magazines, or is this simply the perception of media pundits?

This project seeks to investigate this perception through content analysis of men's magazines before and after *Maxim*, which debuted in spring 1997. In addition to *Maxim*, covers from *Details*, *Esquire*, *GQ*, and *Rolling Stone* are also studied from 1995 through 2000. By analyzing all images of women and men, including their dress, pose, and sexual tone, this study seeks to

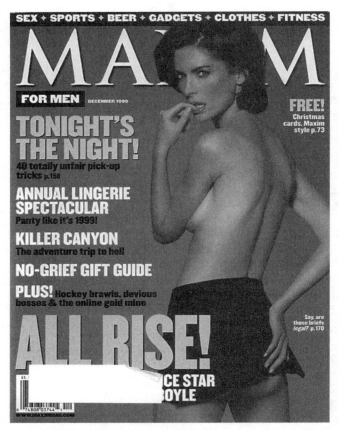

FIG. 5.1. *Maxim's* formula of a B-list actress, sexually dressed and posed, December 1999.

trace whether these other magazines followed *Maxim's* successful formula. As important, this analysis provides information about how images of women, especially those on magazine covers, are used to sell magazines to young adult males. Last, this study contributes to limited research on magazine covers and their role in marketing and branding publications (Johnson, 2002).

MAXIM AND MEN'S MAGAZINES

There is little doubt that images of women and their bodies have been— and continue to be—used as adornments in the marketplace. Much documented research exists that convincingly demonstrates that sexualized images of women are used to sell not only branded goods such as fragrances and fashion (Reichert, Lambiase, Morgan, Carstarphen, & Zavoina, 1999), but also media products such as music via music videos (Hansen & Hansen, 2000; Signorielli, McLeod, & Healy, 1994), television programming via promos (Walker, 2000), and movies via movie trailers and DVD packaging (Oliver & Kalyanaraman, 2001). Mainstream consumer magazines are certainly no exception. Sexual and decorative images of women adorn covers and editorial content in magazines targeted to both women and men (Brinkley & Fowler, 2001; Malkin, Wornian, & Chrisler, 1999). Most recently, *Maxim*, a men's general lifestyle magazine, began exclusively to use women's images on provocative covers, thus altering the face of men's general-interest magazines.

In April 1997, *Maxim* magazine first hit the shelves of American bookstores. The magazine, first successfully published in the United Kingdom by U.K.-based Dennis Publishing, can be characterized by its tagline "Sex. Sports. Beer. Gadgets. Fashion." According to Gremillion (1997), *Maxim* has achieved success because it has "devoted its covers to B-list female celebs, with an accent on cleavage and come-hither looks . . . and fashion spreads with lots of buxom models as set dressing" (p. 28). It is an invariable editorial formula. Since its debut, each *Maxim* cover has featured a scantily clad woman (or two). Often these women, photographed in a style that accentuates their voluptuous bodies, make eye contact with the camera as they caress themselves, pull down their shoulder straps, or push aside already scanty clothing on their bottoms. These images are continued inside the magazine with three or four layouts of different women, as well as tips for picking up women or pleasing one once you have her home.

More notable, and perhaps less surprising, the formula worked. In a 2-year span, *Maxim*'s circulation not only rivaled those of well-established men's magazines, but also in some cases doubled or tripled them. Circulation grew to 2.5 million subscribers by the second half of 2000, which was more than a 47% increase over the second half circulation of 1999 (Fine, 2001). Its single copy sales rose 22% for the same time period. *Maxim*'s success left the other men's magazines reeling. They were faced with decreased circulation and advertising revenue as marketers placed their media buys with *Maxim*. Each had been battling to maintain circulations between 400,000 and just over a million subscribers: *Details* (446,000), *Esquire* (679,000), *GQ* (899,000), and *Rolling Stone* (1.25 million; Fine, 2001).

One result of *Maxim*'s success was the supposed adoption of the *Maxim* formula by its competition. Much of the speculation at that time and since has focused on changes on the covers of *Rolling Stone*, *GQ*, *Details*, and *Esquire*, supposedly brought about by *Maxim*'s influence (Munk, 2001;

Sullivan, 2000; Walker & Golden, 2001; Warner, 1997). Many of these articles and others featured industry sources who discussed the competition among men's magazines in terms of tension between long-form and short-form journalism, between content and a form that is visually stimulating (Jacobson, 2002; Loeb, 2000; Mnookin, 2001; "Thriving Market," 2001). Almost all of these articles mentioned that sex was selling *Maxim* and that other men's magazines, in an effort to stay competitive, were marketing themselves using sexualized women on their covers.

In February 1999, for example, three of the magazines in this study—*Maxim*, *Details*, and *Esquire*—used scantily dressed women on their covers, prompting a *Newsweek* writer to observe that "[m]en's magazines today practically have to come in a plain brown wrapper" (Turner, 1999, p. 52).

FIG. 5.2. *Esquire*, February 1999, employs *Maxim*'s formula. This same month, *Details* used a similar cover, prompting one writer to observe that "[m]en's magazines today practically have to come in a plain brown wrapper" (Turner, 1999, p. 52).

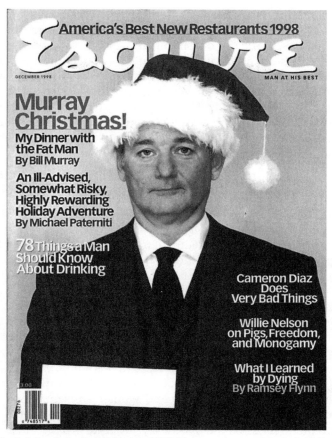

FIG. 5.3. A fully clothed and flat-faced Bill Murray on a non-Maximized *Esquire* cover, December 1998.

When *Details* first seemed to jump on the *Maxim* bandwagon, media observers noticed. One *Time* analyst wrote:

> Now all the fellows are slapping cleavage on their covers—in homage, it would appear, to *Maxim*. Whereas *Details* used to feature the stubbly likes of Stephen Dorff, the current number is graced by Elizabeth Hurley, touched up in such an unsubtle way that her breasts fairly leap off the page; it's as if they were eyeballs in a Tex Avery cartoon, ogling themselves. (Handy, 1999, p. 75)

Similar accusations were leveled at *Rolling Stone*. Criticism began in summer 2002 when *Rolling Stone* hired a new editor, Ed Needham, who had in 2000 started an American version of *FHM* (*For Him Magazine*), itself a clone of *Maxim*. Press accounts depicted the editor change at *Rolling Stone* as an attempt "to save the aging rock bible, famed for its long, in-depth articles, from the onslaught of a brash, new brand of magazine, filled with short articles, bright graphics and a humorous, 'beer-and-babes' attitude" (Jacobson, 2002). And, after a 2-year stint at *Rolling Stone*, Needham was named editor of *Maxim* in mid-2004 (Carr, 2004). Yet even before Needham's arrival in 2002, *Rolling Stone*'s cover in 1999 of a provocatively dressed Britney Spears became the magazine's biggest seller of that year ("Best and Worst," 2000), and she has appeared on the cover at least a half dozen times since then.

MAGAZINE COVER LITERATURE

Research focusing on magazine covers alone is extremely limited and isolated within academic disciplines (Johnson, 2002). Historically, "playful women" were featured on mainstream magazine covers to gain the attention of upwardly mobile men in the first half of the 20th century, when play was seen as "sin—whether in the form of alcohol or illicit sex" (Kitch, 2001, p. 58). An analysis of covers in the latter part of the 20th century found that strategies had changed little for mainstream, middle-class magazines over the century (Malkin et al., 1999). Of 123 covers on 21 men's and women's magazines from 1996, 94% of women's magazines featured a thin female model or celebrity on their covers, with only 3% featuring male models or celebrities on covers. For men's magazines in this study, women appeared on half the covers and men on 28% of covers, with the authors concluding that "visual images on both men's and women's magazine covers tend to portray what women should look like and what men should look for. There is minimal focus on the male body" (Malkin et al., 1999, p. 654).

Another study by Brinkley and Fowler (2001) reviewed covers of American women's and men's magazines in the latter half of the 1990s, coding for the sexual explicitness of the cover subject's dress and for words used in cover text. The study found that covers tended to feature more women than men, that women dressed more explicitly than men, and that more text messages on women's magazines focused on self-improvement than did text on men's magazine covers. Overall, these findings match industry views that fashion–beauty–lifestyle magazines for women in the 1990s competed by featuring sexy celebrities on their covers and by using more "candid" language there, and that men's magazines were starting to borrow this same cover formula (Span, 1998).

Maxim and other "lad mags" such as *FHM* and *Stuff* may seem to be descended most directly from their same-name predecessor publications in the United Kingdom. An argument could be made, however, that all these so-called magazines copied their cover formulas from women's fashion–beauty–lifestyle magazines such as *Cosmopolitan* and *Glamour* and perhaps even from soft pornographic publications such as *Playboy*, which uses a brown wrapper. One North American grocery store chain now uses brown wrappers to cover *Cosmopolitan*, which laid down a formula for attracting readers and attention with sexually suggestive women's bodies on its covers ("Women's Magazines," 2000). More recently, one large discount chain will no longer sell *Maxim*, and some stores are using shields to hide most of *Maxim*'s cover photos ("Wal-Mart banishes," 2003).

That sexy cover models sell magazines is taken for granted by some in industry circles. The mantra that "sex sells" appears to carry currency in the current men's magazine market and beyond. In fact, former *Maxim* and *Details* editor Mark Golin has said he relies on the same formula wherever he works in the industry, whether at *Cosmopolitan*, *Maxim*, or *Prevention* magazine ("The Joy," 2000). Indeed, one academic study that assessed the effects of sexy cover content found that sexual attractiveness of the cover model, and the subsequent sexual arousal it generated, were related to interest in the magazine (Reichert, in press).

In sum, whereas there are few academic studies of magazine covers, industry experts and the popular press offer clues about the cover's importance to branding and sales success, especially newsstand sales. Empirical research on magazine covers, such as this present study, can shed light on shifts among competitors in how they use covers to brand and to sell their publications. As important, this study may demonstrate how these magazines used images of women to position a magazine that was slightly different from competing magazines but targeting the same market or demographic.

RESEARCH QUESTIONS

Based on past magazine cover research and information gleaned from media reports about *Maxim* and its perceived effect on men's magazines, the following research questions were posed for study of covers of *Maxim*, *GQ*, *Esquire*, *Details*, and *Rolling Stone*. Specifically, this study sought to determine if, over time (from 1995 through 2000), the covers of these magazines came to mirror the sexualized *Maxim* formula characterized by women displayed in revealing attire and poses.

RQ1: From 1995–2000, the period including *Maxim*'s debut in 1997, did the covers of men's magazines become similar to *Maxim* as asserted by the popular press?

RQ2: Did men's magazine covers follow *Maxim*'s formula before *Maxim*'s debut (January 1995 to April 1997) compared to after (May 1997 to December 2000)?

Based on previously cited research (Brinkley & Fowler, 2001; Malkin et al., 1999) as well as decades of media-portrayal research, it is expected that females will be portrayed in a more sexual manner and in a more decoratively revealing manner than males regardless of adoption of the *Maxim* cover formula.

H1:   Female and male depictions on the covers of men's magazines will differ in terms of pose, body view, attire, and sexual tone.

METHOD

Sample Selection

All covers of *Details*, *Esquire*, *GQ*, and *Rolling Stone* from January 1995 through 2000 were included in the sample ($n = 359$). All are published monthly, except for *Rolling Stone*, which is published every other week; in Spring/Summer 2000, *Details* ceased publication for several months when it changed formats. All issues of *Maxim* were coded, from spring 1997 through 2000, including joint July/August issues in its first 2 years ($n = 36$). The total sample consisted of 395 covers ($N = 395$).

These magazines were selected based on their inclusion in popular press reports about *Maxim* and based on circulation and gender readership categories. All were well-established magazines published primarily for men before the advent of *Maxim*; *Rolling Stone* does not fit the general interest category as do the others, and yet it was constantly perceived by the press as a competitor for *Maxim*-like readership.

Variables

Variables were selected to represent common elements on *Maxim* covers, namely cover models. These variables included gender and number of cover models as well as how the models were portrayed (pose, body view, amount and style of clothing, and sexual tone). The coders first noted whether a cover contained a primary subject or subjects, and coding continued if a cover featured at least one female or one male subject. The model or most prominent model was coded as female(s), male(s), heterosexual couple, many models, or no model. Overall, most covers with people on them (98%) featured only one model (81%).

How the cover models were portrayed overall was assessed with four variables. Two variables provided an indication of the model's positioning: pose and body view. Pose consisted of whether the model was standing, sitting, or reclining, with a "face only" view coded as standing. Body view represented how much of the model's body was shown, ordered from "body" shots (full-body and three-quarter shots) to "head and torso" shots to "face" shots (head and shoulder, and head shots).

How the models were portrayed sexually was assessed with two variables. One involved dress: the amount and style of clothing worn by the model. Each female or male cover subject was classified into one of four categories for dress: demure, suggestive, partially clad, or nude. Demure was defined as "everyday dress" such as walking shorts but not short shorts or underwear (Soley & Reid, 1988). Suggestive dress was defined as clothing that partially exposed the upper body, such as muscle shirts or unbuttoned shirts, and included very short shorts. Cover subjects were considered partially clad if they were shown in underwear or swimsuits. If the suggestion of nudity was present (a cover subject holds a surfboard in front of his genitals) or subjects were nude but in silhouette, they were coded as nude.

The second sexuality variable required coders to make a subjective judgment about whether the cover model could be considered by potential buyers as being "sexy," with choices of "no," "somewhat," and "yes." Judgment was based on a gestalt reading of the cover that included dress, eye contact, facial expression, posture, and other factors. For the purpose of analysis, the categories "somewhat" and "yes" were combined to indicate the cover model was sexually portrayed.

Overall, most issues were coded by two trained, graduate-student coders, both women, who worked independently. Training consisted of providing each coder with the content categories and of practice sessions using and discussing the categories. After coding, all discrepancies were discussed by the coders until agreement was reached. One of the authors coded the 2000 issues of *Rolling Stone* as well as several magazine covers that were unavailable during the initial coding session.

RESULTS

The first research question (RQ1) sought to assess the men's magazine cover landscape before and after *Maxim*'s debut in 1997. This analysis included all magazines in the study (*Details, Esquire, GQ, Maxim,* and *Rolling Stone*) with only female(s) or male(s) on the cover (91% of all covers). Overall, there were several significant changes (all tests were chi-square with alpha level set at .05). First, there was a relationship between cover model gender and year, $\chi^2(5, N = 361) = 20.87$, $p < .001$, $\Phi = .24$. Over time, women were more likely to appear on magazine covers than men (see Table 5.1). For example, men occupied 75% of covers in 1996 compared to only 44% in 2000.

Second, there was no change between cover models' pose and time, $\chi^2(10, N = 361) = 15.83$, $p > .10$, $\Phi = .21$. For example, there was no

TABLE 5.1
Magazine Covers: Men's Magazines and *Rolling Stone* (including *Maxim*)
1995–2000

	Year					
Primary Model	1995	1996	1997	1998	1999	2000
*Gender**						
Female(s)	24.6%	31.5%	41.8%	53.0%	53.8%	56.3%
Male(s)	75.4%	68.5%	58.2%	47.0%	46.2%	43.8%
Pose						
Standing	82.5%	83.3%	78.2%	83.3%	64.6%	75.0%
Sitting	15.8%	11.1%	16.4%	10.6%	21.5%	21.9%
Reclining	1.8%	5.6%	5.5%	6.1%	13.8%	3.1%
*Body View**						
Body Shot	45.6%	35.2%	27.3%	30.3%	63.1%	68.8%
Head & Torso	24.6%	33.3%	43.6%	39.4%	27.7%	25.0%
Head Shot	29.8%	31.5%	29.1%	30.3%	9.2%	6.3%
*Clothing**						
Demure	68.4%	61.1%	54.5%	50.0%	33.8%	32.8%
Suggestive	15.8%	14.8%	20.0%	19.7%	15.4%	34.4%
Partially Clad	3.5%	16.7%	23.6%	22.7%	36.9%	25.0%
Nude	12.3%	7.4%	1.8%	7.6%	13.8%	7.8%
*Sexual Tone**						
No	61.4%	64.8%	52.7%	47.0%	33.8%	21.9%
Yes	38.6%	35.2%	47.3%	53.0%	66.2%	78.1%
Total	$n = 57$	$n = 54$	$n = 55$	$n = 66$	$n = 65$	$n = 64$

Note. Magazines include *Details, Esquire, GQ, Maxim*, and *Rolling Stone*. Only covers with females or males were included in the table ($N = 361$; 91% of all covers).
*Chi-square, $p < .001$

change in the proportion of models shown sitting, reclining, or standing from 1995 to 2000. There were, however, significant relationships between time and how the models were portrayed with regard to body view, clothing, and sexual tone. The view of the model was significantly related to year, $\chi^2(10, N = 361) = 45.36, p < .001, \Phi = .35$: Covers emphasizing "body" and "head and torso" shots increased from 70% in 1995 to 94% in 2000. Similarly, cover models were more likely to be sexually dressed over time, $\chi^2(15, N = 361) = 43.89, p < .001, \Phi = .35$, with 32% appearing suggestively dressed, partially clad, or nude in 1995 compared to 67% in 2000. Last, cover models were more likely to be portrayed sexually over time, $\chi^2(5, N = 361) = 33.03, p < .001, \Phi = .30$.

The second research question (RQ2) sought to more closely examine the nature of magazine covers before and after *Maxim*'s debut (see Table 5.2).

TABLE 5.2
Magazine Covers: Men's Magazines and *Rolling Stone*
(excluding *Maxim*) 1995–2000

Primary Model	Before Maxim (n = 126)	After Maxim (n = 199)	Female(s) on Cover (n = 124)	Male(s) on Cover (n = 201)
Gender				
Female(s)	27.8%	44.7%	–	–
Male(s)	72.2%	55.3%	–	–
	p < .01			
Pose				
Standing	80.2%	78.9%	68.5%	86.1%
Sitting	16.7%	15.6%	23.4%	11.4%
Reclining	3.2%	5.5%	8.1%	2.5%
	NS		*p* < .001	
Body View				
Body Shot	38.9%	49.2%	64.5%	33.3%
Head & Torso	29.4%	31.7%	31.5%	30.3%
Head Shot	31.7%	19.1%	4.0%	36.3%
	p < .05		*p* < .001	
Clothing				
Demure	65.9%	47.7%	7.3%	84.1%
Suggestive	15.9%	22.6%	38.7%	8.5%
Partially Clad	9.5%	20.6%	37.1%	3.5%
Nude	8.7%	9.0%	16.9%	4.0%
	p < .01		*p* < .001	
Sexual Tone				
No	63.5%	43.2%	4.0%	80.1%
Yes	36.5%	56.8%	96.0%	19.9%
	p < .001		*p* < .001	

Note. Magazines include *Details, Esquire, GQ,* and *Rolling Stone* (*Maxim* was excluded). Only covers with females or males were included in the table (*N* = 325).

This was done by removing *Maxim* covers from the analysis. *Details, Esquire, GQ,* and *Rolling Stone* issues published through April 1997 (Before) were compared to issues published from May 1997 through 2000 (After). Overall, the findings were similar to those for RQ1: Women were more likely to appear on covers after *Maxim*'s debut, $\chi^2(1, N = 325) = 9.39$, $p < .01$, $\Phi = .17$; there was no change in cover models' pose, $\chi^2(2, N = 325) = 1.0$, $p > .05$; but there were significant relationships for how much of the cover person's body was revealed, $\chi^2(2, N = 325) = 7.11$, $p < .05$, $\Phi = .15$; clothing worn by cover models, $\chi^2(3, N = 325) = 12.20$, $p < .01$, $\Phi = .19$; and sexual portrayal, $\chi^2(1, N = 325) = 12.69$, $p < .001$, $\Phi = .20$. The findings suggest that after *Maxim* was published women were more likely to appear on covers and that more of their body was shown, they wore less clothing, and they were portrayed sexually.

The hypothesis predicted that women would be portrayed in a more sexualized and decorative manner than men. Overall, this hypothesis was supported. Despite no differences in the two previous analyses, cover model pose was significant between women and men, $\chi^2(2, N = 325) = 14.97$, $p < .001$, $\Phi = .22$. Thirty-one percent of women were shown sitting or reclining compared to 14% of men. Similarly, most women were shown in "head and torso" or "full body" shots than men, $\chi^2(2, N = 325) = 49.83$, $p < .001$, $\Phi = .39$. The analysis revealed that 96% of women were shot in this way compared to 64% of men. Even more significant, women were much more likely to be dressed sexually (93%) than men (16%), $\chi^2(3, N = 325) = 185.29$, $p < .001$, $\Phi = .76$. Similarly, there was a significant relationship between sexual tone and gender, $\chi^2(1, N = 325) = 177.58$, $p < .001$, $\Phi = .74$. Again, close to 96% of women were shot in a sexual manner compared to 20% of men. These findings and their implications are discussed in more detail in the following section.

DISCUSSION

A primary purpose of this study was to assess changes in the covers of men's magazines and *Rolling Stone* from 1995 through 2000. Overall, we found several striking differences. The first research question (RQ1) sought to determine if the magazines examined in this study adopted the *Maxim* cover formula by featuring women with emphases on their bodies (pose, body view) and sexuality (clothing and sexual tone). The results suggest that, overall, the formula was steadily adopted over time. In an almost perfect upward trend, images of women on covers increased from 25% to 56% from 1995 to 2000 (see Table 5.1). Demure dress for all cover subjects on all magazines dropped from 68% to 33% during those years, and emphasis on the body of cover subjects increased. Body shots increased from 46% to 69% over the 5-year period, and head shots decreased from 30% to 6%. Because this analysis included *Maxim*, there is some bias in the direction of change. At the very least, however, this analysis provides an overview of the shift in positioning of men's magazines as a whole in a competitive environment in which each magazine is vying for a similar audience while trying to brand itself as slightly different and better than its competitors. An examination of non-*Maxim* covers provides, perhaps, a less biased perspective from which to answer the remaining research question.

The second research question (RQ2) sought to determine if there was a difference between the covers of *Details*, *Esquire*, *GQ*, and *Rolling Stone* "before" and "after" *Maxim*'s debut. Results suggest that—similar to the results for RQ1—these magazines adopted a *Maxim*-style format, at least in terms of cover persons (see Table 5.2). For example, women were much more likely to appear on magazine covers after *Maxim*'s introduction (45%) than before (28%; see Table 5.2). Although "pose" was similar both before and after—most persons were shown standing—body view, lack of clothing, and sexual tone increased after *Maxim*'s debut. For instance, 32% of covers contained "head shots" beforehand, compared to only 19% afterward. Perhaps in association with the use of women on covers, the four magazines used more sex-tinged images overall, as coders responded to the images as being sexy 37% of the time before *Maxim* and 57% of the time after.

A closer look at gender differences was illuminated by the hypothesis, which sought to distinguish the nature of portrayal between women and men on covers. The analysis revealed several striking differences. In the overall sample of the four magazines, 84% of men who appeared on the covers were dressed demurely, with only 7% of women dressed demurely. In essence, 54% of women on covers were partially clad (37%; bikinis, lingerie) or nude (17%) in the style of *Maxim* itself. It is important to reiterate that during the study period, not one *Maxim* cover featured a demurely dressed woman. In addition, not only were women wearing less than men, but their bodies were also emphasized more than men's bodies: Across the 1995–2000 time span for the four magazines, just 4% of female cover subjects were emphasized for their faces or head, with the remaining 96% of depictions of women's head and torso or body. For men, the highest view category was head, with 36% of all depictions. Body shots for men accounted for 30% and head and torso for 33% of all depictions for the four magazines. Given the nature of these findings, it is not surprising that almost all women on these magazine covers (96%) were depicted sexually compared to men (20%).

Taken as a whole, these findings are consistent with related research. For example, Brinkley and Fowler's (2001) analysis of men's and women's magazine covers in the latter half of the 1990s also revealed that more women appear on covers than men and that women are dressed more explicitly. This pattern was certainly evident in the present research. Our findings are somewhat inconsistent with those of a study that examined 1996 covers (Malkin et al., 1999). In that study, women were present in half of men's magazine covers, with men appearing on 28% of covers. In our 1996 sample, two thirds of covers featured only men (see Table 5.1). The discrepancy could be explained by sample selection. In the present research, leading men's general-interest magazines were selected in addition to *Rolling Stone*. Our findings were similar, however, in that when males appeared on covers, there was minimal focus on their bodies compared to women (see, for example, Figs. 5.4 and 5.5).

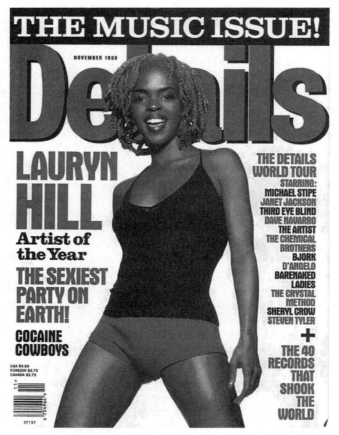

FIG. 5.4.   A body shot of Lauryn Hill on *Details*, November 1998.

IMPLICATIONS

The rise in macho culture may explain *Maxim*'s success, its reliance on images of sexualized women, and its competitors' changing strategies. A *GQ* art director once criticized *Maxim* as serving "men who not only move their lips but drool when they read" (Foege, 2002); but despite such criticism, *Maxim* has relished its macho status as a "safe place for guys to be guys" (Blanchard, 1998, p. 14). Joining *Maxim* in the macho culture trend are television shows such as "The Man Show," sports talk radio that resembles locker-room conversation, as well as movies and music ("Macho Culture," 2000). Men's magazine covers simply may be one effect of macho culture's reach and influence, but *Maxim*'s publisher objects to charges that

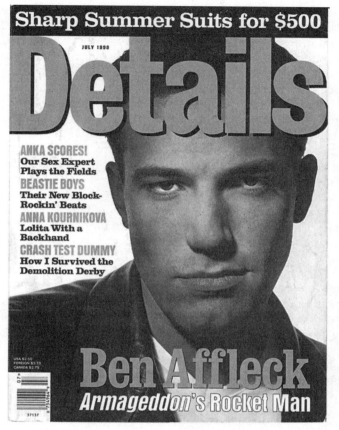

FIG. 5.5. A head shot of Ben Affleck, *Details*, July 1998.

the magazine appeals to "the lowest common denominator. I say we aim for the largest. We're trying to create entertainment value. Make it short. Make it funny" (Gremillion, 1997, p. 28). Golin says the magazine is "like your best buddy that your wife or girlfriend hates. But she can't actually scream at a magazine, so you're safe" (Newman, 1999, p. 46). It is important to remember, however, that this "funny" and "safe" environment also works to construct and constrict its audience, that "[m]edia industries and patriarchal differentiations work hand in hand to keep gender in line" (Steinman, 1992, p. 203). Part of the cultural work performed by *Maxim's* covers and similar publications is the hardening of categories, the sanctioning of the male/female binary as true and good.

Feminist studies have thoroughly addressed concerns about objectification of women's bodies and the damage this does to all women, even to those women who embrace and exploit their objectification while believing they have been empowered by their "exposure," at least superficially. Their images, feminist scholars would say, are representations "of a male-defined ideal; we might argue that men find it easier to 'consume' depersonalised images than to relate to 'real' women, and that this consumption enhances their perceptions of their own power" (Dickey, 1987, p. 75). These images, too, represent a larger phenomenon of women as willing, self-policing subjects. Sandra Lee Bartky calls this "a saving in the economy of enforcement: since it is women themselves who practice this discipline on and against their own bodies, men get off scot-free" (1988, p. 81). *Maxim's* interviews with the women featured on its covers almost uniformly and explicitly express the "cooperative" nature of these representations, of publishers and models/actors working together to produce the ideal look. Interviews with Melissa Joan Hart, Jennifer Love Hewitt, and Lara Flynn Boyle give just that impression. Their voices do change their own objectified images into speaking subjects, yet their stand-alone images on the cover still serve also as signs of oppression, of bodies without "self-defined desires" (Neal, 1992, p. 107). While these women's pillow-talk perspectives may make their objectification seem more ambiguous or benign, their cover displays are nothing but traditional stereotypes of sexualized, commodified females.

In several press accounts about *Maxim's* success, the editors of *Esquire, GQ, Details,* and *Rolling Stone* deny they are trying to be like *Maxim* (Jacobson, 2002; Walker & Golden, 2001). Yet *Details'* hiring of a *Maxim* editor and *Rolling Stone's* hiring of an *FHM* editor—who after his *Rolling Stone* stint then became *Maxim's* editor—belie this stance. In fact, *Details'* failure as a *Maxim* clone demonstrates that adopting the cover and editorial formula of a more successful competitor is not easy. In the case of *Details,* a magazine that radically embraced *Maxim's* look, publishers temporarily ceased publication in the face of rapid circulation declines. It could be that established readers objected to the change and canceled subscriptions while new readers, lured by provocative covers, were disappointed by the lack of corresponding content (e.g., layouts, pictorials, sex advice). On the other hand, *Maxim* clones such as *FHM* and *Stuff*—magazines replete with pictorials and sex-tinged editorial content—experienced rapid circulation gains (Fine, 2001). This is simply more evidence that *Maxim's* retro formula works, that of female bodies selling and branding products (see Fig. 5.6).

LIMITATIONS AND DIRECTIONS FOR FUTURE RESEARCH

The purpose of this study was not to demonstrate that *Maxim* was a causal factor in changes occurring at four other men's magazines. Indeed, that task is nearly impossible because complex economic factors, cultural trends, and editorial personalities join together to affect any single magazine's

FIG. 5.6. The formula continues at *Maxim*, July 2004, and circulation remains at 2.5 million.

purpose and branding strategy. Instead, this study sought to trace changes at *Details*, *Esquire*, *GQ*, and *Rolling Stone* during the rise of *Maxim*, which surely can be said to have exerted some influence in editorial decisions made in the men's magazine market from 1997 to 2000, however ambiguous and indirect. Although several popular magazines in the men's market were analyzed, this study obviously did not include all of them, and so results may be generalized to only those magazines in the study. Furthermore, the sexual tone of a cover was a subjective judgment by coders, unlike the other categories used in this content analysis. Although this judgment was based on a gestalt reading, some interpretation was necessary.

Future research might include a correlation analysis of men's magazine covers and newsstand sales, to help provide a link between editorial decisions about covers and the results of those decisions. A future qualitative study could connect the cover strategies used by *Playboy* magazine in its heyday with *Maxim*'s more recent strategy, with the aim of discerning similarities and differences in their approaches and audiences. Comparison and contrast studies could also be conducted between men's and women's magazines and the ways they may influence each other.

CONCLUSION

When a competitor storms a well-established men's magazine market, changes occur and the popular press takes notice—especially when the changes are salacious. In the case of *Maxim*'s debut and spectacular increase in circulation, speculation ran high that the "lad mag" had transformed the market. This study confirms that although changes did occur, these were different from the "cloning" claims made by observers, more subtle than simply copying the formula, but profound nonetheless. The results of this study show that, as a whole, men's magazine covers became more sexualized from 1995 to 2000. Much of the sexual nature can be attributed to the increased presence of women on covers, from 25% in 1995 to 56% in 2000, women whose bodies were invariably characterized by revealing poses and clothing. Overall, this study found that basic format changes on covers of *Maxim*'s competitors occurred after that magazine's debut and success.

ACKNOWLEDGMENTS

The authors thank Alan Albarran and Stacy Anderson at the University of North Texas; Beth Clark and Lei Zhang, graduates of the UNT Mayborn Graduate Institute of Journalism; and Fei Xue, a doctoral student at the University of Alabama, for their assistance with this project. Jacqueline Lambiase received support for this study from a research grant at the University of North Texas.

REFERENCES

Bartky, S. L. (1988). Foucault, femininity, and the modernization of patriarchal power. In I. Diamond and L. Quinby (Eds.), *Feminism and Foucault: Reflections on resistance* (pp. 61–86). Boston: Northeastern University Press.
Best and worst sellers of '99. (2000, March 6). *Consumer Magazines* (in *Adweek*), M84.
Blanchard, K. (1998, March). Editor's letter. *Maxim*, p. 14.
Bounds, W. (1999, January 3). Editor leaves, and magazine spins hamster–shotgun–chain saw tale. *Wall Street Journal*, p. B1.
Brinkley, A., & Fowler, G. (2001, November). The politics of aesthetics: A comparison of appearance-driven messages on men's and women's magazine covers.

Paper presented at the annual meeting of the Southwest Education Council for Journalism and Mass Communication, Tulsa, OK.

Carr, D. (2004, July 10). A top *Rolling Stone* editor is lured to *Maxim* magazine. *New York Times*, p. B2.

Dickey, J. (1987). Women for sale: The construction of advertising images. In K. Davies, J. Dickey, and T. Stratford (Eds.), *Out of focus: Writings on women and the media* (pp. 74–77). London: The Women's Press.

Fine, J. (2001, February 10). Data center: Circ still slow for magazines. *Advertising Age*, p. 12.

Foege, A. (2002, March 1). Lad in charge. *Mediaweek*. Retrieved November 1, 2002, from http://mediaweek.com/mediaweek/search/search_display.jsp? vnu_content_id=1357181.

Gremillion, J. (1997, February 17). What men really want. *Mediaweek*, p. 28.

Hagan, J. (2002, February 1). Cover Creation 2002. *Folio*. Retrieved November 1, 2002, from http://foliomag.com/ar/cover_creation/index.htm.

Handy, B. (1999, February 15). Bosom buddies: Today's men's magazines all share a common interest—can you tell? *Time*, p. 75.

Hansen, C. H., & Hansen, R. D. (2000). Music and music videos. In D. Zillmann & P. Vorderer (Eds.), *Media entertainment: The psychology of its appeal* (pp. 175–196). Mahwah, NJ: Lawrence Erlbaum Associates.

Jacobson, A. (2002, July 15). Old guard, new guard: Graying magazines revamp to keep up with the newcomers. *Newsday*, B6-B7.

Johnson, S. (2002). The art and science of magazine cover research. *Journal of Magazine and New Media Research*, 2. Retrieved November 1, 2002, from http://aejmcmagazine.bsu.edu/journal/Summer_2002/Sjohnson1.htm.

Kitch, C. (2001). *The girl on the magazine cover: The origins of visual stereotypes in American mass media*. Chapel Hill: University of North Carolina Press.

Loeb, M. (2000). Sex, sports, beer, gadgets, clothes: The magic and menace of *Maxim*. *Columbia Journalism Review*, May/June, 68–69.

Macho culture. (2000, January 10). *Talk of the nation*. New York: National Public Radio.

Malkin, A. R., Wornian, K., & Chrisler, J. C. (1999). Women and weight: Gendered messages on magazine covers. *Sex Roles, 40*, 647–655.

Mnookin, S. (2001, August 20). Breaking the last taboo: *Details* takes it all off in Puff Daddy photo spread. Retrieved July 24, 2002, from http://inside.com/prod...3E4A2D-91F3-98B82D4BD2D3&CONTENT=Article.

Munk, N. (2001, May 1). Dennis the menace. *Vanity Fair*, 108–114.

Neal, L. (1992). *The female nude: Art, obscenity and sexuality*. London: Routledge.

Newman, J. (1999, March 8). Men will be boys. *Consumer Magazines* (in Adweek), 45–49.

Oliver, M. B., & Kalyanaraman, S. (2001). Appropriate for all viewing audiences? An examination of violent and sexual portrayals in movie previews featured on video rentals. *Journal of Broadcasting & Electronic Media, 46*(2), 283–299.

Reichert, T. (in press). Do sexy cover models increase magazine sales? Investigating the effects of sexual response on magazine interest and purchase intention. *Journal of Promotion Management*.

Reichert, T., Lambiase, J., Morgan, S., Carstarphen, M., & Zavoina, S. (1999). Beefcake or cheesecake? No matter how you slice it, sexual explicitness in advertising continues to increase. *Journalism & Mass Communication Quarterly, 76*(1), 7–20.

Signorielli, N, McLeod, D., & Healy, E. (1994). Gender stereotypes in MTV commercials: The beat goes on. *Journal of Broadcasting & Electronic Media, 38,* 91–101.

Soley, L., & Reid, L. (1998). Taking it off: Are models in magazine ads wearing less? *Journalism & Mass Communication Quarterly, 65,* 960–966.

Span, P. (1998, December 30). Between the covers: As their editors switch positions, women's magazines unveil a familiar look. *Washington Post,* D1–D2.

Steinman, C. (1992). Gaze out of bounds: Men watching men on television. In S. Craig (Ed.), *Men, masculinity, and the media* (pp. 199–214). Newbury Park, CA: Sage.

Sullivan, A. (2000, June 26). Dumb and dumber. *The New Republic,* p. 6.

The joy of sex. (2000, March 6). *Consumer Magazines* (in *Adweek*), M82.

Thriving market captures attention of younger men. (2002, April). *PR Week,* 12.

Turner, R. (1999, February 1). Finding the inner swine. *Newsweek,* p. 52.

Walker, D., & Golden, R. (2001, March 5). The fall and rise of *Details. Adweek Special Report,* SR58–SR59.

Walker, J. (2000). Sex and violence in program promotion. In S. Eastman (Ed.), *Research in media promotion* (pp. 101–126). Mahwah, NJ: Lawrence Erlbaum Associates.

Wal-Mart banishes bawdy mags: Retailer takes *Maxim, Stuff* and *FHM* off the shelves, citing complaints over racy content. (2003, May 6). Retrieved June 15, 2003, from http://money.cnn.com/2003/05/06/news/companies/walmart_mags/.

Warner, M. (1997). Sexy Brit mag invades U.S. *Fortune, 135,* 27–28.

Women's magazines: Are the teasing covers going too far? (2000, January 23). *Dallas Morning News,* 24A.

Chapter 6

From Sideline to Centerfold: The Sexual Commodification of Female Sportscasters

Jamie Skerski
Indiana University

> They don't call it the boob tube for nothing. Why else would Lisa Guerrero be talking into a microphone while sashaying down the sidelines of *Monday Night Football* on ABC–TV? With ratings gone flaccid in recent years, network honchos got the urge to inject something into *Monday Night Football* that every red-blooded American male likes even more than football . . . sex. (Kiszla, 2003, p. D1)

> Don't get me wrong, I felt a tad embarrassed for Mr. Namath when he wanted to plant a wet one on ESPN sideline snoop Suzy Kolber. That said, in his moment of "indiscretion" Mr. Namath exposed just what a farce—not to mention waste of time—these sideline "reporters" are. (Raissman, 2004, p. 4)

Lisa Guerrero's debut as *Monday Night Football's* newest sideline reporter in 2003 resulted in a flood of criticism. After her first broadcast, she was publicly ridiculed by several ESPN *Sportscenter* anchors for making the mistake of identifying a player with the wrong team. Veteran female sports reporter, Leslie Visser, declined to comment specifically on Guerrero's publicized mishap, but she did offer a generalization about women in sports, stating, "There are two kinds—those of us who love sports and end up in TV, and women who love TV and end up in sports" (Hiestand, 2003, p. 2C).

Joe Namath's infamous flirtation with female sports reporter Suzy Kolber during a live broadcast in 2003 is indicative of a larger trend within professional sports—the attempt to capitalize on the incorporation of female sex appeal. Namath, who was visibly intoxicated during the sideline interview, slurred words and told Kolber twice he wanted to kiss her ("Namath Gets Help," 2004). While the Namath blunder was a temporary embarrassment for the NFL, it was also an unforeseen consequence of incorporating women into a domain traditionally defined by masculinity.

FIG. 6.1.   CBS reporter Bonnie Bernstein working the sidelines.

Tune into any nationally televised NFL or college football game and you will likely encounter images of attractive young women interacting with players and coaches on the sidelines (see Fig. 6.1). These sexy sideliners deliver injury reports and player gossip to the fans watching at home, before handing it back to the men in the broadcast booth to resume the play-by-play commentary. With *Monday Night Football* experiencing some of its lowest ratings since it began in 1970, and the added competition of cable sports stations, networks have been forced to reconsider marketing strategies. Incorporating sex appeal into the football broadcasts and pregame shows has become a trend—and it seems to be working. In fact, FOX's *NFL Sunday's* self-described "Weather Broad," Jillian Barberie, and her flirtatious interactions with her male counterparts have helped elevate the pregame show to its highest ratings in 5 years (*For Him Magazine*, 2002).

Female sportscasters are undoubtedly capturing the attention of the male viewer, and judging by the exposure they receive in men's magazines, their popularity is largely due to sex appeal. Ultimately, the networks profit from the sportscaster's popularity, enjoying an increase in television ratings and, hence, an increase in advertising revenue. More is at stake, however, than just ratings and advertising dollars, and this chapter confronts the implications of the female sportscaster's movement between sideline and centerfold.

SPORTS CULTURE

Sports news coverage has evolved from a tradition that had been trivialized as mere entertainment. Recently, however, sports have been reconsidered as an important site of cultural production. Scholars from the fields of anthropology, sociology, and media studies, as well as others, are beginning to recognize that "more—much more—is going on in sports than fun and games" (Polumbaum & Wieting, 1999, p. 70). This shift in the conceptualization of sports

> as frivolous and marginal to important human affairs has become hard to sustain. Many sports stories are no longer just sports stories; they may be labor, legal, or lifestyle stories as well. Major sports are big business and, when it comes to public investments in sports facilities, also public business. Sports have become an arena for scrutinizing larger social problems, including racial tensions and gender inequities. (Polumbaum & Wieting, p. 69)

An analysis of the contemporary female sportscaster offers a perspective on understanding the maintenance of a normative gender order that continues to privilege men over women. The inclusion of female sportscasters illustrates a form of strategic absorption. Social systems dominated by masculinity, such as professional football, may incorporate the challenge of female participation by including women, without having to significantly alter the underlying masculine structure and value systems. This inclusion results in increased visibility—more women are sportscasters—but the underlying value systems remain intact.

The professional sports industries—and football, in particular—remain cultural contexts defined by masculinity and patriarchal values (Sabo & Panepinto, 1990). As *Sports Illustrated*'s Sally Jenkins puts it, "Sports remains a bunch of boys observing what a bunch of boys do together" (Cramer, 1994, p. 159). While the inclusion of female sportscasters in this primarily male domain appears to be a step in the right direction for gender equity, I suggest that their inclusion may also be at the expense of systematic social progress. This chapter takes a critical cultural perspective in the evaluation of the contemporary female sports personality, arguing there are detrimental consequences stemming from the commodification and circulation of the female sportscaster image. To begin, I offer a brief history of women in sportscasting, contextualizing their current position in terms of their sexual value. Next, I describe the role of the sportscaster through the lens of primary themes, or prevalent tropes. Finally, I discuss the implications for the network rationale perpetuating the movement of female sportscasters between sideline and centerfold.

FROM SIDELINE TO CENTERFOLD

Phyllis George, named Miss America in 1971, became the first female sportscaster in 1975 when CBS hired her for its pregame show, *The NFL Today*. A few women were able to break into sports broadcasting in the subsequent years, but it certainly was not easy. Many of the pioneers speak of the difficulty of entering a male-dominated industry. Hannah Storm, one of the more respected contemporary commentators, recalls her job-search frustrations in the late 1980s: "I had a name and a lot of experience, and one sports news director said he wouldn't hire a woman over his dead body" (Garcia, 1998, p. 1C). In 1989, after she passed a quiz testing her knowledge about sports, supposedly a requirement for all applicants, CNN finally hired Storm. Later she discovered that not one of her 75 male colleagues had been tested (Garcia, 1998, p. 1C).

Title IX and the women's movement of the 1970s were instrumental in increasing the number of women who were able to pursue sports broadcasting, but the industry is still primarily a masculine domain. Title IX increased opportunities for female participation in youth and collegiate sports, while also creating an "expansion of career opportunities for women in the world of sports," including sports broadcasting (Storm, 2002, p. 12). However, a particular component—the locker room—made it difficult for female sportscasters to match the work of their male counterparts. Access to the locker room was crucial for game-day coverage, yet it remained an inaccessible space for many women. When access was granted in the early 1990s, women still faced the potential of harassment or male athletes who refused to speak to them (see Disch & Kane, 1996). Today, the locker room continues to be a necessary evil for the female reporter. One female reporter remarked, "I go in there, do what I have to do, and get the hell out. I make sure my eyes don't stay anywhere too long so people don't get the wrong idea" (Cramer, 1994). It is interesting to consider that the locker room *does not have to be* the primary place for athlete contact—in fact, many women's professional sports do not allow access to player locker rooms, opting for a postgame press conference atmosphere. Yet, the male locker room remains a site of status and power, despite the difficulties for women in the industry. Maintaining locker-room interviews both perpetuates and reinforces the women's disadvantage in male-dominated territory.

Women who successfully enter the realm of sports broadcasting endure increased scrutiny. Female reporters are aware that if they make a mistake, people will regard it as incompetence, whereas errors committed by male counterparts are dismissed as isolated incidents (Cramer, 1994). Andy Rooney, a *60 Minutes* commentator, vocalized his displeasure with the female reporters in a televised interview, remarking, "The only thing that really bugs me about television's coverage is those damn women they have down on the sidelines who don't know what the hell they're talking about" ("Women sportscasters bristle," 2002). Similarly, well-known NFL coach Bill Parcells insisted that female reporters "don't know whether the ball is pumped or stuffed" (Kimball, 2001). The Rooney and Parcells comments reflect the uneasiness regarding the presence of women in a masculine domain. The women seem to be either objects of criticism or objects of adoration—and yet the networks continue to gamble by increasing the number of women in sports broadcasting.

The trend of incorporating female sportscasters on the sidelines began in the mid-1990s. And, despite public debate about their popularity, women are increasingly appearing on game-day television, both on the sidelines and on pregame programming. In 1991, *Sports Illustrated* reported fewer than 50 female sportscasters were on the air, while a decade later *USA Today* counted 127 (Klaffke, 2003). These game-day reporters tend to roam the sidelines and deliver nonessential information to the viewer at home—adding emotional appeal to the play-by-play discourse and sex appeal to the game aesthetic. Other female football personalities, such as the "Weather Broad," Jillian Barberie, on the FOX pregame show, simply add sex appeal to a sports show otherwise dominated by middle-aged men. In Barberie's particular case, there is little disguise of the pseudo-meteorologist's purpose, as illustrated by this description accompanying her photoshoot in the men's magazine, *FHM [For Him Magazine]*:

> "Lookit, I'm just a delicate flower, Terry," Fox *NFL Sunday's* self-described "weather broad" said as she patted her left butt cheek in response to Terry Bradshaw's question about the floral pattern on her skirt. It's the kind of sexually charged exchange that delights testosterone-laden football fans of all ages and helped to launch the pre-game program to its highest ratings in its five years on the air. Fox analyst Howie Long put it best when he said, "I know my three boys have gotten more interested in the weather." Haven't we all? ("*FHMUS Online*," 2002; see Fig. 6.2)

Twenty-five years after Phyllis George broke the gendered barrier to televised sportscasting, *Playboy* magazine reinforced the aesthetic appeal of the female sportscaster by launching a contest in which readers could vote to determine the Sexiest Sports Babe (*Playboy.com*, 2000). Readers were invited to vote online and the winning sportscaster was to be offered $1 million in exchange for a nude photo spread in the magazine. Over 200,000

FIG. 6.2. Jillian Barberie, Fox *NFL Sunday's* Weather Broad, works to keep it hot in an *FHM* layout.

votes were cast, making it *Playboy's* most popular contest to date. CBS college football sideline reporter, Jill Arrington (see Fig. 6.3), was crowned the winner with 57,643 votes, edging out *Monday Night Football's* Melissa Stark's 51,574 votes. Arrington, to the dismay of the magazine's editors, chose not to do the photo shoot, stating, "Of course I won't pose. I consider myself a serious journalist" (Kimball, 2001). However, Arrington did not renounce her title. In fact, several contestants who criticized the contest as "demeaning" ended up sending *Playboy* better photographs of themselves because they did not like the ones the magazine was using to promote the contest (Kimball, 2001). Bonnie Bernstein, another CBS sideliner and contest finalist, protested to a *New York Daily News* columnist (see Fig. 6.1), saying, "I never asked to be a part of this," but Bernstein admitted she was keeping tabs on the vote (Kimball, 2001, p. 25). As a side note, since being crowned the winner, Arrington has posed for several men's magazines, including *Maxim* and *FHM*.

Undoubtedly, the *Playboy* contest was a catalyst for the circulation of the female sportscaster image within popular culture. Prior to the contest, there was little coverage, or even recognition, of female sportscasting in the mainstream press. After the contest, their sexuality overshadowed all other aspects of coverage. For example, during the 2000 football season, several developments were taking place for women in sports broadcasting. ESPN's Pam Ward became the first woman, *ever*, to do play-by-play in a national college football broadcast. The game was not nationally televised, but it was still an impressive stride for a woman to make it into the broadcast booth. Within a few weeks of Ward's historic broadcasting opportunity, several other sportscaster-related events took place: (a) An announcement was made that 26-year-old Melissa Starks was going to replace 46-year-old Leslie Visser on *Monday Night Football*, (b) sideliner Jill Arrington drew media attention to herself for wearing a revealing tank top during a college football broadcast, and (c) the *Playboy* contest went public. As could be expected, little was mentioned about Ward's historic achievement, and the news coverage revolved around those developments related to the women's sex appeal.

Overall, it is important to note that women have had the opportunity to report on a variety of professional and college competitions, including impressive media events such as the Super Bowl and NCAA Final Four. However, the role of the female sportscaster for major sporting events is supplementary to the commentary of her male counterparts. Thus, because these reporters are seldom primary analysts, it is common practice for them to report on a variety of sports year-round. For instance, Bonnie Bernstein serves as NFL sideline reporter, covers NCAA basketball and track and field, cohosts the *At the Half* basketball program, and reports occasionally on the U.S. Open Tennis tournament. As mentioned earlier, despite the wide range of athletic competitions that have incorporated female sportscasters, the women who work within the football industry receive, by far, the most outside media publicity. This is evident in the amount of newspaper coverage about the football sideliners, the frequency of appearances in men's magazines, and even the number of fan Web sites dedicated to these particular football women.

From beginnings of a former Miss America in 1975 to the *Playboy* contest of 2000, the evolution of the female sportscaster's function is fairly transparent. The numbers of women have increased dramatically, but their social function remains that of sexual object. Before considering broader social implications of these portrayals, let us examine the primary tropes, or themes, that define the role of the contemporary female sportscaster.

FIG. 6.3. Sideliner Jill Arrington making headlines for turning heads.

CHEERLEADERS, SEX APPEAL, AND GOSSIP

Cheerleaders With Microphones

For nearly 30 years, the cheerleader has been the primary female figure associated with professional football. Although the Baltimore Colts were the first NFL team to employ women as professional cheerleaders, it was the Dallas Cowboys who famously catapulted the image of the cheerleader into the international spotlight in 1976, creating the "first pin-ups in modern

FIG. 6.3. *(Continued)*

sport" (Pratt, 2002, p. 30). Tex Schramm, the Cowboys' general manager at the time, realized football was becoming as much entertainment as sport and decided to introduce a squad of talented dancers wearing go-go boots and hot pants (Pratt, 2002). The success of the cheerleader is still evident 30 years later, as they remain on the sidelines, now joined by reporters. Cheerleaders entertain (male) fans attending the contest at the stadium, while the young and sexy female sportscasters provide similar supra-competition entertainment for the (male) television viewer at home or local sports bar. This connection, or articulation, to the cheerleader is integral to the production of meaning for the female sportscaster. That is, what the female sportscaster *means* is reliant, in part, on the way other women have been defined in the context of football—as people on the sidelines of the main event.

The concept of articulation has recently been adopted by several communication scholars as a way for theorizing how meaning is produced within the relationships among different ideas. Articulation can be defined as "any practice establishing a relation among elements such that their identity is modified as a result of the articulatory practice" (Laclau and Mouffe, 1985, p. 105). Simply put, the connection between cheerleader and reporter significantly affects the identity of the female sportscaster. Cheerleaders have increasingly earned respect for the athleticism necessary for participating, but "there's no doubt that they are viewed by most players and fans as mere sex objects" (Pratt, 2002, p. 32). Cheerleaders are employed for their sex appeal and entertainment value, and as Pratt notes, "the fact that the Dallas Cowboys and Miami Dolphins cheerleaders publish swimsuit calendars does little to atone for their sexpot image" (2002, p. 32). The sexualized reputation of the cheerleader alters the perception of the reporter, whereas the identity of the cheerleader is not disturbed by the relation to the sportscaster. The sportscaster's role becomes trivialized, if not sexualized, through this articulation to the cheerleader. Both female roles occupy a space, literally, on the sidelines, and provide nonessential components to the competition. Neither the cheerleader's nor sportscaster's actions contribute to driving the progress of the game. Rather, the athletes and male commentators control the pace and movement of the competition, while the cheerleaders and female sideliners react to the actions of the men. The cheerleaders react to certain athlete actions, and the sideliners wait passively to be called upon by the men in the broadcast booth.

Cheerleaders are employed for their entertainment value, and publicity and discourse revolving around the female sportscasters also point to their entertainment and sexual value. For instance, when the *Playboy* contest was unveiled during the 2000 holiday season, a *Monday Night Football* broadcast showed a fan holding a sign that read, *All I want for Christmas is Melissa* (Martzke, 2000). Furthermore, Jill Arrington's clothing has been known to cause some fan reaction, particularly a tank top she wore while sidelining a Virginia Tech–Miami football game. A particular crowd in an Atlanta sports bar was apparently so taken with Arrington's look that they would chant her name every time she appeared on the screen (Ginn, 2001). Arrington seemed surprised by the reaction to her outfit, stating she was more concerned with doing her job than what she was wearing. The viewers, however, seem less concerned with how she does her job than with the way she looks, as the sports bar scene suggests. Many, if not most, sports bars do not even have the volume turned on for televised games. Similarly, the aesthetic components of the cheerleader are more important than their actual cheers. Much like the case of the cheerleader, the fans want to watch—more than they want to listen—to the female sportscasters. The connection to the cheerleader is evident in their mutual placement on the sidelines, their entertainment value, and their nonessential part in the competition. Of course, the component of sex appeal is one of the most important characteristics, specifically, heterosexual sex appeal. The articulation with the cheerleader helps to frame the sportscaster as clearly heterosexual. Promoting her new book on American cheerleaders, author Pamela Bettis explains, "Cheerleading ... avoids the lesbian overtones some people place upon rough and tumble sports such as softball. You don't question the sexual orientation of a cheerleader" (Geranios, 2003, p. C5).

Sex Appeal

Female sportscasters generally embody heterosexual ideals of feminine sexuality. Most sideline sportscasters are tall, slim, and wear heavy makeup and stylish clothes on the field. In short, most of them share the glamorous aesthetic and body type that transfers well to the magazine photo spreads common in men's magazines. They are often protected from the elements in ways that differ from their male sportscaster companions. Rather than bulky jackets in cold weather, they wear stylish coats with matching hats and scarves. It remains important to "look good," in spite of the elements. In the rain, an umbrella resembling a parasol is favored over a practical rain parka so as not to mess with their stylish hair.

A certain type of feminine beauty and sex appeal are clearly a requirement for the job; however, the expectations exceed the realm of simple visual pleasure. The aesthetic requirements of the female sportscaster contribute to the perpetuation of a strict gender dichotomy—one that reinforces masculine strength and feminine passivity. During the actual sideline interviews, the hypermasculine male athlete is paired with the attractive female sportscaster, working to emphasize the sexuality of the sportscaster and the contrast between genders. The image of the sportscaster serves to reinforce ideological messages about strength, wherein women are deemed weaker than men. The conceptualization of strength as being defined by muscle mass (as opposed to being defined by something such as grace or agility) is a type of socially constructed "truth" that has been naturalized through a variety of discourses, primarily Western scientific discourse. The definition of strength *as muscle* has been so ingrained throughout culture that it is difficult to conceptualize strength as anything else. Because muscle mass is associated with maleness, and

FIG. 6.4. Sportscaster Lisa Guerrero exposed. A former NFL cheerleader, she was ridiculed for her "Monday Night Football" mishaps.

not femaleness, it leads to a larger cultural value system that associates females with weakness. This notion is visually reinforced, literally, with female sportscasters on the sidelines. The image includes a small-framed, attractive woman, complete with fashion sense and makeup, standing under the hulking epitome of masculinity and strength—the football player, shoulder pads and all, making him look even "stronger." Cultural studies theorist Stuart Hall (1989) reminds us that female sexuality is stabilized and controlled through the maintenance of this strict gender contrast—the contrast itself is not stable and must be constantly reinforced and reproduced. Hall continues:

> The *construction of difference* as a process, as something that goes on over time is something that feminism has been showing us is never finished. The notion that identity is complete at some point—the notion that masculinity and femininity can view each other as a perfectly replicating mirror

image of each another—is untenable . . . So the notion that identity is outside representation—that there are our selves and then the language in which we describe ourselves—is untenable. Identity is within discourse, within representation. (emphasis in original, p. 20)

Hall suggests the (re)construction of systematic patriarchy is an ongoing process—requiring revision and new forms of subordinating the feminine within a masculine culture. The female sportscaster's role within a male-dominated sports world illustrates one of these revisions. What appears to be a progressive mobility for a few individual women is, unfortunately, often a reinscription of a subordinate feminine sexual identity. The football player's towering masculinity paired with the small-framed feminine sexual ideal upholds the strict gender dichotomy that is most valuable for the upkeep of heterosexual normalcy. However, the masculine athlete and the feminine sportscaster do not hold equitable positions in the upholding of the heterosexual institution. Masculinity benefits from the upkeep of this sexual dichotomy, while the portrayal of femininity works to reinforce the values of a patriarchal system.

As noted earlier, the sex appeal of the female sportscaster, in part, is perpetuated by the women themselves. Although some of them did not agree to participate in the *Playboy* contest, several have gone on to do photo spreads for men's magazines. Additionally, several of them maintain personal Web sites complete with photo galleries. Some of these Web sites are more sexualized than others, as is the case of Jillian Barberie's personal Web site that contains the photo caption, "*Maxim* wanted to feature women in sports in their September issue. I guess because I do the weather for the NFL pre-game show, they figured I knew something about football—WRONG!" ("Jillian's World," 2003). There are also fan Web sites dedicated to these particular women. For instance, Bonnie Bernstein has a fan Web site dedicated to her, because in the words of its creator, Bernstein is a "talented sportscaster, who is also drop dead gorgeous" ("Bonnie Bernstein Fansite," 2004). Sexuality has also been used to promote the upcoming football schedule. In perhaps one of the more distasteful advertisements for FOX's pregame show, *NFL Sunday,* Barberie is shown taking a bath, and she is startled when she realizes she is being watched. The glimpse into her bathtub is then followed by a list of Sunday's game. The images of the sportscaster we consume point to her sexual objectification, but her discourse also places her into a feminized and trivialized role.

Gossip

The female sportscaster further contributes to the upkeep of gender assignments through her discourse. As mentioned earlier, the sideliners provide nonessential commentary on the game, which can be easily characterized within the feminized genre of communication known as "gossip." Brenneis believes that even without scandal, "gossip has a somewhat illicit air, as gossipers are telling someone else's story, one to which they have no right" (1992, p. 150). Essentially, gossip is not to be taken seriously—it is not of importance and trivial. The sportscasters, then, by talking about others, add "soft" news and "fluff" information—contrasted to the "hard" facts and analysis in the broadcast booth. One reporter even referred to the women as "sideline snoops" who have no business being there (Raissman, 2004).

The content of the sideline contributions generally range from injury reports to emotional appeal to the somewhat ridiculous. For instance, early in the 2003 season, Lisa Guerrero reported from the sideline during a Green Bay Packers game that she had talked to Packers quarterback Brett Favre prior to the game. She asked him whether he had plans to return to the game someday as a head coach. Then, she asked him "whether he would be a baseball hat-wearing coach, a visor-wearing coach, or would he not wear anything on his head at all." Pregame interviews tend to also fall into the "gossip" genre. For example, Melissa Starks conducted a pregame interview with Donovan McNabb, the Philadelphia Eagles quarterback who missed most of the 2002 season with a broken ankle. The interview took place as McNabb was about to make a dramatic late-season comeback. Stark's pressing question: "If someone were to make a soap opera about the events of this season—your injury and comeback—what would the soap opera be called?" Clearly, the insights these women provide are tangential to the actual competition, ranging from "Smith is being taken to the locker room for X-rays," to "Mitchell's wife delivered a healthy baby boy last night."

Representation of the female sportscaster can be characterized by her connection to the cheerleader, sexualized sidekick, and feminized "gossip." The combination of these tropes is detrimental to potential systematic progress for those women who desire to be taken seriously as sports journalists. The sexual appeal and circulation of that sex appeal into numerous media outlets—including men's magazines, Web sites, and the popular press—are of value to the networks. The sportscaster's utility is slim, because she contributes little content to the drive of the broadcast, yet her exchange value is enormous. The popularity of these women outside the realm of the broadcast is what is important to the networks.

It is the sportscaster's sexuality that is being commodified for the television audience, sufficiently diminishing the agency of the individual women. Thus, even those women who take their jobs seriously must become a part of the larger circulation of their generic sexualities. Ultimately, they are relegated to stereotypical female roles for the visual consumption of men in order to generate economic profit. The strategic incorporation of these women to increase ratings results in the confinement of women within a particular social order. Whatever their intentions may be, serious journalist or not, these women are enveloped in a discourse that is beyond their control. None of the women in *Playboy's Sexiest Sports Babe* contest volunteered to participate, yet the status of the generic female sportscaster made all of them eligible for the patriarchal circulation of their sexuality. Therefore, although the proliferation of female sportscasters may appear progressive for women, I argue that it is only about appearance, not substance.

CONCLUSIONS AND IMPLICATIONS

During this research, I searched for any and all depictions of female sportscasters in popular magazines. Quickly, it became apparent these women were most frequently featured in magazines targeted at men. Both *Playboy* and *Maxim* had issues dedicated to a version of the "Sports Babe," and female sportscasters have graced the cover of several other men's magazines. When mainstream magazines discussed the role of the female sportscaster, the features often revolved around the ways they were being visually consumed. For instance, *Sports Illustrated* ran an article about the sportscasters, but it was all reaction to the poll *Playboy* was sponsoring—it had nothing to do with their professional abilities. The *Playboy* poll was consistent with the theme found in most magazine and newspaper coverage. Regardless of magazine content or genre, the coverage of the female sportscasters revolved around their sexuality, whether explicitly or implicitly. This sexualizing trend resulted in newspaper headlines such as "Looking good...too good?" in the *St. Petersburg Times* and "TV Execs give us *Playboy* babes" in *USA Today*, or "Sports Babes are catching on," in the Canadian paper *The Calgary Herald*.

Even more interesting, the sportscaster phenomenon is occurring not only in the United States. Canada is also experiencing a similar trend with its female hockey commentators. *The Montreal Gazette* reported, "Taking a page from *Playboy*, which ran a reader survey rating American women sportscasters in January 2001, *Canada's Urban Male Magazine* went after Canada's female hockey sportscasters to photograph in provocative poses." The article mentioned the struggle of female sportscasters to remain "above the market demand for breasts and buttocks" (Cornacchia, 2002, p. A3). Notably, the female sportscasters who are most sexualized seem to come from the more violent sports—football and hockey. Perhaps future research should interrogate this link between sexy sportscasters and aggressive games.

In an era in which political correctness has promoted the illusion of progressive politics, it is important to examine the subtle ways dominant powers remain rather peacefully at the helm. The role of the female sportscaster is a unique site for exploring the ways in which female bodies are maneuvered by and for male-dominated social systems. For centuries, women have been tokens of exchange for men. Gayle Rubin refers to this as the "trafficking" of women. Men maintain and increase their social status by exchanging women. Women merely circulate. Marriage is thought of as the ultimate form of gift exchange, recognized in the familiar custom of the father giving away the bride to the prospective husband, while the daughter serves both a functional and ritualistic purpose. Rubin (1975) writes:

> The "exchange of women" is a seductive and powerful concept. It is attractive in that it places the oppression of women within social systems, rather than in biology. Moreover, it suggests that we look for the ultimate locus of women's oppression within the traffic of women, rather than in the traffic of merchandise. . . . Women are given in marriage, taken in battle, exchanged for favors, sent as tribute, traded, bought, and sold. Far from being confined to the "primitive" world, these practices seem only to become more pronounced and commercialized in more "civilized" societies. (p. 175)

Rubin's mention of practices in "civilized" societies resonates with the role of the female sportscaster in contemporary American popular culture. The female sportscaster's primary role in the political economy of the media industries is to attract male viewers and, hence, advertising dollars. The networks capitalize when the female sportscaster image is circulated within other masculine domains. The *Playboy* contest is only one example, but these women have been circulated in a variety of men's magazines as sexual objects, been used in television commercials to promote programming, and are certainly part of the conversation on weekend afternoons between male football viewers.

That being said, the current meaning enveloping the female sportscaster is not permanent and is subject to transformation and change. As Polumbaum and Wieting (1999) remind us, "Sports stories do not have changeless meanings through time and, in any given period, may serve a variety of rhetorical purposes in carrying moral values." In order to transform the current sexualized position of the female sportscaster, we first must realize that each media image we consume is tailored to meet a particular need. Images and representations of gender and sexuality are framed in ways that ask us to accept a particular reality over another. In this case, it is important to keep in mind that the function of the sideline female sportscaster was the creation of an industry dominated by masculinity.

We live in a media-saturated society that tends to equate an increase in representation as an increase in political progress or tolerance.

Sidestepping this common reaction and understanding that *visibility does not necessarily change the values* allow us to consider other ways in which dominant structures are able to absorb challenges to the system without having to substantially alter the system itself. Incorporating the sexy sportscasters allows a hypermasculine sports industry to incorporate the challenge of female participation without having to alter a sexist belief system underlying industry motivations. The sportscaster allows one to consider how members of underrepresented groups inadvertently participate in their own marginalization by illuminating the ways in which serious journalists are enveloped in a sexualized environment beyond individual control. Finally, it brings to attention the fact that popular culture does have significant impact on social relations. Sport has been trivialized as mere entertainment, a realm not to be taken seriously. However, this study reinforces the notion that mediated sport is an arena in which critical social and political conditions are being reproduced. The seemingly small role of the female sportscaster can, in fact, illuminate some of the subtle ways in which large oppressive systems maintain their dominance.

To conclude, it appears that female football sportscasters will continue to make headlines based on their ability to turn heads. Notably, Lisa Guerrero again became a news story herself after being fired from ABC's *Monday Night Football* after one season (Tierney, 2004, p. 2C). Apparently, Guerrero's good looks could not mask her limited football knowledge. Guerrero's replacement was another woman, Michele Tafoya, who supposedly has both sports knowledge and good looks. Yet, as one newspaper reporter put it, "Whether ABC's turnabout bodes ill for the next bimbo waiting in the wings is unclear. A segment of the sports audience always will dismiss the football sideline reporter as window dressing and would rather the networks recruit from a Hooters wait staff" (Tierney, 2004, p. 2C). Unfortunately, the reporter's remarks work to predetermine the newest sideliner's fate, while demonstrating the uphill battle women continue to fight in a masculine sports industry.

REFERENCES

Berger, K. (2003, December). Joe's lips get him in trouble. *Newsday*, p. A60.
Bettis, P., & Adams, N. (2004). *Cheerleader! An American icon.* New York: Palgrave.
Billings, A., Halone, K., & Denham, B. (2002). "Man, that was a pretty shot": An analysis of gendered broadcast commentary surrounding the 2000 men's and women's NCAA Final Four Basketball Championships. *Mass Communication & Society, 5,* 295–336.
Bonnie Bernstein Fansite (2004). Retrieved June 8, 2004, from http// bonniebernstein.freeservers.com.
Brennan, C. (2000, December 7). TV execs give us *Playboy* babes. *USA Today*, 3C.

Brenneis, D. (1992). Gossip. In R. Bauman (Ed.), *Folklore, cultural performances, and popular entertainments: A communication-centered handbook* (pp. 150–153). New York: Oxford University Press.

Cornacchia, C. (2002, October 11). Sports babes idea shut out: Female telecaster refuses to be photographed in provocative poses for male magazine. *Montreal Gazette*, A3.

Cramer, J. (1994). Conversations with women sports journalists. In P. J. Creedon (Ed.), *Women, media, and sport: Challenging gender values* (pp. 159–180). Thousand Oaks, CA: Sage.

Disch, L., & Kane, M. (1996). When a looker is really a bitch: Lisa Olson, sport and the heterosexual matrix. *Signs: Journal of Women in Culture and Society, 21*, 278–308.

For Him Magazine Online-US version (2002). *Covergirls: Jillian Barberie*. Retrieved May 24, 2002, from http://www.fhmus.com/girls/covergirls/133.

Garcia, A. (1998, July 26). Doors open, microscopes intense for media women. *San Antonio Express*, 1C.

Geranios, N. (2003, January 3). Assessing a sport's rah-rah materials. *The Washington Post*, C5.

Ginn, S. (2001, January 9). Looking good . . . too good? *St. Petersburg Times*, 1C.

Hall, S. (1989). Ethnicity: Identity and difference. *Radical America, 23*, 9–20.

Hiestand, M. (2003, December 22). Namath steps over line on ESPN. *USA Today*, 2C.

Jillian's World (2003). *Gallery*. Retrieved June 8, 2004, from http://www.jilliansworld.com/frameset.htm.

Kimball, G. (2001, January 18). Familiar issue for female TV presenters. *Irish Times on the Web*. Retrieved May 24, 2002, from http://Ireland.com/newspaper/sport/2001/018/spo3.htm.

Kiszla, M. (2003, September 10). Why Guerrero is bad news for MNF. *Denver Post*, D1.

Klaffke, P. (2003, February 3). "Sports babes" are catching on. *Calgary Herald*, C9.

Laclau, E., & Mouffe, C. (1985). *Hegemony and socialist strategy: Towards a radical democratic politics*. London: Verso.

Martzke, R. (2000, December 6). *Playboy* picks take poll in stride. *USA Today*, 2C.

Martzke, R. (2003, September 17). "Sportscenter" anchors unfairly put joke on Guerrero. *USA Today*, 2C.

Maxim Online (2002, September). Retrieved September 16, 2002, from http://maximonline.com.

Messner, M., Duncan, M., & Jensen, K. (1993). Separating the men from the girls: The gendered language of televised sports. *Gender & Society, 17*, 121–137.

Namath gets help for alcohol abuse (2004, January 23). *USA Today*, 15C.

Playboy.com (2000). *A league of their own*. Retrieved November 21, 2002, from http://www.playboy.com/sports/features/sportscasters/index.html.

Polumbaum, J., & Wieting, S. (1999, Summer). Stories of sport and the moral order: Unraveling the cultural construction of Tiger Woods. *Journalism & Communication Monographs, 1*(2), pp. 68–117.

Pratt, S. (2002, October 6). Observer sport monthly. *Observer Sports Magazine, 30.*

Raissman, B. (2004, January 11). Sideline chats more pain than pleasure. *Daily News,* 4.

Rubin, G. (1975). The traffic in women: Notes on the "political economy" of sex. In R. Reiter (Ed.), *Toward an anthropology of women* (pp. 157–210). New York: Monthly Review Press.

Sabo, D., & Panepinto, J. (1990). Football ritual and social reproduction of masculinity. In M. Messner & D. Sabo (Eds.), *Sport, men, and the gender order.* Champaign, IL: Human Kinetics.

Storm, H. (2002, June 22). Title IX offers fair play for all. *Chicago Sun-Times,* 12.

Tierney, M. (2004, May 4). "Monday Night" goes for sideline substance. *Atlanta Journal-Constitution,* 2C.

Women Sportscasters Bristle at Commentator's Remarks. (2002, October 10). ESPN.com. Retrieved October 28, 2002, from http://espn.go.com/nfl/news/2002/1010/1443917.html.

Chapter 7

Selling Spanish-Language Programming: A Comparison of Sex and Gender in Univision and NBC Promotional Announcements

Jami A. Fullerton
Oklahoma State University

Alice Kendrick
Southern Methodist University

Today, more than one in eight people in the United States is of Hispanic origin. In addition, Hispanics are the fastest growing ethnic group in the United States, increasing over 17% from 2000 to 2004 to more than 41 million, or 14% of the total population. With the rapid growth of Hispanic households, advertising targeted to this group is increasing as well, up 4 percent in 2002 to about $2.2 billion. Most of the ads intended to reach Hispanics appear on Univision, the largest Spanish-language television network and the fifth largest television network overall (Hall, 2002). Univision experienced double-digit increases in annual revenue in 2002 to more than $1.5 billion (Romano, 2003).

It takes only a few minutes of watching its programming to realize that Univision is not simply a Spanish-language translation of U.S. general market television. Not only does the programming sound different—all dialogue is in Spanish—but it also looks different from general market TV; however, few studies can be found that quantify these differences. The purpose of the present analysis, therefore, is to compare the content of programming on Spanish-language television (Univision) to U.S. general market television (NBC) with a particular emphasis on sexual content and gender portrayal in promotional announcements.

Previous research that examined role portrayal in Spanish-language television (Fullerton & Kendrick, 2001b) suggested that Univision promotional announcements (promos) contained an abundance of sexual content and stereotypical role portrayal. The present study attempts to compare the same promos with general market television and to describe the extent to which both Univision and NBC use sexual content to attract viewers and build audiences.

The importance of examining role portrayal and gender stereotyping in television content has been documented in numerous studies. Cultivation theory (Gerbner, 1998) suggests that as people view television over time, they begin to accept what they see as reality. Researchers have suggested that even brief exposure to the depiction of women in overtly sexual and submissively dependent roles in the mass media may reinforce negative stereotypes (Bretl & Cantor, 1988) and can contribute to even more serious social problems such as sexual harassment and eating disorders (Lavine, Sweeney, & Wagner, 1999).

PREVIOUS RESEARCH

Hispanic Culture and Media

The term "Hispanic" is commonly used to refer to residents of the United States who trace their family origin to Spain or one of the Spanish-speaking Latin American nations (Marin & Marin, 1991; Foster, 1995). Although Hispanic is an ethnic group, not a racial label, most Hispanics are a racial mix of white Europeans, Indigenous Indians, and Africans. Though they come from different countries of origin, they are tied together by similar cultural values, customs, and language (Valdes & Seoane, 1995).

Recently, Hispanic culture has received high-profile exposure in U.S. mainstream pop culture through music, fashion, media, and movies (Navarro, 1999; La Ferla, 2001; also see Soldow, this volume). Popular Latin entertainers such as Selma Hayek, Jennifer Lopez, and Ricky Martin have created a fascination with Hispanic style (Feuer, 2000). Overall, however, Hispanic culture is relatively distinct from general U.S. culture and has been described as a "country within a country" (Valdes & Seoane, 1995). Though many second- and third-generation Hispanics, particularly those who are younger, are more fully acculturated into mainstream America, many consider themselves a part of both cultures by retaining the heritage and language of their grandparents (Gardyn, 2001).

Sex roles in the Hispanic culture are considered to be traditional, conservative, well defined, and rigid (Gonzalez, 1982; Marin & Marin, 1991; Kranau, Green, & Valencia-Weber, 1982). A patriarchal-authoritarian structure exists in many traditional households. The father is the master and sole breadwinner (Gowan & Trevino, 1998); the wife cares for the household and children while serving her husband (Pavich, 1986).

Culturally prescribed sex roles for Hispanic men and women are commonly referred to as "machismo" and "marianismo." While no longer widely practiced by acculturated families (Gowan & Trevino, 1998), sex roles continue to influence sexual behavior (Wood & Price, 1997). Machismo is a social behavior pattern in which Hispanic men are dominant and demand subservience of women. In addition, males are considered to be sexual aggressors and are applauded for their sexual conquests and extramarital affairs. By contrast, "marianismo" is a social behavior pattern by which traditional Hispanic females relate to Mary (the mother of Jesus Christ) and consider themselves to be morally superior and more spiritual than men (Wood & Price, 1997). As a *good* woman, she is a dutiful wife who engages in sexual intercourse only for procreation. Perhaps as a result of piety, another stereotypical female sex role emerges—the mistress. She is

FIG. 7.1. Univision promos for telenovelas often contain images of sexual behavior and romantic intrigue.

a *bad* woman who is free to engage fully in sexuality with men (Barkley & Salazar-Mosher, 1995; Pavich, 1986).

Regarding media use, readership of Hispanic newspapers and magazines tripled between 1992 and 1999 (Haegele, 2000), but in 2001 only 20% of Hispanics were regular newspaper readers (Raymond, 2002). Therefore, marketing professionals believe that TV and radio are the most effective means of reaching Hispanic consumers (Kim & Kang, 2001). As a group, Hispanics watch as much English-language as Spanish-language television (Valdes & Seoane, 1995). Hispanics use Spanish-language television not only for entertainment, but also to stay connected to the Hispanic community and to receive news from their native countries (Valdes & Seoane, 1995).

In terms of popularity, Hispanic television has exploded over the last decade. Univision, with its new sister station Telefutura, comprises the largest all-Spanish broadcasting group with 90% penetration among Hispanic households, followed by NBC-owned rival Telemundo (Hall, 2002). As previously mentioned, Univision programming is exclusively Spanish-language and consists of popular telenovelas, talk shows, and entertainment-oriented variety shows (Romano, 2003; Fullerton & Kendrick, 2001b). Most programming on Univision is supplied by companies outside the United States such as Venezuela's Venevision and Mexico's Grupo Televisa, both large producers of Spanish-language programming (Bowser, 1998; Hall, 2002). In addition to Univision programs, the average viewer sees from 12 to 15 minutes of nonprogramming per hour during prime time. This time is roughly split between commercials and station promotional announcements (Fullerton & Kendrick, 2001b).

Sex and Sex-Role Portrayals in Network Promos

Since the 1950s, researchers have studied the sexual and violent content on general market television programming and advertising. Regarding sexual stereotypes, female characters are typically portrayed as housewives and mothers (Courtney & Lockeretz, 1971; Courtney & Whipple, 1983) or as decorative sex objects (Dominick & Rausch, 1972), while males appear outdoors or in business settings and as advisors to women. Research revealed that although women's roles in society were expanding, their roles on television remained narrow (Schneider & Schneider, 1979). Additional studies provide similar conclusions that advertising often portrays women in inferior, domestic, or sexual roles (Bretl & Cantor, 1988; Craig, 1992; Ferguson, Kreshel, & Tinkham, 1990; Fullerton & Kendrick, 2000; Kaufman, 1999; Riffe, Place, & Mayo, 1993; Signorelli, McLeod, & Healy, 1994).

Several analyses of network promotional content reveal that sexual language and imagery are common devices. For example, Soley and Reid's

(1985) analysis of advertising in *TV Guide* found that sex (20.8%) and violence (19.9%) were predominant features in television program advertising, especially ads for network programs. Davis and Walker (1991) reported that 12% of promos contained sexual content and that NBC promos featured the most sexual behavior. Similarly, Sapolsky, Tabarlet, and Kaye (1996) found that about 20% of general market network promos contained sexual acts or references, and that NBC promos featured the most sexual content. In the most recent analysis, Walker (2000) found sexual behavior (21.5%) and sexual language (23.4%) present in a comprehensive sample of 1998 network promos.

Relatively, fewer academic studies have assessed the effects of program promos on audiences, and the results of those studies are mixed. Eastman, Newton, and Bolls (2003) found that certain content variables within promos, though not sex appeal of the characters, contributed modestly to intention to view featured programs. A correlational analysis of *TV Guide* advertising found that sex and violence "do have a positive impact on a program's rating" (Williams, 1989). Conversely, Shidler and Lowry (1995), in a study of network promos and ratings, found no link between program ratings and sexual content in promos. At this point, it is clear that network promos contain sexual content but the effect of that content remains to be established.

There is a body of literature that examines the portrayal of Hispanics in general market media (Dixon & Linz, 2000; Mastro & Greenberg, 2000; Tamborini et al., 2000; Vargas & DePyssler, 1998; Fitzgerald, 1998; Taylor & Bang, 1997; Taylor, Lee, & Stern, 1995; Soruco, 1996; Faber, O'Guinn, & Meyer, 1987; Greenberg et al., 1983). This research generally reveals that Hispanics are underrepresented in the mass media, with only 3% of characters on general market television identified as Hispanic (Mastro & Greenberg, 2000), and that those who are present are often portrayed as criminals, poor immigrants, or "sultry seductresses or buffoons" (Vargas & DePyssler, 1998). Recent studies do show improvement in the portrayal of Hispanics in TV drama (Tamborini et al., 2000; Mastro & Greenberg, 2000). However, Mastro and Stern (this volume) found in their analysis of 2,880 commercials that Hispanic females were commonly depicted as "young adults, extremely thin, and highly likely to engage in alluring behaviors and sexual gazing."

Three studies examine sex-role portrayal on Spanish-language television (Fullerton & Kendrick, 2000; Fullerton & Kendrick, 2001a; Fullerton & Kendrick, 2001b). Fullerton and Kendrick (2000) found that women were portrayed in sex-stereotypical roles with men seldom cast as a parent or homemaker. The researchers noted that many ads on Spanish-language television are simply dubbed versions or "retreads" of general market commercials. A follow-up study directly compared Univision commercials with network ads in the same market (Fullerton & Kendrick, 2001a). The findings indicated that a predominance of White, male professionals appeared in network ads compared to the prevalence of female characters in Univision commercials. Characters on both networks were portrayed in a stereotypical manner, with women more frequently cast in parental or domestic roles than men. In an analysis of prime-time promos, Fullerton and Kendrick (2001b) found a large presence of sex-role stereotyping, sexual dress, and sexual content. For example, 40% of the Spanish-language promos contained sexual content or contact—much more than that reported in general market TV by either Davis and Walker (1991) or Sapolsky et al. (1996).

PURPOSE

The current study builds on Fullerton and Kendrick's (2001b) study of Spanish-language promotional ads by directly comparing simultaneous broadcasts of Univision prime-time promos with NBC prime-time promos in the same market. Specifically, the study is designed to describe the portrayal of gender, sex roles, and sexual content appearing in the promos and to analyze any differences.

METHODOLOGY

Sample

The sample consisted of 21 hours (seven evenings) of prime-time programming (7–10 P.M., CST) aired on NBC and Univision affiliate stations in the Oklahoma City DMA from November 1 through November 11, 1998. All sampled programming was recorded, but for this project it was edited to include only station promotional announcements (promos). Promos were defined as nonprogram content, which did not constitute paid advertising or public service announcements. Consistent with previous research (Sapolsky et al., 1996), promos for local news were not included in the analysis.

Overall, there were 459 promos in the 21-hour Univision sample and 152 in the NBC sample. Coders were instructed to analyze each promo, which meant that they coded several promos more than once. Inclusion of duplicate promos was intentional so as to provide a complete picture of the type and quantity of promotional announcements aired during prime time.

Variables and Coding

Each promo was coded using a protocol designed to assess variables related both to the type of program being promoted and the portrayal of adult actors (Fullerton & Kendrick, 2001b). Coding schemes from the advertising content analysis literature were employed, including Craig (1992) for "characters present" and Goffman (1976) for "male/female" relationship roles. The Goffman role definitions allowed for traditional roles where the male is dominant, reverse roles where the female is dominant, and equality roles where neither sex is dominant. Some promos did not show men and women together and therefore were coded as lacking any relationship role.

To assess sexuality in the promos, three variables were analyzed. Coding for sexual contact and degree of dress employed Soley and Kurzbard's (1986) operationalizations. Sexual contact included simple contact such as holding hands and more intimate contact such as kissing, hugging, and playful wrestling. Promos showing men and women embracing while in a prone position or while nude together in bed were coded as intercourse. Regarding clothing, demure dress was defined as typical clothing styles such as business suits, sportswear, and casual clothing. Suggestive dress included open blouses, exposed cleavage or midriffs, tight clothing, short shorts, and miniskirts. Partially clad models were those wearing bathing suits, underwear, and opaque lingerie, and nudity was represented as unclothed bodies and models wearing only a towel or translucent lingerie. Last, the presence or absence of sexual content was recorded as a gestalt variable that encompassed sexual language, sexual contact, sexual dress, or sexual behavior such as an actor staring seductively into the camera or tight shots of intimate body parts. For this variable, sexual content was either evident or absent in each promo.

To determine individual roles, McArthur and Resko's (1975) definitions were used to categorize "primary role" as the "everyday role in which they (the primary characters) were cast." Primary roles adapted for the present research included professional, homemaker, lover, parent, show host, and "other."

Overall, 16 variables were recorded for each promotional announcement (e.g., length in seconds), followed by 21 variables for up to two primary adult male actors and two primary female adult actors. A primary character was one who was on camera for at least 3 seconds or had at least one line of dialogue (Schneider & Schneider, 1979).

The Univision commercials were first translated into English and then independently evaluated by two coders: a bilingual Hispanic male advertising executive and an English-speaking female advertising professor. The same female advertising professor and two advertising graduate students evaluated the NBC promos. Each spot was viewed at least three times before each coder made independent evaluations. Results were compared, disagreements were recorded and subsequently resolved by discussion, and a single set of data was used for the analysis. Using Holsti's (1969) formula, a .96 coefficient of intercoder reliability was computed, with a range from .89 to .99 for all coded variables.

TABLE 7.1
Type of Programs Featured in Promotional
Announcements by Network (in Percent)

Program Type*	NBC (n = 152)	Univision (n = 459)
Variety Show	5.3	19.4
Novela	0.0	18.7
Talk Show	5.9	16.8
Movie	11.8	10.2
Game Show	0.0	9.4
Situation Comedy	41.4	7.4
Real Video	1.3	7.0
Magazine Format	3.3	6.3
Sports	2.6	4.8
Dramas	27.0	0.0

*χ^2, $p < .01$

FINDINGS

Structural Variables

Overall, more than three times as many promotional spots existed for Univision ($n = 459$) than for NBC ($n = 152$). Situation comedies and dramas dominated the type of promos on NBC (see Table 7.1). By contrast, Univision viewers witnessed a mix of program promos, with variety shows, talk shows, and novelas comprising more than half of all program types. The difference between programming content between both networks was significant, $\chi^2(9) = 279.3$, $p < .001$.

Length. Promos on Univision averaged 21 seconds in length, significantly more than those on NBC, which averaged 18 seconds (t-test, $p < .001$). Thirty-one percent of the NBC spots were 10 seconds or less, compared with only 3.4% of those on Univision. Thus, promos on Univision tended to last longer than those on NBC.

Content Variables

Sexual content and contact. Sexual content could be either visual (contact or noncontact) as defined as Soley and Kurzbard (1986) or verbal such as use of the words "hot," "babe," or "sexy" by either on-screen characters or an off-screen announcer. Overall, 40% of Univision promos contained some form of sexual content, compared with 34% of NBC promos (see Table 7.2). Univision viewers were more likely to be exposed to

TABLE 7.2
Sexual Content, Contact, and Dress in Network
Promotional Announcements (in Percent)

	Network	
Type of Sexual Information	NBC	Univision
*Sexual Content**		
Present (both visual and verbal)	8.6	9.8
Present (visual only)	21.1	30.4
Present (verbal only)	4.6	0.0
No sexual content	65.8	59.9
Sexual Contact		
Intimate (kissing, petting)	27.0	19.3
Holding hands	0.7	5.6
Eye contact	2.0	5.4
No contact	70.4	69.6
*Dress**		
Nude	0.0	0.0
Partially clad	0.6	11.8
Suggestively clad	6.9	15.3
Demurely clad	92.5	72.9

*χ^2, $p < .01$

visual-only sexual references than were viewers of NBC. Regarding sexual contact, images of sexual behavior were noted in about 30% of promos on both stations, with somewhat more subtle modes of contact such as hand holding and eye contact on Univision, and more kissing and touching on NBC—coded as "intimate" contact.

Dress. Although the majority of actors featured in both NBC and Univision promos were not dressed in a sexual manner, viewers on Univision were three times more likely to witness either suggestively clad or partially clad characters, $\chi^2(2) = 30.5$, $p < .001$ (see Table 7.2).

Characters. On both Univision and NBC, viewers were most likely to see both a male and female in each promo, though NBC viewers were more likely than Univision viewers to see station promos featuring all males [13.2% versus 5.0%; $\chi^2(6) = 35.4$, $p < .001$].

Goffman sex roles. While more than one in four Univision promos featured men and women in Goffman's traditional roles, NBC promos which could be coded according to Goffman categories were as likely to feature men and women in reverse traditional roles or equal roles as they were to show Goffman's traditional roles.

TABLE 7.3
Character Gender and Sex Roles in Network
Promotional Announcements (in Percent)

	NBC	Univision
*Characters**		
All male	13.2	5.0
All female	1.3	5.0
All adults	65.1	66.4
All children	0.0	0.9
Male with children	0.7	0.0
Mix of sex and ages	15.8	22.6
No characters	3.9	0.2
Goffman Relational Roles		
Traditional	7.9	25.8
Reverse	7.2	3.3
Equality	7.2	5.6
No Roles Recorded	76.3	65.3
*Roles**		
Professional	44.8	17.2
Homemaker	0.6	0.0
Lover	27.0	13.4
Parent	2.9	4.6
Show Host	0.0	32.4
Other	24.7	32.4

$^{*}\chi^2, p < .01$

Male and female roles. Viewers of both NBC and Univision were shown a variety of characters in a number of different roles (see Table 7.3), but they were more likely to see professionals depicted on NBC promos and show hosts on Univision [$\chi^2(5) = 109.2$, $p < .001$]. One in four NBC promotional characters were featured as lovers, compared with 13% of characters on Univision.

Gender, race, and age. Overall, a total of 547 characters were coded, with 373 of them appearing on Univision promos and 174 on NBC promos. Univision promos primarily featured female characters while actors on NBC promos were predominantly male. More specifically, of the 373 Univision characters, 212 (56.8%) were female and 161 (43.2%) were male; while only 60 (34.5%) of the NBC characters were female and 114 (65.5%) were male.

Regarding race, all of the characters on Univision promos were Hispanic, while over 90% of the characters were White on NBC (6.3% Black, 1.1% Hispanic, 1.1% other). Obviously, the percentage of Hispanics appearing in NBC promos is far lower than their demographic incidence in the population as a whole. The mean age for main characters on both stations was between 31 and 40, with Univision characters appearing somewhat younger than their NBC counterparts (*t*-test, $p = .06$). Twenty-nine percent of Univision characters were under the age of 30, compared with only 18% of those on NBC.

DISCUSSION

This analysis compared the content of promotional announcements aired on a major network (NBC) and a Spanish-language station (Univision), and represents the first direct comparison of its type. Both networks offer a relatively steady diet of sexual content and contact—40% for Univision and 34% for NBC—in their promos. These findings were somewhat higher than those reported in previous studies of network promos (Sapolsky et al., 1996; Davis & Walker, 1991; Walker, 2000), which reported sexual content in the 10–20% range. However, direct comparisons are difficult to make given differences in coding schemes and sampling. In addition, the level of sexual content in promos appears notably higher than those in Fullerton and Kendrick's (2001a) analysis of prime-time commercials on Univision and NBC. Commercials on both networks appear to be more conservative when compared to the more provocative content of promos. This difference suggests that marketers are less likely to use "sex to sell" in their ads than broadcasters who readily include sexual imagery to attract viewers to their programs.

Generally speaking, the Univision promos were even more sexually charged than those on NBC, which has been criticized as the most provocative of the general market networks. The Univision spots were significantly more likely to feature suggestively dressed women than were those on NBC. This finding, coupled with the sheer volume of the promotional spots on Univision compared with NBC, indicates that the Spanish-language television viewer is exposed to a large dose of sexual imagery when watching television.

A close examination of the promos reveals not only a difference in the levels of sexual content, but also a difference in type of sexual imagery on the two networks. For example, the Univision promos featured more women overall than those on NBC. Many of the Univision promos were for variety shows featuring scantily clad dancing girls thrusting their voluptuous, pulsating bodies at the camera. Others were for telenovelas featuring romantic scenes of innocent kissing and hand-holding. In contrast, NBC promos were dominated by men and promoted situation comedies using sex jokes to grab attention and prime-time dramas featuring considerably less romantic coupling. In addition, the sexual content on NBC tended to involve sexual innuendo, lusty intercourse, and body organ humor while Univision's promos showcased physically alluring women.

FIG. 7.2. Talk shows and variety programs are heavily promoted on Univision.

Differences in the type of sexual content between the networks may be a reflection of cultural variation in Hispanic and general market attitudes toward sex. When considered in the context of the Hispanic culture, the sexual portrayals revealed in this study support the concepts of machismo and marianismo. For instance, the partially clad, sexy women on display may be a stereotypical portrayal of the *bad* woman who exists for the pleasure of men. The image of the *bad* woman in promos may be acceptable to a Hispanic audience because she is pleasurable to men, and television is primarily a source of entertainment. Furthermore, the study found that when men and women were shown together in Univision promos, they were typically depicted in traditional sex roles. This finding could be evidence of the portrayal of the *good wife* (marianismo) who is obedient and subservient to her husband.

In the general market culture, where the influences of modern feminism prevail, the use of women as decoration or entertainment for men could be considered exploitative, and the blatant use of dancing girls in bikinis considered sexist. Keeping with the general market's attitudes toward sex and the role of women, sexual content in NBC promos tended instead to take the form of humor or graphic sexual acts between men and women. The study found female dominant relationships as prevalent as male-dominant relationships in NBC promos, though both were at a relatively low level, suggesting nontraditional portrayals of women were as common as traditional ones.

One interesting finding was that viewers of Univision during the week chosen for analysis were exposed to more than three times as many station promos as viewers of NBC. This finding appears notable in and of itself, especially when considered with Fullerton and Kendrick's (2001a) finding that the same NBC affiliate ran almost twice as many minutes of commercial spots as did its Univision counterpart. The net effect for the viewer of Univision is that in-program and between-program breaks are dominated by station promos, whereas breaks on NBC primarily contain ads for products and services. Advertising to the Hispanic market, though increasing at a rapid pace, represents only a fraction (about 15% in 2002) of the amount spent on general market media (Romano, 2003). As a result, excess time inventory on networks like Univision is filled with station promos.

Using sexually laced promos is widely considered one of the best ways to attract and maintain more viewers (Walker, 2000), which could eventually lead to more advertising. Certainly, there is a downside to an abundance of sex-filled promos. For example, Walker (2000) contended that the influence of sexual content of on-air promotions is significant because repeated airings result in exposure to large and diverse audiences. Frequent repetition of promos also increases potential impact on viewers, and the brevity of most promos precludes the "context of the larger story" available in the full program, and therefore may be misunderstood, especially by young children.

In conclusion, the direct comparison of Spanish-language and general market television suggests that programming is to a large extent a reflection of the culture of the audience to which it is targeted. Further research is needed to examine this point more closely, but evidence from this initial comparative content analysis seems to suggest that the differences seen on NBC and Univision may be a result of the different societal attitudes and economic realities that exist both in Hispanic culture and the culture at large.

REFERENCES

Barkley, B. H., & Salazar-Mosher, E. (1995). Sexuality and Hispanic culture: Counseling with children and their parents. *Journal of Sex Education & Therapy, 21*(4), 255–267.

Bowser, A. (1998, November 9). Univision rules with telenovelas. *Broadcasting & Cable*, 34–35.

Bretl, D., & Cantor, J. (1988). The portrayal of men and women in U.S. television commercials: A recent content analysis and trends over 15 years. *Sex Roles, 18*(9–10), 595–609.

Courtney, A., & Lockeretz, S. W. (1971). A woman's place: An analysis of the roles portrayed by women in magazine advertisements. *Journal of Marketing Research, 8*, 92–95.

Courtney, A., & Whipple, T. (1983). *Sex stereotyping in advertising*. Lexington, MA: Lexington.

Craig, R. S. (1992). The effect of television day part on gender portrayals in television commercials: A content analysis. *Sex Roles, 26*(5–6), 197–211.

Davis, D., & Walker, J. (1991). Sex, violence, and network program promotion: A content analysis. A paper presented at the annual meeting of the Speech Communication Association, Atlanta, GA.

Dixon, T., & Linz, D. (2000). Overrepresentation and underrepresentation of African Americans and Latinos as lawbreakers on television news. *Journal of Communication, 50*(2), 131–154.

Dominick, J., & Rausch, G. (1972). The image of women in network TV commercials. *Journal of Broadcasting, 16*, 259–265.

Eastman, S. T., Newton, G. D., & Bolls, P. D. (2003). How promotional content changes ratings: The impact of appeals, humor and presentation. *Journal of Applied Communication Research, 31*(3), 238–259.

Eaton, B. C. (1997). Prime-time stereotyping on the new television networks. *Journalism and Mass Communication Quarterly, 74*(4), 859–872.

Faber, R., O'Guinn, T., & Meyer, T. (1987). Televised portrayals of Hispanics: A comparison of ethnic perceptions. *International Journal of Intercultural Relations, 11*, 155–169.

Feuer, J. (2000, December 18). Latin quarter. *Adweek*, 11.

Ferguson, J. H., Kreshel, P. J., & Tinkham, S. F. (1990). In the pages of *Ms.*: Sex role portrayals of women in advertising. *Journal of Advertising, 19*(1), 40–52.

Fitzgerald, M. (1998, July 4). TV network news tunes out Hispanics. *Editor & Publisher*, 4.

Foster, G. M. (1995). Contemporary Hispanic American culture: The product of acculturation. In Antoinette Sedillo Lopez (Ed.), *Latinos in the United States, historical themes and identity* (pp. 17–25). New York: Garland.

Fullerton, J. A., & Kendrick, A. (2000). Portrayal of men and women in U.S. Spanish-language television commercials. *Journalism & Mass Communication Quarterly, 77*(1), 128–142.

Fullerton, J. A., & Kendrick A. (2001a). Comparing content of commercials from general market and Spanish-language television. *Southwestern Mass Communication Journal, 17*(1), 53–62.

Fullerton, J. A., & Kendrick, A. (2001b). An analysis of role portrayal in U.S. Spanish-language television promotional announcements. *Southwestern Mass Communication Journal, 17*(1), 63–75.

Gardyn, R. (2001). Habla english? *American Demographics, 23*(4), 54–57.

Gerbner, G. (1998). Cultivation analysis: An overview. *Mass Communication and Society, 1,* 175–194.

Goffman, E. (1976). *Gender advertisements.* Cambridge, MA: Harvard University Press.

Gonzalez, A. (1982). Sex roles of the traditional Mexican family: A comparison on Chicano and Anglo students' attitudes. *Journal of Cross Cultural Psychology, 13,* 330–339.

Gowan, M., & Trevino, M. (1998). An examination of gender differences in Mexican-American attitudes toward family and career roles. *Sex Roles, 38*(11/12), 1079–1093.

Greenberg, B. S., Burgoon, M., Burgoon, J. K., & Korzenny, F. (1983). *Mexican Americans and the mass media.* Norwood, NJ: Ablex.

Haegele, K. (2000, March). Hispanic Americans. *Target Marketing, 23*(3), 97–99.

Hall, L. (2002, November 25). Special report: Hispanic television—Telemundo targets Univision. *Electronic Media,* 12.

Holsti, O. R. (1969). *Content analysis for the social sciences and humanities.* Reading, MA: Addison-Wesley.

Kaufman, G. (1999). The portrayal of men's family roles in television commercials. *Sex Roles, 41*(5/6), 439–459.

Kim, Y. K., & Kang, J. (2001). The effects of ethnicity and product on purchase decision making. *Journal of Advertising Research, 41*(2), 39–48.

Kranau, E. J., Green, V., & Valencia-Weber, G. (1982). Acculturation and the Hispanic woman: Attitudes toward women, sex-role attribution, sex-role behavior and demographics. *Hispanic Journal of Behavioral Sciences, 4*(1), 21–40.

La Ferla, R. (2001, April 15). Latino style is cool, Oh, all right: It's hot. *New York Times,* 9, 1.

Lavine, H., Sweeney, D., & Wagner, S. (1999). Depicting women as sex objects in television advertising: Effects on body dissatisfaction. *Personality and Social Psychology Bulletin, 25*(8), 1049–1058.

Marin, G., & Marin, B. (1991). *Research with Hispanic populations.* Newbury Park, CA: Sage.

Mastro, D. E., & Greenberg, B. (2000). The portrayal of racial minorities on prime time television. *Journal of Broadcasting & Electronic Media, 44*(4), 690–703.

Mastro, D., & Stern, S. (this volume). Race and gender in advertising: A look at sexualized images in prime-time commercials. In T. Reichert & J. Lambiase (Eds.), *Sex in consumer culture: The erotic content of media and marketing.* Mahwah, NJ: Lawrence Erlbaum Associates.

McArthur, L. Z., & Resko, B. G. (1975). The portrayal of men and women in American television commercials. *Journal of Social Psychology, 97,* 209–220.

Navarro, M. (1999, October 4). After a summer of high-profile coverage of Hispanic culture, some wonder if it will last. *New York Times,* 17.

Pavich, E. G. (1986). A Chicana perspective on Mexican culture and sexuality. *Journal of Social Work & Human Sexuality Special Issue: Human Sexuality Ethnoculture and Social Work, 4*(3), 47–65.

Romano, A. (2003, September 8). Finally, some new advertisers turn to Latin TV. *Broadcasting & Cable,* 36.

Raymond, J. (2002). Tienen numeros? *American Demographics, 24*(3), 22–25.

Riffe, D., Place, P. C., & Mayo, C. M. (1993). Game time, soap time and prime time TV ads: Treatment of women in Sunday football and rest-of-week advertising. *Journalism Quarterly, 70,* 437–446.

Sapolsky, B. S., Tabarlet, J. O., & Kaye, B. K. (1996). Sexual behavior and references in program promotions aired during sweeps and nonsweeps periods. *Journal of Promotion Management, 3*(1/2), 95–106.

Schneider, K. C., & Schneider, S. B. (1979). Trends in sex roles in television commercials. *Journal of Marketing, 43,* 79–84.

Shidler, J. A., & Lowry, D. T. (1995). Network TV sex as a counterprogramming strategy during a sweeps period: An analysis of content and ratings. *Journalism and Mass Communication Quarterly, 72*(1), 147–157.

Signorielli, N., McLeod, D., & Healy, E. (1994). Gender stereotypes in MTV commercials: The beat goes on. *Journal of Broadcasting & Electronic Media, 38,* 91–97.

Soley, L. C., & Kurzbard, G. (1986). Sex in advertising: A comparison of 1964 and 1984 magazine advertisements. *Journal of Advertising, 15*(3), 46–54.

Soley, L. C., & Reid, L. N. (1985). Bating viewers: Violence and sex in television program advertisements. *Journalism Quarterly, 62,* 105–110, 131.

Soruco, G. R. (1996). *Cubans and the mass media in South Florida.* Gainesville: University Press of Florida.

Tamborini, R., Mastro, D. E., Chory-Assad, R. M., & Huang, R. H. (2000). The color of crime and the court: A content analysis of minority representation on television. *Journalism and Mass Communication Quarterly, 77,* 639–653.

Taylor, C. R., & Bang, H. (1997). Portrayals of Latinos in magazine advertising. *Journalism and Mass Communication Quarterly, 74*(2), 285–303.

Taylor, C. R., Lee, J., & Stern, B. (1995). Portrayals of African, Hispanic, and Asian Americans in magazine advertising. *American Behavioral Scientist, 38*(4), 608–621.

Valdes, M. I., & Seoane, M. H. (1995). *Hispanic market handbook.* Detroit, MI: Gale Research.

Vargas, L., & DePyssler, B. (1998). Using media literacy to explore stereotypes of Mexican immigrants. *Social Education, 62*(7), 407–412.

Walker, J. R. (2000). Sex and violence in program promotion. In S. T. Eastman (Ed.), *Research in media promotion* (pp. 101–126). Mahwah, NJ: Lawrence Erlbaum Associates.

Williams, G. A. (1989). Enticing viewers: Sex and violence in *TV Guide* program advertisements. *Journalism Quarterly, 66,* 970–973.

Wood, M., & Price, P. (1997). Machismo and marianismo: Implications for HIV/AIDS risk reduction and education. *American Journal of Health Studies, 13*(1), 44–52.

PART II

Sexualizing Products

Chapter 8

Sexual Content of Television Commercials Watched by Early Adolescents

Carol J. Pardun

Middle Tennessee State University

Kathy Roberts Forde

University of Minnesota

When Justin Timberlake ripped Janet Jackson's bodice, exposing her breast during the MTV-produced Super Bowl half-time show in 2004, parents, educators, and network executives entered into a heated debate about appropriate content for national network television. Comments typically ranged from outrage to a simple shrug; the concern generally centered on younger viewers who were unwittingly exposed to the daring stunt. The incident also focused attention on the program's advertising as being crass, oversexualized, and inappropriate for young audiences (Smith & Simon, 2004). Fallout from this media "event" highlights how little we know about the content of television that children consume—and that we know even less about the content of embedded commercials in those programs. This chapter attempts to close that gap by focusing on one specific age group—early adolescents—and the sexual content of the commercials that run during their most-watched shows.

LITERATURE REVIEW

Sex in the Media

Sexual images in the media have long been a concern of mass media researchers. Much of the early research concentrated on the content analysis of sex on prime-time television in an attempt to paint an accurate picture of the type and amount of sexual content portrayed during the most heavily watched time slot.

Spanning the second half of the 1970s, these analyses established that sex was primarily portrayed through reference and innuendo (Franzblau, Sprafkin, & Rubinstein, 1977), and that the incidence of such references generally increased from year to year (Greenberg, Graef, Fernandez-Collado, Korzenny, & Atkin, 1980; Sapolsky, 1982; Silverman, Sprafkin, & Rubinstein, 1979). Throughout the 1980s, analyses indicated that the incidence of sexual content in television programming rose consistently. For the first time, actors seemingly engaging in sexual intercourse, formerly portrayed exclusively through reference, were depicted directly (Lowry & Shidler, 1993; Sapolsky & Tabarlet, 1991). Even though television's portrayal of sexual content increased, its portrayal of the risks and possible negative consequences of sexual activity remained infrequent (Lowry & Shidler, 1993).

The 1990s witnessed an explosion of televised sexual content not only in prime-time broadcast television but also across time periods and cable channels. Over time, television depicted or strongly implied sexual intercourse with increasing frequency (Kunkel & Cope, 1999; Kunkel et al., 1999). By 2000, a Kaiser Family Foundation study found that the incidence of sexual content on television had risen to two out of every three shows and that these shows averaged more than four scenes with sexual content per hour; in addition, in all shows depicting sexual behavior, only one in 10 made reference to the risks and responsibilities of sexual activity (Kunkel, Cope-Farrar, Biely, Farinola, & Donnerstein, 2001; see also Farrar et al., 2003).

Sex in Advertising

Since the late 1960s, the use of sex in advertising—a controversial practice much discussed among practitioners, scholars, activists, and the public— has also been investigated. Seminal studies analyzed the effects of nudity in print advertisements: who among viewers responded to the sexual appeal and how the appeal affected brand recall and viewer attitudes toward the brand (Alexander & Judd, 1978; Steadman, 1969). In comparative analyses of sexual portrayals in magazine advertisements in 1964 and 1984, scholars found that while the percentage of sexual appeals did not increase, the types of sexual portrayals did, with the sexual appeal becoming more overt (Soley & Kurzbard, 1986). In addition, women were portrayed in a sexually suggestive manner more in 1984 than in 1964, a reflection the authors attributed to "[c]hanges in society's sexual attitudes and behaviors" (Soley & Reid, 1988, p. 966).

In a comparison of magazine advertisements in 1983 and 1993, scholars found a significant increase in the proportion of sexual appeals, with both genders portrayed more explicitly, although women were three times as likely as men to be portrayed as such (Reichert, Lambiase, Morgan,

Carstarphen, & Zavoina, 1999). While the preponderance of sex appeal studies has centered on magazine advertisements, attention has turned more recently to the use of sex appeals in television commercials. For example, Lin (1998) found that while the sexual appeal accounted for a small fraction of television commercial appeals, three fourths of sexual appeals in the sample presented women as sex objects.

In addition to the sexual appeal, the depiction of gender roles has been a major research interest related to the study of sex in advertising. A prevailing assumption is that constant exposure to stereotyped gender roles in the mass media fosters and reinforces gender-typed views and behaviors. In a pioneering analysis of television commercials, McArthur and Resko (1975) found that men appeared more frequently than women and that women were portrayed as lacking expertise and independent identities. Follow-up studies revealed that while women were portrayed as frequently in television commercials as men by the mid-1980s (Bretl & Cantor, 1988), voiceovers were dominantly male (Bretl & Cantor, 1988; Knill, Pesch, Pursey, Gilpin, & Perloff, 1981; Lovdal, 1989), and women were mainly portrayed in the conventional roles of mother and housewife (Knill et al., 1981; Lovdal, 1989). These studies also reveal that a significant proportion of women are portrayed as sex objects. For example, a study of gender roles in magazine ads found symbolic and institutionalized sexism (Cortese, 1999), while an analysis of portrayals of women in ads in 15 years of *Ms.* magazine found that, even though *Ms.* policy precludes the publication of ads harmful or insulting to women, advertising in the magazine increasingly portrayed women as sex objects (Ferguson, Kreshel, & Tinkham, 1990).

The Role of the Media in the Lives of Children and Teens

Furthermore, in recent years, scholars have begun to systematically examine the role of the media—including advertising—in the lives of children and teens. Many researchers have been concerned in particular with the media's portrayal of sexual behavior and its effect on beliefs and attitudes. As early as 1963, Bandura and Walters suggested that children and adolescents, due to a lack of other information sources, turn to the mass media to learn about sexual behavior. As Bandura's (1977) conception of social learning theory suggests, adolescents are neither the passive dupes of the media nor complete free agents in choosing how the media will and will not influence their behaviors, attitudes, and actions. Rather, adolescent behavior is the result of "a continuous reciprocal interaction between cognitive, behavioral, and environmental determinants" (Bandura, 1977, p. vii). Subsequent research has confirmed that the media serve as the primary sex educators in American culture (Courtright & Baran, 1980). As Brown and Keller (2000) asserted, "The mass media—television, music, magazines, movies and the Internet—are important sex educators. Yet, the media seldom have been concerned with the outcome of their ubiquitous sexual lessons" (p. 255).

The prevailing theme in most studies of children and teens is that the sexual images in the media tend to be harmful to impressionable minds. Knowing that teens watch an average of 6 hours of television a day (Klein et al., 1993) causes concern when researchers also know there is a significant relationship between the proportion of sexual matter an adolescent views on television and the level of his or her sexual experience (Brown & Newcomer, 1991). A recent survey of teens by the Kaiser Family Foundation (2002) revealed that nearly three out of four (72%) teens believe sex on TV influences the sexual behavior of their peers, while only one in four (22%) believes it influences their own behavior. When television programming presented mixed messages about sexual behavior, children received confused messages, and even when programs did not explicitly concern sex but included sexual references, children still received sexual messages (Kaiser Family Foundation & Children Now, 1996). In a study of college-age women, Ward (2002) found that regular television viewing predicted subjects' sexual attitudes and assumptions. Other studies have suggested that the media's presentation of the thin body ideal may negatively affect teens' self- and body-esteem (Botta, 1999; Irving, 1990).

A central concern among effects researchers is the media's relative reluctance to portray the negative consequences of risky sexual behavior. Many recent content analyses of prime-time television programming have shown that these programs rarely discuss or portray controversial issues such as sexually transmitted diseases, the use of condoms, AIDS, homosexuality, and unintended pregnancy (Cope-Farrar & Kunkel, 2002; Kunkel, Cope, & Colvin, 1996; Truglio, 1998). Other concerns focus on the context in which sexual attitudes or behavior is depicted. Pardun (2002) found that while little overt sexual behavior occurred in the movies most watched by teens, most romance was depicted without context between couples who either did not know each other well or were not in committed relationships. Indeed, the media's portrayal of sexual behaviors and attitudes can serve as scripts for young people as they learn about themselves as sexual beings (Brown, White, & Nikopoulou, 1993; Cope-Farrar & Kunkel, 2002; Ward, 1995). Therefore, as the American Academy of Pediatrics and others have repeatedly suggested, advocacy for responsible media portrayals of sexual content and the introduction of media literacy programs in schools would do much to empower children and adolescents to make healthy sexual choices (Brown & Keller, 2000; Committee on Communications, 1995; Committee on Public Education, 2001a, 2001b; Hogan, 2000).

However, the literature exploring the effects of sexual media on children and teens is rather incomplete and inconclusive. Few studies, for example, have examined in detail the sexual images that are portrayed. Kunkel and Cope studied the sexual content of family-hour programming over three decades (in 1976, 1986, and 1996), but did not study in depth the context in which sexual content was depicted (1999). Further, the preponderance of studies has focused on sexual content in television programming (Cope-Farrar & Kunkel, 2002; Kunkel et al., 1996; Truglio, 1998; Ward, 1995), while relatively few have focused on television advertising or other media.

Although a number of studies use ethnically diverse and gender inclusive samples of the U.S. teen population when studying effects (Kaiser Family Foundation, 2002; Kaiser Family Foundation & Children Now, 1996; Ward, 2002), few have examined the differential effects between genders or among ethnic groups. In addition, few scholars have used media lists that were derived from the population itself. More common is to use published lists, such as Nielsen data or magazine lists of top-grossing films, to determine the television programs (Cope-Farrar & Kunkel, 2002; Ward, 1995) and movies (Greenberg et al., 1993) teens most attend. While media critics have castigated the advertising industry for the negative effects of much advertising content—including sexual content—on children and teens (Committee on Communications, 1995), relatively few studies have actually examined the advertising that appears within the programs that these early adolescents (12-to-14-year-olds) watch. The following questions were advanced as an initial effort to inform this area of research:

RQ1: What types of sexual imagery are found in television commercials embedded in television programs that early adolescents indicate they watch regularly?

RQ2: What are the differences in exposure to sexual content according to race or gender?

METHOD

The present analysis is part of the Teen Media Study, a much larger project funded by the National Institute for Child Health and Development. Teen Media, a 5-year longitudinal examination of the impact of media on adolescents' sexual health, gathered and analyzed data from adolescents about their media usage and health, and content analyzed sexual content in adolescents' frequently viewed television programs, movies, CDs, magazines, newspapers, and Internet sites. Analyses indicate that adolescents' sexual media diets are significantly associated with their sexual attitudes, beliefs, and behaviors.

In the first phase of the study, 3,250 seventh and eighth graders (65% of the sample surveyed) were asked several questions about their media use, including the television programs they watched on a regular basis (L'Engle,

TABLE 8.1

Type and Proportion of Sexual Content in Commercials
Aired During Programs Most Watched by Early
Adolescents

Type of sexual content	Percentage of total sexual content in commercial
Sexual emphasis on body	61.8
Light romantic touch	17.6
Dating and relationships	11.5
Sexual innuendo (verbal)	5.1
Marriage	3.6
Passionate kissing	2.3
Reference to sexual intercourse	1.2
Public health messages (sex-related)	0.6
Crushes or flirting	0.3

Pardun, & Brown, 2004). Respondents chose from a list of 140 television programs, which was created by combining Nielsen lists, focus-group results, and a program list derived from pilot testing with the seventh and eighth graders not in the major study. The teens were also given an opportunity to report any additional programs not on the list that they viewed regularly. For this current study, each television program that was mentioned by at least 10% of each subgroup (boys, girls, Blacks, and Whites) was included in the sample. This sampling method yielded 71 programs. Our test sample comprised one episode of each program aired in the fall of 2001 that was collected as closely as possible to the time the teens completed the questionnaires. These 71 episodes collectively contained a total of 1,783 commercials, each of which was analyzed for sexual content (see Table 8.1).

Sexual content was categorized in several ways. We began with a protocol first developed by Kunkel et al. (1999), which focuses on risks and responsibilities of sexual messages. We expanded the protocol to include sexual issues that would have particular interest to early adolescents (12-to-14-year-olds). For example, we allowed for "lighter" sexual encounters (such as light kissing and flirtations). In addition, we specifically searched for positive sexual health messages that would be pertinent to teens such as pregnancy prevention, negative consequences of unplanned sex, and healthy relationships between committed partners.

The unit of analysis was a camera cut, which could be as short as 1 or 2 seconds. Nearly one fourth of the televised sexual content (both commercials and content) was double coded to calculate Scott's *pi* for intercoder reliability. The sexual content was coded at two levels: manifest and latent. Manifest content consisted of overt sexual characteristics such as "crushes or flirting," "light kissing," "reference to sexual intercourse," and "dating," as well as long-term relationships (for example, a commercial depicting a married couple and anniversary diamond rings). In addition, the manifest categories accounted for emphasis on the body in a sexual way, which included nudity or partial nudity and revealing clothing. A separate category for sexual innuendo was created that allowed for innuendo (e.g., "size really does matter") common in advertising content.

Latent content represented a deeper description of the coding choice selected from the manifest category. For example, if "dating" was chosen, then second-level coding would be a choice between "pleasurable consensual relationship between married couple," "pleasurable consensual relationship between unmarried couple," or "divorce or deteriorating relationship." Manifest content categories resulted in a Scott's *pi* of .85, and latent content achieved a reliability of .84. Because the unit of analysis (a camera cut) was so brief, only one dominant theme for manifest and latent content was coded for each unit.

RESULTS

Research question 1: In the 1,783 commercials examined in this study, a total of 1,796 sexual incidences were identified and analyzed. Each examined episode of the adolescents' favorite television programs was found to have at least one commercial with sexual content. Nearly two thirds of the sexual content in the commercials (61.8%) sexually emphasized the body. The second most common category (17.6%) represented light romantic touches. There were only eight incidences of passionate kissing in the entire sample, and only one incident involving sexual intercourse. Even sexual innuendo, which is often part of the negative critique of "sex in advertising," represented only 5.1% of advertised sexual content.

As previously discussed, much of the advertising literature criticizes the objectification of women in advertising. Therefore, it would be logical to predict that the majority of commercials featuring an emphasis on the body would be focused on women. While this study does reveal that sexualized body instances were mostly of women (58%), it should be noted that 37.5% of the content focused on men, and 12.6% focused on both genders equally. This, of course, may not mean that women are less objectified than in the past, but that male models are now experiencing objectification. Further research would be needed to explore this nuance.

Because many scholars consider the media as a social learning tool for adolescents, we were particularly interested to note how couples were portrayed in the commercials. There were 536 incidences of couples shown in the commercials. Out of those, only 11.9% of the interactions between the couples showed the couple as married; conversely, 88.1% of the incidences were unmarried couples. In addition, when the incident depicted a couple (married or unmarried), it was coded as to whether either partner expressed love to each other verbally. Versions of "I love you" were expressed only 9 times out of the total 546 events. Further, in only one of these instances was the couple depicted as married.

Again following social learning theory, we paid close attention to any form of public health message portrayed in the commercials. Even though we had several categories for public health messages (including information about sexual maturity, condom use, preventing pregnancy, negative consequences of unprotected sex, and regret), all were collapsed into just one category labeled "public health" messages because such messages were so infrequent. In fact, of the 1,796 incidences of sexual messages, only nine occurrences of a public health message of any kind were recorded.

Research question 2: Elsewhere we discuss the racial and gender differences in television programming choices (Brown & Pardun, 2004). In that study, we organized the 140 sampled television shows by gender and race categories. We found that, for the most part, Blacks and Whites and girls and boys reside in different television worlds. For example, only four shows were watched by more than one third of *each* group (*Who Wants to Be a Millionaire*, *The Simpsons*, *Boy Meets World*, and *Malcolm in the Middle*). More common were shows such as *The Hughleys*, watched by 78% of the Black teens and only 11% of the White teens.

To a lesser extent, the sexual content in commercials is considerably varied. When looking at sexual content in the commercials in the top 10 shows as described in Brown and Pardun (2004), there was no significant difference among commercials viewed by Blacks, Whites, males, or females. In some ways, this finding is not surprising, given advertisers' need to reach mass audiences across several different programs as well as the networks' typical rigorous examination of commercial content for regulation pitfalls, such as deception and indecency. However, it is worth noting the interesting patterns that emerged in specific programs. For example, when the 71 television programs most watched by these early adolescents are categorized according to network and cable stations, analysis shows greater variation of sexual content in the commercials. Table 8.2 provides a breakdown of network and cable station by the average number of seconds of sexual content in commercials from the sampled programs.

Among the "Big Four" networks, NBC had, on average, more seconds (64 seconds per show) of sexual content in its commercials than the other major networks. The WB, a network that has positioned itself with programming for younger audiences, had an average of 75 seconds of sexual commercial content per show (see Table 8.2).

Given the Janet and Justin Super Bowl scenario described at the beginning of this chapter, it should come as no surprise that MTV—with 111

TABLE 8.2
Sexual Content in Seconds Per Television Program Watched by Early Adolescents (By Network or Cable Station)

Station	Number of programs	Average seconds of sexual content in commercials per program	Average seconds of commercials per program	Percentage of sexual content per program
NBC	5	64	902	7.09%
CBS	4	32	758	4.22%
ABC	9	42	808	5.19%
FOX	10	29	451	6.43%
UPN	8	48	622	7.71%
WB	12	75	689	10.88%
BET	1	69	1417	4.87%
Nickelodeon	4	14	217	6.45%
MTV	4	111	746	14.87%
Comedy Central	1	108	430	25.11%
Cartoon Network	5	18	462	3.89%
Disney	1	20	431	4.64%
ESPN	1	41	1221	3.35%
FOX Family	1	29	2371	1.22%
TBS Superstation	1	7	394	1.77%
PAX	1	24	874	2.74%
The Learning Channel	1	33	830	3.97%
Syndication	2	51	960	5.31%

seconds—was ranked highest in average number of seconds of sexual content in commercials per program. What might come as a surprise to parents of 12-year-olds, however, is that shows on MTV (e.g., *Total Request Live*) are watched regularly by this age group, and the program and its embedded commercials contain a relatively heavy dose of sexual content.

Tables 8.3 and 8.4 highlight the differences between the amount of sexual content in the commercials and the programming of the top 10 television programs watched by Black, White, male, and female early adolescents across race and gender (Brown & Pardun, 2004). Although the sexual content in both the commercials and programs watched by girls is relatively low (with the exception of the program *Cribs*), in half the programs there was more sexual content proportionally in the commercials than in the programs. With boys, 7 out of 10 programs had more sexual images in the commercials, and with Whites, it was 8 out of 10. Black early adolescents have a different experience, however, with 8 out of 10 programs containing more sexually oriented content than the embedded commercials.

TABLE 8.3

Percentage of Sexual Content in Commercials and Programs of Top 10 Programs Watched by Black and White Early Adolescents

Program	Percentage of Blacks who watch regularly (N = 1,338)	Percentage of sexual content in commercials	Percentage of sexual content in program
Parkers	85.0	2	15
Martin	81.4	2	10
Hughleys	78.8	4	4
Moesha	78.8	1	7
106 and Park	78.4	5	27
Wayan Brothers	71.6	2	3
Parenthood	70.6	37	22
One on One	70.3	7	12
Steve Harvey Show	69.0	8	5
Living Single	67.0	1	1
	Percentage of Whites who watch regularly (N = 1,604)		
Simpsons	51.5	9	1
Boy Meet World	50.2	6	4
Whose Line Is It Anyway?	48.5	7	3
Friends	47.8	11	9
Who Wants to Be a Millionaire?	43.2	5	0
Seventh Heaven	40.2	6	11
Sabrina the Teenage Witch	39.9	4	3
Malcolm in the Middle	37.8	4	1
Survivor	36.7	4	12
Lizzy McGuire	35.5	5	1

DISCUSSION AND CONCLUSION

Our first research question explores the types of sexual imagery found in television commercials embedded in television programs most watched by early adolescents. As discussed earlier, past studies of magazine advertisements have documented the increasing prevalence of sex appeals and the sexual objectification of women from the 1960s and 1970s to the present. This magazine research has led to the general assumption in media effects work that much contemporary advertising is drenched with sexuality. Our study, however, corroborates Lin's (1998) pioneering study of sexual content in television commercials: Overall, television commercials contain a relatively light dose of sexual content. In our study of commercials most watched by early adolescents, sexual intercourse is almost never depicted or implied, passionate kissing is rare, and sexual innuendo is infrequent.

TABLE 8.4

Percentage of Sexual Content in Commercials and Programs of Top 10 Programs Watched by Early Adolescent Boys and Girls

Program	Percentage of boys who watch regularly (N = 1,485)	Percentage of sexual content in commercials	Percentage of sexual content in program
Simpsons	62.9	9	1
Who Wants to be a Millionaire?	44.4	5	0
Rocket Power	44.3	6	4
Jackass	43.6	26	7
South Park	42.5	25	8
DragonBallZ	42.3	3	1
Malcolm in the Middle	41.7	4	1
Cribs	41.3	11	33
Celebrity Deathmatch	40.9	7	8
WWF Smackdown	40.7	10	20
	Percentage of girls who watch regularly (N = 1,776)		
Sabrina the Teenage Witch	59.6	4	3
Boy Meets World	57.3	6	4
Seventh Heaven	54.1	6	11
Moesha	52.5	1	7
Who Wants to be a Millionaire?	51.3	5	0
Clueless	50.1	12	2
Cribs	47.5	11	33
Parkers	47.5	2	15
Lizzy McGuire	47.2	5	1
Braceface	46.5	6	6

Although our study found 1,796 sexual incidences in the 1,783 examined commercials—what at first glance might seem to be a one-to-one correspondence—it must be remembered that our unit of analysis was the camera cut, not the commercial. Thus, when a single commercial did contain sexual content, it typically contained a small number of sexual incidences. And, these sexual incidences—mostly consisting of sexual emphasis on the body and light romantic touches—tended to be relatively minor in nature. Of course, social learning theory suggests that young adolescents' body images may be informed by messages they receive from commercials about the body and its sexuality. Given the alarming prevalence of eating disorders in American youth, further research in this area is needed. Also, most of the messages about relationships in the examined commercials involved unmarried couples. Because many young adolescents are beginning to explore the role of romantic relationships in their own lives, social learning theory suggests that research is needed to explore the messages about romantic relationships contained in these commercials and their potential effect on young adolescents' relational scripts.

Our second research question examined the differences in exposure of young adolescents to sexual content according to race and gender. Although there is relatively little variation in the total amount of sexual content in television commercials consumed by these groups, there is greater variation in the proportion of commercial sexual content to programming sexual content. Media effects research has traditionally assumed that television programming contains more sexual content than commercials, but our research shows evidence that this assumption may be invalid. Although girls' programming contains more sexual content than the embedded commercials, boys' programming contains less sexual content than the commercials. It may be that girls' programming is responding to the popular perception that adolescent girls are more interested in learning about romantic relationships than are adolescent boys. Girls' most-watched programming thus explores relationships more—and contains more sexual content—than boys' programming does. The starkest variation occurs between White and Black adolescents' media diets: For Whites, the majority of programs contained less sexual content than the embedded commercials, and for Blacks, the majority of programs contained more sexual content than the commercials. Overall, then, Black adolescents consume more sexual messages in their television diets than their White peers do. Why the disparity, and what Black youth are learning about sexual relationships from these messages, are questions future research needs to explore more fully.

While media scholars, parents, and politicians often talk about whether adolescent exposure to television is problematic, the discussions rarely focus on advertising. Assumptions range from "all ads are evil" to "no one pays attention to advertising anyway." But, clearly, adolescents' daily media diets include a large dose of commercials. Some of this commercial content is clearly inappropriate for early adolescents.

Parents, if they choose, can use the controversial (and certainly not flawless) rating system that is available to decide whether a certain program is appropriate for their children to watch. But, the rating system does not pertain to the embedded commercials in those programs. While this study shows a relatively light overall dose of sexual content in commercials that run in programs that early adolescents watch regularly, in some programs, there is more sexual content in the commercials than the programs. Although the content may be considered "mild," these adolescents are receiving sexual messages that many in the adult community would question is appropriate. Adolescents are seeing unmarried couples in intimate situations; on the rare occasion when they might see a married couple, it is likely to be in a context like a recent Yoplait yogurt commercial. In the spot, the wife acts like a French maid in a "come on" to her husband. This ad may be rather sophisticated for a 12-year-old to assess.

Additionally, popular shows among this age group, like *Jackass* and *South Park*, have strong discrepancies between the sexual content of the commercials and the sexual content of the television program. Even a show such as *Who Wants to be a Millionaire?*, which has no sexual content and is given the mildest television rating possible ("appropriate for all ages"), contained sexual content in the embedded commercials.

Finally, as adults, we are living in a highly fragmented media world. We should remember that early adolescents' media worlds are just as complicated. Additionally, as media choices become ever more complex, commercials may become the only media connection between these fragmented audiences. It is important, therefore, that we better understand the content that may be providing the glue that connects these diverse groups.

ACKNOWLEDGMENTS

This research was funded by a grant from the National Institute of Child Health and Human Development.

REFERENCES

Alexander, M. W., & Judd Jr., B. (1978). Do nudes in ads enhance brand recall? *Journal of Advertising Research, 18*(2), 47–50.

Bandura, A. (1977). *Social learning theory*. Englewood Cliffs, NJ: Prentice-Hall.

Bandura, A., & Walters, R. H. (1963). *Social learning and personality development*. New York: Holt, Rinehart & Winston.

Botta, R. A. (1999). Television images and adolescent girls' body image disturbance. *Journal of Communication, 49*(2), 22–41.

Bretl, D. J., & Cantor, J. (1988). The portrayal of men and women in U.S. television commercials: A recent content analysis and trends over 15 years. *Sex Roles, 18*(9/10), 595–609.

Brown, J. D., & Keller, S. N. (2000). Can the mass media be healthy sex educators? *Family Planning Perspectives, 32*(5), 255–258.

Brown, J. D., & Newcomer, S. F. (1991). Television viewing and adolescents' sexual behavior. *Journal of Homosexuality, 21*, 77–91.

Brown, J. D., & Pardun, C. J. (2004). Little in common: Racial and gender differences in adolescents' television diets. *Journal of Broadcasting and Electronic Media, 48*(2), 266–78.

Brown, J. D., White, A. B., & Nikopoulou, L. (1993). Disinterest, intrigue resistance: Early adolescent girls' use of sexual media content. In B. S. Greenberg, J. D. Brown, & N. L. Buerkel-Rothfuss (Eds.), *Media, sex and the adolescent* (pp. 177–195). Cresskill, NJ: Hampton Press.

Committee on Communications, 1993 to 1994 (1995). Sexuality, contraception, and the media. *Pediatrics, 95,* 298–300.

Committee on Public Education, 2000 to 2001. (2001a). Children, adolescents, and television. *Pediatrics, 107,* 423–426.

Committee on Public Education, 2000 to 2001. (2001b). Sexuality, contraception, and the media. *Pediatrics, 107,* 191–194.

Cope-Farrar, K. M., & Kunkel, D. (2002). Sexual messages in teens' favorite prime-time television programs. In J. D. Brown, J. R. Steele, & K. Walsh-Childers (Eds.), *Sexual teens, sexual media: Investigating media's influence on adolescent sexuality* (pp. 59–78). Mahwah, NJ: Lawrence Erlbaum Associates.

Cortese, A. J. (1999). *Provocateur: Images of women and minorities in advertising.* Lanham, MD: Rowman & Littlefield.

Courtright, J. A., & Baran, S. J. (1980). The acquisition of sexual information by young people. *Journalism Quarterly, 57,* 107–114.

Farrar, K., Kunkel, D., Biely, E., Eyal, K., Fandrich, R., & Donnerstein, E. (2003). Sexual messages during prime-time programming. *Sexuality & Culture, 7,* 7–37.

Ferguson, J. H., Kreshel, P. J., & Tinkham, S. F. (1990). In the pages of *Ms.*: Sex role portrayals of women in advertising. *Journal of Advertising, 19*(1), 40–51.

Franzblau, S., Sprafkin, J. N., & Rubinstein, E. A. (1977). Sex on TV: A content analysis. *Journal of Communication, 27*(2), 164–170.

Greenberg, B. S., Graef, D., Fernandez-Collado, C., Korzenny, F., & Atkin, C. K. (1980). Sexual intimacy on commercial TV during prime time. *Journalism Quarterly, 57,* 211–215.

Greenberg, B. S., Linsangan, R., Soderman, A., Heeter, C., Lin, C., Stanley, C., & Siemicki, M. (1993). Adolescents' exposure to television and movie sex. In B. S. Greenberg, J. D. Brown, & N. Buerkel-Rothfuss (Eds.), *Media, sex, and the adolescent* (pp. 61–98). Cresskill, NJ: Hampton Press.

Hogan, M. (2000). Media matters for youth health. *Journal of Adolescent Health, 27(Suppl.1),* 73–76.

Irving, L. M. (1990). Mirror images: Effects of the standard of beauty on the self- and body-esteem of women exhibiting varying levels of bulimic symptoms. *Journal of Social and Clinical Psychology, 9*(2), 230–242.

Kaiser Family Foundation. (2002). Survey on teens, sex and TV. Menlo Park, CA: Kaiser Family Foundation.

Kaiser Family Foundation & Children Now. (1996). *The family hour focus groups: Children's responses to sexual content on TV and their parents' reactions.* Menlo, CA: Kaiser Family Foundation & Children Now.

Klein, J. D., Brown, J. D., Walsh-Childers, K., Oliveri, J., Porter, C., & Dykers, C. (1993). Adolescents' risky behavior and mass media use. *Pediatrics, 92,* 24–31.

Knill, B. J., Pesch, M., Pursey, G., Gilpin, P., & Perloff, R. M. (1981). Still typecast after all these years? Sex role portrayals in television advertising. *International Journal of Women's Studies, 4*(5), 497–506.

Kunkel, D., & Cope, K. M. (1999). Sexual messages on television: Comparing findings from three studies. *Journal of Sex Research, 36*(3), 230–236.

Kunkel, D., Cope, K. M., & Colvin, C. (1996). *Sexual messages on family hour television: Content and context.* Menlo Park, CA: Kaiser Family Foundation.

Kunkel, D., Cope, K. M., Farinola, W. J. M., Biely, E., Rollin, E., & Donnerstein, E. (1999). *Sex on TV: A biennial report to the Kaiser Family Foundation.* Menlo Park, CA: Kaiser Family Foundation.

Kunkel, D., Cope-Farrar, K., Biely, E., Farinola, W. J. M., & Donnerstein, E. (2001). *Sex on TV2: A biennial report to the Kaiser Family Foundation 2001.* Menlo Park, CA: Kaiser Family Foundation.

L'Engle, K., Pardun, C. J., & Brown, J. D. (2004). Accessing adolescents: A school-recruited, home-based approach to conducting media and health research. *Journal of Early Adolescent Research, 24*(2), 144–158.

Lin, C. A. (1998). Uses of sex appeals in prime-time television commercials. *Sex Roles, 38*(5/6), 461–475.

Lovdal, L. T. (1989). Sex role messages in television commercials: An update. *Sex Roles, 21*(11/12), 715–724.

Lowry, D. T., & Shidler, J. A. (1993). Prime-time TV portrayals of sex, safe sex, and AIDS: A longitudinal analysis. *Journalism Quarterly, 70*(3), 628–637.

McArthur, L. Z., & Resko, B. G. (1975). The portrayal of men and women in American television commercials. *The Journal of Social Psychology, 97*, 209–220.

Pardun, C. J. (2002). Romancing the script: Identifying the romantic agenda in top-grossing movies. In J. D. Brown, J. R. Steele, & K. Walsh-Childers (Eds.), *Sexual teens, sexual media: Investigating media's influence on adolescent sexuality* (pp. 211–225). Mahwah, NJ: Lawrence Erlbaum Associates.

Reichert, T., Lambiase, J., Morgan, S., Carstarphen, M., & Zavoina, S. (1999). Cheesecake and beefcake: No matter how you slice it, sexual explicitness in advertising continues to increase. *Journalism & Mass Communication Quarterly, 76*(1), 7–20.

Sapolsky, B. S. (1982). Sexual acts and references on prime-time TV: A two-year look. *Southern Speech Communication Journal, 47*, 212–226.

Sapolsky, B. S., & Tabarlet, J. O. (1991). Sex in primetime television: 1979 versus 1989. *Journal of Broadcasting & Electronic Media, 35*(4), 505–516.

Silverman, L. T., Sprafkin, J. N., & Rubinstein, E. A. (1979). Physical contact and sexual behavior on prime-time TV. *Journal of Communication, 29*(1), 33–43.

Smith, L., & Simon, R. (12 February 2004). TV content leads to capitol threat, *Los Angeles Times*, A14.

Soley, L. C., & Kurzbard, G. (1986). Sex in advertising: A comparison of 1964 and 1984 magazine advertisements. *Journal of Advertising, 15*(3), 46–54.

Soley, L. C., & Reid, L. N. (1988). Taking it off: Are models in magazine ads wearing less? *Journalism Quarterly, 65*, 960–966.

Steadman, M. (1969). How sexy illustrations affect brand recall. *Journal of Advertising Research, 9*, 15–19.

Truglio, R. T. (1998). Television as sex educator. In K. Swan, C. Meskill, & S. DeMaio (Eds.), *Social learning from broadcast television* (pp. 7–23). Creskill, NJ: Hampton Press.

Ward, L. M. (1995). Talking about sex: Common themes about sexuality in the prime-time television programs children and adolescents view most. *Journal of Youth and Adolescence, 24*(5), 595–615.

Ward, L. M. (2002). Does television exposure affect emerging adults' attitudes and assumptions about sexual relationships? Correlational and experimental confirmation. *Journal of Youth and Adolescence, 31*(1), 1–15.

Chapter 9

Sexually Oriented Appeals on the Internet: An Exploratory Analysis of Popular Mainstream Web Sites

Artemio Ramirez, Jr.

The Ohio State University

The mention of the words "sex on the Internet" likely conjures images in readers' minds of sexually explicit, pornographic material located on adult entertainment Web sites. Images of scantily clad (if at all) models positioned in provocative poses gazing seductively into the camera also likely come to mind. Less likely evoked are images of these models peddling a product on mainstream popular sites frequented by the average consumer searching for information about news, sports, or entertainment. Despite the fact that scholars have reported on the vast amount of sexual content available on the Internet (see Lambiase, 2003, for a review), the thought that coverage of, for instance, world events, sports competitions, and entertainment gatherings would share the same virtual space with this and other similar images is almost unthinkable to some in the mainstream public. In the virtual world of Wolf Blitzer, Diane Sawyer, Sam Donaldson, and Chris Berman, they would argue that there is no room for such images . . . or is there?

The notion that sex sells and does so very well is not new to advertising and marketing circles (see Reichert, 2003). As chapters throughout this book attest, the use of "sex in advertising," or sexually oriented appeals (SOA), is a commonly employed persuasive approach to selling everything from movies (Oliver & Kalyanaraman, this volume) to music videos (Andsager, this volume), magazines (Lambiase & Reichert, this volume) to alcoholic beverages (Chambers, this volume), as well as many other consumer goods in between. However, less studied has been the idea that sex sells on the Internet. The phenomenal growth of the Internet over the last decade as a marketplace and realm for consumer marketing as well as the development of an increasingly burgeoning body of research examining both topics suggest the Internet may be a venue ripe with opportunities for employing SOA.

This chapter examines the prevalence of SOA on three categories of popular mainstream Web sites: news, sports, and entertainment. The following sections (a) review existing literature on the prevalence of SOA and the characteristics of such ads, (b) report on the results of an exploratory study investigating both aspects of SOA (prevalence characteristics), and (c) discuss the implications of the findings for the study of SOA, in general, and on the Internet in particular.

THE PREVALENCE OF SOA IN MEDIA

Accumulated research examining the prevalence of sexually oriented advertising in traditional print and electronic media provides some insight into its pervasiveness on the Internet. Investigations into the prevalence of such ads in print magazines suggest they are quite common. Soley and Reid (1988) reported that over the 20-year span from 1964 to 1984 the sexual nature of advertising, as indexed by the amount of clothing worn, featuring females increased by approximately 3%, from 31% to 34%. In contrast, sexually oriented ads featuring males during the same period increased 8%, from 6% to 14%. Similarly, findings reported by Reichert, Lambiase, Morgan, Carstarphen, and Zavoina (1999) indicate that not only has the prevalence of sexual content in advertising reported by Soley and Reid (1988) continued to increase, particularly in targeted men's and women's magazines, but also that it has evolved to include more subtle forms beyond the absence of clothing. For example, their results revealed an increase of 32% in the number of ads showing sexual contact between models, from 21% in 1983 to 53% in 1993. At the same time, the number of ads suggestive of "very intimate contact" (e.g., sexual intercourse) increased by 16% during the same period, from 1% to 17%.

Whereas these studies report a fairly high prevalence of sexually oriented advertising in print media, other research suggests their use on television by advertisers is more limited. In a content analysis of prime-time television commercials aired in 1993, Lin (1998) found that a moderate percentage of the models featured in the ads, approximately 18%, were labeled as *very sexy* based on their level of physical attractiveness and style of clothing. A similar analysis conducted by Fullerton and Kendrick (2001) on NBC prime-time commercials aired in 1998 found a relatively low percentage of ads featured females (12%) and males (2%) dressed in sexually suggestive clothing.

Interestingly, networks' own promotional advertising appears to reflect a higher prevalence of sexual content than those of advertisers. An early study of network promotional ads by Soley and Reid (1988) found that more than one third (36%) of the promos aired in 1983 contained some form of sexual behavior or language. Walker (2000) reported sexual behavior/contact in network promotional ads had increased 9% over a period of 8 years, from 12% in 1990 to 21% in 1998. In addition, sexually suggestive language was found in approximately 23% of the promotional commercials. This trend in network promotional ads also appears to extend across cultural programming boundaries. Fullerton and Kendrick's (this volume) analysis of network promotional ads aired on Univision, a Spanish-language network, revealed a fairly high prevalence of sexually oriented promos featured female models/actors (40%) dressed in sexually suggestive clothing.

SOA on the Internet

In contrast to the scholarly attention garnered by SOA in print and traditional electronic media, the prevalence of sexually oriented advertising on the Internet remains largely unexamined. From a pragmatic perspective, studying SOA on the Internet creates certain challenges to researchers that would not normally emerge in other venues. Prospective advertisers utilize cookies, intelligent agents, online surveys, and other information-gathering tools, some of which are employed covertly, to profile consumers. This information is then used to target consumers with advertising content in the form of banner, pop-up, pop under, and embedded ads based on characteristics such as demographic information (e.g., age, sex, etc.) or browsing behavior (Kaye & Medoff, 2001). As Lambiase (2003, p. 257) explained:

> It is this covert advertising strategy that may make the Internet as an advertising venue more difficult to study, in terms of how sexually oriented appeals operate in this evolving environment and by whom they are seen. While pull technology tries to attract appropriate audiences for web content and corollary advertising, push technology is more interesting in terms of sexually oriented appeals. It is used widely on the web to send content and advertising by email to users who fit demographic profiles or who passively provide clues about their interests through cookies. Then, push technology interprets data from surfing profiles to make users into targets for ads about sites with sexualized content, for ads for sex products, or ads with sexualized content.

The net effect is clear: Consumers who fit a particular profile, one that is targeted with sexually oriented advertising content, will experience the same Web sites in a distinct manner from those who do not fit such a profile. Although this is desirable for advertisers in that it aids them in properly targeting messages to audiences, it complicates the ability of researchers to adequately document the effects of advertising approaches.

Nonetheless, other factors point to the Internet as a particularly attractive venue for investigations into the use of SOA. Advertising campaigns directed at traditional media outlets (e.g., newspapers, magazines, and television) frequently include online components such as banner ads or brief streaming video versions of television commercials. Yet, the Internet not only combines characteristics of advertising available in both traditional print and electronic media, but it also does so in a more permissive environment with less constraints on sexual content or explicitness of images (Lambiase, 2003). Ads that may be deemed too "racy" or explicitly sexual in other venues may be given life online. Indeed, much of the technology currently available online to deliver advertising and other content was originally developed to deliver sexually explicit material (Bedell, 2001; Klein, 1999; Needham, 2001). The combination of environment and technology allows advertisers online to "push the boundaries" more so than, for example, on television, where they are more susceptible to the oversight of federal agencies. With respect to SOA, this provides advertisers the opportunity to utilize appeals with a greater degree of sexually tinged content or employ them to a greater extent than they would in traditional outlets.

In summary, whereas studies assessing SOA in print and electronic media suggest they are quite pervasive, predominantly in the form of attractive, primarily female models clad in revealing or suggestive clothing, the lack of complementary investigations on SOA on the Internet precludes proposing hypotheses regarding their prevalence and nature expected to emerge in the present analysis. Thus, the following research questions are posed:

RQ1: How prevalent are SOA on popular mainstream websites?
RQ2: What are the most common features of SOA on popular mainstream Web sites?

METHOD

Sampling

Three general categories of popular Web sites (news, sports, entertainment) were sampled and examined in the present study. However, little agreement exists as to what the most popular or frequently visited Web sites are in each category (for a discussion, see Stempel & Stewart, 2000). This is the result of several influences, including the fact that: (a) no definitive source of popular Web site rankings has emerged, (b) sources that do identify popular Web sites use distinct methodologies or tracking tools, and (c) individual sources typically do not employ more than one methodology for determining their rankings. Because of this, several sources were used to generate an initial list of popular or most frequently visited news, sports, and entertainment Web sites, including reports generated by Internet audience measurement firms such as comScore Media Matrix (www.comscore.com), Nielsen/NetRatings (www.nielsen-netratings.com), and Ranking.com (www.trafficranking.com) on popular Web site properties; lists of most popular search terms tracked by searchenginewatch.com, which includes Google, Yahoo!, Lycos, and other search engines; and lists of popular Web sites published in newspapers (e.g., *New York Times, Chicago Tribune*).

These sources provided a degree of convergence on a set of Web sites within each of the three categories, resulting in an initial sample of 25 sites. However, the initial sample was further reduced because although some of the Web sites that shared parent companies served as a presence for their counterparts in another category, they were not maintained as separate Web sites. For example, in the case of CNN.com and CNNSI.com, the two sites are maintained as separate entities, with the latter more closely linked to the *Sports Illustrated* magazine than CNN news. This is not the case with ABCNews.com and its sports counterpart, ABC Sports—ESPN.com serves as the sports presence for ABC on the Web, and visiting the ABC Sports site redirects visitors to ESPN.com. As a result, the ABC Sports "site" was eliminated from the list as it would provide redundant information. That is, because the design of and advertising located on the homepage of the two sites are not going to differ, the results of the analyses would be skewed since the two pages (in reality) represent one site. Proceeding in this manner resulted in the final sample of 16 Web sites included in the analyses reported below. Table 9.1 shows specific information about the overall sample.

Procedure and Coding

As noted above, analyzing advertising on Web sites introduces complexities that would not normally emerge in other venues. Using information-gathering tools (e.g., cookies and intelligent agents) to profile and target consumers with advertising content based on their background or browsing behavior is normative. As a means of countering these tools, two new computers (one desktop, one laptop) were used to visit and capture the home sites examined in the present study; the computers were used only

TABLE 9.1

Summary Statistics of Advertising of Web Sites and
Sexually Oriented Appeals (SOA) by Category

Category/ Web sites	Ads on the site	SOA Per Visit M	(S.D.)	Proportion of ads
News				
CNN.com	3	.38	(.52)	.13
FoxNews.com	5	.88	(.35)	.20
CBSnews.com	6	.88	(.83)	.15
MSNBC.com	5	1.50	(.53)	.30
ABCnews.com	3	.38	(.52)	.13
USAToday.com	6	.75	(.46)	.13
Category average	4.67	.79	(.42)	.17
Sports				
ESPN.com	2	.50	(.53)	.25
CNNSI.com	5	1.75	(.46)	.35
FoxSports.com	5	.63	(.52)	.13
CBS.sportsline.com	5	.50	(.53)	.17
Category average	4.25	.84	(.61)	.20
Entertainment				
BET.com	4	.50	(.76)	.13
Entertainmentweekly.com	3	1.00	(.76)	.25
Eonline.com	5	1.00	(.93)	.20
ETonline.com	3	.50	(.53)	.17
MTV.com	4	.88	(.35)	.22
WWE.com	3	1.13	(.35)	.38
Category average	3.67	.83	(.27)	.23

Note. The ad space available on site column represents the number
of spaces dedicated to advertising on the homepage. The proportion of
space column is calculated by dividing the number of sexually oriented
ads by the total number of ads on the Web site.

for the purposes of this study during the data collection period. The security settings of the browsers on each computer were set to "high" and Web
sites were not allowed to deposit cookies, which reduced their ability to
track browsing history.

Each selected home site was visited a total of eight times over the course
of a 2-week period. Two steps were taken in order to adequately represent the advertising content on the sites throughout a 24-hour day. First,
each "visit" represented a 3-hour block of time with the combined visits
constituting a 24-hour time period. Thus, each Web site was examined
once over a 2-week period during the 3-hour block of time from 9 A.M. to
12 P.M., then again between 12 P.M. and 3 P.M., and so forth. Days and
times were initially randomly selected for each category of sites. However,

because some of the sites were unavailable during scheduled visits due to a variety of factors (e.g., system maintenance), adjustments were made to the original schedule to ensure the proper number of visits was conducted for each site. Second, snapshots of homepages were taken during each visit and subsequently coded for content.

The Web sites were examined through a two-step process of content analysis. Initially, all of the ads were independently examined by six naïve coders (three males, three females) to determine whether they qualified as SOA. The use of naïve coders in this initial step is consistent with grounded theory approaches for understanding advertising content (see Hirschman & Thompson, 1997) which propose that consumers, not researchers, determine how advertising content is perceived. If an ad was identified as a SOA, the coder was required to provide a brief explanation for the decision. Ads labeled as SOA by a majority of the coders were included in the second step of the coding process.

The second step of the content analysis involved coding each ad according to Reichert and Ramirez's (2000) four categories of sexually oriented appeals. This typology was employed because it recognizes both the explicit and implicit nature of sexually oriented appeals, provides a broad set of categories for determining what constitutes them, and encompasses several other conceptually related schemes (see Reichert & Ramirez, 2000, for discussion). The coding scheme also allows the multiple characteristics of individual ads to be coded into distinct categories.

Two trained assistants independently categorized the ads into four categories based on their features. The first category, *physical features*, includes characteristics of ads that highlight a model's body or clothing. Features such as the presence or absence of clothing, a physically attractive model, and/or a physically fit or appealing body comprise this category. The second category, *movement*, includes characteristics of ads that focus on a model's behavior or demeanor. Features such as the models' posture and attitude as well as the sounds (including voices) that accompany the ad constitute this category. The third category, *context*, includes characteristics of ads that highlight aspects of the ad other than the model. These characteristics include photographic effects used to create the ad (e.g., camera angle) as well as the ad's physical setting, background music, lighting effects, and presence/absence of color. The final category, *proxemics*, includes characteristics of ads that feature the physical distance or relative interaction between models. Features such as close interpersonal distance and an embrace between models are common to ads in this category.

Intercoder agreement, as indexed by Cohen's Kappa, on the four categories was high: physical features (96%), movement (90%), context (87%), and proxemics (92%).

RESULTS

Prevalence of SOA

The first research question (RQ1) asked about the prevalence of SOA on popular Web sites. Table 9.1 summarizes the results associated with the prevalence of SOA on the Web sites assessed in the present study. The first column of the table reports the number of ads present on the Web site. The second column reports the mean number of SOA present on the Web site based on the eight visits conducted as described in the method section. The third column reports the proportion of the ad space available on the site that were coded as SOA; this number can be interpreted as the percentage of SOA present on the site. The overall results show that news sites contained the smallest proportion of SOA, with 17% of their ads categorized as SOA. Entertainment sites contained the highest proportion, with 23% of their ads classified as SOA. SOA constituted 20% of the ads on sports sites. Table 9.1 also shows that the average number of SOA present per visit across the Web site categories was comparable. News sites averaged .79 SOA per visit, sports sites averaged .84, and entertainment sites averaged .83.

Considerable variation also emerged within each category of Web sites. Table 9.1 shows that the prevalence of SOA on news sites ranged from 13% (CNN.com, ABCNews.com, and USAToday.com) to 30% (MSNBC.com) of the ads overall. Both CNN.com and ABCNews.com contained the lowest number of SOA per visit (.38). MSNBC.com contained the highest number (1.50). That is, whereas on an average visit to either of the prior sites (CNN.com, ABCNews.com) .38 of the ads available were classified as SOA, 1.50 of the ads on the latter site (MSNBC.com) qualified as such.

An example of a SOA taken from MSNBC.com is shown in Fig. 9.1. The ad is part of an overall advertising campaign for TrimSpa, a collection of weight-loss products, featuring Anna Nicole Smith, which includes television ads showing her modeling on runways dressed in sexy outfits designed to highlight her *new* body. The ad shown in Fig. 9.1 shows Smith dressed in a revealing negligee, smiling and leaning forward slightly, exposing part of her breasts. Her image is accompanied by a caption declaring, "Anna Nicole revealed—69 lbs. sexier!" The ad then asks "How?" and provides a link instructing interested parties to "Click Here" to find out.

Among the sports sites, the overall prevalence of SOA ranged from 13% (FOXSports.com) to 35% (CNNSI.com). Both ESPN.com and CBS.sportsline.com contained the lowest proportion (.50) of SOA, with FoxSports.com containing a slightly higher proportion (.63). CNNSI.com contained the highest proportion in the category, averaging 1.75 ads per visit; this was also the highest average per visit across the three categories of Web sites.

FIG. 9.1. MSNBC.com advertisement for TrimSpa featuring Anna Nicole Smith.

A caveat to these results, however, is that analysis of CNNSI.com included ads for its own products on the site, including subscription offers for its off-line companion publication, *Sports Illustrated* magazine. Figure 9.2 shows an example of a SOA for *Sports Illustrated* taken from CNNSI.com. One of the magazine's most popular issues is their annual swimsuit issue, which includes photographs of bikini-clad models and athletes typically taken at an exotic beach location. The ad shown in Fig. 9.2 draws upon the popularity of that issue by featuring tennis player/model Anna Kournikova tanned, dressed in a bathing suit, and lying on her side on a beach. Her image is accompanied by a caption stating, "Try 4 free issues of SI and get the 2004 swimsuit DVD free."

FIG. 9.2. CNNSI.com advertisement for *Sports Illustrated* featuring Anna Kournikova.

FIG. 9.3. Eonline.com advertisement for Victoria's Secret Annual Sale.

Entertainment sites also showed significant variation in the prevalence of SOA, ranging from 13% (BET.com) to 38% (WWE.com) overall. WWE.com, a wrestling entertainment site that targets a younger, primarily male audience, averaged the highest number of SOA per visit (1.13), although both Entertainmentweekly.com and Eonline.com contained comparable levels (1.00). As with the CNNSI.com site, WWE.com featured advertising for several of its own products (WWE magazine, events, etc.), which contributed to its overall average. BET.com, the online presence of the Black Entertainment Television network, and ETonline.com, the online presence of Entertainment Tonight television program, averaged the lowest number of SOA per visit (.50).

The Victoria's Secret ad shown in Fig. 9.3 is an example of a SOA found on the Eonline.com Web site. The ad for their semiannual sale shows a seemingly topless and tanned female model lying on her stomach and superimposed on a background of flowing water. The caption accompanying the image states, "Swim Sale" with the statement "20–60% off select styles."

Characteristics of SOA

The second research question (RQ2) asked about the most common features of SOA on popular Web sites. Table 9.2 reports the frequency and percentage of characteristics of SOA by each category of Web sites. Across the three categories, SOA featuring the physical features of the models overwhelmingly represented the most common ad characteristic (93%). SOA highlighting movement (22%) and proxemics (21%) were the next most common characteristics in the ads, with contextual features represented to a lesser extent (14%).

This pattern was consistent within each category of Web sites as well, although the percentages varied considerably. Features of SOA on sports sites highlighted each category of characteristics to a greater extent than did those on news or entertainment sites. Of the SOA present on sports sites, 93% featured the physical characteristics of the models, whereas 88% of them on entertainment and 85% on news sites did so. The movement of the model(s) was featured in 44% of SOA on sports sites, 18% on news sites, and 13% on entertainment sites. The space between models (e.g., proxemics) was featured in 37% of the SOA on sports sites, 25% on entertainment sites,

TABLE 9.2
Frequency Statistics for Each Sexually Oriented Appeal
Coding Category by Web Site Category

| Category | Sexually Oriented Appeal Category | | | | | | | | Total |
| | Physical features | | Movement | | Context | | Proxemics | | |
	n	%	n	%	n	%	n	%	
News	33	85	7	18	4	10	6	15	39
Sports	25	93	12	44	7	37	10	37	27
Entertainment	35	88	5	13	4	10	6	25	40
Overall	99	93	24	22	15	14	22	21	107

Note. Row totals do not equal "Total" column due to the fact that the coding system allowed ads to be coded into multiple categories based on their characteristics.

and 15% on news sites. Contextual features appeared in 37% of the SOA on sports sites, whereas 10% of SOA on both news and entertainment sites highlighted them.

DISCUSSION

The growth of the Internet as a virtual marketplace has opened up new venues for the study of advertising practices including whether sex indeed does sell, in this case online. The present study provides an initial examination of sexually oriented advertising content on mainstream popular Web sites. The results of the present study are fairly straightforward. Sexually oriented advertising on the Internet is quite common to popular mainstream news, sports, and entertainment Web sites. Overall, approximately 20% of the ads examined on the three categories of Internet sites were coded as SOA. In other words, the average consumer who visits one of these sites can expect that approximately 20% of the ads he or she will be exposed to will be sexually oriented in nature. Moreover, consumers could expect a slightly higher percentage when visiting entertainment sites (23%) but slightly lower percentage when frequenting news sites (17%).

Despite the exploratory nature of the study and limited number of Web sites assessed, the results are consistent with previous research investigating SOA in traditional media (e.g., Fullerton & Kendrick, 2001, this volume; Reichert et al., 1999). The present study offers additional support to previously reported findings regarding the most prominent characteristics of SOA. Previous research on sexually oriented advertising

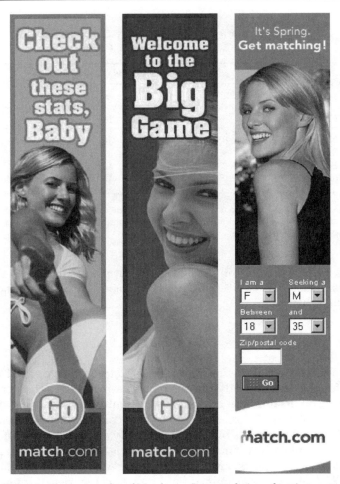

FIG. 9.4. Three examples of Match.com Internet dating advertisements.

in traditional media reports that physical features of models (e.g., attractiveness, appearance, athletic body, tan, clothing, etc.) are the most common characteristics of print and television ads (Lin, 1998; Reichert, 2003; Soley & Reid, 1988). Overall, 93% of the ads identified as SOA in the present study highlighted the physical features of one or more models. Although SOA on sports sites were more likely to emphasize this characteristic, ads appearing on news and entertainment also did so at relatively high degrees (see Table 9.2). As the examples shown in Figs. 9.1 through 9.3 illustrate, female models or actors were prominently featured in most of these ads. Of the 107 SOA identified in the present study, females were featured in

83% ($n = 81$), males in 9% ($n = 10$), and mixed-sex pairs in 15% ($n = 16$) of them. Thus, the results suggest that, as in other media outlets, images of females appear to be the dominant form of SOA on the Internet.

Whereas the examples of SOA provided in Figs. 9.1 through 9.3 appeared on the specific Web sites discussed above (e.g., unique to a given site), other SOA surfaced on multiple sites. Particularly notable was the prevalence of sexually tinged advertising for online dating services that appeared on several sites across the three categories (news, entertainment, sports). Figures 9.4 and 9.5 show SOA for the online dating services of Match.com and Great Expectations. The ads illustrate how online dating sites utilize SOA to attract consumers' attention online. With the subtly flirtatious heading of "Check out these stats, baby," one of the ads in Fig. 9.4 features an attractive, smiling female model dressed in a bathing suit partially turned from the camera, suggesting a playful yet sensual tone to the ad. Similarly, a second Match.com ad features another smiling, attractive female model peering over her shoulder, with her chest disappearing out of the ad. The image is accompanied by the sexually suggestive line "Welcome to the big game," with the word "big" appearing in a larger font than

FIG. 9.5. Example of Great Expectations Internet dating advertisement.

the rest of the words and to be possibly interpreted as a having a double meaning. The ad shown in Fig. 9.5 departs from the previous examples by featuring a couple embracing in an apparent passionate kiss, accompanied by the question, "Is finding an attractive and intelligent person too much to ask?" Interested consumers are then invited to "click here" to connect to the Great Expectations site.

Taken together, the overall results appear to indicate that the Internet is simply another venue for the use of SOA, closely paralleling previous investigations of off-line advertising in traditional media outlets. However, it must be emphasized that the sites examined were virtual spaces that the average Web user seeking information might frequent and not sites that would typically be associated with conceptions of SOA (e.g., gendered sites). News sites such as CNN.com, sports sites such as ESPN.com, and entertainment sites such as ETonline.com are popular mainstream sites frequented by consumers representing a diversity of socioeconomic backgrounds, ages, races, and sex.

Not included in the study were sites that cater specifically to one demographic or another (e.g., sex), which would be expected to reflect higher levels of SOA than that reported above (see Lambiase, 2003, for a discussion). For example, sites such as Maxim.com, which is the magazine's online presence, contain ads directed specifically at males and include a variety of SOA for its own products as well as those of its advertisers. In the present study, an argument can be made that WWE.com, which reflected an elevated level of SOA for its category, is a similar type of site that primarily targets young males. Yet, the overall results revealed that it did not contain the highest level overall of sexually tinged ads. Indeed, CNNSI.com, a sports site, and MSNBC.com, a news site, both exceeded it in terms of their average per visit and overall proportion of SOA (Table 9.1). Although only suggestive, these results imply that mainstream sites may contain comparable levels of SOA to those of "gendered" sites. Unfortunately, this question must be left to future study.

Limitations and Directions for Future Research

An important limitation of the present study is the small set of Web sites examined. This was necessitated by the desire to focus on categories of popular mainstream sites identified through the convergence of multiple factors discussed in the method section. Other approaches would likely identify a distinct set of sites, although some overlap should emerge, and potentially result in different results from those reported. Another limitation is the trade-off between the decision to control the utilization of cookies and other information-gathering tools during data collection and the extent to which SOA appeared on the sites examined. As noted above, information-gathering tools are employed as a means of targeting ads to consumers so that those who fit a certain profile are exposed to them more often than those who do not. This leaves open the possibility that the results reported are in fact *conservative* estimations of the extent to which SOA are employed on popular mainstream Web sites. Another potential limitation involves the number of visits to each Web site included in the analysis. Each site was visited eight times, each visit conducted at 3-hour windows and cumulatively representing a 24-hour period. It is possible that a greater number of visits could produce greater variation in content. That is, more than one visit per 3-hour period may provide more insight into the advertising content contained by each site. It is worth noting that supplemental analysis of the Web sites' content according to the time period of when the data was collected using a liberal p-value ($p = .25$) failed to reveal any systematic differences. Although not conclusive, this suggests that the degree of SOA shown on the sites does not vary as function of the timing of the visit (morning, daytime, evening, night).

The results of the present study also suggest several directions for future study. The results reported herein should be viewed as only an initial modest step in examining SOA online. Clearly, replication of the results with a larger sample is needed and indeed welcome. Left unaddressed in the present study was the extent to which consumers perceived the SOA identified on the news, sports, and entertainment sites as appropriate to each venue and effective in marketing the product featured. Future research on these aspects stands to advance important information about the role SOA play online in influencing consumer behavior. As this and other chapters indicate, the use of SOA is quite common and prevalent in many media outlets. This raises the question of whether consumers exposed to SOA online eventually reach a saturation point where such ads lose their effectiveness (or are even ignored), if only because of the sheer amount of sexual content available. Given that exposure to SOA online is embedded in a larger context of exposure to such ads in traditional print and electronic media, an integrative approach to understanding the interplay between the use of SOA in *both* traditional and new media is warranted. Moreover, the fact that many of the sites examined in this chapter correspond to off-line media outlets suggests a more integrative approach to understanding SOA would be a logical next step.

In closing, this chapter began with the question of whether in the virtual world of Wolf Blitzer, Diane Sawyer, and others there was room for SOA. The results reported indicate that not only is there room for SOA, but also that they are quite common to news, sports, and entertainment sites. Indeed, sex does sell online—just as it does elsewhere.

REFERENCES

Bedell, D. (2001, April 26). Unlikely innovators: Many online technologies were first perfected by the adult industry [Electronic version]. *Dallas Morning News.* Retrieved January 21, 2004, from http//www.dallasnews.com.

Chambers, J. (this volume). Taste matters: Bikinis, twins, and catfights in sexually oriented beer advertising. In T. Reichert & J. Lambiase (Eds.), *Sex in consumer culture: The erotic content of media and marketing.* Mahwah, NJ: Lawrence Erlbaum Associates.

Fullerton, J., & Kendrick, A. (2001). Comparing content of commercials from general market and Spanish-language television. *Southwestern Mass Communication Journal, 17,* 53–62.

Fullerton, J., & Kendrick, A. (this volume). Selling Spanish-language programming: A comparison of sex and gender in Univision and NBC promotional announcements. In T. Reichert & J. Lambiase (Eds.), *Sex in consumer culture: The erotic content of media and marketing.* Mahwah, NJ: Lawrence Erlbaum Associates.

Hirschman, E. C., & Thompson, C. J. (1997). Why media matter: Toward a richer understanding of consumers' relationships with advertising and mass media. *Journal of Advertising, 26,* 43–60.

Kaye, B. K., & Medoff, N. J. (2001). *Just a click away: Advertising on the Internet.* Boston: Allyn & Bacon.

Klein, M. (1999). The history and future of sex. *Electronic Journal of Human Sexuality, 2.* Retrieved January 21, 2004, from http//www.ejhs.org.

Lambiase, J. J. (2003). Sex—online and in Internet advertising. In T. Reichert & J. Lambiase (Eds.), *Sex in advertising: Perspectives on the erotic appeal* (pp. 247–272). Mahwah, NJ: Lawrence Erlbaum Associates.

Lambiase, J., & Reichert, T. (this volume). Sex and the marketing of contemporary consumer magazines: How men's magazines sexualized their covers to compete with *Maxim.* In T. Reichert & J. Lambiase (Eds.), *Sex in consumer culture: The erotic content of media and marketing.* Mahwah, NJ: Lawrence Erlbaum Associates.

Lin, C. A. (1998). Uses of sexual appeals in prime-time television commercials. *Sex Roles, 38,* 461–475.

Needham, K. (2001). Porn star Danni shows her e-business skill [Electronic version]. *Sydney Morning Herald.* Retrieved February 1, 2004, from http//www.smh.com.au/news/0107/21/national/national17.html.

Oliver, M. B., & Kalyanaraman, S. (this volume). Using sex to sell movies: A content analysis of movie trailers. In T. Reichert & J. Lambiase (Eds.), *Sex in consumer culture: The erotic content of media and marketing.* Mahwah, NJ: Lawrence Erlbaum Associates.

Reichert, T. (2003). *The erotic history of advertising.* Amherst, NY: Prometheus.

Reichert, T., & Ramirez, A., Jr. (2000). Defining sexually-oriented appeals in advertising: A grounded theory approach. In S. J. Hoch & R. J. Meyer (Eds.), *Advances in consumer research* (vol. 27, pp. 267–273). Provo, UT: Association for Consumer Research.

Reichert, T., Lambiase, J. J., Morgan, S., Carstarphen, M. G., & Zavoina, S. (1999). Beefcake and cheesecake: No matter how you slice it, sexually explicit advertising on the rise. *Journalism and Mass Communication Quarterly, 76,* 7–20.

Soley, L., & Reid, L. (1988). Taking it off: Are models in magazine ads wearing less? *Journalism and Mass Communication Quarterly, 65*, 690–966.

Stempel, G. H., & Stewart, R. K. (2000). The Internet provides both opportunities and challenges for mass communication researchers. *Journalism and Mass Communication Quarterly, 77*, 541–548.

Walker, J. R. (2000). Sex and violence in program promotion. In S. T. Eastman (Ed.), *Research in media promotion* (pp. 101–126). Mahwah, NJ: Lawrence Erlbaum Associates.

Chapter 10

Taste Matters: Bikinis, Twins, and Catfights in Sexually Oriented Beer Advertising

Jason Chambers
University of Illinois, Urbana-Champaign

A radio contest to promote Sam Adams beer before 10 million listeners certainly sounded like an excellent idea to Jim Koch, CEO of Boston Brewing. The promotion did not require any significant financial contribution from the company, and it had the possibility of a high return in terms of brand image. In addition, the company had been involved with promotional efforts on the shock-radio show "Opie and Anthony" in years past with no problems. Because the radio hosts had a history of sexually themed, on-the-edge promotions, the program was popular with 18- to 35-year-old men, a demographic Koch wanted to reach for Sam Adams beer. This new partnership between the radio station and Boston Brewing resulted in "Sex for Sam," a contest requiring couples to have sex in public places to acquire points. The couple with the most points would win an expense-paid trip to Boston for a brewery tour (Chura, 2002a; Weaver, 2002).

The "Sex for Sam" promotion was in its third year in 2002, with Koch well aware of the stipulations of the contest, when it attracted attention to Sam Adams for the wrong reasons (Chura, 2002a; Hyatt, 2002). That spring, a couple attempted to have sex in St. Patrick's Cathedral in New York City during a Catholic holiday, with Koch in the studio during the broadcast, laughing over reports of the couple's efforts. After the pair was arrested, Boston area bar owners organized a boycott of Sam Adams beer and Koch issued a public apology for the incident (Burger, 2002). The hosts of the radio show were fired and the parent company, Viacom, received a substantial fine from the FCC (Hyatt, 2002; "Viacom Fined," 2003).

Despite the FCC fine and product boycott, Boston Brewing was unhurt by the scandal because the company's relationship to the promotion was never clearly established and because the radio hosts received the brunt of the criticism. Furthermore, Boston Brewing controlled less than 1 percent of the beer market in the United States, resulting in limited national attention. In terms of impact on the brand, "the people who most identify Sam Adams with what happened . . . think it's kind of 'cool.' A lot of people doing most of the complaining are Chardonnay drinkers," according to a professor at Syracuse University (Chura, 2002b, p. 3).

Thompson accurately identified the importance of consumer perception and image building for beer products. While few brewers are as bold in their marketing as Koch was in the "Sex for Sam" promotion, it nonetheless illustrates the comfortable role for sexuality in the image creation for beer brands. The beer industry, like that of cigarettes and soft drinks, is one where competing products have few areas for significant differentiation. Anecdotal evidence abounds in all three industries of product-loyal consumers who, when tested, were unable to tell the difference between their favorite brand and its competitors. Therefore, advertising for these brands was not based solely on logic, but included the creation of an image for the product that attracted consumers. As one advertising executive admitted, "You don't sell [beer] on taste. You've got to sell on image" (Chura, 2001, p. 36). For beer, the image often conveyed has been one that included heavy doses of sexuality and sexual innuendo.

Although several hundred brewers operate in the United States, the top three brewers—Anheuser-Busch, Coors, and Miller—dominate the industry. In 2001, those three accounted for nearly 80 percent of all sales and their annual collective advertising spending approached $1 billion (Dunn, 2003a). Brewers continually battle one another for market share, and advertising is the primary mechanism through which brewers create the brand image to attract consumers. Consequently, other brewers tend to follow whatever advertising efforts work for the major brands. At the very least, critics view the efforts of the three major companies as representative of the entire industry.

This chapter examines the contemporary history of sexuality in beer advertising by focusing on three campaigns for major brands: the "Swedish Bikini Team" for Old Milwaukee, the "Twins" for Coors Light, and the "Catfight" series for Miller Lite. Each effort has contributed to the development and use of sex in beer advertising, and each included a substantial media budget from its parent company. Accordingly, each campaign received more national attention than the "Sex for Sam" promotion and each had the potential for widespread imitation by other brewers. It also illustrates social and cultural changes that transformed "safe" or "acceptable" images into those viewed as reprehensible. After the Swedish Bikini Team ads, major beer manufacturers avoided overt uses of sexual imagery for nearly 10 years, a time period labeled as visual "celibacy" (Reichert, 2003a, p. 298). Executives at Coors renewed the trend among major brands when they began using the "Twins" in their beer advertising. And, there may once again be a departure from overt uses of sexuality after the controversy surrounding Miller Lite's recent commercial series: "Catfight."

In advertising, the use of sexuality is most common in products fitting these criteria: "new brands, dying products, or ones with small ad budgets" (Chura, 2001, p. 1). To these three, a fourth category may be added: brands needing reinvigoration. Examining these three campaigns provides a lens on the specific decisions and rationale behind the switch to the sexual sell in the beer industry. Prior to overt uses of sexuality, each of the three brands used little or no sex in its advertising. Sex is an attention grabber, and sexual appeals, like humor, are a popular advertising technique. Sexual advertising has rescued brands from obscurity and companies from bankruptcy (Reichert, 2003a).

Yet, the actual sales impact of sexualized advertising divides scholars. On the one hand, there is considerable evidence of the positive sales impact of sexuality in advertising. On the other hand, several studies have shown that while sex increases attention to the product advertised, it diverts cognitive resources used to make the purchase decision. So, sex arrests viewers' attention but it does not necessarily lead them to purchase (Lang et al., 2003; Steadman, 1969).

SEX AND BEER ADVERTISING

Sex and the marketing of beer are virtually inseparable. Beer promotional events are often tinged with sexuality when bikini-clad women distribute samples or appear on printed materials. Additionally, beer advertising often uses both overt and implied arguments that link a particular brand with a higher likelihood of sexual encounters. For example, during the 1980s Michelob told viewers "the night belongs to Michelob." The use of sexuality in this way crosses racial lines. African American actor Billie Dee Williams told viewers to buy Colt 45 and then go to "a good-time place" that invariably involved beautiful women and sex.

A review of advertising research revealed five major types of sexual content: nudity, sexual behavior, physical attractiveness, sexual referents, and sexual embeds (Reichert, 2003b). Nudity might include full or partial nudity and includes the style of clothing being worn. Sexual behavior deals with the mannerism depicted or the level of sexual interaction between the characters. Physical attractiveness involves the beauty of various body parts including the face, hair, legs, and stomach. Sexual referents might involve the use of double entendre in the images or words used and may include music or the photographic techniques of the advertisement. Sexual embeds are types of sexual content only recognized at the subconscious level.

Scholars have also concluded women are far less likely to be shown as whole characters in advertising. Instead, women are presented as parts, in a kind of "body-ism," when individual physical segments are shown but not a whole person. While men's faces and entire bodies are often shown, representations of women are a visual conglomeration of their legs, breasts, faces, and hair. Such depictions reduce women to a less than human state because they are not shown as whole persons. Hence, women are not presented as intelligent and active persons, but instead as attachments for men or as peripheral to the situation being depicted (Iijima Hall & Crum, 1994).

The three campaigns discussed in this chapter fit many of the categories of sexual content and also present women as parts. By connecting beer and attractive women, both male and female viewers are targeted. Men are led to believe that the consumption of the brand in question will help them attract the types of women shown, while women are led to believe that consuming the beer will both help them look like the women shown and attract men (Dunn, 2003a; Lambiase & Reichert, 2003).

Sexuality in beer advertising often is directly correlated to the target market, with most major brands focusing sales efforts on 20-something males who consume more than 25 percent of all beer sold. Furthermore, it is commonly assumed by the industry that most men by their late 20s have chosen the brand they will loyally drink throughout their lives. This demographic focus, however, has led some to accuse beer advertisers of a "frat boy" mentality that in some cases includes little more than the inclusion of a pair of breasts and a beer bottle (Dunn, 2003a).

While convincing consumers to adopt a particular brand for life is difficult, getting them to change their image of a brand is even more problematic. For example, it would be difficult to change the perception of a "blue-collar" brand to a premium brand consumed by professionals. In the early 1990s, however, executives at the Stroh's company tried to do just that with its Old Milwaukee brand, and the lead campaign in that effort was the Swedish Bikini Team.

THE SWEDISH BIKINI TEAM

When Stroh's Brewing purchased the Joseph Schlitz Company and its Old Milwaukee brand, Stroh's was already in trouble. It had gone into considerable debt to make the purchase, its flagship brands of Stroh's and Stroh's Light faced declining market share, and it was caught in a price war with other major brewers. Furthermore, promotional efforts to lift sales, such as bonus packs and lower prices, had led to devaluation of the flagship brands and the common perception that they were "cheap." For its part, Old Milwaukee was clearly established as a blue-collar brand, but by itself, it did little to lift the image of the company's product mix. Additionally, younger consumers viewed the beer as one consumed primarily by older men. Consequently, in the late 1980s, Stroh's executives approached their advertising agency, Hal Riney & Partners/San Francisco, for ways to invigorate the image of the brand family (Woodruff, 1989).

The task for rejuvenating interest in Old Milwaukee fell to Patrick Scullin, creative director for the account. With a 50-percent increase in the advertising budget, Stroh's executives had five requirements for the new campaign: to continue the appeal to blue-collar men; to incorporate outdoor activities; to create "high-energy" commercials; to use the theme line, "It doesn't get any better than this"; and to convey fun through beer consumption. The result of Scullin's creative deliberations was the Swedish Bikini Team, five blond, bikini-clad women who brought beer and good times to men (McKelvey, 2003, Reichert, 2003a).

Though the Swedish Bikini Team ads became a catalyst for public debate regarding sexuality and beer, their level of sexuality and sexual innuendo was not considerably different from advertising and promotional efforts by other major brewers. For example, Miller Brewing produced an insert for college newspapers titled *Beachin' Times*, aimed at the male spring break crowd. The 16-page booklet featured images of beer-fueled parties replete with gorgeous women and text gave pointers on how to "scam...babes" and "turn spring break into your own personal trout farm" (Lanpher, 1992, p. 39). While protests limited distribution of the insert, its very production illustrated the lengths brewers were willing to go to in order to reach the younger demographic (McKelvey, 2003; Riordan, 1989; Institute for Public Strategies, 2002).

Scullin was well aware of the conventions of beer advertising and its use of women. He later argued that he conceived the Swedish Bikini Team as a "joke" and a "spoof" of traditional beer advertising. The team, five American actresses in blond wigs, extended the Old Milwaukee campaign since it used outdoor imagery common to earlier advertising, but inclusion of bikini-wearing women was a break from prior commercials. In the first commercial in 1991, male campers remark, "Guys, it doesn't get any better than this," then see the "team" float down a nearby river (see Fig. 10.1). Then, five bikini-clad women join the men at their campsite as cases of Old Milwaukee float from the sky. As the commercial concludes, the men and women dance while various shots of the women's body parts, especially their breasts, fill the screen and verify that things can indeed get better (McKelvey, 2003; Reichert, 2003a).

The Swedish Bikini Team promised targeted viewers an unbeatable combination: beer, women, and enough distance from the rest of

FIG. 10.1.   A shot of Old Milwaukee's Swedish Bikini Team coming to enliven the camping trip.

civilization that their activities would go unreported. Future variations of the commercials made slight alterations to the initial theme. Sometimes the cases of Old Milwaukee float from the sky, sometimes they are replaced with members of the team dropping from the sky, and in others, lobsters appear on cue as though from the heavens. Still, the core of all these commercials is the same: Recreation with friends is good, but recreation with five blondes, an ample supply of beer, food, and even live music is far better.

The commercials encompassed three of the five major categories of sexual content. The attire of the female models was limited at best, the models were all attractive and well-endowed, and the references to sexuality were palpable. The women had no specific reason for inclusion in the commercials other than for the interests and attraction of men. Furthermore, the repeated focus on their hair, breasts, and legs communicated that they were not whole persons, or, at least not persons who could think beyond swaying to a rock music beat or the delivery of beer.

Initially it appeared as though the spots would be a tremendous hit. Writers at *TV Guide* referred to the campaign positively and compared its popularity to that of the famous "Energizer Bunny." The team also appeared on late-night television, including *The Tonight Show* (McKelvey, 2003). Problems that eventually engulfed the Old Milwaukee campaign, however, began in other areas of society, but directly influenced its public perception. In 1991, two high-profile cases about the treatment of women received intense media scrutiny; one involved the alleged rape of a young woman by a member of the Kennedy family, and the other involved testimony by lawyer Anita Hill against Supreme Court nominee Clarence Thomas. Consequently, the Swedish Bikini Team arrived at a time of national discussion about sexual harassment and violence that resulted from the two cases. Therefore, a campaign that may have been seen as merely a "joke" in another year became the poster child for all that was wrong with sexual relations. Furthermore, the commercials were named in a sexual harassment lawsuit filed by Stroh's female employees (Reichert, 2003a).

These employees' attorney charged that Old Milwaukee ads depicted women as "stupid party playthings that have nothing better to do than shake their boobs" (Teinowitz & Geiger, 1991, p. 48). These impressions were not "just pinups that you can pull out of *Hustler* or *Playboy* or something, it's stuff your own company is saying (that) 'this is what women are.' Here it is coming from the top of the company saying a woman's just tits and ass" (Lanpher, 1992, p. 39). Linking the case to a popular national advertising campaign elevated what would likely have been a regional story into a national one.

For their part, Stroh's executives tried to weather the storm. But, despite protestations of innocence from company representatives, problems for the campaign mounted. Ironically, the first incident would, in another time period, have been a major coup for the campaign—the arrangement by the team members for a pictorial spread in *Playboy* magazine (see Jamie Skerski's chapter, in this volume, on sideline sports reporters and *Playboy*). Members of the team appeared on the cover of the January 1992 *Playboy*, with photographs inside featuring the women scantily clad and fully nude. Not only did the magazine put the brand in front its target market, but also the publicity was worth hundreds of thousands of dollars and signaled that the bikini team had become an element of popular culture. However, an appearance that in other times would have been a benefit became a further indication that the campaign represented what was wrong with depictions of women in advertising. Following the filing of the lawsuit and the *Playboy* appearance, other events led directly to the retirement of the Swedish Bikini Team campaign.

Near the time of this adverse publicity, the U.S. Surgeon General asked beer manufacturers to stop including sexual imagery in their ads because the images attracted underage drinkers. The Texas attorney general began an investigation into the link between advertising and underage drinking. And, the Center for Science in the Public Interest gave the Swedish Bikini

Team campaign its "irresponsible advertising" award (Cortez & Teinowitz, 1991). Clearly, the campaign was caught in a vortex of negative publicity from which it seemed impossible to escape. Stroh's executives decided to avoid taking chances and replaced the team with a flannel-wearing male duo named "Jack and Andy." The only female clearly visible in the new ads was a park ranger who saved the duo from a grizzly bear (Cortez & Teinowitz, 1991).

After the controversy surrounding the Swedish Bikini Team, other major brewers announced a shift away from the "women as bimbos" approach. August Busch IV, brand manager for Budweiser, announced new advertisements would treat women and men equally (Teinowitz, 1991, p. 1). Other less well-known brands changed their advertising as well. Brewers were trying not only to stay away from negative publicity, but also to reach out to female consumers. Their efforts gained the approval of *Wall Street Journal* columnist Joanne Lipman (1992), who concluded that the new beer ads portrayed "women as real people rather than sex toys" (p. B2).

The negative publicity surrounding the Swedish Bikini Team campaign affected the manner and style of beer advertising for nearly 10 years. Beer advertising now featured humorous situations with men as comic foils. Examples include the male character of "Johnny" for Bud Light, who begged friends and family for the beer by exclaiming, "I love you, man." Additionally, animals such as frogs, bears, and lizards replaced women in a variety of settings as major brewers conspicuously avoided images and situations that could be defined as sexist (Reichert, 2003a). It was not until 2001 that another major brewer initiated a campaign for a major brand with sexuality as a central component. Rather than a full team, however, and perhaps in a nod to restraint, the brewer settled for twins.

COORS LIGHT

In 2001, annual spending by Anheuser-Busch, Coors, and Miller was in excess of $900 million. Industry-leader Anheuser-Busch, however, spent nearly as much as Coors and Miller combined. Neither Coors nor Miller had the capital reserves to outspend Anheuser-Busch and the two companies refocused their efforts against one another, including aggressive pursuit of a younger demographic (Dunn, 2003a). These brewers were also battling the growing category of "malternatives," the sweet, fruit-flavored malt beverages increasingly popular among young consumers who had not yet acquired the taste for beer. This new category also meant Miller and Coors had to consider ways to make their beer advertising more attractive and relevant to younger drinkers (Elliot, 2002).

For Coors executives, the shift toward a younger demographic came with a high price tag and led to two key departures for the traditionally fiscally and philosophically conservative company. First, the firm paid $300 million for a 5-year agreement to become the national sponsor for the National Football League (NFL), a figure more than double the offers by Anheuser-Busch and Miller (Beirne, 2003). Second, the youthful ads were a break from the traditional advertising used for Coors Original that featured company chairman Peter Coors walking through snow-covered mountains extolling the virtues of the Rocky Mountain water used to make the beer. While the new ads were for Coors Light rather than Original, they signaled the willingness of Coors executives to take on their rivals in the fast-growing light beer category.

Much of the impetus behind Coors' new marketing effort came from the prodding of Ron Askew, chief marketing officer for the company. After joining the firm in late 2001, Askew concluded that Coors had "lost traction" with the 21- to 25-year-old male demographic. Consequently, he instructed the company's advertising agency, Foote Cone & Belding of Chicago (FCB), to develop an "anthem for what guys really like" (McCarthy, 2003b). The result? A song titled "Rock On," extolling things that men in the target demographic supposedly enjoyed: football, television, parties, friends, women, and beer. While the music formed an important linkage among the advertisements in the campaign, the figures at the center of several ads were sisters Diane and Elaine Klimaszewski, the "Coors Light Twins." The two sisters fit the traditional model of women in beer advertisements: attractive, blond, physically fit, and buxom. In ads featuring the sisters, three central elements were used: the rock anthem, the twins, and a toast at the end that focused on one of the things that men love.

The first commercial featuring the twins focused on summer. Images of beaches, pool parties, and attractive people were displayed over the driving rhythm of the "Rock On" anthem. The singer intoned: *I love workin' on my tan, That girl from the taco stand, Lotsa' long weekends, And twins!* When twins were mentioned, the sisters emerged from a pool wearing red bikinis while fireworks exploded behind them. The camera then zoomed closer to the pair, showing them only from the waist up. The sisters writhed to the beat and they suggestively leaned forward and used their upper arms to squeeze their breasts together. After additional images associated with summer as well as another shot of the twins, the commercial ended with the phrase "Here's to *summer*" and the Coors Light logo.

A second advertisement in the series incorporated Coors' sponsorship of the NFL. The imagery was changed to a football setting with the lyrics of the anthem altered to reflect the singer's love for football—and twins (see Fig. 10.2). The twins were dressed in black cheerleader attire complete with pom-poms and fireworks. Their images were interspersed with those of ongoing games, rabid fans, and other minimally clad cheerleaders. The commercial ended with the phrase "Here's to *football*."

FIG. 10.2. Coors Light's "Twins" cheering for the team.

The third commercial, "Fast Forward," was a combination of images from other commercials in the series. The difference was the focus on the twins themselves. The scene was presented as though it were a recorded tape and the viewer was fast-forwarding through all parts that did not include the twins. The voice of the singer was sped up to a chipmunklike squeak, but not so much that the words of the anthem were indecipherable. At the end of the commercial, the "viewer" repeatedly used the rewind button in order to linger on the final image of the twins, who were dressed in halter tops and shorts. The "toast" at the end of the commercial read: "Here's to *the remote*."

In terms of recognition, Ron Askew, chief marketing officer at Coors, reported the commercials to be "the highest scoring spots in Coors history" (McCarthy, 2003b). Although there were complaints about the ads, they were popular among their target demographic. An Ad Track poll conducted by *USA Today* found that 40 percent of consumers in their 20s liked the ads "a lot," the highest possible response category. The ads also received a high "dislike" score, but researchers found that number driven by females and consumers over the age of 65, all persons outside of the target demographic (McCarthy, 2003b; Dunn, 2003b).

Moreover, unlike the case with the Swedish Bikini Team, negative responses to the campaign have largely been telephone calls and e-mail messages to Coors, rather than significant public debate (McCarthy, 2003b). But, lack of significant public response may not be due to viewers' failure to recognize the obvious sexual imagery and referents in the ads. Viewers certainly understood the double entendre inherent in the anthem's references to "twins," meaning the sisters and most certainly the slang word for breasts. When asked about a commercial featuring the duo, one 25-year-old male said, "I don't know if I'd even call them twins—it's more like quadruplets" (Dunn, 2003b). Thus, in many ways the ads for Coors Light were not too different from those featuring the Swedish Bikini Team, but the public reaction was considerably so. What accounts for the difference?

The central difference separating commercials featuring the twins from those for the Swedish Bikini Team (and especially the "Catfight" series, discussed later in this chapter) was the setting. The twins were depicted as part of summertime and football games, environments where minimal clothing was accepted and expected. Other women appeared in the ads along with the twins, and these other women were depicted as central and whole actors in the scenes. In the football ads, female fans screamed alongside men, with both viewing the action over scantily clad cheerleaders. Members of both sexes were depicted consuming the beverage. Also, shots inclusive of the more fully dressed women were complete, showing them from head to toe rather than as a conglomeration of body parts. Askew believed that part of the positive response was because women were not "followers" in the ads but were a central part of the situation. He observed "the women are in control. They're the ones inviting you into the party at 4 A.M." (McCarthy, 2003b). Though Askew overstated the case, he accurately described how women in the ads had a purpose other than to be ogled at by male viewers. That subtle addition to the framework of the commercial has allowed Coors to avoid the negative publicity received by other brewers.

In addition, the ads for Coors Light were based in a measure of believable reality, with the twins part of what may be termed *situational sexuality*. While they are there for reasons of sexual attraction, the situation in which they are placed, as cheerleaders, for example, grants their depiction a higher measure of acceptability. This situation is different from the Swedish Bikini Team members, whose situation was incongruent with the setting and whose central purpose in the ad was sex. In commercials featuring the twins, though clad in bikinis, the entirety of the spot was in harmony with their appearance. Minimally dressed cheerleaders have been a part of the NFL ever since team General Manager Tex Schramm founded the Dallas Cowboys Cheerleaders in the 1970s. And, while cheerleaders may be an adolescent male fantasy, they fit into the context of the commercial. Consequently, the appearance of the twins in the ad differed little from the reality of a professional football game.

The ads for Coors Light are unique among the campaigns analyzed here, not only for the situational settings but also in the lack of negative publicity surrounding their airing. How all women were depicted was certainly a major factor in the public's reception of the Coors Light campaign. Following this popular campaign, however, have been the "Catfight" ads from Miller Lite, which to many observers were seen as a true return to the days of gratuitous sexuality in beer advertising. Their arrival made the Coors commercials seem tame and innocuous.

MILLER LITE

After Coors' effort reopened the door to incorporating sexual imagery into major brand beer advertising, executives at Miller Brewing willingly followed suit. Executives reasoned that beer advertising's reliance on humorous appeals had made all advertising nearly indistinguishable from brand to brand, and consequently, sex was one way to cut through the white noise and be unique (Reichert, 2003a).

In addition to the widespread use of humor, cultural shifts in other forms of media became another reason for the renewed inclusion of sexuality. Television shows such as "Son of the Beach" and "The Man Show," magazines such as *Maxim* and *Stuff*, and radio shock jock Howard Stern and others were utilizing risqué forms of sexuality that faced not backlash, but often widespread popularity. Society, it seemed, was once again willing to accept something more than funny situations and cute animals in beer advertising (Reichert, 2003a).

Cultural changes aside, however, Miller executives had other reasons to consider a shift in advertising in 2001 as Miller Lite was a brand in decline. Since the mid- to late-1990s, Miller Brewing had initiated several efforts to increase sales. The company introduced new brands (in the process further diluting the product mix), lowered prices, changed the packaging, and tried a bevy of different advertising approaches, all to no avail (Gallun, 1999).

This "try anything" strategy was somewhat surprising for Miller Lite. After all, the introduction of Miller Lite in the early 1970s had helped start the light beer craze. Some of the most popular beer commercials in history were associated with the brand via the "All-Stars" campaign that featured ex-professional athletes and celebrities. That campaign had driven the success of the brand for nearly 15 years. But, shortly after Bud Light eclipsed the category leadership from Miller Lite, the "All-Stars" campaign was retired. From that point on, Miller Lite executives struggled to find a campaign that mirrored the popularity and sales impact of the "All-Stars." Like other executives who had faced declining market share, Miller Lite executives willingly turned to the sexual sell in order to attract consumer attention (Baue, 2000).

The shift toward the inclusion of sexuality into Miller advertising began in 2000 and was visible across several brands. For example, a spot for Miller Genuine Draft features a woman caught disrobing in a laundry room by a man. At first, there is an awkward moment as neither knows exactly what to do or say until the man produces a six-pack of Genuine Draft. The commercial closes with the woman tossing her bra into the washing machine as the slogan appears on the screen: "Never miss a genuine opportunity" (Reichert, 2003a).

For the flagship brand, Miller Lite, the sexual content is left to a viewer's imagination. One ad features two young women arriving home to their apartment, only to find that their roommate has left the signal not to enter. As they sit in the hallway, moaning noises emanate from the apartment and one muses, "Why don't they just get a room?" After a pause in the noises, the other young woman states, "She's going to be sore after this one." Next, a young man exits the room buckling his pants. The two women then enter their apartment and hand a beer to their friend, who is wearing yoga tights and involved in a class rather than a sexual encounter.

So, in advance of the "Catfight" series, Miller Brewing had introduced some sexuality into its brand advertising, but especially in the case of Miller Lite, the viewer was required to make the sexual connections in his or her own mind. As had been the case with other campaigns, the new efforts did not visibly affect sales. In early 2001, Miller Lite dropped from the top three brands in terms of overall beer sales, a position it had held for 25 years. Consequently, as sales continued to flounder, executives were emboldened to take additional steps to increase sexual content (Gallun, 1999).

In 2002, South African Breweries (SAB) purchased Miller Brewing from Philip Morris. Whereas Miller constituted less than 5 percent of the total business for Philip Morris, it accounted for nearly half the business for SAB. When the new owners observed that they lagged behind Coors in advertising expenditures, they immediately corrected the imbalance. In addition to increased dollars, SAB executives wanted to increase the brand presence of Miller Lite, and they aggressively pushed the envelope on sexual imagery in order to do so. As one beer distributor candidly observed, "SAB is willing to take chances Philip Morris was not" (Chura, 2003).

The first notable Miller Lite spot following the purchase appeared during the 2003 NFL playoffs. The commercial, dubbed "Catfight," featured a return to the "Tastes great, less filling" slogan made popular during the "All-Stars" campaign. The scene opens with two attractive women, a blonde and a brunette, at a table debating the reasons to drink Miller Lite. As one exclaims it "tastes great," the other vehemently responds it is because it is "less filling." The pair begin slapping and clawing at one another, and they end up wrestling in a pool of water and tearing each other's clothes off. The scene then abruptly shifts to a bar with two young men, one who approvingly nods to the other: "Now, that would make a great commercial." The fight is actually the fantasy of the two men, and a viewer's stunned reaction to this ploy may be reflected in the open-mouthed stares and sideways glances of two "real" women at the bar with these men, who are still fantasizing. At the end of the commercial, the scene returns to the still-fighting females, who fall into a pool of cement locked in a physical embrace. In the version of the advertisement played on cable and late-night television, one breathlessly suggests to the other, "Let's make out," as the commercial ends.

From the very beginning, the "Catfight" commercial generated considerable attention. Veteran *Advertising Age* columnist Bob Garfield (2003a) quipped that the spot made the "Swedish Bikini Team look like the little sisters of the poor." Garfield's witty condemnation aside, the spots attracted attention. The advertisements were replayed on a variety of television shows, sometimes in a vigorous debate of its merits, other times in humor and appreciation. The company concluded that coverage of the single "Catfight" spot exposed even more viewers to the ad, perhaps more than 80 million viewers. Due to the buzz, Miller Lite executives announced that they were planning several additional commercials for the series; three new spots were actually produced and aired (Chura, 2003).

The first ad to follow the original was an obvious attempt to balance the sexism in the ad and to help show the intended humor behind them. It features a setting like the original with the battling women replaced by two men. Like the women, they start arguing about the beer, but instead of fighting they profess their desire to "communicate" with one another and form a "supportive" friendship. The pair embrace and the scene cuts back to the bar setting, this time with the two females in mental control of the fantasy much to the chagrin of the men. Rather than a fantasy with two buxom females, the women praise the merits of "hot guys expressing emotion." The scene then shifts back to the pool scene as the two men remove their shirts and expose muscular upper torsos.

The third commercial features not the blond female in the original pool scene, but one of the fantasizing men from the bar. He goads the brunette into chasing him into the fountain by repeatedly exclaiming, "tastes great, tastes great." Unable to stand the affront, she growls, "less filling," rips off her clothes and makes her point by wrestling with him much to his obvious delight. At one point, she pulls him out of the water with his face just inches from her breasts. After the requisite bar scene with the four friends, the commercial ends with the man emerging from the water to find not the gorgeous brunette, but, in a seeming nod to prison movies, a hulking man standing over him.

The final commercial in the series, dubbed "Pillow fight," features the blonde and brunette from the original commercial. The two again begin to fight over the benefits of Miller Lite, but this time the fight moves to a hotel room. Awaiting them as they collapse onto one of the beds is Pamela Anderson, an actress with enhanced breasts whose fame is based on her role on the television series "Baywatch" and as the star of a homemade pornographic film that circulates on the Internet. She huskily asks the women if she can join them, and they readily agree. The trio then engages in the ultimate "catfight": three women in a hotel room wearing little more than undergarments as the camera provides multiple shots of their breasts, legs, torsos, and faces. The three women gleefully hit each other with pillows and feathers float around the room. The scene shifts back to the bar, with the men once again pleased with their fantasy creation and the women with them visibly less so. The commercial closes with another scene from the hotel room, and one of the women sets off the sprinkler system. The spray douses the three women as they continue to dance and their ecstasy makes them oblivious to the water.

Like Stroh's executives defending the Swedish Bikini Team campaign, Miller executives claimed the Miller Lite ads were a parody of beer advertising. They claimed that since the ads featured men as central caricatures, the company's campaign lampooned both sexes equally and that no harm was meant. They also pointed out that the women were the fantasy of two men, who were barely sophisticated enough to be with the women in the bar, let alone the two beauties who formed the crux of the commercials. Furthermore, because the relationship between the men in the bar and their female companions was not clearly defined, the disgusted reaction of the females to the obviously sexist fantasy was sufficient condemnation (Crain, 2003; Garfield, 2003b).

These explanations are suspect for several reasons, especially since it is arguable that any of the ads, even the first, featured men as the primary focus. One of the latter ads that featured the male from the bar wrestling with the brunette was an additional step, not toward parity, but toward a violent kind of sexual intercourse. All of the three later ads in the series catered to nearly every adolescent male fantasy imaginable: attractive, large-breasted women willing to fight each other or to wrestle with a man over the merits of beer. Furthermore, the final ad in the series placed the duo in a bedroom with another female, opening at least the fantasy door to a female same-sex threesome.

The "Catfight" series is unique among the three brand campaigns examined here because it is the only one to feature overtly sexual behavior, and even violent behavior. While the other two campaigns referred to a level of sexual behavior, they remained at the level of implication. The "Catfight" ads, especially the final one in the series, include a specific setting for sex as well as three willing women to engage (violently) in the act.

For Miller Lite, a brand that was in dire need of a new image or identity to encourage consumers to select it over its rivals, the "Catfight" advertising series was an absolute failure. The ads offered few reasons to consume the brand and instead went for cheap gags. Even the Swedish Bikini Team campaign exhibited some continuity with the overall theme of the campaigns that had preceded it. While it utilized a long-time slogan, the "Catfight" series otherwise was a complete break with the ads that had come before, and it did nothing to build Lite's brand image. To add insult to injury, many consumers simply found the ads offensive and distasteful (McCarthy, 2003a). Confronted with criticism from both consumers and the trade as well as a steady sales decline, executives eventually pulled the provocative campaign.

CONCLUSION

In the world of advertising, sex and beer are inseparable. Industry executive Dean Philips candidly observed, "[Sex] is indeed the easy and the effective way. It's hard to be in this business and not look at the success of beer advertisers and argue that it doesn't work" (Chura, 2001, p. 36). While there may be a periodic reduction in its use, as was the case in the years following the Swedish Bikini Team campaign, sexuality often reappears when brand executives try to attract attention, like Boston Brewing, or increase market share, like Miller Lite. Simply put, sex sells. Certainly not in every instance, since there have been failures and apologetic public statements by industry executives. Or, as in the case of Miller Lite, executives simply admit the failure of the campaign to impact sales and they move on to other approaches (McCarthy, 2003a).

The three campaigns examined here utilized four of the five major categories of sexual content in advertising. All featured scantily dressed women, but full nudity has yet to be broached in any advertising campaign in the United States. But, with full-frontal male nudity now being used in some campaigns in France, it seems likely that the nudity barrier will fall at some future point. Whether it will be beer marketers who broach that final taboo in the United States, however, remains to be seen.

Manufacturers in the beer industry must use marketing to build an image for and awareness of their brand. With little real difference between competing products, consumer decision-making must be influenced through other means such as pricing, distribution, packaging, and, especially, advertising. Still, the Swedish Bikini Team campaign and the "Catfight" ads form the bookends of the depiction of sexuality in beer advertising, as each is considered the height (or depth) of bad taste in beer advertising. Yet, taste issues aside, the three campaigns also came from brewers seeking to attract attention to their brand and illustrate the lengths they will travel to do so. With sales levels stagnant in the industry, there will likely be no retreat from using sexualized appeals, like that in the years following the Swedish Bikini Team. Instead, ads like those in the "Catfight" series and the ads coming from some of the so-called malternative brands are more likely to become fodder for commentary rather than for the elimination of sexual images, as each manufacturer tries to draw consumer attention. Furthermore, as the culture and especially media forms continue to push the boundary toward more sexualized content, advertisers will continue to follow suit.

REFERENCES

Baue, W. D. (2000). Miller time campaign. In T. Riggs (Ed.), *Encyclopedia of major marketing campaigns* (pp. 1117–1121). Detroit: Gale Group.

Beirne, M. (2003). Coors twins greet NFL, halloween. *Brandweek, 44*(30), 6.

Burger, J. (2002). *Rejecting apology, Boston pubs boycott Sam*. Retrieved from http://www.ncregister.com/Register_News/090402sam.htm.

Chura, H. (2001). Spirited sex. *Advertising Age, 28,* 1, 36.

Chura, H. (2002a). *Beer exec apologizes for sex show involvement*. Retrieved from http://www.adage.com.

Chura, H. (2002b). Sam Adams unlikely to be hurt by scandal. *Advertising Age, 73*(35), 3, 27.

Chura, H. (2003). Miller set to roll catfight sequels. *Advertising Age, 74*(7), 1, 35.

Cortez, J. P., & Teinowitz, I. (1991). More trouble brews for Stroh bikini team. *Advertising Age,* 45.

Crain, R. (2003). "Relevance" is operative word in "catfight" or chip-dip ads. *Advertising Age, 74*(4), 20.

Dunn, J. (2003a). *The light stuff*. Retrieved from http://www.westword.com/issues/2003-01-23/feature.html.

Dunn, J. (2003b). *Twin peeks*. Retrieved from http://www.westword.com/issues/2003-01-23/sidebar.html.

Elliot, S. (2002, September 12). Sales of malternatives show an early peak. *New York Times*, p. 17.

Gallun, A. (1999). *Miller brewing regroups amid declining sales*. Retrieved February 8, from http://milwaukee.bizjournals.com/milwaukee/stories/1999/02/08/story2.html.

Garfield, B. (2003a). Garfield's ad review: Miller Lite's latest is a return to the bad old days of beer ads. *Advertising Age, 74*(3), 3.

Garfield, B. (2003b). Oversexed Miller spots show little regard for overall brand. *Advertising Age, 74*(12), 57.

Hyatt, J. (2002). *Business unusual*. Retrieved from http://www.fortune.com

Iijima Hall, C. C., and Crum, Matthew J. (1994). Women and "body-isms" in television beer commercials. *Sex Roles, 31*(5/6), 329–337.

Institute for Public Strategies. (2002). *Advocating responsibility in sex-themed alcohol ads*. National City, CA.

Lambiase, J., & Reichert, T. (2003). Promises, promises: Exploring erotic rhetoric in sexually oriented advertising. In L. Scott & R. Batra (Eds.), *Persuasive imagery: A consumer perspective* (pp. 247–266). Mahwah, NJ: Lawrence Erlbaum Associates.

Lang, A., Wise, K., Lee, S., & Cai, X. (2003). The effects of sexual appeals on physiological, cognitive, emotional, and attitudinal responses for product and alcohol billboard advertising. In T. Reichert & J. Lambiase (Eds.), *Sex in advertising: Perspectives on the erotic appeal* (pp. 107–131). Mahwah, NJ: Lawrence Erlbaum Associates.

Lanpher, K. (1992, November). A bitter brew. *Ms., 3*, 36–41.

Lipman, J. (1992). Farewell, at last, to bimbo campaigns? *Wall Street Journal*, p. B2.

McCarthy, M. (2003a). *"Catfight" ad's appeal pits men against women*. Retrieved February 16, 2003, from http://www.usatoday.com.

McCarthy, M. (2003b). *Coors' twins ads a hit with target market*. Retrieved from http://www.usatoday.com/money/advertising/adtrack/2003-03-02-coors_x.htm.

McKelvey, K. (2004). *All that glitters is not sold: True tales of great creative that never made the public eye*. Retrieved from http://www.telefim-south.com/Georgia/Oz/Oz10-5/allisglitter.html.

Patwardhan, A. (1994). Old Milwaukee. In J. Jorgensen (Ed.), *Encyclopedia of consumer brands* (Vol. 1, pp. 418–421). Detroit: St. James Press.

Reichert, T. (2003a). *The erotic history of advertising*. Amherst, NY: Prometheus Books.

Reichert, T. (2003b). What is sex in advertising? Perspectives from consumer behavior and social science research. In T. Reichert & J. Lambiase (Eds.), *Sex in advertising: Perspectives on the erotic appeal* (pp. 11–38). Mahwah, NJ: Lawrence Erlbaum Associates.

Reske, H. J. (1992). Stroh's ads targeted. *ABA Journal, 78*, 20–21.

Riordan, T. (1989, March 27). Miller guy life. *New Republic*, 16.

Sellers, P. (1990, January 15). Busch fights to have it all. *Fortune*, 81–88.

Steadman, M. (1969). How sexy illustrations affect brand recall. *Journal of Advertising Research, 9*(1), 15–19.

Strnad, P. (1989). Light leftists. *Advertising Age*, 72.

Teinowitz, I. (1991). This Bud's for her. *Advertising Age*, 1, 49.

Teinowitz, I., & Geiger, B. (1991). Suits try to link sex harassment, ads. *Advertising Age*, 48.

Viacom fined over sex contest. (2003). Retrieved from http://money.cnn.com/2003/10/02/news/companies/viacom_fine.reut/index.htm.

Weaver, J. (2002). *Sam Adams apologizes for sex stunt*. Retrieved from http://www.msnbc.com/news/0801557.asp?cp1=1.

Woodruff, D. (1989, May 15). A sip of Stroh's could turn into a gulp. *Business Week*, 37.

Chapter 11

From Polo to Provocateur: (Re)Branding Polo/Ralph Lauren With Sex in Advertising

Tom Reichert

University of Georgia

Tray LaCaze

Practical Advertising, Inc.

Corporate America invested a massive sum—more than $250 billion—in domestic advertising in 2004, and the motive for that huge investment is more than selling products in the short term. Advertising also helps to build corporate brand images and, over time, fortify those images in the minds of consumers. Through repetition and consistency, advertising can shape perceptions of what a product means to consumers and how it compares to similar products. According to Aaker (1991), the strongest brands have maintained consistent brand images for 20 or 30 years, or even longer, while less successful brands are seen altering their strategies for short-term gain. To survive, however, organizations may need to adjust their brands' identities in response to changing market conditions, consumer tastes, and competitive action (Park, Jaworski, & MacInnis, 1986). These pressures might explain why Polo/Ralph Lauren, a leading design house and marketer of aspirational brands, is sexing up its image (see Fig. 11.1).

Primarily through its strong brand image, Polo/Ralph Lauren has become one of the top 100 global brands ("The 100 Top Brands," 2004). The brand's association with wealth and affluence has been nurtured and reinforced in its advertising since the 1970s when Ralph Lauren began building a brand based on the symbolic representation of the polo player—refined,

FIG. 11.1. Polo/Ralph Lauren ads, like this one, have become more sexualized since the early 1990s.

affluent, aristocratic, stylish, esteemed, and athletic (Trachtenberg, 1988). Despite the company's well-cultivated image, a cursory review of its recent ad campaigns suggest that urban settings are slowly displacing homes in the Hamptons, and that grungy models have moved in with Polo's country club set. Many of these new models are younger and more sexualized than in past ads, despite Lauren's inclination to abstain from sexuality in his advertising. This investigation examines and documents the nature of imagery in Polo/Ralph Lauren advertising in *GQ* magazine from January 1980 to December 2000 to verify any shift in brand direction. In addition, several reasons are proposed to explain why well-established, aspirational brands such as Polo attempt to modify their brand images.

BRANDING, ADVERTISING, AND POLO/RALPH LAUREN

Tom Peters once said, "It's a new brand world" (1997, p. 83). Humorously eloquent, he captured the state of contemporary America. No longer do people buy a shirt; they buy a Hilfiger. And, the holidays are no longer just holidays; it is a Martha Stewart Holiday Experience. Branding and brand building are essential concepts in the communication and marketing plans of profitable firms. These concepts have become so important that commonly a company's brand equity is more than its total assets. For example, when Philip Morris purchased Kraft for $13 billion, it paid six times Kraft's book value because of the perceived worth of the brand name (Cobb-Walgren, Ruble, & Donthu, 1995).

Although it is an often overused buzzword, branding—creating a strong and distinct identity for a product—can effectively position a product, provide a hedge against competition, and enhance financial performance (Park et al., 1986). Brand images are defined by Keller (1993) as "a set of associations linked to the brand that consumers hold in memory" (p. 2). As such, brand images reside with consumers, and firms attempt to enhance those perceptions through a variety of means, with advertising being one of them. According to Park et al.'s (1986) brand management framework, firms actively manage the brand concept to maintain and control the brand's identity through the product's life cycle. The firm begins by establishing a brand concept; operationalizing it into images, messages, designs, and actions; and then communicating it to specified audiences. In other words, the brand concept is the embodiment of the brand's intended identity, or what that brand is supposed to mean. Essentially, a product's brand image comprises all interactions consumers have with a product and their understanding that results from these encounters (Park et al., 1986).

An important consideration regarding the role of advertising in building brand images is that this form of marketing communication is completely within the firm's control. Marketers either create ad messages in-house or hire professional agencies to create them. As a result, advertising constitutes a fairly unfiltered indicator of the brand concept the firm wishes to construct. The deliberate use of visuals, text, and message strategies (e.g., functional, symbolic, experiential benefits) provide useful clues for consumers (and researchers) as to who are intended users of the brand, how the brand should be used, and in what situations it should be used. Given some degree of congruence and believability (Gwinner & Eaton, 1999), the meanings in these ads influence the brand's image (McCracken, 1986; Messaris, 1994; Schroeder & Borgerson, 2003; Schroeder & McDonagh, this volume). In other words, the meaning in the ad is transferred to the brand by pairing the two together to create associations between them (see Friedmann & Zimmer, 1988; Kates & Goh, 2003; Smith & Engel, 1968). As such, the images in Polo/Ralph Lauren's ads allow us to analyze the meanings this firm intends to infuse with its brand.

Ralph Lauren: The Man and the Brand

Polo/Ralph Lauren is a leader in the design, marketing, and distribution of premium lifestyle products. For more than 30 years, Polo's reputation and distinctive image have been developed across an expanding number of brand extensions and global markets. The company, still directed by its founder Ralph Lauren, believes it is "an original idea, built on the universal and enduring appeal of the American lifestyle," and that its products "seem always to be the perfect expression of how people want to live" ("Annual Report," 2000).

In a true rags-to-riches story, Lauren, born Ralph Lifshitz in 1939 in the Bronx, New York, was raised in a family with modest means. While waiting tables at resorts during his teens, Lauren was exposed to a lifestyle he desired to emulate—one exemplified by wealth and status. Evidently he did not keep his wish a secret because the only word listed under his senior high school yearbook photo was "Millionaire." In 1967, after a stint in sales at Brooks Brothers, Lauren began designing neckties. By 1968, he had formed Polo Fashions, Inc., so named because polo was a rich man's game and it conveyed the image of money, style, and exclusivity that he wanted to associate with his designs (Pendergast, 1994).

Initially, Lauren struggled to remain profitable without compromising the style or image of his products. Asked by Bloomingdale's to make his ties narrower and remove his name from the label, Lauren refused. Soon thereafter, Bloomingdale's became a regular buyer of Polo merchandise. His products consisted of a full men's clothing line, a smaller line of women's clothing, and Chaps, a Polo fragrance introduced with a national ad campaign in 1978. After costuming *The Great Gatsby* and *Annie Hall*, Lauren found himself at the forefront of a classic fashion revival, one that was congruent with the style he strove to project.

Today, Polo/Ralph Lauren, which went public in 1998, represents more than Polo fragrance, ties, and oxford shirts—it represents a mega-brand. The company consists of three integrated operations: wholesale, retail, and licensing. Polo's wholesale business is divided into two groups: Polo brands and Ralph Lauren Collection brands. The Polo brand group operates, distributes, and markets Polo by Ralph Lauren, Polo Sport, Ralph Lauren Polo Sport, RLX Polo Sport, and Polo Golf. Through licensing alliances, Polo creates and markets most of its products. As of 2004, Polo had 20 product lines and 10 international licensing partners for its apparel and accessory lines. No longer a fledgling business, Polo/Ralph Lauren is a sizeable corporation with an estimated brand value of $2.1 billion.

Polo/Ralph Lauren Advertising

From the beginning, Lauren's advertising portrayed an upscale, high-quality appearance. Annual advertising budgets in the 1970s, averaging $400,000, were used to purchase blocks of pages in major magazines once or twice a year. Lauren justified this practice by saying, "When we appear, we'll be a star. It's like Frank Sinatra. If you see him once a year on TV, it's an event. If you see him every week, it's no big deal" (Trachtenberg, 1988, p. 213).

Today, Polo/Ralph Lauren's global marketing efforts—at over $100 million—are managed by a centralized, in-house advertising and public relations department. The company creates advertising for all its products, conveying a particular message for each brand within the context of Polo's core themes. Ads portray lifestyles rather than specific items, and each ad may contain a variety of products offered by both the company and its licensing partners. Polo's primary advertising medium is print, with multiple-page ads appearing regularly in consumer magazines (see Fig. 11.2), with marketing efforts also consisting of commercials and a Web presence.

FIG. 11.2. Not all Polo ads are sexual, as this recent ad exemplifies.

To cultivate the company's brand image, Polo/Ralph Lauren campaigns utilize themes such as affluence, conservatism, family, and elegant living. Ad images also reflect costumes and scenes from films that feature sophisticated characters (e.g., *The Thomas Crown Affair*). The brand was built on ad images that exuded sophistication and privilege, with the Polo logo signifying the wealth and status associated with country clubs, expensive automobiles, and English manors. According to one observer, Polo's "multi-page ads catch wealthy, attractive people during a weekend at their country estate or on a safari in Africa" (Pendergast, 1994, p. 437).

Somewhat surprising for a designer in the last quarter century, Lauren's ads were devoid of sexual imagery (Reichert, 2003). At a time when competitors such as Calvin Klein were featuring shocking sexual images in ads for jeans and fragrances, Lauren refused to use sexually suggestive imagery in ads for Polo. According to Trachtenberg (1988), Lauren disdained sex in advertising and chose to promote his products without employing nudity and sexual innuendo. More recently, however, images in Polo/Ralph Lauren advertising are less prudish. Perusal of its ads reveal images of young men and women in revealing displays. A recent analysis by *Adweek* critic Barbara Lippert (1999, p. 34) described a Lauren ad this way:

> It's highly stylized to look trashy—the hair and the tattoo, mostly—but what makes the picture so different is the focus: the eye goes naturally to the largest expanse of skin in the picture, the sensual arc of the small of his back. (Partly and artfully covered bodies are much more erotic or, in this case, homoerotic, than nude ones).

Lippert was describing a two-page spread for Polo underwear featuring an unclothed male model reclining on a cot (see Fig. 11.3). Lippert's observation suggests that imagery and lifestyle scenes in Polo ads are not the same as they once were. Recent ads feature young men and women, some scantily clad, in grungy urban settings. Shirttails are untucked and the models' hair is mussed. Why might a very profitable organization with a well-entrenched brand identity attempt to change its image in this manner?

A few reasons that may compel a company to reposition its brands include competition, the nature of media, and brand extensions (Upshaw, 1995). Certainly, competition is a catalyst for advertising modification. Successful organizations are quick to adapt to competition pressures (Park et al., 1986). A common ad strategy among Polo's competitors includes sex in advertising. Over the past few years, fashion houses such as Abercrombie & Fitch, Calvin Klein, Guess, DKNY, Tommy Hilfiger, and Perry Ellis have built or revived brands with attention-getting nudity and sexual imagery (Reichert, 2003). Polo/Ralph Lauren may be mirroring these approaches in an attempt to maintain share among younger

FIG. 11.3. A 1999 ad for men's underwear. *Adweek* critic Barbara Lippert noted the ad's homoerotic tone.

audiences. The shift to sexual themes may also be a response to ad-saturated media. Americans are exposed to more than 500 commercial messages a day (Bovee & Arens, 1996), and more than half of consumer magazines consists of advertising. As a result, "commercial" clutter may reduce the effectiveness of individual ads unless they grab attention (Elliott & Speck, 1998). In addition, there has been an increase in Polo brand extensions, especially for fragrances, swimwear, intimates, and underwear. Some or all of these factors, as well as others, may account of a shift in brand concept as reflected in Polo's advertising strategy.

Hypotheses

The purpose of present investigation is to determine if, as expected, a well-known brand has indeed moved away from its quintessential, well-established image of affluence and sophistication to that of urban youth characterized by tattoos, long hair, and diverse ethnic backgrounds.

H1: From 1980 to 2000, lifestyle images (including race and age) in Polo ads have transitioned from a conservative, country club image (e.g., country club settings, traditional clothing) to that of an urban hip image (e.g., urban settings, tattoos, long hair).

In addition, it is anticipated that images in Polo/Ralph Lauren ads have become more sexualized over time. According to a *Time* magazine article: "Even Ralph Lauren who previously confined himself to Aryan youth on sailboats...has succumbed this fall to the aggressively sexual" (Carlson, 1995, p. 64). Based on observations like this one, it is expected that images in Polo's ads have become more sexual as well.

H2: Polo ads have become more sexually provocative from 1980 to 2000, especially in regard to sexual dress and sexual behavior between models.

METHOD

The investigation involved examining all Polo/Ralph Lauren ads in *Gentlemen's Quarterly* (*GQ*) from 1980 to 2000. Variables were chosen to assess lifestyle image and sexual imagery. For Hypothesis 1, lifestyle, race, and age were analyzed, while nudity and sexual contact were coded for Hypothesis 2.

Sample

The sample included all Polo ads containing images of people that appeared in *GQ* from 1980 through 2000 (*N* = 237). Ads were coded only if a model was observable and if enough of the model was shown to identify race, age, and sex. Overall, 283 Polo ads appeared in *GQ*, the quintessential voice for men's fashion (Nixon, 1996). Since its inception in 1958, *GQ* has positioned itself as "essential reading for a particular kind of man—a lifestyle manual for the professional who has achieved success with style" (Nixon, 1996, p. 142). The magazine emphasizes male-oriented style and fashion issues, making *GQ* the choice of designers who wish to showcase their products. Polo ads in *GQ* per year ranged from 1 ad in 1980 to 30 ads in 1995.

Variables

Lifestyle. To ascertain differences between "country club" and "urban hip" images, variables such as lifestyle, race, and age were coded. Models' clothing style, activity, and appearance represented an overall lifestyle for each ad. In addition, the background elements and the activities of the models contributed to lifestyle determination. Ads were coded into three categories: country club, urban, and undetermined. The country club category depicted scenes and models that exhibited an association with wealth, influence, and luxury featuring models shown in upscale dress or clean-cut appearances participating or observing polo, yachting, sailing, equestrian activities, and formal functions. The "urban" category was present if scenes, settings, and models were urbanized but did not depict wealth and affluence. These ads were set in lofts, buildings, cities, and forests (e.g., camping). While the country club category included scenes of camping, its scenes included private lodges instead of tents. Overall, urban hip scenes had a rugged look. Models had long hair, beards or stubble, and tattoos. Those ads not fitting either category were labeled as "undetermined."

For race/ethnicity, each ad containing at least one model was coded as (a) White, if all models were White; (b) African American, if at least one model was African American; or (c) other, if at least one person was of ethnic descent and no African Americans were present. Models were also categorized by age (young adult, adult, or mature adult). Models assumed to be younger than 26 were considered young adults, while those 40 years of age or older were considered mature adults. Age was estimated by appearance and context.

Sexuality. To test the second hypothesis, the sexual nature of the ad was coded. Nudity was operationalized according to Soley and Reid's (1988) categorization of dress: (a) demure, (b) suggestive, (c) partially clad, and (d) nude. Demure dress is represented by everyday or nonsexual clothing. Suggestive clothing provides coverage of the model's body while exposing specific areas such as cleavage, thighs, and biceps. Partially clad includes models photographed in bathing suits or underwear. Partially clad also included models depicted shirtless or in an unbuttoned shirt. Nude models include those assumed to be unclothed, but with covering (e.g., towel, blanket). Sexual interaction between models was evaluated according to an adapted version of Soley and Kurzbard's (1986) categorization pertaining to physical contact between heterosexual adult couples. The classification order was (a) nonsexual (e.g., no contact, holding hands) and (b) sexual (e.g., embracing, kissing, suggestion of intercourse or other sexual acts).

Coding. Two coders working independently analyzed each ad. Agreement for each variable ranged from .72 to .98: Race, age, and lifestyle agreement was .98, .89, and .85, respectively. Agreement for nudity and sexual interaction was .86 and .72.

RESULTS

Hypothesis 1: Lifestyles

Hypothesis 1 predicted that Polo ads in *GQ* transitioned from a conservative country club lifestyle to that of an urban hip lifestyle. This hypothesis was supported with regard to lifestyle (e.g., country club scenes and up-scale clothing vs. urban settings and models with tattoos and long hair), race of model, and age of model. Because the variables were either simple groupings or rank-ordered, Spearman's measure of nonparametric correlation was used to test the hypothesized relationships. First, lifestyle image (country club/urban hip) was found to have a positive correlation over time, Spearman $r = .58$, $n = 209$, $p < .001$ two-tailed (see Table 11.1). Over time, Polo/Ralph Lauren images were more likely to display urban hip than country club-oriented lifestyle images. Similarly, there was a positive correlation in regard to race of models (White/Black), Spearman $r = .20$, $n = 233$, $p < .01$. Over the years, Polo models were more likely to be diverse. Last, a negative correlation with age (young

TABLE 11.1
Lifestyle, Race, and Age by Year (in Percent)

Year	Lifestyle* ($n = 109$)		Race* ($n = 233$)		Age* ($n = 235$)		
	Country Club	Urban/Hip	White	Black	Young Adult	Adult	Mature Adult
1980	100	0	100	0	0	0	100
1981	100	0	100	0	0	50	50
1982	—	—	—	—	—	—	—
1983	100	0	100	0	0	100	0
1984	100	0	100	0	0	89	11
1985	100	0	100	0	0	100	0
1986	100	0	100	0	100	0	0
1987	100	0	100	0	0	100	0
1988	100	0	100	0	0	91	9
1989	100	0	100	0	9	91	0
1990	100	0	100	0	0	100	0
1991	100	0	92	8	15	85	0
1992	88	13	100	0	10	80	10
1993	43	57	100	0	13	87	0
1994	56	44	90	11	0	100	0
1995	27	73	83	17	0	100	0
1996	31	69	68	32	0	90	11
1997	25	75	57	44	22	78	0
1998	42	58	84	16	11	79	11
1999	14	86	95	5	26	74	0
2000	32	68	94	6	6	89	6
	$n = 19$	$n = 90$	$n = 205$	$n = 28$	$n = 20$	$n = 205$	$n = 10$

Note. Percentages may not equal 100% due to rounding. No models were present in 1982 ads.
*Spearman r, $p < .05$.

adult/adult/mature adult) over the two decades suggests that models in Polo ads were younger over time, Spearman $r = -.13, n = 235, p < .05$. Overall, these findings show that in the past 20 years, Ralph Lauren ads have become more urbanized and the models more racially diverse and younger.

The pattern of lifestyle change over time is evident in Table 11.1. According to the table, images in Polo ads were exclusively "country club" until 1991. Two years later, urban/hip lifestyle images were present in 57% of all ads. While the percentages of urban/hip images varied each year after 1991, it remained high with most averages above 65%. Likewise, racial minorities made a breakthrough in 1994 with 10.5% representation. While the appearance of Blacks in Polo advertising was lower in 1999 and 2000, they were present in ads in the 1990s. Regarding age, the "adult" category consistently ranged from 70% to 100% for most years. Young adult models (under the age of 26) are intermittently absent until 1997.

Hypothesis 2: Sexual Content

The second hypothesis predicted that Ralph Lauren's ads in *GQ* from 1980 to 2000 became more sexually provocative. This hypothesis also was supported. Regarding dress (demure, suggestive, partially clad, nude), there was a positive correlation over time, Spearman $r = .35, n = 235, p < .001$. According to Table 11.2, sexually explicit clothing increases after 1992. In 1991, suggestive dress makes its first appearance at 23.1%, followed by partially clad in 1994 at 10%. Nudity began consistently to appear in 1997. For the first 10 years, Polo/Ralph Lauren advertising was almost exclusively demure, but this category dropped to less than half (44.4%) by 2000. A positive correlation, Spearman $r = .46, n = 71, p < .001$, was also found for the sexual interaction variable (no contact/contact). As the years progressed, a higher percentage of models were shown engaging in intimate contact after 1992.

DISCUSSION

As previously discussed, advertising contributes to the creation and maintenance of brand images. By examining the lifestyles and models in Polo ads during the last two decades of the 20th century, it is possible to identify possible shifts in brand-concept expression. The analysis reveals that while Polo/Ralph Lauren styles have remained essentially consistent, its advertising has not. Following is a discussion of each hypothesis, reasons that may explain the pattern of findings, and suggestions for future research.

TABLE 11.2
Nudity and Sexual Contact by Year (in Percent)

Year	Nudity* (n = 235)				Sexual Contact* (n = 71)	
	Demure	Suggestive	Partially Clad	Nude	No	Yes
1980	100	0	0	0	0	0
1981	100	0	0	0	50	50
1982	—	—	—	—	—	—
1983	100	0	0	0	100	0
1984	100	0	0	0	100	0
1985	100	0	0	0	100	0
1986	100	0	0	0	100	0
1987	100	0	0	0	100	0
1988	100	0	0	0	75	25
1989	91	0	0	9	100	0
1990	100	0	0	0	0	0
1991	77	23	0	0	0	0
1992	100	0	0	0	100	0
1993	87	12	0	0	67	33
1994	85	5	10	0	100	0
1995	63	13	21	4	67	33
1996	74	21	5	0	100	0
1997	57	9	22	13	67	33
1998	74	11	11	5	100	0
1999	68	11	11	11	43	57
2000	44	28	22	6	25	75
	n = 181	n = 24	n = 21	n = 9	n = 51	n = 20

Note. Percentages may not equal 100% due to rounding. No models were present in 1982 ads.
*Spearman r, $p < .001$.

Lifestyle

The first hypothesis pertained to the lifestyle changes depicted in Polo's advertising. The results were such that country club imagery, characterized by affluent lifestyles, has been partially supplanted by images of young, gritty urbanites. Traditionally, Polo advertising displayed what Thomas and Treiber (2000) defined as affluence in advertising: images that associate wealth, elite style, and tastes with executive status, power, and conservatism. According to the present findings, Polo's early advertising clearly reflects that look. Typical ads in the 1980s showcased country club imagery with conservatively dressed White models. Other early ads depicted scenes that could have appeared in photo albums of English gentry and the idle rich. Settings were spacious homes and mansions with elegant decor. Models were impeccably dressed in semiformal or formal clothing, and men wore clean-cut hairstyles that resembled styles from the 1930s and 1940s. Of all the ads examined in the present investigation, only one in 1984 contained copy. The text, appearing in a five-page magazine spread, exemplified the essence of Lauren's lifestyle themes at that time. It read as follows:

> There is a way of living that has a certain grace and beauty. It is not a constant race for what is next, rather an appreciation of what has come before. There is a respect for the quality recognition of what is truly meaningful. These are the feelings I would like my work to inspire. This is the quality of life I believe in. Ralph Lauren

Based on the present analysis, Lauren must have experienced a change of heart. Images in his contemporary ads are hip and trendy. Models have long shaggy hair and tattoos, not oxfords and chinos. For example, a 1993 ad featured two models, a male and a female, with dreadlocks. Their messy, tangled hair and cold deadpan stares lack any resemblance to Polo's earlier images. While some ads are still set around elitist sports, such as lacrosse, the models are young and rugged. They have "carefree" hairstyles, 3-day beard growth, and muscles. Their clothes are unbuttoned and loose—a radical style shift from earlier ads.

Findings also reveal an increase in racial diversity beginning in 1983, although only African Americans appeared in any Polo ads. Lauren's use of Tyson Beckford, a Black supermodel, is notable—especially when only Whites appeared until then (see Fig. 11.4). Beckford's use, however, is limited to that of a muscular, athletic Black male donning sportswear and underwear. As a result, the analysis revealed that most non-White models were depicted as partially clad or nude. For example, a typical ad for Ralph Lauren underwear in the 1990s depicted a group of men standing on the beach in their underwear (Beckford among them). Another ad, for Polo Jeans Co., highlighted Beckford's muscular bicep and shoulder (and tattoo), although no clothing is visible in the ad. Overall, the findings suggest that current lifestyles portrayed in Polo ads are dissimilar from early ads that positioned the brand as purely affluent and aristocratic.

Sexual Content

Aside from lifestyle display, Polo's ads are also more sexually provocative than in the past. The analysis revealed that sexual imagery (sexual dress and interaction) was more common in the 1990s than in the 1980s. Polo's early ads featured fully clothed models with shirts and blouses buttoned

FIG. 11.4. Tyson Beckford, and his torso, were showcased in mid-1990s Polo Sport ads.

to the collar. Ties and jackets were de rigueur. Even models shown walking off the cricket field wore buttoned-up shirts.

Recent ads are more likely to feature sensual images. First, models are wearing more revealing clothing, or no clothing at all, compared to earlier models. The percentages in Table 11.2 regarding dress reveal an interesting trend. Beginning in 1989, models were shown with chiseled chests revealed by unbuttoned shirts, or only in their underwear. In a frequently appearing ad, a group of underwear-clad muscular men are shown on a beach. In another ad for Polo Sport, a muscular male model is wearing only a beach towel around his hips. The ad is cropped so that the model's head is not shown, drawing attention to his torso. As mentioned before, several columnists noted the presence of skin in Polo ads: "Stick your nose in GQ this month and find yourself smack in the middle of a taut male

FIG. 11.5. A recent ad for Polo jeans showcases supermodel Gisele Bundchen as well as her attire.

torso spread across two full pages, pictured only from the region of his belly button to the region of his Polo briefs" (Carlson, 1995, p. 64).

Provocatively dressed women are present as well. Revealing clothing includes skimpy blouses, bikini tops, and intimates (see Figs. 11.1, 11.2, and 11.5). In one ad, for instance, a man is resting his head on a woman's bare back. On the opposite page, the same woman is shown standing in a bikini with her hands behind her head—emphasis is placed on her breasts and torso. The woman is posed so that she is standing in the water with her legs spread slightly as she gazes at the camera. Such images would have been out of place in Polo's 1980s advertising as there was no sexual contact until 1988. Early forms of contact were nonsexual and primarily limited to children with their parents. As nudity in the ads increased in 1994, so, too, did sexual interaction between the models. In a 1997 ad for Ralph Lauren Home Collection, a nude couple is shown in bed. The man is lying behind the woman with his arms around her. Her hand wraps back to touch his hair. The image illustrates how the well-orchestrated scenes of models and photographers can be captured as if they were personal intimate moments. That the man's jeans are shown jumbled on the floor next to the bed suggests the couple has recently engaged in a sexual encounter.

Reasons and Implications

As content analysis can only document manifest trends when they exist, not the causes for those trends, the following reasons for the (d)evolution of Polo advertising are only conjecture. For example, Polo's brand concept may have changed because the market was changing. Instead of hanging on to graying Yuppies who boosted his brand in the 1980s, Lauren may be attempting to appeal to the Y generation (Pendergast, 1994). According to *Business Week* writers Neuborne and Kerwin (1999), "[Y] is the first generation to come along that's big enough to hurt a boomer brand simply by giving it the cold shoulder—and big enough to launch rival brands with enough heft to threaten the status quo" (p. 82). It is doubtful that today's fashion-conscious youths find stuffy, stiff-shirt images very appealing.

Similarly, Polo ads may be getting sexier because its products are competing with established brands and fashion upstarts that use sexual imagery in their advertising. Rarely do Calvin Klein ads *not* contain provocative imagery, and competitors such as Levi's, Guess, Gap, Abercrombie & Fitch, and Banana Republic rely heavily on sensual ad appeals. As Polo/Ralph Lauren competes with these brands, its advertising may need to contain sexual imagery just to get noticed as one of these trend-setting fashion companies. In addition, the "look" of models has changed since the 1980s. According to Cortese (1999), 90% of male models in the late-1990s were "working class—rough around the edges and beefy, not as frail, thin, or chiseled as their predecessors" (p. 58). Models like those described by Cortese are a far cry Polo's classic look: "the patrician snob appeal that Polo epitomized in the 1980s, [wasn't] so coveted in the practical 1990s" (Agins, 1996, p. B1).

Another reason for change may be Polo/Ralph Lauren's "business" model. Like other designers, Lauren's company has gone public. No longer in the private realm, he now must answer to stockholders and their demands for consistent revenues. To meet Wall Street expectations, Lauren signed a number of licensing agreements for variety of products, and these extensions may have been advertised differently. For example, both Safari fragrance for women and men's underwear were introduced in 1990 (Pendergast, 1994), and these two types of products have historically lent themselves to eroticism (Reichert, 2003). These introductions—along with a campaign for Lauren intimates in the mid-1990s—coincide with the increase in sexuality in Polo advertising.

Limitations and Future Research

An obvious limitation is that ads in only one magazine were analyzed. As such, the results of this analysis may not fully reflect Polo/Ralph Lauren's overall advertising plan. Examining a variety of magazines would enhance the generalizability of this study's findings. Another limitation is the exclusive emphasis on print advertising. Whereas most Polo ads appear in print, the company does utilize other forms of marketing communication (e.g., Web site, in-store displays) that can contribute to brand image. Similarly, distinctions between the various brand extensions within the Polo/Ralph Lauren umbrella were not considered. As mentioned, sexual appeals for only a few products could have influenced the overall findings.

In addition, this chapter examines sexual content by coding nudity and contact. Based on the analysis, it was apparent that sexuality is more than dress and interaction. Other aspects of sexual representation such as gaze, eye contact, and body positioning are also important to consider (see Reichert & Ramirez, 2000). Future research should broaden the scope of sex in advertising to heighten validity (see Gould, 2003; Lambiase & Reichert, 2003; Schroeder & McDonagh, this volume). Future studies should also examine how major fashion brands like Polo/Ralph Lauren integrate race into their advertising. In this study, it appeared that Black models were primarily used to promote sport and athletic products (e.g., Polo Sport). Last, an extension of the present research would be to test and examine the effects of various ad images on brand perceptions (see Gwinner & Eaton, 1999). Such research would be valuable for illustrating how the market's image of a brand can be influenced by its advertising.

CONCLUSION

Advertising contributes to brand identity and differentiation. While some marketers strive to maintain a consistent brand identity through advertising, others respond to shifting lifestyles and cultural changes. Styles and preferences in the fashion industry not only change each year, but can change each season. As such, successful brands can either adapt to these trends (see Kates & Goh, 2003) or hope for the best. It appears that Polo/Ralph Lauren has attempted to do both. While its products are still positioned as aspirational, its advertising has adapted, perhaps, to reflect product introductions and to appeal to younger consumers more interested in urban hip styles than country club exclusivity.

This chapter reports how Polo/Ralph Lauren's advertising has evolved over time with a content analysis of all its advertisements appearing in *GQ* from 1980 to 2000. The analysis revealed that Polo images shifted from images of country club lifestyles to images of young, sexualized urbanites. The analysis also suggests that recent Polo advertising features more nudity and sexual interaction than before, despite Lauren's initial tendency to eschew eroticism. By examining Polo's brand concept expressed through its advertising, it is hoped that this study contributes to a greater understanding of the connection between advertising and brand image. Polo's strategy appeared to be working; the company increased its global brand value by 5% in 2004 ("The 100 Top Brands," 2004). In some cases—especially with regard to designer fashion—changing a company's identity from polo players to sexy urbanites may prove to be a successful brand-image adaptation.

REFERENCES

Aaker, D. A. (1991). *Managing brand equity: Capitalizing on the value of a brand name.* New York: Free Press.

Agins, T. (1996, April 24). Ralph Lauren tries to bring Polo to the masses. *Wall Street Journal*, B1–B2.

Annual Report (2000). Polo.com: Ralph Lauren [online]. Retrieved October 17, 2002, from http://www.corporate-ir.net/media_files/NUS/RL/reports/00ar/polo2000-gatefold1-8.pdf, p. 3.

Bovee, C., & Arens, W. (1996). *Contemporary advertising* (5th ed.). Homewood, IL: Irwin.

Carlson, M. (1995, September 11). Where Calvin crossed the line. *Time, 146,* 64.

Cobb-Walgren, C. J., Ruble, C., & Donthu, N. (1995). Brand equity, brand preference, and purchase intent. *Journal of Advertising, 24,* 26–39.

Cortese, A. (1999). *Provocateur: Images of women and minorities in advertising.* Boulder, CO: Rowman & Littlefield.

Elliott, M., & Speck, P. (1998). Consumer perceptions of advertising clutter and its impact across various media. *Journal of Advertising Research, 38,* 29–41.

Friedmann, R., & Zimmer, M. R. (1988). The role of psychological meaning in advertising. *Journal of Advertising, 17,* 31–40.

Gould, S. J. (2003). Toward a theory of advertising lovemaps in marketing communications: Overdetermination, postmodern thought and the advertising hermeneutic circle. In T. Reichert & J. Lambiase (Eds.), *Sex in advertising: Perspectives on the erotic appeal* (pp. 151–170). Mahwah, NJ: Lawrence Erlbaum Associates.

Gwinner, K. P., & Eaton, J. (1999). Building brand image through event sponsorship: The role of image transfer. *Journal of Advertising, 28,* 47–57.

Kates, S. M., & Goh, C. (2003). Brand morphing: Implications for advertising theory and practice. *Journal of Advertising, 32,* 59–68.

Keller, K. L. (1993). Conceptualizing, measuring, and managing customer-based brand equity. *Journal of Marketing, 57*, 1–22.

Lambiase, J., & Reichert, T. (2003). Promises, promises: Exploring erotic rhetoric in sexually oriented advertising. In L. Scott & R. Batra (Eds.), *Persuasive imagery: A consumer perspective* (pp. 247–266). Mahwah, NJ: Lawrence Erlbaum Associates.

Lippert, B. (1999, April 19). Here's the beef. *Adweek, 40*, 34–36.

McCracken, G. (1986). Culture and consumption: A theoretical account of the structure and movement of the cultural meaning of consumer goods. *Journal of Consumer Research, 13*, 71–84.

Messaris, P. (1994). *Visual literacy: Images, mind, and reality.* Boulder, CO: Westview.

Neuborne, E. and Kerwin, K. (1999, February 15). Generation y. *Business Week*, 80–86.

Nixon, S. (1996). *Hard looks: Masculinities, spectatorship and contemporary consumption.* New York: St. Martin's Press.

Park, C. W., Jaworski, B. J., & MacInnis, D. J. (1986). Strategic brand concept-image management. *Journal of Marketing, 50*, 135–145.

Pendergast, T. (1994). Polo/Ralph Lauren. In J. Jorgensen (Ed.), *Encyclopedia of consumer brands*, vol. 2 (pp. 435–440). Detroit: St. James Press.

Peters, T. (1997). The brand called you. *Fast Company*, 10, p. 83.

Reichert, T. (2003). *The erotic history of advertising.* Amherst, NY: Prometheus.

Reichert, T., & Ramirez, A. (2000). Defining sexually oriented appeals in advertising: A grounded theory investigation. In S. J. Hoch & R. J. Meyer (Eds.), *Advances in consumer research*, vol. 27 (267–273). Provo, UT: Association for Consumer Research.

Schroeder, J. E., & Borgerson, J. L. (2003). Dark desires: Fetishism, ontology, and representation in contemporary advertising. In T. Reichert & J. Lambiase (Eds.), *Sex in advertising: Perspectives on the erotic appeal* (pp. 65–87). Mahwah, NJ: Lawrence Erlbaum Associates.

Schroeder, J. E., & McDonagh, P. (this volume). The logic of pornography in digital camera promotion. In T. Reichert & J. Lambiase (Eds.), *Sex in consumer culture: The erotic content in media and marketing.* Mahwah, NJ: Lawrence Erlbaum Associates.

Smith, G. H., & Engel, R. (1968). Influence of a female model on perceived characteristics of an automobile. *Proceedings of the 76th Annual Convention of the American Psychological Association, 3*, 681–682.

Soley, L., & Kurzbard, G. (1986). Sex in advertising: A comparison of 1964 and 1984 magazine advertisements. *Journal of Advertising, 15*, 46–64.

Soley, L., & Reid, L. (1988). Taking it off: Are models in magazine ads wearing less? *Journalism Quarterly, 65*, 960–966.

The 100 top bands. (2004, August 2). *Business Week*, 68–71.

Thomas, M. E., & Treiber, L. A. (2000). Race, gender, and status: A content analysis of print advertisements in four popular magazines. *Sociological Spectrum, 20*, 357–371.

Trachtenberg, J. A. (1988). *Ralph Lauren: The man behind the mystique.* Boston: Little, Brown.

Upshaw, L. B. (1995). *Building brand identity: A strategy for success in a hostile marketplace.* New York: Wiley.

Chapter 12

Where Are the Clothes? The Pornographic Gaze in Mainstream American Fashion Advertising

Debra Merskin

University of Oregon

The woman looks you straight in the eye, defiantly and suggestively. Her hands reach to her inner thighs, parting her legs as she straddles the drive-train hump in the backseat of the big blue car. While it sounds like a scene straight out of a pornographic magazine, it instead is a description of a recent Bebe clothing advertisement in *Vogue* magazine (see Fig. 12.1).

This type of portrayal is not unusual, and others like it are so common-place that many of us fail to notice them. In this chapter, I present an inter-disciplinary analysis of pornographic themes in fashion advertising that draws upon film, communication, and fashion theories. For the purposes of this chapter, fashion includes apparel (including shoes and accessories) as well fragrances and jewelry. The goal is to discuss what constitutes pornography, as we traditionally think about it, to apply a framework that identifies elements of pornography in media text, and to consider the consequences of the pornographication of mainstream American fashion advertising. An examination of advertisements from *Vogue, Elle,* and *W* suggests the cultivation and perpetuation of these ads weaken women's power by presenting them not only as objects of the male gaze, but also as objects of a *pornographic* gaze. Considered in this light, fashion advertising clearly becomes "the pornography of everyday life" (J. Caputi, 1999, p. 434) wherein the "female image is seen through the lens of male sexual fantasy" (Steele, 1991, p. 92). Furthermore, this predominantly heterosexual eroticization of the female body supports an ideology of male superiority, power, and desire that contributes to "male psychosexual fetishistic formation" (Stratton, 1996, p. 1).

FIG. 12.1. Bebe fashion ad.

A feminist-centered approach is used to analyze visual components of several representative fashion ads including Marc Jacobs (shoes), Prada (jewelry), Gucci, and Versace (clothing). These ads illustrate how sexual referents used in pornography are incorporated into mainstream fashion advertising. The analysis brings together previous discussions of what constitutes pornography in film (Kuhn, 1985) and in video (Jensen & Dines, 1998) and introduces a framework that can be used to unpack the visual elements of what makes an image pornographic. Basic characteristics from visual analyses of pornographic films, such as voyeurism, scopophilia, Mulvey's (1988) male gaze, and Goffman's (1976) semiotic analysis of women's representation in advertising, contribute to this analysis.

The first section of this chapter briefly examines definitions of pornography, followed by a discussion of the intersections of pornography, fashion, and advertising. The second section presents the framework and the descriptive analysis of the ads. I do not claim fashion advertising and pornography are equivalent. Rather, when the visual elements of the ads are examined, less and less differentiates what is available in the checkout line from what is kept behind the counter.

The results of this study are important because identifying materials of everyday life and "stripping away the veil of anonymity and mystery that surrounds advertising is of great value in demystifying the images that parade before our lives" (Jhally, 1995, p. 86). By not seeming strange to us, to paraphrase Goffman (1976), the proliferation of this kind of representation gains acceptance as normal reflections of heterosexuality. Once normalized, so-called high fashion advertising comes to be embraced as a part of "high culture," resulting in abstract acceptance of content. The promise of pornography is thereby satisfied not only through the endurance of hypersexualized images of women, but also through fashion advertising's willing participation in the process.

WHAT IS PORNOGRAPHY?

For many of us, Supreme Court Justice Potter Stewart's response to the question "What is pornography?" aptly sums it up: "I know it when I see it" (*Jacobellis v. Ohio*, 1964). While individual subjectivity is important, for purposes of this study it is important to go beyond individual perceptions of what constitutes "dirty pictures." Since this analysis is based on interpretations of what constitutes mass-market heterosexual pornography, a widely understood definition is appropriate.

The label "pornography," according to McNair (1996, p. 45), signifies: (a) a particular *content* with (b) an *intention* to produce (c) a particular kind of *effect*. As such, three commonly recognized feminist perspectives contribute ways of reading pornography: liberal, socialist, and radical. Liberal feminist definitions for pornography are sometimes as broad as a "depiction of women and men as sexual beings" (McElroy, 1995, p. 51) or, more specifically, as "human beings, individually, in couples, or in groups, engaged in sexual behavior" (McNair, 1996, p. 45), with sexual behavior denoted or connoted. A socialist feminist focused view identifies pornography as "a specific kind of sexual material that reflects and helps maintain the sexual subordination of women" (Dines, Jensen, & Russo, 1998, p. 65). Radical feminism focuses on the "maleness." In their well-known *Minneapolis Ordinance* case, Dworkin and MacKinnon articulated a very specific view of pornography as "the sexually explicit subordination of women, graphically depicted, whether in pictures or in words" (Itzin, 1992, p. 435), and further delineated specific acts (dehumanization, objectification, violence, and degradation) that, according to their argument, should make the production and distribution of pornography subject to civil litigation. I suggest using a combination of these ideas and contend that materials intended to arouse are not limited to pornography as it is typically regarded and found only in sex shops or curtained-off areas of video stores. Rather, for purposes of this chapter, pornography is defined as material that depicts men and women as sexual beings with the purpose of arousing mostly male desire in a way that reflects and helps to maintain the subordination of women.

There are also content differences within the genre of pornography. Erotica, for example, is generally thought of as an "artistic expression of sexuality," and pornography as "trash, produced for profit rather than cultural enlightenment," with these differing not in terms of sex, but rather in terms of power and control (Kuhn, 1985). Sexualized representations occur along a continuum, from mild versions (erotica) where the power relationship between (usually) a man and (usually) a woman is equal to those in which a woman is (allegedly) killed (snuff porn). Furthermore, the pornographic genre is generally divided into soft- and hard-core categories. Soft-core pornography typically presents romantically posed, softly lit young and attractive women on their own (without men). The relationship to the spectator is "private, one-to-one" (Kuhn, 1985, p. 32) and there is little or no exposure of genitals. In some cases, adult women are made to look like girls.

In hard-core pornography, women do not appear alone—one or several men and possibly other women accompany them. Some level of violence is common, with the images made "deliberately *strange*. . . . Hard core girls look like prostitutes or lesbians; they may even be dressed as boys. The lighting is often hard flash, drawing attention to the fact that there is a photographer present" (Steele, 1991, p. 92). Typically, "the harder the porn, the more people—and significantly the more men—in it" (Kuhn, 1985, p. 45), and the more opportunity for the viewer to identify with the protagonist who has power and control.

Pornography pivots on sex and works in specific ways that target particular audiences by cultivating control and desire and the promise of sexual power through the viewing of available bodies. One of the most common forms of pornography is found in photographs (Kuhn, 1985, p. 26) in printed materials such as magazines. The images lend the quality of "visual truth" (Newton, 2001, p. 5), invite the spectator's look, and often offer a return of the male gaze. The male gaze, defined as "the voyeuristic way men look at women" (Evans & Gamman, 1995, p. 13), appeals to the pleasure of seeing what is prohibited in relation to the female body and "projects its phantasy on to the female figure which is styled accordingly" (Mulvey, 1988, p. 62). An image "orchestrates a gaze and its pleasurable transgression. The woman's beauty, her very desirability, becomes a function of certain practices of imagining—framing, lighting, camera movement, angle"

(J. Berger, 1972, p. 43). This "fusion of sexual and ideological issues" supports men as "active, thinking subjects and women as passive, receptive objects" (M. Caputi, 1994, p. 16).

WHAT IS PORNOGRAPHIC ADVERTISING?

> We don't mind nudity if there is a very good reason for it, such as sex, bathing, or autopsy. The problem is, advertising seldom presents a good reason for it. (Garfield, 1999, p. 28)

Female identity in advertising is almost exclusively defined in terms of female sexuality. Schroeder and Borgerson (1998, p. 168) pointed out that "women are objectified in many ways, each suggesting and reinforcing the perspective that women are objects to be viewed voyeuristically, fantasized about, and possessed." Fashion advertising intentionally creates ambiguity that in some ways "transmutes 'the male gaze' into a 'mirrored gaze'" (Goldman, 1992, p. 11). This ambiguity is increased since sexualized women in ads are created for women to look at. While men look at women,

> Women watch themselves being looked at. This determines not only most relations between men and women but also the relation of women to themselves. The surveyor of woman in herself is male: the surveyed female. Thus she turns herself into an object—most particularly an object of vision: a sight. (J. Berger, 1972, p. 47)

In fashion advertising, however, models in the ads frequently return the gaze. Voyeurism, fantasy, and implied participation on the part of the photographed woman work together to create a moment of tension "well-suited to expressing the instinct for pleasure inherent in the libido for looking" (Steele, 1991, p. 96). Similarly, in pornography, it is a gaze that "threatens and undermines society at the same time that it is the fullest expression of society's unspoken desires" (Turner, 1984, p. 83).

Defined as communication "paid for and delivered to an audience via mass media" that "attempts to persuade," advertising is a powerful source of information and relater of culture (O'Guinn, Allen, & Semenik, 2000, p. 9). As a form of cultural text, advertising provides insight into the culture within which it resides and is a useful barometer for measuring sexual permissiveness of a particular era. Today, through the use of branding, advertising is expected to do more than sell a product. Rather than simply telling consumers about the *use-value* of a product (what it can do for you), the emphasis is on a product's *exchange-value* (what you can do with it). Modern advertising "thus teaches us to consume, not the product, but its sign. What the product stands for is more important than what it is"

(Goldman, 1992, p. 19). Ultimately, the voice added by branding imbues an essentially neutral object with qualities and characteristics that are then transferred to the consumer. For example, red lipstick is essentially a 2-1/2-inch tube of wax and oils that, once applied, has significant social meaning. This fetishization of the object "with powers it does not have in itself" creates meaning through "integration into a *system of meaning*" (Jhally, 1990, pp. 28–29). The product-as-fetish, defined as an "iconic element of sexuality in visual culture," contains qualities that, through association, the consumer adopts as his or her own, thereby fulfilling a need or desire (Schroeder & Borgerson, 2003, p. 65; see also Gould, this volume). The fetish "replaces human relations with commodified object relations" and promises satisfaction of desires (Schroeder & Borgerson, 2003, p. 66). Thus, using sex to sell is intimately connected with branding and implied is the transference of particular qualities or opportunities through purchase of a product.

Advertising constructs images of femininity and ideal female beauty and establishes definitions that employ particular codes that help viewers read and understand what being a woman means. This is accomplished in ways that make complete sense, that appear normal and natural. So-called feminine qualities such as softness, beauty, perfection, health, and sexiness are tied to the consumption of products designed to achieve these same ends. The ubiquity of highly sexualized renditions of women further normalizes unrealistic goals and ideas. In this way, advertising takes meaning from a particular context and then uses it to re-create meanings or *re*-present it. Appropriation and reformulation of cultural values "take into account not only the inherent qualities and attributes of the product they are trying to sell," but go beyond this by doing so in ways "in which they can make those properties mean something to us" (Williamson, 1978, p. 12). This "articulation" of meaning in advertising seems to be constructed from direct knowledge based on what appear to be widely held beliefs, perceptions, and values (Hall, 2002). Ads are not about the way men and women actually behave; rather, they are about the ways we think women and men behave (Goffman, 1976). In fashion advertising, sexualized poses have become "so commonplace . . . that their cultural meanings acquire a degree of naturalization" (Kuhn, 1985, p. 38). By constructing what is sexy, fashion advertising works to reinforce gender differences and sex roles and to perpetuate an ideology of the naturalness of female submission and male dominance.

Transgressing moral boundaries of what seems appropriate has been a mainstay of fashion advertising. In the last few years, particularly since the 1980s when 15-year-old Brooke Shields revealed nothing came between her and her Calvins, fashion ads have become increasingly sexually revealing. What makes representations of sexuality in advertising even more powerful is that openness about sex is corroborated in other media representations, such as film, television, and music where "rock stars" grab "their genitals on stage, Abercrombie & Fitch magalogs celebrate nudity and sex, and Madonna's much-publicized masturbation scene in *Truth or Dare*" was "performed in front of multitudes, and perhaps more important, as her father watched" (Ackerman, 1995, p. 244). As pedagogical mechanisms, the shared focus on sex in the media appears to reflect a widely shared level of acceptance in American society. Indeed, nude bodies of women are ubiquitous in advertising because they reflect cultural norms about appearance, control, and attractiveness (Bordo, 1993). Although advertising today "seems to be obsessed with gender and sexuality" (Jhally, 1990, p. 13), according to *Advertising Age* editor Scott Danton, it is also "about being noticed because sexuality provides a resource that can be used to get attention" (Ingrassia, 2000, p. 64) and "nothing cuts through the clutter like sex" (Solomon, 1990, p. 69).

WHAT IS FOR SALE?

Many media literacy scholars agree the starting point of a visual analysis is identification of the text and a description of the problem (A. Berger, 2004; Rose, 2001; Chandler, 2002; Galician, 2004), and the focus is *interpretation* of the meaning of the images. In this study, the unit of analysis is fashion advertisements. Kuhn's (1985, 1995) work with filmed pornography exposed identifiable codes and conventions that communicate with the viewer: caught unawares, bits and pieces, and the invitation. These "gender displays" (conventionalized portrayals) work well as descriptive elements for Jensen and Dines' (1998, p. 66) "elements of the pornographic": hierarchy, objectification, submission, and violence. I have combined Kuhn's (1985) feminist framework for identifying gendered codes in mass-marketed pornography and Jensen and Dines' (1998) four-part "elements of the pornographic" into a single model from which to analyze mainstream fashion advertising. This analysis begs the question "Where are the clothes?" and, by implication, asks and answers, "What is *really* for sale in these ads?"

In the tradition of Goffman (1976), a selection of fashion ads from contemporary, mainstream fashion magazines (*Vogue, W,* and *Elle*) is presented in this section. In the ads, sexual referents, defined as "message elements (visual or verbal) that serve to elicit or induce sexual thoughts" (Reichert, 2003, p. 23), are analyzed. In some cases, this information is conveyed through allusion or innuendo (Reichert, 2003). This method is supported by work in semiotics and art history and criticism (Barthes, 1972; Goffman, 1976; Williamson, 1978; Stokstad, 1995; Schroeder & Borgerson, 1998, 2003).

Hierarchy

A man standing over a woman, standing behind her in the shadows, or even as the implied viewer represents power and control. These "rituals of subordination" include the implication of a parent–child relationship in which a woman is physically positioned in a childlike pose and often dressed in a childlike manner (Goffman, 1976, p. 50). In some cases, she is partially concealed, coyly turning away from the camera, or appears psychologically disengaged from the situation. She may appear shy, fearful, or giggly.

Kuhn's (1985) "invitation" is an example of this type of coding. In this kind of image, the model invites the viewer to look. She is aware of being looked at. Her head is tilted and angular and she teases with a kind of come-on look. Her lips are slightly parted. A two-page ad for Marc Jacob's shoes (see Fig. 12.2) presents a woman on her back, positioned sideways to

FIG. 12.2. An ad for Marc Jacob shoes.

the viewer. She wears a black-strapped dress and black high-heeled shoes. Her right ankle has a tattoo. In both images, she looks directly at the viewer. In the first, she has partially lifted her hips as if to roll over backward like a ball. In the process, her dress has slipped to her waist revealing a tease of white underwear. Her arms are bent over her head, suggesting she is about to roll up and over. In the second image, she has rolled further up and onto her shoulders, elevating her hips, and revealing her bare bottom. In both photographs, she meets the reader's gaze and invites him or her to watch. She is available. She is not walking away. The ad is for shoes.

Objectification

Showing only parts of women's bodies has long been a mainstay of fashion advertising. A leg, an arm, breasts, belly, or bottom only are common referents, regardless if the dismembered part wears or bears the item for sale. Breasts, buttocks, and lips as fetishes are particularly introduced as iconic devices for perfume, jewelry, clothing, and hosiery (Gould, this volume). Sexuality thereby becomes a "catalyst for collapsing the distinct between" high art (the photograph) and popular culture (pornography; McDonald, 2001, p. 81). Often, the model's head is "cut off," her body angled toward the camera, as she offers maximum display of herself to the viewer, who need not feel self-conscious about looking as no one is looking back. These images are common in posters, pinups, and "cheese-cake" photographs in which the woman in the picture, and by extension all women, are interesting because of their body parts. This fragmentation is problematic as it "equates women with their distinctly female body parts," and, as in pornography, the representations "do not merely enhance these female features but presents them in such a way as they stand in for the woman to whom they belong" (M. Caputi, 1994, pp. 18–19). Similarly, fashion advertising draws upon soft-core porn by embracing these conventions through "particular placement of arms, elbows, and hands. The formal arrangement of the body ... solicits the spectator's gaze" (Kuhn, 1985, p. 275). "Voyeurism and exhibitionism" are thereby "as intrinsic to fashion photography as they are to fashion itself" (Steele, 1991, p. 81), and objectification facilitates fetishization.

An example of objectification is an ad for Kieselstein-Cord (see Fig. 12.3). In the ad, we see a woman wrapped in two leather belts and nothing else. Her naked torso is shown from head to hip. She is looking forward with wet and parted lips. In addition, the model's breast and nipple are revealed in the crux of her elbow. Obviously, she is displaying belts, but she is equally displayed as a sex object. Similarly, an ad for Sergio Rossi shoes shows a fishnet stocking-clad model lying on her stomach with her legs crossed at the ankles. Her body is shown only from the waist down, beginning with the thin, black, thong underwear strip between the model's buttocks.

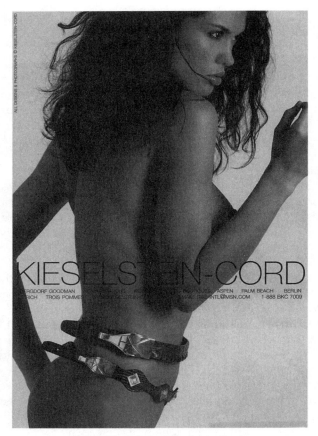

FIG. 12.3. Belts by Kieselstein-Cord.

An ad for Michael Kors shows the button and sides of what appears to be a corduroy jacket opened to reveal the underside of a headless model's breasts and concave belly and abdomen. The photo is gently shaded, emphasizing the flatness of the stomach and the indentation of the navel.

Submission

In 2001, an Yves St. Laurent Opium perfume ad was banned in Great Britain and France because it was considered degrading to women (see Fig. 12.4). Nude, reclining, red-haired "ghostly white" model Sophie Dahl is viewed from the side wearing only a necklace and a pair of high-heeled strappy sandals, "caressing herself into a state of ecstasy" (Baker & White, 2001, p. 47). Dahl is languidly reclining on her back, fondling a breast, and

FIG. 12.4. An ad for Opium fragrance.

apparently enthralled in sexual rapture. Her lips parted, she is clearly "caught unawares" as she enjoys her body and is transported by her pleasure—"two staples of soft-core porn" (Kuhn, 1985, p. 30). She is made available for viewing and faces away from the viewer, whom she seems unaware of since she is so caught up in her own passion. This example of "lawless seeing" encourages voyeurism and embraces not only voyeurism, but also scopophilia. The viewer can gaze for as look as he likes, "permitted by the photo's reassurance that the woman is unaware of his look" (Kuhn, 1995, p. 273). The hierarchy of male power over female objectivity is evident in her vulnerability and positioning.

The classic stereotype of deference, of "lowering oneself physically" (Goffman, 1976, p. 40), is a typical representation that appears to be so normal, that dominant group's use of power over the less powerful seems normal and natural. The model is unaware of the viewer's gaze, her eyes are usually closed, she faces away from the camera, her body is open, her genitals just barely concealed. Other examples include an YSL perfume ad in which the viewer sees a model dressed only in a man's unbuttoned black shirt. Her arms are raised above her head as she looks into a mirror. Her back is arched, revealing most of her breasts, all of her belly, and her bikini underwear. A shirtless young man or boy accompanies her, and the sleeve of a shirt worn by an adult man appears in the corner of the ad. The viewer is invited to watch . . . is it a one-way mirror? A ménage a trois? An incestuous encounter? Is she a prostitute? The story is up to the viewer, but clearly something sexual is, has, or will be happening.

At first blush, a recent print ad for Gucci appears to be a representation of female power. The long-legged model is standing with her feet apart between which a young man (boyish in fact) kneels at her feet. While the boy/man watches, she uses her thumb to pull down the front of her underwear revealing pubic hair shaved in a Gucci "G." She is, however, headless as the image begins at her breasts—revealed by her open robe— and armless, except for what appears to be her left hand pulling down the underwear.

Violence

Collectively, hierarchy, objectification, and submission converge to make the condition of violence possible (Jensen & Dines, 1998). In violent representations, the woman is not in control, or if she is, she is aggressive and working to dominate other people in the ad and, of course, the viewer. Advertisements from a number of fashion houses have used this theme. Often homosexuality is used in violent ads, such as those for Lanvin and Gucci that feature two women. A Gaultier ad shows a woman surrounded by several men; Dolce & Gabbana favors women with whips (which, to my knowledge, are not a fashion accessory they sell); a woman wearing a tight black leather jacket and tight black leather underwear poses in a Bottega Veneta ad, leaning against a sink in a restroom, while a naked man looks on. Guess ads feature a woman overpowered and pressed against a tree by a man or men. Francesco Biasia takes coding of violence and lesbianism a step further in an ad for handbags. At the top of the page, the model is dressed as a vampire and has blood running out of the corner of her mouth. Below, her red Biasia purse is accessorized with cloves of garlic.

A particularly flagrant example of violence is found in a series of Versace advertisements. These are the folks who brought viewers ads in which Madonna appeared to have bitten a poisoned apple and is found lying dead on marble stairs. In one of many sets of Versace mini-series ads, three women are shown in various states of dress and undress, wearing 3- to 4-inch aqua high heels, lying across beds, some with skirts on, some off, some with blouses and some without. The viewer sees the faces of only two of the models; the face and body of the third are turned away. She is seen only from behind. The focus is drawn to her exposed buttocks, emphasized by her black lace thong panties, garters, and hose. Her body is draped across a pillow, slightly raising her hips, making her available for pleasure. The other somnolent women in the cheaply paneled motel room are on beds or in chairs, clearly available and clearly willing to be involved with each other. In one of the ads, a fully clothed man is shown watching. This series of ads presents a scenario that combines voyeurism, hierarchy, objectification, and submission.

The presumed gaze in these ads is not only male, but also White. Mainstream fashion magazines claim to target all races and ethnicities, but ads primarily feature White models. While an analysis of race and ethnicity is beyond the scope of this chapter, it is an important next step. Hierarchy, supremacy, and control are clearly marks of pornography and are evident as well in fashion advertisements. Among the dozens of ads in the magazines, only two included an African American woman. An example is an ad for Chloe in which an African American woman wears a one-piece, V-shaped swimsuit that is open down the middle to a image of a pineapple at the base of her pelvis (see Fig. 12.5). She is kneeling and straddling a small pile of sand. Light shines between her thighs, pubic area, and the sand. She wears sunglasses so the viewer cannot see her eyes, but she is looking directly at the viewer. Her lips are parted, her nails long as talons. She is framed on each side by a horse. The color scheme is brown and gold; the context is animalistic and exotic—she is "the other."

THE PROMISE OF PORNOGRAPHY

In what might be the most important sentence in his classic work *Gender Advertisements*, Goffman pointed out:

> Although the pictures shown here cannot be taken as representative of gender behavior in real life...one can probably make a significant negative statement about them, namely, as *pictures* they are not perceived as peculiar or unnatural. (1976, p. ix)

This chapter presents a study that reveals not only the promise of pornography realized in fashion advertising, but also how normal it seems to be. Such naturalization of female bodies in pornographic poses raises

FIG. 12.5. A sexualized and animalistic representation for Chloe.

several areas of concern: (a) sexualization of children through portrayals of grown women as little girls, (b) normalization of violence, (c) undermining of positive images and artful representations, and (d) the wide availability of these images to young audiences. Each of these concerns is discussed in greater detail in this section.

A plethora of images of the erotic promise of teen girls pervades American culture. Bruce Weber's controversial photographs for Calvin Klein, for example, portray a "youthful eroticism" (Szymanski, 2000, p. 3). Even thinking in those terms and pairing the words "youth" and "erotic" together is deeply disturbing. Advertising imagery that dresses grown women as girls risks pedophiliac appeal. The girl child becomes available in fantasy, but is safely accessed because, in actuality, she is a grown woman. The "pornographication of the American girl" (Junod, 2001, p. 133) is disturbing enough in advertising, but goes beyond commercial messages. For example, porn filmmaker Gregory Dark directs Britney Spears videos. Critic Junod (2001, p. 133) posited that this "seems not so much anomalous as inevitable" as part of what is being called "the lure of jailbait." A *Rolling Stone* cover features Christina Aguilera with shorts unzipped and her "athletic tongue licking her lascivious lips." Presented in this way with such frequency and corroboration, "pornography can be considered mainstream" (Kilbourne, 1998, p. 217) as the "'sex sells' advertising mantra has migrated from other forms" of communication (Lambiase, 2003, p. 247).

The second area of concern is violence (or promised violence) in these ads. In the advertising analyzed as well as in other examples too numerous to include, violence emerged as a dominant and unexpected theme. Violence is certainly about power and is an element used to distinguish between soft- and hard-core pornography. The sex seen in advertising is as separate from love as it can possibly be. Advertising sex, according to Ackerman (1995, p. 242) is "angry, mean, and sad. Sex on display has become tougher and more perverse." This finding begs the question whether fashion advertising has moved not only toward a pornographic gaze but also toward a quasi-hard-core one. If so, the consequences are serious. Advertising helps to create

a climate in which certain attitudes and values flourish, such as the attitude that women are valuable only as objects of men's desires, that real men are always sexually aggressive, that violence is erotic, and that women who are the victims of sexual assault "asked for it." (Kilbourne, 1998, p. 291)

Hood (1998) described the United States as a rape-prone society, in which criminals should not be the targets of assault prevention, but rather "advertisements portraying someone as sex objects" should be. Objectified ideal female beauty, as presented in advertising, turns women's bodies into things, into objects, and "turning a human being into a thing is often the first step toward justifying violence" (Kilbourne, 2001, p. 56). The subtlety with which fashion advertising has moved the line of social acceptability is also problematic. It is increasingly difficult to tell the difference between *Playboy*, *Vogue*, and *Sports Illustrated*'s swimsuit edition based on what we see. This has to be "more damaging to women than frank pornography, which you at least know is pornography" ("Pornographication," 1989, p. 23).

The third concern raised in this study is the promise of the aesthetic (and therefore benign) transgression through the mainstreaming of pornography that undermines positive and artful representations of women. Fashion is a powerful force in shaping popular culture and is reflected in and borrows from fine arts. Tickner (1989) pointed out how art does not just make ideology explicitly, but can be used at a particular historical juncture to rework it. Sexual acts and sexual referents referenced in these ads are not only mainstream, but also *mainstreamed*, earning a place among other media representations as normal and natural interactions between people.

The fourth concern is that images in fashion advertising are easily accessible to all ages, but most importantly to children who are in the process of learning about sex roles. Not confined to behind-the-counter locations, magazines such as *W*, *Elle*, and *Vogue* are widely available, and "small boys who had once searched the *National Geographic* now look to mother's fashion magazines for information" (Fraser, 1992, p. 7). These are the magazines read

> in waiting rooms and libraries, subscribed to by teetotalers and wine tasters, delivered to one's doorstep, devoured in the agreed-upon sanctity of one's home, read in bathtubs and over coffee, left lying around the house for guests to riffle through and children to scissor up for school projects. (Ackerman, 1995, p. 243)

The use of sexual imagery in advertising in general—and fashion advertising in particular—shows no signs of slowing because, if for no other reason, sex has become the commodity used by advertisers competing for consumers' attention. The amount of pornographic imagery has escalated into "sexual clutter" where sexuality is so pervasive, the only way to get noticed is with increasingly explicit imagery (A. Berger, 2000, pp. 66–67). The "sign wars" that advertisers engage in eventually work to naturalize what we see as one company trying to "out sex" the other. Sexual appeals in advertising can been seen as "a sign of a desperate need to make certain that clients are getting their money's worth" (Solomon, 1990, p. 69). Thompson (2000, p. 9) pointed out that "you can still be offended, but I think we can't be shocked anymore. What we've done to the swear word, to taboo subjects, is to use them as if there's no tomorrow" (as cited in Ingrassia, 2000).

The goal of this chapter is to ascertain whether codes and conventions of pornography can in fact be found in mainstream fashion advertising. By drawing upon established codes and categories that satisfy widely held beliefs of what is pornographic (both soft- and hard-core), it is clear that what is presented in fashion ads is pornographic. Since ads, by their very nature, are designed to incite desire (in its many forms) and to draw attention to a brand, the use of sexual appeal is a natural link to deep-seated, fundamentally human urges.

Nevertheless, "we must never underestimate the power of sexual images to affect us in mysterious and powerful ways" (A. Berger, 2000, p. 67). Whether these urges are biological or cultural is beyond the scope of this chapter. However, it appears that advertising draws upon both, the impact of which conflates fashion, photography, advertising, and pornography into a unified whole that normalizes viewing women as only sexual, girls as sexually stimulating and available, and violence as the next level of activity and excitement. "Sex in advertising is pornographic," Kilbourne said (1998, p. 271), "because it dehumanizes and objectifies people, especially women and because it fetishizes products, imbues them with an erotic charge, which dooms us to disappointment since products can never fulfill our sexual desires or emotional needs." And, as promised, this is all available at the local supermarket and bookstore in a society in which the visual is now the privileged mode of discourse.

REFERENCES

Ackerman, D. (1995). *A natural history of love.* New York: Vintage.

Baker, S., & White, C. (2001, July 30). Why "porno chic" is riling the French. *Business Week, 47.*

Barthes, R. (1972). *Mythologies.* New York: Noonday Press.

Berger, A. A. (2004). *Ads, fads, and consumer culture: Advertising's impact on American character and society.* Lanham, MD: Rowman & Littlefield.

Berger, J. (1972). *Ways of seeing.* London: British Broadcasting Corporation.

Bordo, S. (1993). *Unbearable weight: Feminism, Western culture, and the body.* Berkeley: University of California Press.

Bordo, S. (2003). Bodies of work. (Interview). *Bitch, 21,* 52–57.

Caputi, J. (1999). The pornography of everyday life. In M. Meyers (Ed.), *Mediated women: Representations in popular culture* (pp. 57–80). Cresskill, NJ: Hampton Press.

Caputi, M. (1994). *Voluptuous yearnings: A feminist theory of the obscene.* London: Rowman & Littlefield.

Chandler, D. (2002). *Semiotics: The basics.* London: Routledge.

Cortese, A. J. (1999). *Provocateur: Images of women and minorities in advertising.* Lanham, MD: Rowman & Littlefield.

Crary, J. (1990). *Techniques of the observer: On vision and modernity in the nineteenth century.* London: MIT Press.

Dines, G., Jensen, R., & Russo, G. (1998). *Pornography: The production and consumption of inequality.* London: Routledge.

Evans, C., & Gamman, L. (1995). The gaze revisited, or reviewing queer viewing. In P. Burston & C. Richardson (Eds.), *A queer romance: Lesbians, gay men and popular culture* (pp. 13–56). London: Routledge.

Fraser, K. (1992). *On the edge: Images from 100 years of* Vogue. New York: Random House.

Galician, M. L. (2004). *Sex, love, and romance in the mass media.* Mahwah, NJ: Lawrence Erlbaum Associates.

Garfield, B. (1999, April 12). Nudity: Ads for *Shape* get directly to the point. *Advertising Age, 28.*

Goffman, E. (1976). *Gender advertisements*. Cambridge, MA: Harvard University Press.

Goldman, R. (1992). *Reading ads socially*. New York: Routledge

Hall, S. (2002). Race, articulation, and societies structured in dominance. In P. Essed & D. T. Goldberg (Eds.), *Race critical theories* (pp. 38–68). Malden, MA: Blackwell.

Hood, J. (1998). "Let's go girl": Male bodily rituals in America. In M. S. Kimmel & M. Messner (Eds.), *Men's lives* (pp. 431–436). New York: MacMillan/Maxwell.

Ingrassia, M. (2000, September 21). Risqué business: Magazine fashion ads push lewdness to the edge. *New York Daily News*, 64.

Itzin, C. (1992). *Pornography: Women, violence, and civil liberties*. New York: Oxford University Press.

Jacobellis v. Ohio (1964). Supreme Court of the United States. 378 U.S. 184; 84 S. Ct.1676; 12 L. Ed. 2d 793; 1964 U.S. LEXIS 822; 28 Ohio Op. 2d 101. Retrieved Lexis/Nexis January 29, 2004.

Jensen, R., & Dines, G. (1998). The Content of Mass-Marketed Pornography. In G. Dines, R. Jensen, and A. Russo (pp. 65–100).

Jensen, R., Dines, G., & Russo, G. (1998). *Pornography: The production and consumption of inequality*. London: Routledge.

Jhally, S. (1990). *The codes of advertising: Fetishism and the political economy of meaning in the consumer society*. New York: Routledge.

Jhally, S. (1995). Image-based culture: Advertising and popular culture. In G. Dines and J. Humez (Eds.), *Gender, race, and class in media* (pp. 77–87). London: Sage.

Junod, T. (2001, February). Devil Greg Dark. *Esquire*, 130–135.

Kilbourne, J. (1998). Beauty and the beast of advertising. *Media & value*, 121–125.

Kilbourne, J. (1999). Can't buy my love: How advertising changes the way we think and feel. New York: Touchstone.

Kilbourne, J. (2000/2001, December/January). Quoted in C. Simon. Hooked. *Ms.*, 55–59.

Kuhn, A. (1985). *The power of the image: Essays on representation and sexuality*. London: Routledge & Kegan Paul.

Kuhn, A. (1995). Lawless Seeing. In G. Dines & J. M. Humez (Eds.), *Gender, race, and class in media* (pp. 271–278). Thousand Oaks, CA: Sage.

Lambiase, J. (2003). Sex—online and in Internet advertising. In T. Reichert & J. Lambiase (Eds.), *Sex in advertising: Perspectives on the erotic appeal* (pp. 247–269). Mahwah, NJ: Lawrence Erlbaum Associates.

McDonald, H. (2001). *Erotic ambiguities: The female nude in 636332*. London: Routledge.

McElroy, W. (1995). *A woman's right to pornography*. New York: St. Martin's Press.

McNair, B. (1996). *Mediated sex: Pornography and postmodern culture*. London: Arnold.

Mulvey, L. (1988). Visual pleasure and narrative cinema. In C. Penley (Ed.), *Feminism and film theory* (pp. 57–58). New York: Routledge.

Newton, J. (2001). *The burden of visual truth: The role of photojournalism in mediating reality*. Thousand Oaks, CA: Sage.

O'Guinn, T., Allen, C. T., & Semenik, R. J. (2000). *Advertising* (2nd ed.). Cincinnati, OH: South-Western.

Pornographication of the mainstream. (1989). *Women Artists News, 14*, 23.

Reichert, T. (2003). What is sex in advertising? Perspectives from consumer behavior and social science research. In T. Reichert & J. Lambiase (Eds.), *Sex in advertising: Perspectives on the erotic appeal* (pp. 11–38). Mahwah, NJ: Lawrence Erlbaum Associates.

Rose, G. (2001). *Visual methodologies.* London: Sage.

Schroeder, J. E., & Borgerson, J. L. (1998). Marketing images of gender: A visual analysis. *Consumption, Market and Culture, 2*(2), 161–201.

Schroeder, J. E., & Borgerson, J. L. (2003). Dark desires: Fetishism, ontology, and representation in contemporary advertising. In T. Reichert & J. Lambiase (Eds.), *Sex in advertising: Perspectives on the erotic appeal* (pp. 65–87). Mahwah, NJ: Lawrence Erlbaum Associates.

Solomon, J. (1990). *The signs of our times: The secret meanings of everyday life.* New York: Harper & Row.

Steele, V. (1991). Erotic allure. *Aperture,* 81–96.

Stokstad, M. (1995). *Art history.* New York: Abrams.

Stratton, J. (1996). *The desirable body: Cultural fetishism and the erotics of consumption.* Chicago: University of Illinois Press.

Szymanski, K. (2000, July 27). Online commercialism. *Bay Area Reporter.* Retrieved January 29, 2004, from onlinepolicy.org/turing/000727.bar. pnocensorsxy.shtml.

Tickner, L. (1989). The body politic: Female sexuality and women artists since 1970. In R. Betterton (Ed.), *Looking on: Images of femininity in the visual arts and media* (pp. 235–253). London: Pandora Press.

Turner, B. (1984). *The body and society: Exploration in social theory.* Oxford, England: Basil Blackwell.

Williamson, J. (1978). *Decoding advertisements: Ideology and meaning in advertising.* New York: Boyars.

Chapter 13

The Logic of Pornography in Digital Camera Promotion

Jonathan E. Schroeder
University of Exeter

Pierre McDonagh
Dublin City University

> Women in any type of costume usually make excellent photographic subjects.
> —from *Kodachrome and How to Use It,* 1940

Drawing on a theory of the fetish in visual representation, this chapter investigates the interactions of consumption, representation, and sexuality in contemporary digital camera advertising. We introduce the concept *logic of pornography* to theorize how cultural and representational codes of pornography influence other realms, such as advertising and digital photography, and how contemporary branding campaigns express these codes. We discuss the use of voyeuristic images and sexual innuendoes in various print and Internet ads for handheld, cell phone, and tiny video surveillance cameras from companies such as Ricoh, Kodak, Siemens, Pentax, Canon, and Casio, as they raid the referent system of pornography to promote their products.

Producing sexualized pictures requires advanced photographic technology, a conscious effort to photograph the act, and often, especially within pornographic representations, a costumed, scripted, and directed scenario produced for profit—which is itself a central element of commercial culture. We present critical analysis of sexual issues in contemporary advertising via an interdisciplinary reading that brings insights from visual studies, consumer behavior, and social theory to bear on how photography, advertising, and eroticism intermingle in contemporary visual consumption. Many of the ads discussed seem to suggest that consumers can now become producers of pornography for personal pleasure or profit, via the easy access and circulation of images over the Internet. We cover a specific industry sector, but our conclusions resonate throughout the entire spectrum of sex in consumer culture.

We focus on digital cameras for several reasons. First, they have exploded in popularity—digital models' sales now surpass traditional cameras (Photo Marketing Association, 2003; Rijper, 2002), with a worldwide market of about $6.6 billion in 2002 (Imerge Consulting Group, 2003). Concurrently, digital cameras became a surprise "killer application" in the telecommunications industry, spearheading a visual revolution in cell phone technology and consumption. Second, digital camera ads often feature sexually tinged photographs. Photography has traditionally been the province of male desire—cameras represent technologically sophisticated gadgets with which to survey and record at a distance (see Mirzoeff, 2002; Schroeder, 2002; Slater, 1995). Third, by taking a sustained look at the intervisuality of camera advertising—the ads themselves are photographically produced, they show photographic techniques and tools, and they promote a photographic lifestyle—we have a chance to develop new insights into the intersection of photography, advertising, and representations of sexuality.

Just as it is not enough merely to assume that "sex sells," we need to understand why images are considered sexy; what they represent about arousal, sexual desire, and interpersonal relations; and how advertising harnesses these concerns to create brand associations. We emphasize photography by treating it as information technology, consumer behavior, and popular product, and focus attention on photographic conventions and advertising techniques to show how advertising photography depicts sexual themes. We call on several visual genres to enrich our analysis, including pornography, portrait photography, and film.

Consumer research and marketing scholarship often overlook visuality despite the increasing emphasis of the visual in consumer society (Schroeder, 2002). Our interdisciplinary visual method offers a productive, critical analysis, particularly suited to sort out meaning construction in advertising imagery. We introduce several exemplars culled from contemporary digital camera marketing. These images are not meant to be a random representative sample; we chose them precisely because they reveal interesting aspects of sexual positioning in advertising. Digital camera ads employ many other motifs, including photographing children, embarrassing moments, and spectacular scenery—we are not suggesting that sexual themes always appear. However, we argue the logic of pornography that pervades the genre necessarily influences the possibilities and potential of digital photography. We close by discussing conceptual and operational implications of our position. How does advertising represent sexual themes? What does it suggest about the appropriate use of digital cameras? What do advertising images say about human relationships?

ADVERTISING AND PHOTOGRAPHY

We begin with the assumption that advertising and its discourse both reflect and create social ideals. In a powerful critique of advertising, philosopher Richard Lippke argued "the ways in which individuals habitually perceive and conceive their lives and the social world, the alternatives they see as open to them, and the standards they use to judge themselves and others are shaped by advertising, perhaps without their ever being consciously aware of it" (Lippke, 1995, p. 108). In other words, advertising representations influence cultural and individual conceptions of identity, including sexuality and desire, and must be understood as the result of changing cultural norms and social standards. Consequently, our overarching framework views meaning as the result of representational, cultural, and technological practices. In this analysis, we focus on the successful recent introduction of a photographic and market innovation—the amateur digital camera—by looking at marketing strategies, advertising exemplars, and photographic practice.

The analytic approach presented here makes three interrelated assumptions about advertising images. First, ads may be considered *aesthetic objects*. This assumption acknowledges the creativity and thought that goes into the production of most national advertising campaigns, and that consumption has become aestheticized via style, fashion, and integration into culture. Second, ads are *socio-political artifacts*. These two categories, aesthetic and political, are often constituted as mutually exclusive. Our analysis attempts to locate advertisements within a complex visual signifying system that includes the interrelated domains of the aesthetic and the political. Third, we situate advertising within *a system of visual representation* that creates meaning within the circuit of culture, often beyond what may be intended by the photographer and advertising agency. This circuit assumes that advertising both creates and contributes to culture (see Hall, 1997; Schroeder & Zwick, 2004; Stern & Schroeder, 1994). Indeed, illicit, pornographic visual representations infiltrate more acceptable, mainstream forms of representation; advertising straddles this divide, pushing boundaries and appropriating proscribed conventions.

Research on advertising, including sex in advertising, must account for how images appear erotic or look sexy and for how visual representational codes contribute to attributions of sexiness or desirability. The logic of market segmentation needs recalling. What one segment finds sexy may leave another cold, and one consumer's erotic fantasy may strongly offend someone else. "Sexy" must be contextualized. Certainly, there are shared cultural codes of sexual attraction, but these change across consumers, between generations, and over one's own lifetime. We propose that researchers make too many assumptions about what is sexy, how it might be represented, and for whom. Furthermore, pointing alone does not demonstrate an image's sexual aspect. One must visually analyze what makes it sexy, under what conditions, and how this association works.

Advertising photography fetishizes goods by eroticizing and reifying consumer products (e.g., Goldman & Papson, 1996; Miklitsch 1998; Schroeder & Borgerson, 2003). Photographic representation of fetishism depends on three factors: liminality, concepts of the *other*, and visual conventions. Liminality refers to the conceptual divide of nature and culture, a realm *in between* that startles, unnerves, and unsettles—and attracts attention (Schroeder & Borgerson, 2003). Sexualized photographic representations inhabit this liminal zone, and they oscillate between photographing a "natural" act while reminding us of the very artificiality of depicting this act. Taking sexually themed photographs suggests sophisticated equipment, forethought, and a narrative of sexual encounter designed to arouse audiences. Furthermore, the images discussed below hover between illicit and culturally sanctioned forms of representation: between pornography and erotic imagery, smut and salesmanship, and private collections and public expressions.

Erotic photography, pornography, and advertising routinely present images of the *other*—the exotic, sexually ambitious subject that exists for the viewer's imagination (see Borgerson & Schroeder, 2002). Most pornography assumes heterosexual male consumers, although there is a large gay market (much so-called lesbian action porn is produced under a heterosexual gaze). Women, or more accurately, the feminine, generally play the object of desire. Moreover, women of color, Asians, Blacks, "natives," and so on typify the pornographic realm. In addition, standard pornography costumes include tight-fitting fetish clothing, and this pushes many models into the liminal zone between nature and culture (Schroeder & Borgerson, 2003). For example, iconic images of exotic "island girls," complete with primitive, pre-Christian notions about sex and guilt, overpopulate advertising and pornographic imagery that draws on cultural stereotypes about paradisal vacations and "native" practices on "temptation island" (see Borgerson & Schroeder, 2002; Cortese, 1999; Ramamurthy, 2002). Furthermore, photographic conventions such as close cropping, lighting, and depth of field visually fetishize objects via isolation, decontextualization, and reification. The pornography industry developed photographic codes that shape its visual representations, including poses, positions, gestures—including "the money shot"—realist aesthetics, and production values that contribute to the look of porn (cf. Kendrick, 1996; O'Toole, 1999).

Photographs are used so often and so fluidly for scientific, judicial, and civil evidence—what photo historian Peter Hamilton (1997) termed "objective representation"—that it can be difficult to keep in mind that photographs are culturally produced images that exist within shifting planes of meaning and significance. Furthermore, "the range of contexts within which photographs have been used to sell products or services is so enormous that we are almost unaware of the medium of photography and the language which has been created to convey commercial messages" (Ramamurthy, 2002, p. 169). Photographs often appear as if they just *are*, mere visual records of what has happened, how people look, or where events took place. Upon reflection, however, "all photographs are representations, in that they tell us as much about the photographer, the technology used to produce the image, and their intended uses as they tell us about the events or things they depicted" (McCauley, 1997, p. 63). It is important, therefore, to acknowledge this subjective photographic representation, remembering that someone takes a range of photographs and then selects one or two which juxtapose product and text in the frame which we read as an "ordinary advertisement."

Sociologist Erving Goffman (1979) pointed out that ads directly affect lived experience by normatively limiting our conceptions of identity, right and wrong, and the good life. Critically, ads influence how we think about masculinity and femininity, what is sexy, and what will be seen as attractive by desired others. Goffman showed that "every physical surround, every box for social gatherings, necessarily provides materials than can be used in the display of gender and the affirmation of gender identity" (1997, p. 207). Standard advertising poses generally signal men's dominance over submissive women, be it through physical, financial, or psychological superiority (Kilbourne, 2000; Schroeder & Borgerson, 1998; Shields & Heinecken, 2002). By focusing on behavior as *performance*, he challenged the distinction between the image and lived experience. We see in our selection of ads similar performative behavior: acting out scripted scenarios for photographic posterity, grabbing semi-risqué photos of unaware women, and displaying attractive bodies for the camera's gaze.

PHOTOGRAPHY AND PORNOGRAPHY

Pornography pervades the contemporary visual landscape. In particular, the Web embodies what Laurence O'Toole (1999) called "pornocopia" in his apologia for contemporary pornography: "porn is no longer a 'shameful,' 'weird,' 'dark,' out-of-the-way nightmare, but something that has come above ground, that is linked in with the 'straight' communications and media industries, as it is linked in with the private lives of an ever-increasing number of adults" (p. 374). Although we do not wish to elucidate heated debates about pornography, our view is that its overall effects are not conducive to equal and productive human relationships, particularly between men and women (cf. Brod, 1996). We acknowledge that some couples use pornography creatively and lovingly within the bounds of their relationship; that marginalized groups—gays, minorities, fetishists—may find in porn an expressive outlet for constructing, representing, and celebrating identity; and that for some individuals, pornographic material offers a remedy for physical (or mental) dysfunction. However, at the risk of seeming prudish, or worse, passé, we believe that typical pornography, including copycat amateur pornography, exerts a debilitating influence on people's relationships with actual bodies and lovers and infects our sexual imagination (see Carter, 1978; Dines, Jensen, & Russo, 1998; Wells, 2002).

Pornography implies pictures. Moreover, pornographic photography always implies material bodies, digitally transformed and manipulated. Current pornographic expression includes digital photographs; online pornography, which includes magazines, still photographs, streaming videos, live webcams, and CD-ROMs; as well as "spy," surveillance, and cell phone cameras that spawn "upskirt" Web sites (photographs of women, generally, taken without their awareness or consent, posted on the Internet). *Newsweek* reported that porn-site visits comprise a third of all Internet usage (Databank, 2000). Pornography dominates the Web's commercial sector, driving many technological e-commerce "advances," including billing capacity, video streaming, and image database management (Cone, 2002: Marshall, 2002; Oliver, 2002).

Photographic practice, including practices promoted in ads discussed here, implicates a larger politics of power and representation articulated within the social psychological process of the *gaze*. To gaze signals more than to look at. It implies a social psychological relationship of power in which the gazer is superior to the object of the gaze. Pornography has been called an extreme expression of the male gaze, producing sexist representations of women, the good life, and sexual fantasy from a male point of view (cf. Kendrick, 1996; Stern, 1991; Williams, 1999). Interpersonally, the gaze "corresponds to desire, the desire for self-completion through another" (Olin, 1996, p. 210). The gaze limits both the gazer and the gazed upon. Recent theoretical treatments of the gaze acknowledge the myriad forms it may take, including a female gaze (see Schroeder, 2002; Schroeder & Zwick, 2004).

In pornography and other representational genres, women and their bodies serve iconic functions; these images celebrate and sexualize while they survey and circulate. Pornography and its more prissy cousin, glamour photography, both developed codes of representation and subgenres such as softcore, hardcore, fetish, and so on. Pornographic photography depends on stereotypical classification into recognizable types—the inexperienced babysitter, the enthusiastic nymphomaniac, or the stern dominatrix; "in this way it makes different women appear sexually available to a presumed heterosexual male viewer" (Henning, 2002, p. 225). Internet porn features "the time-tested formula of women's bodies displayed for men's eyes . . . heartily embraced by those developing marketing strategies for the Web, despite egalitarian or postmodern hopes for the medium overall" (Lambiase, 2003, p. 262). The Web offers almost anything imaginable online, but most pornographic "content" remains sexist, racist, and stereotypical, hardly the liberating expressive force many foresaw.

Recent developments shift digital photography production to private hands, enabling consumers to shoot, view, print, post, and e-mail photographs from home. Enterprising shutterbugs can now produce porn, send upskirt images to friends and colleagues, and effortlessly circulate images on the World Wide Web (cf. Slater, 2002). This brave new world animates latent fantasies of glamour photography: The "original lure of photographic technology has become distanced: the readers of porn magazines could only imagine themselves as a real glamour photographer, but now they have a hands-on relationship with technology at the very point of consumption of pornography" (Graham, 1995, pp. 82–83). In this way, photographing a woman came to be associated with having sex with her (e.g., Pultz, 1995).

Although there are many "amateur" sites—private people who post provocative photos—commercial porn operations swarm the Net, employing such annoying gimmicks as "mouse traps," "misleading meta tags," and spam, all unscrupulous technological tricks that lure surfers to their sites (Cone, 2002; Marshall, 2002). Visual theorist Suren Lalvani presciently reminds us that pornography exists always for public display even if it is intended for private consumption (Lalvani, 1996). In any case, photography has for its relatively short history enjoyed a fascination with the gaze, bodies, and new possibilities of representing desire. Pornography centers around public circulation of private desire.

Photography theory urges us to consider photographs as social texts, not mere pictures that accurately record faces, families, or familiar sites. Digital photography can be seen as a qualitative shift in image production, one that fueled the growth of the World Wide Web and enabled photography consumers to more easily become producers.

SEX IN ADVERTISING: SOME REFLECTIONS

We contend that the logic of pornography profoundly marks advertising and its representation of the good life, especially how marketing connects brands to sexual themes. This logic of pornography includes the sale (or circulation) of sexual expression, the commodification of human bodies, and the (persistently) stereotyped portrayal of male and female roles. Pornography underscores the generalized relationships between sex and commerce, between bodies and money, and between men and women, structuring how many conceptualize the ideal life. Although we do not discuss the broader implications of pornography within culture here, we note that others contend that pornography, particularly Internet porn, feeds directly into other forms of sexual exploitation (e.g., Hughes, 2000).

Sex in advertising is not the same as sex, no matter how realistic it may appear. As graphic designer Sarah Dougher pointed out, "sexuality is not solely the sex act. Rather, it is how desire is expressed and represented over various contexts. Sexuality has an object—even if that object is the self—and, consequently, its relationship to consumer objects is of primary importance" (2003, p. 39). Furthermore, pornography is not the same as sex either, it is generally a staged drama produced by professionals for profitable distribution.

Many analyses of "sex in advertising" or "sexual appeals in advertising" point to images that are considered sexy, and perhaps count their appearance in one medium or another, but spend little time articulating why they are "sexy" or "arousing." Often, this is due to the use of a naïve "picture theory" of photographic representation, that is, photographs are mere pictures of reality and thus need little analysis or explanation in order to understand what they "show" and how they work (see Schroeder, 2002). In this way of thinking, "sex is a natural attention-getter," as one recent advertising textbook—*Advertising and the Mind of the Consumer*—put it (Sutherland & Sylvester, 2000, p. 102). But, what is "sex"? And, how is it visually represented? The book reproduces three examples, including one for Jewelry.com that shows a woman aggressively "making the moves" on a man, her long pearl necklace dangling over his lips. "Results may vary" reminds the ad, in an ironic reference to advertising convention. None of these ads is discussed within Sutherland and Sylvester's text; thus, the "sex in advertising" they purportedly show remains unexamined—as if they are "natural" examples of sex and sexual appeals as "attention-getting" devices that require no further explanation (cf. Reichert, 2003). But, what about these ad images is sexy? Why do they require no discussion, no careful analysis, as many of the other ads in this otherwise serviceable book do? They miss how advertisers "use the edges of the sex act—the body part, the innuendo, the bed, the lingerie—to make their points and to evoke the meaning of sex without actually showing the act. Through these acts of design, the regular world becomes sexual, and sex—every kind of sex—is naturalized into the regular world" (Dougher, 2003, p. 157). Sex in advertising works by association to cultural and representational codes, not by merely showing "sexy" pictures.

We think it is essential to attempt clarity in discussing photographic representations of sex, sexy images, pornography, and pornographic images, as much as these concepts intermingle (see also Solomon-Godeau, 1991; Weitman, 1998). In the images assembled for this analysis, the body itself fuels the fetish engine, along with its bodily representation (cf. Fernbach,

2002). To demonstrate what we mean, we turn now to a set of ads, culled from mainstream lifestyle magazines, a fetish magazine, and the Internet.

THE IMAGES

Our analysis focuses on photographic style, cultural conventions, representational codes, and comparative associations to bring forth possibilities of meaning, not to fix one meaning or impose an orthodox interpretation. We offer thick descriptions of several ads, followed by interpretative analysis informed by our theoretical framework of the fetish in visual representation. These examples were assembled specifically to illuminate this chapter's concepts, as well as for their compositional connections (for a full explication of our method, see Schroeder, 2002; Schroeder & Borgerson, 1998; or Stern & Schroeder, 1994). We do not claim that they are representative, rather, we argue that each is a meaningful, compelling image worthy of close analysis. In this way, we follow interpretive work that focuses on a limited range of materials in order to make broader points about sexuality, photography, and representation in contemporary advertising. We do worry that by reproducing these images, we may inadvertently reinforce and reinscribe sexist attitudes; however, we did not produce the images, we follow others' work in this vein, and we believe that awareness is part of the solution.

We present our most spectacular image first, a recent ad for a full-featured Ricoh digital camera (see Fig. 13.1). This Ricoh ad appeared in *Skin Two*, a glossy fetish magazine sold, among other places, in mainstream outlets such as Tower Record stores (see Schroeder, 2004, and of course the requisite Web site: www.skintwo.com). Not explicitly pornographic, in that it does not portray nudity or sexual intercourse, *Skin Two* has been described as "a stylish fetish magazine which was instrumental in making the sexual underground trendy in the '90s" (Baddeley, 2002, p. 213). *Skin Two* mimics pornographic titles, with its shiny, heavy printing stock, photographic layouts, and high production values. The ad copy, running in capital letters across the two-page spread, reads: *Total Multimedia. Total Digital Camera. Total Control. Total Manipulation.* Then, down the right side: *No Film. No Processing. No Waiting. No Censorship!* The payoff line appears below: *Digital Solutions for Demanding Situations.* Small print, under a large photograph of the camera, states: *Ricoh Digital Cameras Download Image Direct to Mac or PC, direct to disc, direct to printer and direct to Internet.*

The ad exhibits the camera's buttons and switches, the "live" button prominent among them, but another image attracts our attention. The Ricoh's digital monitor shows two women: One wears a black bra, thong, garter belt and stockings, standing crouched with her back to the viewer;

FIG. 13.1. Ricoh "Total Manipulation."

and another, in black thigh-high stockings, thong, and lacy top, rests somewhat precariously on her knees. The setting looks anonymous, since heavy red curtains hang in the background. The first woman's nearly bare buttocks loom toward the viewer, her head cropped so we just see the tips of her chin-length hair, her legs lopped to accentuate the iconic black stockings (see Schroeder & Borgerson, 2003). The second woman smiles coyly and looks off-screen, her head tilted in a rather strange manner. Her body leans into the other woman (and to the viewer), revealing her breast. She seems to be crawling. Perhaps she plays the submissive partner—is that a leather leash? Upon closer inspection, it may be that the first woman wields a riding crop, a staple S & M prop.

Although it may appear "natural" as if it was just photographed as it happened, we would describe this image as a clearly stylized, ritual performance of what is typically scripted for male heterosexual pornography, complete with fetishized "sexy" outfits, salacious accessories, and opportunistic viewer perspective. In other words, this picture and its poses are *informed* by pornographic practice, in which everything within the frame expresses a strategically limited range of visual possibilities. This same picture appears, smaller, on the ad's right side, and a detail of the "submissive" woman hovers in the background of the entire two-page spread. Another detail bleeds off the bottom of the ad, a cropped version of the original picture, repeated in a way that visually mimics a reel of movie film, alluding to another of the camera's capabilities. Thus, this ad expresses a formal condition of representation that visual theorist Nicholas Mirzoeff (2002) called *intervisuality*: "the simultaneous display and interaction of a variety of modes of visuality" (p. 3). Photographic representation provides several spheres of meaning: the product itself (Ricoh digital cameras), the repeated photograph of the two women (assumed to be taken by a Ricoh), and the photograph that constitutes the ad itself (probably not taken by the Ricoh).

One might be tempted to describe the models as "sexy," and we certainly believe that they were intended to be sexy. However, what is sexy about the models, their clothing, and their posed interaction? A quick turn to art history affords many visual connections; the famous French painter Jean Auguste Dominique Ingres' *Bather*, which he painted over and over, classical depiction of the *nymph*, "a young and beautiful nude woman" (West, 1996, p. 670), or the *graces*, a good excuse to portray several near naked women frolicking about. To us, it does not appear to be an amateur photo, capturing a "real" sexual act. Rather, it looks more like an erotic scenario, performed expressly for the camera. Thus, photography constitutes and constructs the scene. It is the reason it exists. This is not to imply that we are privileged viewers who can "tell" just by looking that these two women are or are not "really" sexual partners. We call attention to the performed, aestheticized qualities of the image. For example, it appears in an ad, it is arguably intended to demonstrate both product performance and potential emotional (and practical) benefits of using Ricoh digital cameras, and it is similar to many other images within the pornographic genre. A Google search will quickly reveal that two women photographed playing S & M games provide a rather typical trope.

Turning to the text, we find the "no censorship" product attribute captivating. This product promise alludes to the newly won "freedom" to produce photographic images without intermediaries, those pesky photo lab clerks who might report pornographic images or at least snicker at the erotic auteur who comes to pick up his prints. With Ricoh digital cameras, one can produce pleasing pornography at will, without worrying about George Orwell's Big Brother-style surveillance. It sounds liberating, but there may be a darker side to this particular product attribute. Who shot this saucy scene?

The depicted scenario, in both the ad and in the digital camera within the ad, places the spectator in a privileged position—a stylistic approach that Kokonis (2002) calls a "window within a window"—and invites viewers to share the spectacle at a distance. One might argue the ad's framing owes more to the spectacle of filmmaker Richard Cronenberg's *Videodrome* than just purely sadomasochist, dominatrix-fueled erotic enjoyment. It can be read as male voyeurism, raiding the pornographic referent system and sensationalizing the "no censorship" logic of the pornographic. Thus, the

Ricoh ad appropriates and transforms the sociolegal conundrum of censorship, conflating political struggle with personal sexual photography. We do not mean to deny the importance of sexual rights, sexual expression, and sexual choice, yet we suggest that Ricoh drains the cultural history of censorship. These types of images have been readily available, uncensored, for a long time. Additionally, the ad text avoids any suggestion of improper (or illegal) usage, such as child pornography, forced participation, nonconsensual use or circulation, and so on, with the exception of the curious copy "total manipulation," which, we assume, refers to digital image manipulation, not human manipulation. Furthermore, buying Ricoh offers a way to celebrate freedom of expression, what might constitute a state or community concern seemingly solved by private consumption.

Next, we turn to that global photo icon, Kodak. This 2000 ad for Kodak's DC4800 Zoom Digital Camera resembles Ricoh's effort in its use of capitalized, declarative sentences, a dominant single image, and a crisp picture of the product itself (see Fig. 13.2). *For beautiful digital pictures, just add light and your imagination. Kodak DC4800 Zoom Digital Camera.* "The possibilities are endless," we read, as the ad exhorts "experience greater creative freedom" and "all you have to do is supply the imagination." We see a small picture of a woman who appears to be standing in a doorway, with her arms out, touching the frame. She is young, White, and she looks "glamorous." Why? Well, she sports dark sunglasses and a tight, shiny, zipped-up leather jacket that both reflect the bright studio lights. Her hair is severely pulled back, her bright red lips are parted to barely reveal her teeth, and she has been glamorously posed, like a model or a stripper. Her appearance mirrors the pornographic logic of male audience, female subjects, of men viewing women. The door does not seem to lead outside, and thus wearing this jacket is a bit unusual. Her position in the doorway begs the question: Is she coming or going? Doors are familiar props from photographic history (see Alfred Stieglitz's famous image on the front cover of John Szarkowski's *Looking at Photographs*, 1999). Doors represent possibilities, as in going through doors, opening doors, and so on; thus, this visual image reinforces "possibilities are endless" copy. Doors also represent the liminal zones between inside and outside, private and public, past and future. In addition, the doorway or windows to brothels are fixations of Dutch society consumed in the global tourist gaze. In this context, it seems reasonable to assume that this Kodak print might represent the first in a quickly snapped series that culminates with her disrobed, in the room within. We do not expect all viewers to make these connections, but we insist that they inform the production and consumption of ads.

Pentax transformed the 35-millimeter market with affordable, small, high-quality cameras, and they have aggressively marketed digital products. In a 2003 ad, we see a vaguely dark-skinned woman trying on lingerie

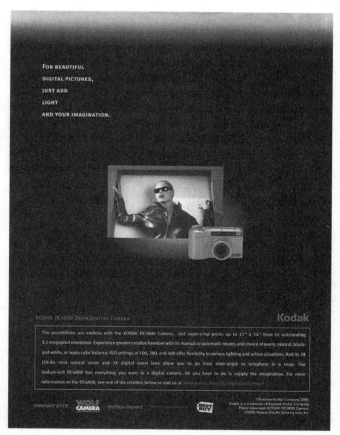

FIG. 13.2. Kodak DC4800 Digital Zoom Camera "the possibilities are endless."

and a fully clothed man holding several items on his arm, while she pon-
ders her (his?) choice (see Fig. 13.3). Her skimpy thong resembles the Ricoh
model's. Arms akimbo, she fastens (or unfastens) her bra, making her hands
appear as if pinioned behind her. "Pentax for your precious moments"
reads the copy, underscoring this shot's intimate quality, apparently dis-
rupted by photographic activity. A mirror reflects her image, showing her
slightly blurred upper body and black bra to the man, the photographer,
and us, the viewers. Subtly supporting distinct gender roles (women appear, men look; women wear sexy lingerie, men watch them wearing it;
women shop, men buy), this image builds upon a host of visual, gender,
and commodity conventions that we invite readers to consider. For example, the mirror stands as a traditional trope of vanity, narcissism, lust,
and pride in Western art. Usually, mirrors are linked to women, revealing,

FIG. 13.3.   Pentax "all the right accessories" (Sweden).

reflecting, and reinforcing the feminine attributes of beauty and vanity (Hall, 1979; see also Schroeder & Zwick, 2004). In this ad, the mirror plays a double role, allowing both the man and the viewer visual access to her lingerie-modeling body and providing an intervisual subtext for the image.

This Pentax ad clearly commodifies "the perfect female form," "with all the right accessories" as well as the lingerie-clad model, undressing as she seeks acceptance from a male voyeur (cf. Kilbourne, 2000). Its appearance in retro, hyper-masculine male lifestyle magazines further reinforces this message. The scene has cinematic referents to the movie *Pretty Woman*, specifically the narrative where the male protagonist (played by Richard Gere) dresses the female (Julia Roberts, in the role that made her a superstar), thus saving her from life on the street. Although the man appears to play a subservient role within the image, as dressed in business clothes, he radiates more power than her, undressed. One might imagine him paying for her clothes. He appears older, more successful than her, who is literally stripped of all professional or public identity. Is he waiting for her to wear these outfits as his escort? Is she a dutiful wife doing as she is told? Or, did she drag him, kicking and screaming, to the dreaded lingerie department, unsettling his masculinity, then reaffirming it via sexy purchases? In any case, we suggest that this image, along with hundreds like it, reinforces cultural expectations commonly found in pornography, reiterating social stereotypes of the domesticated subject, that freely sexually available female object at the male's beck and call.

In a Siemens Mobile ad, the spy camera comes into its own powerful realm with the offer to "Expose more" (see Fig. 13.4). This ad, which appeared in a popular men's fashion magazine, features a large pixilated

FIG. 13.4. Siemens "expose more" (England).

image in the top portion of the frame, with a photographed Siemens S55 cell phone inset below. It is difficult to decipher this low-resolution picture, and only upon inspecting the rest of the ad does it make much sense. On the phone's screen, the image comes into clearer view: a woman's nearly bare back. Her head is cropped, her face turned away, and she appears unaware of the photographer or (his) surreptitious snapping. Her back seems sunburned, and the straps of her low-cut dress reveal a pattern from wearing a t-top in the sun, perhaps a one-piece bathing suit.

The tabloid-like headline, "Expose more," appears just over the larger picture's nearly naked shoulders, motivating several conclusions. First, the ad encourages women to take off clothes and to expose more of their bodies. Second, it commands the viewer–photographer to take more (revealing) photographs, with an archaic reference to exposing film to light. Third, it signals the phone's functional capability to store more pictures with its 8080 pixels, in this case, more of the undressing woman. The proud owner could expose more detailed poses of the woman with a S55 phone than other models, publicly displaying her body for male inspiration. The camera's small size illustrates possibilities to take pictures without drawing attention to the fact, perhaps appealing to furtive, forbidden desires. Furthermore, Siemens offers consumers pornographer potential via sending digitized pictures, music and text instantly to friends, increasing the shared voyeuristic thrill, engaging in a heterosexually affirming group ritual, and completing the digital disembodiment of the subject.

Lest the reader think only women feature as sex objects in digital camera ads, we present Canon's ad for its high-end Digital IXUS400 (see Fig. 13.5). Here, we see a man and a woman, both with no visible clothes, a Canon camera their only accessory. The camera serves as an updated, technological fig leaf. "You don't need anything else," Canon tells us. Like the Ricoh ad, this picture recurs three times: first as the main image; smaller, emerging from a printer; and smaller still within the camera monitor. Perhaps more subtle than the previous examples, this ad nevertheless quivers with sexual possibilities; its hedonistic portrayal of the tanned body is equally at home in the porn movie as in a nudist beach. We could be awaiting a film director's "action" call. What will the young, healthy, physically fit couple do with two cameras and no clothes?

DIGITAL VOYEURISM AND COMMODITY FETISHISM

This cross-section of ads seemingly offers consumers a chance to assume the role of glamorous fashion photographer or pornographer, for whom women willingly undress, tapping into cultural fantasies about voyeurism, career opportunities, looking, and technological life. Digital cameras rework consumers' interaction with photographic fetishism: "the original

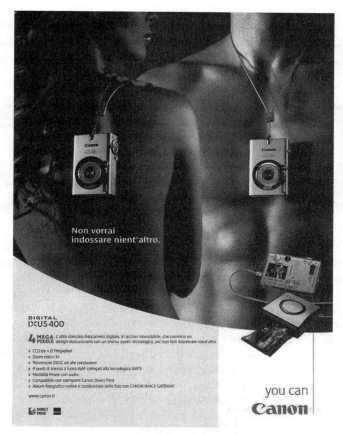

FIG. 13.5. Canon Digital IXUS400 (Italy).

lure of photographic technology has become distanced: the readers [sic] of porn magazines could only imagine themselves as a real glamour photographer, but now they have a real hands-on relationship with technology at the very point of consumption of pornography" (Graham, 1995, pp. 82–83). We do not claim that all digital camera buyers rush home and hook up their sexed-up photos to the Net. Rather, pornography and its insistent production, circulation, and commodification of human images extensively affect the digital photography domain, offering consumers opportunities to become producers of pornography. Furthermore, we argue that these associations foster connections between technological agility and sexual ability, between cutting-edge cameras and cutting-edge sexuality.

Obviously, many ads invoke sexual imagery to inject products and services with meaning. Digital camera ads offer rather blatant examples that

FIG. 13.6.   Digital Camera Girls—a porn site.

help clarify general issues of sex and advertising. We do not contend that these ads are necessarily extreme examples, nor do we argue that they are particularly offensive. Indeed, "it may well be that the most insidious and instrumental forms of domination, subjugation and objectification are produced by mainstream images of women rather than by juridically criminal or obscene ones" (Solomon-Godeau, 1991, p. 237; cf. Kilbourne, 2000). We point to the liminal flows between licit and illicit representational forms, and how each interacts with and informs the production, consumption, and circulation of the other (Lambiase, 2003; Schroeder & Borgerson, 2003).

The digital camera retails to a male world as a pornographic enabling device (see Fig. 13.6). Digital camera ads borrow from popular conventions associated with soft porn and the representations of sexuality—depicted in popular texts such as *Playboy*, porn sites, and sexist advertising. The marketing strategies behind the ads appropriate the pornographic, although the advertisers may contest this, claiming celebratory impulses about socioerotic relationships and consumer desire. These ads function within the visual domain of the fetish; they draw upon liminality, otherness, and photographic techniques to produce spectacular scenes of stereotyped sexuality. Moreover, they can be read as racist, elitist, and sexist, reinforcing power relations from a conservative masculine perspective. They appear at a time when consumer society celebrates reality television and "fly on the wall" documentaries.

Digital photography, like photography before it, profoundly influences the representational realm. Digital technology further disembodies the human form. Moreover, it supports the myth of individual choice (see Fitchett & McDonagh, 2000), with invitations to expose more, add imagination, and fly in the face of censorship. Paradoxically, digital photography does more to confirm a surveillance society and Winokur's (2003) discussion of Foucault's codes of cyberspace and the panopticon than a noncensorship-based consumer society (see also Hackley, 2002).

These ads' messages promote a mode of interacting with others, a way of seeing them, and a method for capturing their image; "photographs do not simply speak of 'the body' but of particular bodies, of social groups and the relationships of power between them" (Henning, 2002, p. 247). Like so many advertising campaigns, these ads unite product and woman within an image of desire. Without contextual analysis, however, these issues fade, and we are left with what appears to be fun, sex-filled, attention-grabbing imagery—pure tabloid titillation. Ads must be looked at from outside the "text": "the problems of oppression, subordination, and objectification do not exclusively reside in the given contents of an image. Images, in other words, do not causally produce a world of female objects and male subjects; rather, they may articulate, naturalize, and confirm an oppressive order whose roots lie elsewhere" (Solomon-Godeau, 1991, p. 221). We turn to broader dimensions of culture, history, and representational conventions to understand how these ads produce compelling, yet controversial images as well as sites for oppositional discourses (see also Desmond, McDonagh, & O'Donohoe, 2000; Holt, 2003).

CONCLUSION

This chapter reviewed photography as information technology, the marketing of digital photography, and how the logic of pornography affects digital camera advertising from an interpretive, interdisciplinary perspective. What we term the logic of pornography concerns how its ideals—including sexual representations made for profit, the commodification of human sexual expression, and the stylized reproductions of traditional sex roles and myths—interact with advertising and consumer culture. Pornographic and illicit representation infiltrates more acceptable, mainstream media forms, infecting it with often troubling visions of social relationships, sexual desires, and representational practice.

Cameras create most advertising imagery, yet few studies within marketing or advertising research employ a sophisticated view of photography, informed by the growing body of photographic writing and visual theory. Largely due to photography's realism, combined with technological and artistic expertise, advertising images produce powerful, persuasive simulations of a real world (cf. Goldman & Papson, 1996). Photography remains inextricably intertwined with our notions of attraction, desirability, and sexuality; marketing campaigns routinely tap into these sensual associations (cf. Dobers & Schroeder, 2001). Photographic conventions, while appearing natural and spontaneous, evolved within historical contexts of visual representation—pornography, glamour photography, and fashion photography each developed its own internal logic and set of practices (Schroeder & Zwick, 2004). As photography theorist Michelle Henning stated, "seeing through the camera is different from seeing without it, and, since photography, seeing is a changed practice" (Henning, 2002, p. 240). Much of the difficulty in comprehending and interpreting photography lies in the medium's surface realism. We must remind ourselves that advertising models in ads are posed, paid, and pampered. Despite their "natural" appearance, advertising images "are not 'reality' but an artfully arranged manipulation of visual elements. Those elements are, however, arranged precisely to arouse desire, fantasy, and longing, to make us want to participate in the world they portray" (Bordo, 1997, p. 122). Digital camera advertising plays upon these conventions, creating compelling, complex images of desire, fetishism, and voyeurism.

Contemporary digital camera branding campaigns reveal the interconnections between photographic technology, pornography, and consumer culture, shedding light on the inexorable intertwinement of sexuality, consumption, and photography. The ubiquitous promise of digital cameras— so small and unnoticeable, hidden within an innocuous cell phone, instantly connected to the Internet—surely illustrates Foucault's panoptic society (Winokur, 2003). Bodies, especially women's bodies, formerly under constant display and scrutiny, are now continuously available as photographic subjects and are digitized voyeuristic images easily appropriated by the World Wide Web, posted at "upskirt" sites, or traded among technological trophy hunters.

At a broader level, these campaigns herald contemporary, sophisticated attitudes toward sexuality, sexual expression, and pornography. Adopting a technologically advanced camera coincides with expressing contemporary attitudes about social conventions and sexual standards. These ads, as many do, make light of sexual relationships, without acknowledging the emotional, physical, political, and cultural complications of sexual activity. They tend to denigrate the specialness of sex and inadvertently place limits on how consumers view sex, sexual expression, visual representation, and human relationships. This ad genre conflates voyeurism, fetishism, and commodification in ways that may be socially harmful.

Marketers appropriate, transform, and harness photography as a dominant communication technology. Ads for photographic products offer complex analytic sites, pulsing with signification. Visual consumption analysis provides important tools for problematizing social relations in consumer society. As information technology diffuses within culture, its purpose, content, and form often evolve under the purview of commercial concerns (see also Schroeder & Borgerson, 2002). What we have called the logic of pornography includes reproduction and reproducibility, which digital photography readily supports, plus the Web enhances via its circulatory power. Within this "logic," capacity to consume magically signifies sexual ability, and technological prowess energizes erotic power.

ACKNOWLEDGMENTS

The first author thanks the Jan Wallanders and Tom Hedelius Foundation for support. Thanks also to Lars Jonsson for his insight into the Siemens Mobile ad, and to Jacob Östberg, Sven Bergvall, and Janet Borgerson for comments on this project.

REFERENCES

Baddeley, G. (2002). *Goth chic: A connoisseur's guide to dark culture.* London: Plexus.

Bordo, S. (1997). *Twilight zones: The hidden life of cultural images from Plato to O.J.* Berkeley: University of California Press.

Borgerson, J. L., & Schroeder, J. E. (2002). Ethical issues of global marketing: Avoiding bad faith in visual representation. *European Journal of Marketing, 36,* 570–594.

Brod, H. (1996). Pornography and the alienation of male sexuality. In L. May, R. Strikwerda, & P. Hopkins (Eds.), *Rethinking masculinity: Philosophical explorations in light of feminism,* 2nd ed. (pp. 237–254). Lanham, MD: Rowman & Littlefield.

Carter, A. (1978). *The Sadeian woman and the ideology of pornography.* New York: Pantheon.

Cone, E. (2002, February). The naked truth about Internet porn. *Wired, 10*(2), 100–103.

Cortese, A. J. (1999). *Provocateur: Images of women and minorities in advertising.* Lanham, MD: Rowman & Littlefield.

Databank. (2000, June 12). Selling sex on the Web. *Newsweek,* 76J.

Desmond, J., McDonagh, P., & O'Donohoe, S. (2000). Counter-culture and consumer society. *Consumption, Markets & Culture, 4*(3), 241–280.

Dimitri, I. (1940). *Kodachrome and how to use it.* New York: Simon & Schuster.

Dines, G., Jensen, R., & Russo, A. (1998). *Pornography: The production and consumption of inequality.* New York: Routledge.

Dobers, P., & Schroeder, J. E. (2001, November). Representing IT: Embodying the electronic economy. Paper presented at the Digital Communities conference, Chicago.

Dougher, S. (2003). *XXX: The power of sex in contemporary graphic design.* Gloucester, MA: Rockport.

Fernbach, A. (2002). *Fantasies of fetishism: From decadence to the post-human.* New Brunswick, NJ: Rutgers University Press.

Fitchett, J., & McDonagh, P. (2000). Relationship marketing, e-commerce and the emancipation of the consumers. In A. Sturdy, I. Grugulis, & H. Wilmott (Eds.), *Customer service* (pp. 100–125). London: Palgrave.

Goffman, E. (1979). *Gender advertisements: Studies in the anthropology of visual communication*. New York: Harper & Row.

Goffman, E. (1997). *The Goffman reader*. Malden, MA: Blackwell.

Goldman, R., & Papson, S. (1996). *Sign wars: The cluttered landscape of advertising*. New York: Guilford.

Graham, B. (1995). The panic button (in which our heroine goes back to the future of pornography). In M. Lister (Ed.), *The photographic image in digital culture* (pp. 77–94). London: Routledge.

Hackley, C. (2002). The panoptic role of advertising agencies in the production of consumer culture. *Consumption Markets & Culture, 5*, 211–230.

Hall, J. (1979). *Dictionary of subjects and symbols in art*, revised ed. Boulder, CO: Westview.

Hall, S. (Ed.) (1997). *Representation: Cultural representations and signifying practices*. London: Sage/Open University Press.

Hamilton, P. (1997). Representing the social: France and Frenchness in post-war humanist photography. In S. Hall (Ed.), *Representation: Cultural representations and signifying practices* (pp. 76–150). London: Sage/Open University Press.

Henning, M. (1995). Digital encounters: Mythical pasts and electronic presence. In M. Lister (Ed.), *The photographic image in digital culture* (pp. 217–235). London: Routledge.

Henning, M. (2002). The subject as object: Photography and the human body. In L. Wells (Ed.), *Photography: A critical introduction* (pp. 217–250). London: Routledge.

Holt, D. B. (2003). What becomes an icon most? *Harvard Business Review*, March, 43–49.

Hughes, D. (2000). The Internet and sex industries: Partners in global sexual exploitation. *Technology & Society*, Spring, 35–42.

Imerge Consulting Group (2003). The worldwide consumer digital camera market forecast and market overview, 2002–2007. Retrieved September 22, 2003, from http://www.imergeconsulting.com.

Kendrick, W. (1996). *The secret museum: Pornography in modern culture*. Berkeley: University of California Press.

Kilbourne, J. (2000). *Can't buy my love: How advertising changes the way we think and feel*. New York: Simon & Schuster.

Kokonis, M. (2002). Postmodernism, hyperreality and the hegemony of spectacle in new Hollywood: The case of the *Truman Show*. Retrieved October 29, 2003, from http://genesis.ee.auth.gr/dimakis/Gramma/7/index_en.html.

Lalvani, S. (1996). *Photography, vision, and the production of modern bodies*. Albany: State University of New York Press.

Lambiase, J. (2003). Sex–online and Internet advertising. In T. Reichert & J. Lambiase (Eds.), *Sex in advertising: Perspectives on the erotic appeal* (pp. 247–269). Mahwah, NJ: Lawrence Erlbaum Associates.

Lippke, R. L. (1995). *Radical business ethics*. Lanham, MD: Rowman & Littlefield.

Lister, M. (2002). Photography in the age of digital imaging. In L. Wells (Ed.), *Photography: A critical introduction* (pp. 303–347). London: Routledge.

McCauley, E. A. (1997). Photography. In S. Barnet (Ed.), *A short guide to writing about art*, 5th ed. (pp. 61–71). New York: Longman.

Marshall, G. (2002, June). Secrets of attraction. *.net, the Internet magazine*, (98), 52–57.

Miklitsch, R. (1998). *From Hegel to Madonna: Towards a general economy of "commodity fetishism."* Albany: State University of New York Press.

Mirzoeff, N. (2002). The subject of visual culture. In N. Mirzoeff (Ed.), *The visual culture reader* (pp. 3–23). New York: Routledge.

Olin, M. (1996). Gaze. In R. S. Nelson & R. Schiff (Eds.), *Critical terms for art history* (pp. 208–219). Chicago: University of Chicago Press.

Oliver, D. (2002, June). Online porn stripped bare. *.net, the Internet magazine*, (98), 47–51.

O'Toole, L. (1999). *Pornocopia: Porn, sex, technology and desire*. London: Serpent's Tail.

Photo Marketing Association (2003). *The path from pixels to prints: The challenge of bringing digital imaging to the mass market*. Jackson, MI: Author.

Pultz, J. (1995). *The body and the lens: Photography 1839 to the present*. New York: Harry Abrams.

Ramamurthy, A. (2002). Constructions of illusion: Photography and commodity culture. In L. Wells (Ed.), *Photography: A critical introduction* (pp. 165–216). London: Routledge.

Reichert, T. (2003). What is sex in advertising? Perspectives from consumer behavior and social science research. In T. Reichert & J. Lambiase (Eds.), *Sex in advertising: Perspectives on the erotic appeal* (pp. 11–38). Mahwah, NJ: Lawrence Erlbaum Associates.

Rijper, E. (2002). *Kodachrome: The American invention of our world 1939–1959*. New York: Delano Greenidge Editions.

Schroeder, J. E. (2000). Édouard Manet, Calvin Klein and the strategic use of scandal. In S. Brown & A. Patterson (Eds.), *Imagining marketing: Art, aesthetics, and the avant-garde* (pp. 36–51). London: Routledge.

Schroeder, J. E. (2002). *Visual consumption*. London: Routledge.

Schroeder, J. E. (2004). Branding the body: Skin and consumer communication. In S. Brown & D. Turley (Eds.), *European advances in consumer research, 6*, 23–28.

Schroeder, J. E., & Borgerson, J. L. (1998). Marketing images of gender: A visual analysis. *Consumption Markets & Culture, 2*(2), 161–201.

Schroeder, J. E., & Borgerson, J. L. (2002). Innovations in information technology: Insights from Italian Renaissance art. *Consumption Markets & Culture, 5*(2), 153–169.

Schroeder, J. E., & Borgerson, J. L. (2003). Dark desires: Fetishism, ontology, and representation in contemporary advertising. In T. Reichert & J. Lambiase (Eds.), *Sex in advertising: Perspectives on the erotic appeal* (pp. 65–87). Mahwah, NJ: Lawrence Erlbaum Associates.

Schroeder, J. E., & Zwick, D. (2004). Mirrors of masculinity: Representation and identity in advertising images. *Consumption Markets & Culture, 7*, 21–52.

Shields, V. R., & Heinecken, D. (2002). *Measuring up: How advertising affects self-image*. Philadelphia: University of Pennsylvania Press.

Slater, D. (1995). Domestic photography and digital culture. In M. Lister (Ed.), *The photographic image in digital culture* (pp. 129–146). London: Routledge.

Slater, D. (2002). Making things real: Ethics and order on the Internet. *Theory, Culture & Society, 19*(5/6), 227–245.

Solomon-Godeau, A. (1991). *Photography at the dock: Essays on photographic history, institutions, and practices.* Minneapolis: University of Minnesota Press.

Stern, B. B. (1991). Two pornographies: A feminist view of sex in advertising. *Advances in Consumer Research, 18,* 384–391.

Stern, B. B., & Schroeder, J. E. (1994). Interpretive methodology from art and literary criticism: A humanistic approach to advertising imagery. *European Journal of Marketing, 28,* 114–132.

Sutherlund, M., & Sylvester, A. K. (2000). *Advertising and the mind of the consumer.* London: Kogan Page.

Szarkowski, J. (1999). *Looking at photographs.* New York: Bulfinch.

Weitman, S. (1998). On the elementary forms of the socioerotic life. *Theory, Culture & Society, 15*(3), 71–110.

Wells, L. (Ed.). (2002). *Photography: A critical introduction.* London: Routledge.

West, S. (Ed.). (1996). *The Bulfinch guide to art history.* New York: Little, Brown.

Williams, L. (1999). *Hard core: Power, pleasure and the frenzy of the visible.* Berkeley: University of California Press.

Winokur, M. (2003). The ambiguous panopticon: Foucault and the codes of cyberspace. Retrieved March 13, 2003, from http://www.ctheory.net [Article A124].

PART III

Sexualizing People

Chapter 14

Erotic Encounters: Female Employees and Promotional Activities

Jacqueline Lambiase

Texas Tech University

The Maserati and Ferrari display at the 2004 Auto Show stood at the center of the Dallas Convention Center, a barely controlled hive of activity just 75 feet from the show's main entrance. Border ropes along the display's perimeter kept people from freely entering the display space. Instead, visitors needed appointments to enter or could wait in line to see the latest Maserati and Ferrari car models. And, a second set of models was just as important to the buzzing success of the display.

Six women in their 20s and 30s served as escorts for visitors wishing to enter the display to learn more about Maserati's and Ferrari's newest cars. All were professional models and actors hired through a local company for the weeklong auto show. They were not experts on foreign automobiles, but good at memorizing a script, and they were an important part of selling the automakers' image to the public. Each new visitor or small group seeking entrance to the display was assigned a personal female attendant dressed in high heels and a closely fitted pantsuit. Once inside, visitors were offered hors d'oeuvres and champagne served by a waiter in white gloves. The booth's atmospherics, like no other at the auto show, generated cocktail-party and call-girl vibes.

Cars and women may be a nostalgic coupling, considering that automakers for years used cheesecake frequently in print advertising. Beyond automakers, many trade-show displays, restaurants, retailers, and companies of all sorts utilize a branding approach that still relies on an old formula. This formula is not that sex sells, but that it both attracts attention and becomes an important part of a brand and its atmospherics, mostly an appeal to enliven lifestyle choices through consumption of the brand. The spectacle at the auto show provides some proof of this marketing assumption.

Spectacle, along with good face-to-face or handshake-to-handshake contact, becomes the goal of many promotional activities. In the Maserati/Ferrari example, signs of exclusivity, including the cars themselves, provide the spectacle. Face-to-face contact is ceded to models and professional actors rather than to auto salesmen and saleswomen. The scene is an inversion of the usual car-buying experience. It is an illusion. Instead of anxious sellers pushing emotional buttons in order to make a sale, anxious spectators—the majority of them men—wait in line for a quite different emotional experience. Eros is mixed into a clever concoction that is part woman, part car.

This qualitative study focuses on the erotic codes and scripts used for many live promotional or selling activities and uses semiotic protocols to interpret these behaviors. First, ethnographic analysis of live promotional events captured descriptions of this erotic code in action, such as the Maserati/Ferrari example above. Based on these observations, the researcher developed story prompts and a topic guide for narrative interviewing of female workers and models. These participants were asked to tell stories about their experiences with promotional activities.

Research questions for the project were these:

- How do companies combine physically attractive employees with sexualized contexts to attract attention, brand their products, and sell merchandise in the marketplace?
- What are the codes and scripts of these sexual appeals in commercial spaces?
- What constitutes sexiness, based on perceptions of promotional professionals and models, as well as the expectations of their employers?

REVIEW OF LITERATURE

Physical Attractiveness

Physical attractiveness research in the fields of social psychology and marketing has contributed many studies that confirm the "beautiful is good" stereotype (Ashmore, Solomon, & Longo, 1996; Dion, Berscheid, & Walster, 1972; Patzer, 1985; Reingen, Ronkainen, & Gresham, 1981). General findings in social psychology conclude that, when compared to people with lower physical attractiveness, people with higher physical attractiveness have greater social power, are better liked, possess more favorable characteristics, and "have different effects on others and receive different responses" in interpersonal relationships (Patzer, 1985, p. 42). This "attractive is good" stereotype is also problematized in terms of a "dark side," when attractive people are seen as self-centered or vain (Dermer & Thiel, 1975; for review, see Eagly, Ashmore, Makhijani, & Longo, 1991).

Differences exist between women and men in their perceptions of physical attractiveness, including that men are more likely to believe that beauty is a subjective judgment, requiring little or no input from others' opinions (Graziano, Jensen-Campbell, Shebilske, & Lundgren, 1993). Men are more likely to "emphasize sexuality in appraising female good looks" (Ashmore, Solomon, & Longo, 1996, p. 1110). Also, men's ratings of women's beauty were found to be especially consistent, and "this consensus probably contributes to the impressive influence of physical attractiveness in social life" (Marcus & Miller, 2003, p. 334). Both men and women, however, link the trait of "sexual warmth" to physical attractiveness in women more than in men (Feingold, 1990, p. 991). This kind of sexualized communication has been studied by symbolic interactionists, who trace how "female-gender role expectations emphasize and reinforce the importance of personal appearances and having romantic partners, but at the same time, [how] society negatively evaluates women who seem too sexually liberated" (Longmore, 1998, p. 49).

Interpersonal Contacts and Personal Selling

In terms of interpersonal contacts, men are more likely than women to perceive interpersonal situations as sexually oriented (Shotland & Craig, 1988). When attractive models are placed within a context for interpersonal exchange, they "contribute in limited but important ways toward increasing a communication's effectiveness" (Joseph, 1982, p. 22). In addition, part-time female employees are believed to have higher communal qualities than men (Eagly & Steffen, 1986). Traditional gender roles may cause women to work harder to appear socially competent, which may also account for "women's greater interest in their personal appearance" (Eagly, Ashmore, Makhijani, & Longo, 1991, p. 122). This chapter is particularly interested in further scrutiny of this cycle of physical attractiveness, sexual contexts, and expected gender roles during communication that is both interpersonal and promotional.

Without a doubt, the "attractive is good" stereotype extends into personal selling contexts. Within these contexts, a "personal selling atmospheric" is created for interactions between sellers and buyers, including the physical selling environment and the physical characteristics of the seller (McElroy, Morrow, & Eroglu, 1990, p. 31). This theoretical model suggests that "salesperson atmospherics can create customer arousal" (p. 38). Furthermore, when "buyers attribute more favorable dispositions to attractive sellers than to unattractive ones," then people were more likely to comply with a request when it came from an attractive person

(Reingen, Ronkainen, & Gresham, 1981, p. 78). In a study of fast-food workers, women were most likely to work at drive-through windows because that task required smiling and deference, and because men did not enjoy "swallowing one's pride and accepting abuse calmly" (Leidner, 1991, p. 163).

A review by the author of current trade-show advice books, as well as of topics discussed at trade-show industry conferences, found that these information sources generally avoid the topics of gender and sexuality, physical attractiveness, and the use of female models as promotional workers. One recommendation suggests bringing nonsales staff members who are "more comfortable initiating conversations with strangers" (Levinson, Smith, & Wilson, 1997, p. 137). Male and female exhibit staff members should wear simple professional clothing that focuses on a business's image, "not on being sexy," with women warned not to "look like floozies, unless the only differentiation your product has is 'the girls in the exhibit'" (Levinson, Smith, & Wilson, 1997, p. 168).

Sexual Scripts

Using scripting theory as a foundation, Simon and Gagnon (1986) developed three levels for considering scripts in terms of sexual behavior: (a) cultural scenarios, which "provide for understandings that make role entry, performance, and/or exit plausible for both self and others" (p. 98); (b) interpersonal scripting, which must be improvised based on cultural scenarios in action; and (c) intrapsychic scripting, a symbolic reorganization of reality that realizes "the actor's many-layered and sometimes multivoiced wishes" (p. 99). Cultural scenarios and intrapsychic scripting are linked when sexual behavior seems "natural," but is in fact embedded in cues from the external environment (p. 106). Negotiations among the three levels may be complex, somewhat flexible, and often simplified into the "very conservative, highly ritualized, or stereotyped character that sexual behavior often takes" (p. 110).

Flirtation is one sexual script interpreted through the cultural scenario, and its tactics demonstrate the ambiguity of Simon and Gagnon's model since flirting allows an actor to assess interest without losing face (Metts & Spitzberg, 1996). Flirtation has been socially ascribed as sexual behavior, even if sexual intercourse is not the ultimate outcome, and flirting may serve "numerous manipulative ends aside from sex" (Metts & Spitzberg, p. 53). One survey of nearly 800 college students found that 66% of the women had used sexual teasing with no interest in culminating the teasing with sexual intercourse, while 65% of the men reported experiencing sexual teasing from women who did not want more than teasing or flirting to occur (Miller & Marshall, 1987).

More broadly, sexual scripts depend upon traditional gender roles in which women act as gatekeepers and men act as initiators of sexual relations (Rose & Frieze, 1993; Ryan, 1988; Simon & Gagnon, 1986). When women are the objects of desire, rather than the subjects who desire, then physical attractiveness is emphasized more for women than for men (Rose & Frieze, 1993). Stereotyped behavior for flirting, dating, and other sexual scripts includes conversation and alcohol consumption (Ryan, 1988), and fleeting glances, smiling, self-grooming, head tilt, exposure of neck (Givens, 1983). Men's proactive behavior typically includes requesting dates, driving, opening doors, and starting sexual interaction such as initial physical contact and kissing, while women's reactive behavior includes grooming, being picked up for the date, and responding to sexual overtures made by men (Rose & Frieze, 1993).

METHOD

Ethnographic analysis of the sexualized or gendered spaces of trade shows, consumer goods displays, retailers, and restaurants was undertaken by the author in 2003–2004 to develop a topic guide and questions for in-depth narrative interviewing of women who work in these spaces. Spaces were considered to be sexualized or gendered when all workers for specific tasks were women, when employees were mostly women and customers were mostly men, or when employees were dressed in form-fitting clothing or other kinds of sexualized dress. Interviews were garnered by contacting a Dallas/Fort Worth-area modeling agency, by seeking participation from students on a Texas university campus, by asking employees at trade shows to participate, and by using a snowball method of obtaining more names from women and men who had been interviewed.

For this study, four interviews were selected from among others in a larger study (Lambiase, 2004), each representing a female worker from a specific area of promotional work: (a) a model and convention specialist for trade shows, (b) a restaurant server and bartender, (c) a retail sales associate, and (d) an assistant to a high-yield broker. To be included in this particular study, each participant answered "yes" to these questions: Do you believe you were hired for this job because of your physical attractiveness? Do you think the use of sexual appeals is (or was) a part of your expected job duties? Beyond these questions, each participant was asked to describe typical working conditions, to tell stories about interactions with customers, and to describe the expectations of their employers about dress codes and the use of sexuality in the workplace. A short demographic profile of each participant is included in Table 14.1; each woman is identified by a fictitious first name to ensure confidentiality.

TABLE 14.1
Female Participants in Study of Erotic Codes Used in Corporate Promotional Activities

Designated Name for Study	Description
"Cathy," convention specialist	A 40-year-old professional model for print advertising and for trade show work, with more than 20 years' experience. Says she is sometimes referred to as a "booth babe."
"Amy," retail sales associate	A 22-year-old woman who worked for Abercrombie & Fitch for 1 year, hired while shopping after a manager said, "Hey, she's cute. Give her an application."
"Gina," restaurant server and bartender	A 22-year-old bartender and server who was hired on the spot without filling out an application. Told by boss to dress, to style hair, and to wear makeup as if "date ready."
"Nicole," assistant to high yield broker	A 23-year-old woman with 2 years of experience, calling herself a "corporate cheerleader" who accompanies clients to sporting events and on overnight trips.

Each participant signed a consent form, which promised her privacy and confidentiality and which stated that the study had been approved by a committee for the protection of human subjects at the author's university. Interviews, which were audiotaped and lasted from 30 minutes to an hour, took place in privacy at a modeling agency office or in the author's campus office.

Texts generated by these interviews were then placed under rhetorical, theme, and semiotic analyses to find patterns of working conditions and to discover both first-order and second-order meanings. Focus was placed on words, phrases, and stories that defined the women themselves, their jobs, their connection to the products or companies involved, and the ways that their sexuality and physical attractiveness had been used to attract customers, to maintain relationships with customers, and to promote brands.

RESULTS

Texts generated by the narrative interviews revealed (a) hiring practices used by these four women's employers, (b) expectations about employee demeanor, (c) expectations about employee dress code, (d) linkages between employee's appearance and corporate branding, and (e) correlations between expected behavior of employees and dating rituals. Analysis also revealed meta discourse used by these four women to discuss and to understand their own subject positions as sexualized employees.

Hiring Practices

Both the restaurant server and retail sales associate were identified as desirable and hired almost on the spot for their jobs. Amy's story was a straightforward case of being identified as a potential employee while she was shopping: "I really wanted to work at Abercrombie because I loved the clothes, and everything, so I went in there one day and I heard some guys say, 'Hey, she's cute, give her an application.'" For the interview, she was told "to wear something Abercrombie," and one of the managers asked her how much she weighed. Amy also discussed how others were screened by managers before hiring:

> After working there a while, and a girl came in, she was kind of heavier set, not fat, but kind of thick, and she came in asking for an application, and he was like, "Does she really think she's going to get a job here?" [And it was] just because she was a little bit bigger.

Gina's story of becoming employed is similar to Amy's. After working as a bartender, she entered Razzoo's, a Cajun food restaurant chain, looking for a job as a server. "I just walked in and said I needed a job," she said. "I never even filled out an application. Just two guys wait tables, two guys as bartenders. . . . They only like girls working for them." When she worked at a previous job as a bartender at a tourist location, Gina said, the manager would watch female customers in the bar and say, "She is so good looking. I need to get her on."

Nicole's hiring as a broker's assistant followed more standard procedures, at least at first. She was the only female employee working with five male brokers in a branch of a firm based in New York. At the interview, she said, there was no mention of nighttime work. "Basically, 8 to 5, I did paperwork kind of stuff, kept up with general stuff in the office. But almost every weekend and sometimes, multiple nights during the week, we'd have client events, entertainment, dinners, games, box seating, and I was always expected to go." After 2 years, Nicole left the firm to return to college, and she was asked to help hire her own replacement. She said she chose five women with degrees in finance who would make strong broker's assistants, and these women were interviewed by the brokers. "Somehow in the interview process, these guys had gotten out of [two of] them they [had been] cheerleaders," she said. Ultimately, the brokers hired someone on Nicole's recommendation, who "was cute, not very attractive" and who worked only 3 months before being fired. The brokers later communicated with Nicole that they could not believe she had "done this to us." Nicole, in the research interview, said that the woman had fit the job description perfectly, but "she didn't do weekends. I'm surprised she didn't sue them. There was no good reason for them to fire her."

Cathy, a longtime convention specialist, has had many more hiring experiences, since she relies on modeling photographs and her convention resume to garner dozens of short-term jobs in a year. She explained the hiring process in this way:

> My [management agency] is very good about submitting information and being able to talk through what [the client is] looking for. Some of it is just an age thing. "We want 20- to 25-year-old girls," and boom, that's it. Or "We want someone over 30, no matter what" because they know the demographics of who's going to be at the convention, and what their background is or what their theme is, and they are still playing a part for them.

Cathy said companies with trade-show displays sometimes do want to hire "a headturner," but that "for conventions, you've got to be more than that, because you have to speak. There's nothing worse than having a gorgeous girl surrounded by men . . . because then it becomes very difficult to sort out who's serious about their business."

Expectations About Employee Demeanor

Cathy said several times during the narrative interviewing process that a convention specialist needed to be knowledgeable about a company's basic information, "playful and open to everybody," and then aware of when to direct a prospective client to a senior company executive for discussions of high-dollar contracts. "You don't want the same personalities [handling both tasks]," she said. Some companies, she said, may expect a woman to dress suggestively, while keeping up "a cold front," which is "missing a big opportunity. You can still be courteous and still draw the line on being professional and still be dressed very sexy."

At her Abercrombie & Fitch location in the upper Midwest, Amy said, managers expected sales associates to be "cold." Other retailers usually expect employees to approach customers in a friendly manner, Amy said, but at Abercrombie & Fitch "you do not approach your customer, you wait until they approach you. You walk around with a stuck-up, bitchy look, don't say thank you, you just run the credit card and say 'here you go.'" When asked if that expectation might have been the decision of a local manager, Amy said a friend had the same experience as an employee in California and that she had observed that behavior in southern stores, too.

Opposite of the cold demeanor is the expectation of Gina's employers at the bar to interact with customers in a flirtatious way, or beyond, with direct sexualized contact. "People all the time were taking body shots off of me," Gina said, which entails customers drinking from glasses wedged between her breasts or nestled in her navel, while she lays on the bar. "And if it brings in money, [the manager] is all about making sure that everyone is happy. That's in the service industry in general. You're not supposed to tell the customer no." In Nicole's experience in the investment industry, she knew clearly the expectations about her demeanor on the job. When attending events with clients, Nicole "met a lot of other corporate cheerleaders . . . they're pretty, they're peppy, and they're pumped about the company." She was expected to "talk with [clients] semi-intelligently, not about business, because you didn't want to talk about business."

Expectations About Employee Dress Code

The brokers bought gifts to upgrade the appearance of their assistant, Nicole, presenting her with a Kate Spade purse, visits to spas, and other "very expensive things," she said. "I was like, 'Hey thanks, I could never afford that on my own.'" Once the purse was presented to Nicole, she was expected to carry it daily, even though she had wanted to "save it for special occasions." "They said, 'No, we think you need to be carrying [the new purse],'" she said. For one event, Nicole's boss asked her what she had planned to wear and when she replied "a pantsuit," he asked her, "Don't you want to wear a skirt?" Later, when she appeared at the event in the pantsuit, he said, "Oh, I thought you were going to wear a skirt." Just after she started working at the brokerage firm, Nicole was presented with a gift certificate for free tanning, which the brokers claimed she had won while she was at lunch. When Nicole questioned them about how that was possible, "they kind of joked about it, [saying] 'We noticed you were kind of pale, and summer's coming up.'"

Dress codes for the retail and restaurant workers were also part of an unwritten organizational culture enforced by management suggestions. At Abercrombie & Fitch, sales associates were required to wear the company's clothing, but nothing off the sales racks. "Sometimes you had to show a little skin," Amy said, "your stomach a little bit, for women, and your clothes couldn't be too baggy. If you had baggy pants on, you had to have a little tight shirt on." Men at the store were "preppy," and women were "sexy and sporty." To show off the clothes, "you have to be good looking," Amy said, "and you have to have a good body." Even on the coldest winter days, Amy said, she was expected to wear tiny, tight T-shirts.

For Gina, the restaurant had an official dress code that required a certain style of jeans from the Gap, but an unwritten dress code was also enforced.

How would she put the unwritten code into words? "Look good, look like you'd look if you were going out to impress someone, to find a guy, or if you're seeing one and going out," Gina said. "Date ready. When you walk in, they say 'date ready,' you have to fix your hair, you have to wear makeup." When Gina worked as a bartender at a tourist hotspot, women working for beer companies would visit several times a month, and she described their appearance:

> They're wearing skin-tight black leather-looking pants, little bitty shirts with their whole stomach showing, and they're real low cut, and most of them have huge boobs and fake blond hair. And they just walk around, sometimes they have free beer . . . I cannot look at them, I'm like, oh my gosh, because they are above and over the top.

These beer-company representatives dressed consistently in the same kind of oversexed uniform, Gina said.

A convention specialist, on the other hand, wears a variety of clothing depending on the temporary job's requirements, usually handled through a management agency. Sometimes, Cathy said, she wears "a business suit, because even in a business suit, I still have my legs looking really good with my killer high heels, the sexiest shoes I can wear. But not to come across as that, because my look is so conservative, [with] my skirt an inch above the knee because I might need to sit down." She said it is important to "look a step above the person just walking the show floor, because some of those business women look sharp and put together and their skirts are short and tight." One request Cathy received was quite unusual, however:

> I had a client fax something that was very bizarre. I had to have a beige business suit, that looked very conservative. Now most of the time, like I said, [suits] are a little bit more fitted. He wanted a blue shirt underneath it, and of all things he wanted a blindfold because he wanted me to walk around and I had to be able to see through the blindfold . . . it was one of the technical companies, and it was so funny, and I was dressed so conservative.

Wearing this outfit along with the blindfold, Cathy was expected to walk the aisles of the trade show, handing participants a flyer asking whether they "were going blindly through some new regulations" and would be in need of legal assistance from the booth's attorneys, she said.

Employees' Appearance and Corporate Branding

At the tourist hotspot and bar, Gina wore tight T-shirts and was asked to arrive early on weekends so that she and another female bartender could first walk through the streets, passing out brochures and wearing the bar's name on the T-shirts. Only young women were assigned this promotional duty, she said. In addition, "they put us in the middle of an ad, to use us as part of [their image]," Gina said. "Bad ass music, bad ass beers, and these two girls are working here." Alcohol or alcohol companies, she said, often use sexual appeals to sell products. The restaurant employs attractive women, Gina said, for much the same reason, but "in finer dining places, they aren't really like that. They have a whole different marketing strategy."

On the corporate side, the brokerage firm coupled business with the presence of women. "It was just babysitting men all the time," Nicole said. "I met a ton of assistants, people with these great titles and that's not what they did . . . that's mainly a man's field and that's what they want. They want pretty girls around them all day long. They talk money all day, and at night, they want to be around pretty women."

For Cathy at trade shows, guidelines for dressing and behavior are dictated by the company and its brand. "With Ford, we wore [khaki shorts] with very little makeup, with sneakers," she said, "and what I made sure was my legs were tanned and if you can't wear makeup, your hair has got to look great. There's a way to look polished and look like I'm having fun." The use of attractive convention specialists definitely reflects a company's image, she said. "That's what sells every TV commercial—good-looking women. And also the twist on having some fun." Alcohol companies are one example of coupling beautiful, happy people with products. "They just want people to have a good time," Cathy said, "and to associate their liquor product with [people] having a good time." Often at trade shows, she said, "you are just kind of a prop or an accessory to their company."

Correlations Between Expected Behavior of Female Employees and Dating Rituals

Three of the workers in this study served, at least some of the time, as components of a party scene: Cathy, the convention specialist; Gina, the bartender and wait staff member; and Nicole, the broker's assistant. Nicole and the brokers provided party atmospherics at several events, dinners, and sporting events every week and often on extended weekend trips with clients. "[The company] took care of my room, a really nice room . . . and I had a driver," Nicole said of a trip to New York City. "We had clients, and they would say, 'Where are you staying? We'll meet you at the bar for drinks,' so since you were staying at a nice hotel, then they could meet you at your hotel." In San Diego, the brokers' group "chartered a boat, stayed in an expensive hotel, with thousands and thousands of dollars spent on trips, and there's a lot of weird stuff on expenses. I was never asked to do anything inappropriate [because they would drop me off first], but they would almost always end up in titty bars at the end of a day."

At first, Nicole said, the party life was fun. "That was a major hook for me, the money," she said. "To me, single female, no degree, this was great. At that time, I didn't care too much ... sure I'll tag along, and it was fun for a few months, but then it wasn't a gift. It was 'Hey, you're going on this trip.' I was expected to do those things. It wasn't a perk anymore, it was an expectation."

At trade shows, the booth and its atmospherics may be "a showpiece for [a company's] regular clients," said Cathy, who says that booth visitors make requests such as "Can I bring my friends back?," "Can we take pictures and email them?," and "Can we come back later?" They may also ask for her phone number or ask, "Where are you going tonight?" Cathy, who is married, said she would never meet with participants after a show, but she says booth workers do not have to offend visitors by turning them down. "Some of them are just there and that's just their personality to hit on women," she said. "And especially if a girl is having fun and looks like they'd be the fun type—we make them believe that we just love what we're doing."

After working at several restaurants and bars, Gina said, she has learned that a casual restaurant with a bar scene is likely to hire attractive women as both wait staff and bartenders, "because more men go in there, go in to hang out at the bars." At Razzoo's, where "date ready" is the watchword, managers are pleased when a female wait staff member has "regulars who would ask to sit in our sections." One incident related to customer relationships at the restaurant was unpleasant, though, Gina said:

> I had a guy come in, and it totally freaked me out. He came in after we closed, and there was nobody in the restaurant. He sat at the bar, he was talking to my manager, and he said [that I] was his waitress tonight. He wanted to talk with his waitress. [The manager said to me], "He's cute, go talk to him," and I said, "No." She said, "I'm not going to go out there and tell him to leave. He's our guest." And I said, "No, go tell him to leave, [because] this is so weird." So, I had to go talk to him and tell him, "Hi, how's it going," just because she [wouldn't] tell him to go.

Again, Gina commented, the service industry is about making customers happy.

For Amy, the retail associate at Abercrombie & Fitch, no such demands were made. Her implicit guidelines from management, however, were to play customer relationships as hard to get, as "stuck-up and bitchy."

Meta-Discourse About Their Roles as Sexualized Workers

Each of the four women expressed at least brief comments about their positions as employees who had been sexualized or placed in sex-tinged working atmospheres. Amy, the retail associate, said that after a year of working for Abercrombie & Fitch, "that was enough." When she heard one young girl wanting to dress like the style worn on a mannequin, Amy said she thought to herself, "You do not want to look like that. If I had a kid, I definitely wouldn't want to bring them in there."

Gina said that in her experience as a restaurant server, "I think that sex sells." When a table of men and a table of women come into the restaurant, she would rather wait on the men, "in a heartbeat, because I would have a better chance of getting more money from them." In a more upscale restaurant not focused on the bar scene, she said, then tables of men and tables of women would tip about the same.

The other two women in the study offered different insights into their subject positions as sexualized employees. Nicole, the broker's assistant, said after a while, she realized that "I wasn't going anywhere [as an employee]. I was exactly where they wanted me to be" in terms of working hard during the day and being constantly available in the evenings and on weekends for meeting with customers. While some of the men were "good guys," most of them "are good at business but bad at life—it's wild," she said. "I would say that it's disappointing, that it's bad that this is how it is. I don't think it's going to change a lot."

Cathy, with many more years of experience in the working world, was more philosophical. She says that some women working as contract employees at trade shows think that "their looks will get them by." But her professionalism, and that of her management agency, sets a high standard for her performance as a convention specialist. Before a show opens, she studies her note cards like an actor memorizing a script, so that she will know the basics of the company and the names of its executives who are present at the show. "That way, I know ahead of time, off the tip of my tongue, if someone comes up and asks if so-and-so is at this show," she said. And if a female convention specialist doesn't professionally approach the job, then she's "sitting there going, 'I don't know, I'm just a booth babe, uh, it's not my problem . . . am I pretty enough?" Cathy said facetiously. Her critique of this strategy is sound, theoretically, because "saleswomen who were perceived to act in accordance with the gender stereotypes were also perceived to be less effective on the job (Comer & Jolson, 1991, p. 56).

DISCUSSION AND CONCLUSIONS

All of the women interviewed for the study sensed not only that they benefited from their physical attractiveness by being hired for jobs, but also that they and their jobs were defined and perhaps limited by that same attractiveness. While Gina derived some feelings of power by using her sexuality to gain higher tips from tables of men or to serve drinks in provocative ways, she also was pressured to use those same tactics when it was not her choice to do so, when her manager forced her to talk with a male customer after hours. Amy, the sales associate, simply tired of working through her body to sell a company's clothing and image, which she had slowly come to see as exploitive and inappropriate.

Nicole felt trapped by her role as a company escort for the brokers' business prospects, even while she took pride in her daytime work as an assistant who was successful despite the fact that she had not yet earned a college degree. Although Nicole's official job title designated her as a broker's assistant, she often served as a kind of consort for the brokers themselves, who presented her with expensive gifts while placing huge demands on her free time. Cathy's experiences as a convention specialist belie the flatness of that job title, for she acknowledged being used to attract attention and to serve as an escort or gatekeeper for executives in the booth. Her years of experience, however, had given her a repertoire of responses to defend herself against unwanted queries from male customers.

In all, the job titles and official policies governing these women's jobs are out of alignment with management's expectations for performance and appearance. In at least one of these cases, Nicole's, she was led to believe the job was about its 8-to-5 duties, but she soon discovered the subtextual or second-order requirements of her job description. She needed a tan, an expensive purse, and other accoutrements to fulfill hidden job requirements that made her into an objectified employee. Cathy experienced the most straightforward hiring experience of the four women, since her jobs were handled by a management company, but even she had to navigate a fine line between friendly attractiveness and too much sex appeal. As described above, once she was required to walk around wearing a blindfold, which is a sign for fetishized sexual behavior usually conducted in much more intimate settings than a trade show. Dressed in that way, Cathy was the object of voyeurs much more overtly than in her usual booth duties and she was powerless to look back. Gina's duties as a walking billboard for her bartending job meant that her body served as the real message, cloaked as it was under a tight-fitting T-shirt that was emblazoned with the bar's name. Amy's body, too, was part of the message and branding for Abercrombie & Fitch—like Gina and Cathy, her body signified the brand.

These sex-tinged commercial encounters mirror private dating rituals and support the theories posited by scholars who see women as gatekeepers in these rituals and men as initiators of contact (Rose & Frieze, 1993; Ryan, 1988; Simon & Gagnon, 1986). In this study's narrative examples, women were gatekeepers not only of their companies through service duties or entertainment assignments, but they were also in several cases gatekeepers of their own bodies, allowing or disallowing access according to their levels of comfort through body shots, photographs, or suggestions by men of private encounters. While these women's sexuality may have empowered them to gain employment and to attract attention for their companies, their male customers picked up cues from atmospherics of these sexualized commercial spaces to initiate further sexualized contact within and outside of the spaces.

Furthermore, these stories provide evidence of Simon and Gagnon's (1986) three-level theory for considering scripts in terms of sexual behavior. Two of these levels, cultural scenarios and intrapsychic scripting, are linked when ritualized or stereotyped sexual behavior seems "natural," but is in fact embedded in cues from the external environment (p. 106). Environments or personal selling "atmospherics" (McElroy, Morrow, & Eroglu, 1990, p. 31) are intended to spark customer arousal through emotions, and these environments have been carefully crafted by the corporate spaces described by the four female workers in this study. Sanctioned flirting or sexualized contact did occur in these commercial environments, as one part of the cultural scenario, allowing customers to assess interest without losing face (Metts & Spitzberg, 1996) and allowing these women, at least most of the time, to act as gatekeepers of their own sexuality.

Implications and Limitations

The stories told by these four women may be seen as case studies, which often are used to illuminate and to support or to generalize theory (Yin, 1994), as in the connections made between their narratives and sexual scripting and dating rituals. Of course, like all qualitative research, these narratives are not generalizable to populations but instead serve as examples of behavior that is sanctioned by these particular employers and that is a hint of corporate patterns in the use of sexual appeals across a variety of industries. In addition, measures of external validity may be found for these women's stories. Abercrombie & Fitch's hiring practices for its "brand representatives" or sales associates have resulted in a class-action lawsuit concerning racial discrimination filed in November 2003 and in investigative journalistic accounts of its demands for physical attractiveness, including CBS News' *60 Minutes* in December 2003 (for review, see "Top stories," n.d.). Financial services firms such as Morgan Stanley, Smith Barney, Merrill Lynch, and others have also faced lawsuits and paid settlements resulting from allegations of sexual harassment and sexual discrimination, with women comprising just 15% of brokers in such firms (Thornton, 2004).

Through narrative and theme analyses, this study shows how four female employees experienced their employers' efforts to combine physically attractive women with sexualized contexts to attract attention, brand their products, and sell merchandise. The codes of sexualized dress, entertainment environments, and flirtatious behavior may not have conformed with written policies at these companies, but these women's testimony reveals the powerful hidden directives that management issued to get female employees to conform to sexualized atmospherics in these commercial space. Through these directives, these women became objectified employees, and sexual appeals were intentionally used hand-in-hand with more traditional, sanctioned selling behaviors to build a brand and to attract attention.

ACKNOWLEDGMENT

The author expresses thanks to Blake Morgan of the University of North Texas for his assistance with this project.

REFERENCES

Ashmore, R., Solomon, M. R., & Longo, L. (1996). Thinking about fashion models' looks: A multidimensional approach to the structure of perceived physical attractiveness. *Personality and Social Psychology Bulletin, 22*(11), 1083–1104.

Comer, L. B., & Jolson, M. A. (1991). Perceptions of gender stereotypic behavior: An exploratory study of women in selling. *Journal of Personal Selling and Sales Management, 11*(1), 43–59.

Dermer, M., & Thiel, D. L. (1975). When beauty may fail. *Journal of Personality and Social Psychology, 24*, 1168–1176.

Dion, K., Berscheid, E., & Walster, E. (1972). What is beautiful is good. *Journal of Personality and Social Psychology, 24*, 285–290.

Eagly, A. H., Ashmore, R. D., Makhijani, M. G., & Longo, L. C. (1991). What is beautiful is good, but . . . : A meta-analytic review of research on the physical attractiveness stereotype. *Psychological Bulletin, 110*(1), 109–128.

Eagly, A. H., & Steffen, V. J. (1986). Gender stereotypes, occupational roles, and beliefs about part-time employees. *Psychology of Women Quarterly, 10*, 252–262.

Feingold, A. (1990). Gender differences in effects of physical attractiveness on romantic attraction: A comparison across five research paradigms. *Journal of Personality and Social Psychology, 59*(5), 981–993.

Givens, D. B. (1983). *Love signals*. New York: Crown.

Graziano, W. G., Jensen-Campbell, L. A, Shebilske, L. J., & Lundren, S. R. (1993). Social influence, sex differences, and judgments of beauty: Putting the interpersonal back in interpersonal attraction. *Journal of Personality and Social Psychology, 65*(3), 522–531.

Joseph, W. B. (1982). The credibility of physically attractive communicators: A review. *Journal of Advertising, 11*(3), 15–24.

Lambiase, J. (2004). [Narrative interviewing of trade show participants, managers, and employees of other promotional activities]. Unpublished raw data.

Leidner, R. (1991). Serving hamburgers and selling insurance: Gender, work, and identity in interactive service jobs. *Gender and Society, 5*(2), 154–177.

Levinson, J. C., Smith, M. S. A., & Wilson, O. R. (1997). *Guerrilla trade show selling: New unconventional weapons and tactics to meet more people, get more leads, and close more sales.* New York: Wiley.

Longmore, M. A. (1998, February). Symbolic interactionism and the study of sexuality. *Journal of Sex Research, 35*(1), 44–58.

Marcus, D. K., & Miller, R. S. (2003). Sex differences in judgments of physical attractiveness: A social relations analysis. *Personality and Social Psychology Bulletin, 29*(3), 325–335.

McElroy, J. C., Morrow, P. C., & Eroglu, S. (1990). The atmospherics of personal selling. *Journal of Personal Selling & Sales Management, 10*(Fall 1990), 31–41.

Metts, S., & Spitzberg, B. H. (1996). Sexual communication in interpersonal contexts: A script-based approach. In B. R. Burleson (Ed.), *Communication yearbook 19* (pp. 49–91). New Brunswick, NJ: International Communication Association.

Miller, B., & Marshall, J. C. (1987). Coercive sex on the university campus. *Journal of College Student Personnel, 28*, 38–47.

Patzer, G. L. (1985). *The physical attractiveness phenomena.* New York: Plenum.

Reingen, P. H., Ronkainen, I. A., & Gresham, L. G. (1981). Consequences of the physical attractiveness stereotype in buyer–seller interactions: Affect, intention and behavior. In P. H. Reingen and A. G. Woodside (Eds.), *Buyer seller interactions: Empirical research and normative issues* (pp. 75–87). Chicago: American Marketing Association.

Rose, S., & Frieze, I. H. (1993). Young singles' contemporary dating scripts. *Sex Roles, 28*(9/10), 499–509.

Ryan, K. M. (1988). Rape and seduction scripts. *Psychology of Women Quarterly, 12*, 237–245.

Shotland, R. L., & Craig, J. M. (1988). Can men and women differentiate between friendly and sexually interested behavior? *Social Psychology Quarterly, 51*(1), 66–73.

Simon, W., & Gagnon, J. H. (1986). Sexual scripts: Permanence and change. *Archives of Sexual Behavior, 15*(2), 97–120.

Thornton, E. (2004, September 20). Fed up and fighting back: After years of discrimination, women on Wall Street are turning up the heat. *Business Week Online.* Retrieved September 30, 2004, from http://www.businessweekasia.com/magazine/content/04_38/b3900111_mz020.htm.

Top stories (n.d.). Retrieved September 30, 2004, from http://www.abercrombielawsuit.com/news.html.

Yin, R. (1994). *Case study research: Design and methods.* Thousand Oaks, CA: Sage.

The Fetishization of People and Their Objects: Using Lovemaps to View "Style" From the *New York Times Magazine*

Stephen J. Gould

Baruch College, The City University of New York

> For that matter, how can we think of fetishism without the impact of cities, of certain streets and parks, of redlight districts and "cheap amusements," or the seductions of department store counters, piled high with desirable and glamorous goods ... ? To me, fetishism raises all sorts of issues concerning shifts in the manufacture of objects, the historical and social specificities of control and skin and social etiquette, or ambiguously experienced body invasions and minutely graduated hierarchies. (Rubin & Butler, 1994, p. 79)

The history of the fetish is probably as old as history itself. However, its presence and even its prevalence in advertising are not well heralded or understood. Nor has the fetish been considered in relation to people who are themselves "the fetish." This chapter aims to remedy these deficiencies by considering fetishization as a theoretical process of representation, since sexually charged consumer phenomena are embodied in fetishized advertising. The sexualized fetishization phenomenon in advertising simulates that in everyday life. This is not to say that fetishization is altogether sexual and, as noted in the quote above, may apply to any form of projection onto an object and related practices. Indeed, the renowned psychoanalyst Jacques Lacan (1968) indicated that projected unconscious desire inhabits (and fetishizes through) all language and thought so that our understandings of objects are framed in terms of fetish. With respect to sexuality, the traditional psychoanalytic view has dealt with the process whereby individuals ritualistically displace sexual feelings toward other people to an object, the fetish, as well as therapeutic processes to void certain fetishes (e.g., Abraham, 1959). A nontherapeutic extension of this view with respect to advertising is found in the work of Schroeder and Borgerson (2003), who suggested that the fetish is a psychological phenomenon which directs sexual energy somewhere other than to the genitals of another person.

Here, I further draw on a perspective based on the fetish and pornographic communities, which moves beyond material objects to ways in which various types of people are objectified personally, on the Internet, or through other media. For example, Wise and Kalyanam (2000) described the case of a man who became attracted to amputee women while in his teens through looking at pictures of them in his physician father's textbooks. His amputee fetishism, as it is called, led him into various sexual adventures and the collection of pornography related to this fetish. This case also illustrates how people can trace the evolution of their fetish from an early age and compose a narrative describing their fetish acquisition. Finally, whereas amputee fetishism may not be that familiar to many people, it is typical in its treating of a type of person as a fetish.

Similar to this illustrative case, pornography explicitly labels as fetishes people's preferences for different sexual types. For example, pornographic Internet sites are promoted based on fetish types such as ethnicity (e.g., European, African American, Mexican), age (old, young), relationship (e.g., wife, husband, lover), sexual orientation (e.g., straight, gay, lesbian), lifestyle (e.g., rich, poor, Yuppie, blue-collar, promiscuous, virginal, sexually aggressive), degree of fame (e.g., celebrity, amateur), attractiveness (beautiful, ugly), body size (e.g., tall, short), bodily characteristics (e.g., size of sexual organs, fat, thin), or states of being (e.g., pregnancy). Related fetish processes and objects include such things as different types of physical sex (vaginal, oral, anal), different sexual positions, applying various styles of adornment (e.g., bejeweled or not), displaying various states and styles of dress or undress, different sensory stimuli (visual, aural, olfactory), bondage, domination, sadomasochism, and the use of sex toys and ritual sexual objects (e.g., dildos, whips; for example, see Lance, this volume). On the basis of these types and processes, it is argued that in using pornography consumers match themselves with the types of people and processes they find desirable (c.f. Mosher, 1988). Indeed, when viewed from this perspective, any sexual content that objectifies and draws consumers to sexual types may be seen as involving fetishes, regardless of its conventionality.

Moreover, Schroeder and Borgerson (2003) discussed photography itself as a fetish expressing the viewer's desire. But, I also consider any or all media as fetishized when they depict a consumer's sexual desires (c.f. Lillie, 2002). Often, this perspective takes the form of rendering females as fetish objects for the male gaze as when, for instance, Lara Croft is fetishized in computer games (Schleiner, 2001). Most important, fetishes can consist of people, especially in terms of depicting a certain type; the objects adorning or surrounding the person; the discourses applied; and the medium in which people, objects, and discourses are displayed. In fact, generally the combination of these elements comprises common fetishes in advertising. As Lillie (2002) noted, the "carnal density" of sexualities is fetishized with respect to specific media and discourses. In that regard, sexualized media content is a fetishization by both its producer and consumer. Advertising producers aim to create mimetic desire (Zorach, 2001), in which the ad attempts to induce the consumer to imitate the depicted narrative by projecting herself into the scene—to fetishize the scene in terms of arousal and desire. Thus, the fetish and fetishization process as I conceive them include not only the traditionally defined fetish object in which people invest sexual energy, but also reflect a broadened multilevel theorization informed by both sex research and the pornographic-fetish community in which types of people are fetishized, as well as by media research that defines people in fetishistic terms.

This process is illustrated in the remainder of this chapter by considering prototypical images placed in the Sunday *Style* section of the *New York Times Magazine*. The *Style* section runs a series of related photographs involving stylish clothing and upscale products, embedded in editorial content. The section should be seen as a hybrid promotional tool in which editorial copy and images resemble advertising in a format similar to product placements (Balasubramanian, 1994). Since it resembles advertising, this promotional editorial content lends itself to analysis using the concept of the advertising lovemap.

TOWARD A THEORY OF FETISHIZATION AND LOVEMAPS

I begin by discussing the theoretical concept of the lovemap, which I have employed as the central organizing principle of consumer sexually related behavior and which both includes and helps to map the fetish (Gould, 1991, 1992, 1995, 2003). Lovemaps frame how one approaches sexuality in terms of what to do, feel, and think. From a marketing communications viewpoint, the lovemap can be viewed at various levels. These include the general, consumer, advertising, and cultural consumer lovemaps. As named and developed by leading sex researcher John Money (1984, 1986), the general lovemap concerns all aspects of an individual's sexuality as a biopsychological concept. As derived from his work by Gould (1995), the consumer lovemap involves all aspects of an individual's sexuality that have consumption components, such as purchases and use of products related to attracting a mate or to enhancing one's sexuality or the sex act itself. The advertising lovemap describes how consumers respond to sexuality in advertising (Gould, 2003). Specific themes or targets enter into this strategy, since men and women respond differently to sexual ads and advertisers target them with different ads corresponding to their gendered lovemaps. The advertising lovemap may also be used by advertisers as a blueprint for how consumers respond to sexual advertising. The cultural consumer lovemap concerns how consumers within a culture or unit of culture (i.e., subcultures, lifestyle groups) respond to sexuality in consumption and related advertising terms (e.g., cultural differences in the display of sexual explicitness in ads).

Given these various levels of the lovemap, the fetish is only one component—but a powerful and pervasive component—for constructing meaning in advertising. In addition, the fetish can become sexually charged in its own right or serve as an accessory to the sex act with a sexual partner. For example, a shoe may become an object of sexual arousal without the presence of a foot or it may be an accessory to the sex act with another person. In either case, the shoe is fetishized. However, more radically, I argue that beyond relations with nonhuman physical objects, humans and human types may also be fetishized. This point draws from the universe of the fetish world, which as a culture of sexual practices often depicted in pornography, parallels and shadows both popular culture and the advertising universe, and which influences behavior in fetish terms. As noted above, this fetish world is not merely one that fetishizes objects such as whips or shoes, but also one that includes types of people and sexualized fetish processes. Thus, what might be regarded as "normal" or everyday sexual behavior is just as susceptible of being fetishized as would more extraordinary fetishized behavior. Needless to say, the world of advertising fetishism is more subtle than its parallel pornographic cousin, but this does not mean an absence of connection. These two worlds evolve in tandem, and trends in one may influence the other (for example, see Elliott, 2003). Most important is that the fetish world and its portrayal in pornography suggest the possibility of mapping fetishism in advertising by various types of people and fetish processes. However, these types may or may not correlate with those in the fetish world per se. In fact, advertising fetishes may indicate an expansion of the concept of fetishism rather than a diminution.

The interplay between advertising and pornography is further explained from a number of perspectives ranging from associative learning to arousal transfer. Whereas a full explication of how fetishes function in the lovemaps is beyond the scope of this chapter, I address one salient approach implicated in all lovemaps, namely that various parts of speech can be implicated in the process of simulative representation. A particularly useful part of speech to consider is metonymy, referred to here as the contiguity of one thing to another, which explains how relationships are formed in a person's mind (Schleifer, 1990). For example and similar to findings in sexual lovemap research (Money, 1984, 1986), a child may encounter people engaging in sex, notice an object such as a shoe or one of the people as especially arousing, and fixate on that object or person-type as sexual, thus forming a fetish about it. This is a metonymic process in that through a process of thought, the shoe or person-type is sexualized through emotional linkages and sexual energy displacement.

With respect to advertising—and similar to other textual representations in film, magazines, and books (unless they themselves are the fetish)—the fetish is a distal representation of the sexual act although it serves to arouse actual sexual feelings and thoughts. More to our point here and as noted earlier, Schroeder and Borgerson (2003) suggested that photos with sexual material can be treated as fetishes. Metonymic processes are central to understanding such fetishization in advertising, not to mention the overall relationship between advertising and sexuality. Fetishes may emerge almost incidentally from the juxtaposition of a sexually charged someone or something with people or things lacking a sexual charge, such as a sexy model shown with a product. Of course, these processes may occur long before the fetish appears in an ad. In fact, ads often reenact the process of metonymic fetishization by building on the ongoing culturally embedded relationships between sexuality and fetishized people or objects. Thus, over time, ads refer to sexual play and sexual play is informed by advertising and the products in it. In a sense, these processes also may be linked to sign play and the formation of disembodied signs in which the original source of the sign is lost or forgotten (Baudrillard, 1983). For example, an adornment worn by a model may carry its original sign-meanings from the past that are lost in the consumer's consciousness but remain active in arousing her.

Beyond parts of speech, fetishization may be seen to comprise a process of narrativity such that each fetish embodies a story (c.f. Wise & Kalyanam, 2000). A fetish is not a mere object, but suggests a network of stories that is part of the fetish beholder's consumer lovemap. For example, a person who has fetishized shoes has a series of stories of how shoes function to arouse him or her and may have various objects, characters, situations, and plots in these stories. That person may have an original story of how shoes became a fetish as well as developmental stories on their use as sexual objects. Evidence for these stories appears in research (Wise & Kalyanam, 2000), as well as anecdotally within the fetish community when participants graphically describe their personal fetishes.

On a cultural level, consumer lovemaps embody narratives that cultures and subcultural groups share. In this instance, intertextuality indicates references that one narrative makes to another, in effect rendering our understanding of fetishism as a hybridized phenomenon. Thus, reflecting the multiple cultural sites of fetishism, fetishism in advertising is linked to fetish art, mainstream cinema and television, pornography, and contrasting narratives from everyday life, among others. For example, a fetishized narrative on shoes may refer to more everyday stories about the ordinary use of shoes. This point is illustrated in examples from the *Style* section of the *New York Times Magazine*, where many references between fetish narratives and other areas of life are made. Within the *Style* section, there are at least three types of intertextual fetishization: (1) the intertextuality of fetishized images and sex play, including pornography; (2) the intertextuality of everyday situations with fetishized advertising; and (3) the intertextuality of people as types and advertising. In many cases, these intertextualities overlap, but it still is useful to identify them as guides to creating this sort of editorial content and its intertextual relationship with advertising campaigns.

FETISH EXEMPLARS FROM THE *STYLE* SECTION OF THE *NEW YORK TIMES MAGAZINE*

The blurring of entertainment and advertising that has been noted as a promotional trend (Balasubramanian, 1994) is very apparent in the *Style* section of the *New York Times Magazine*. Within this section, various tongue-in-cheek expressions of humor and mock seriousness are laid out in a framework of overarching sophistication. A high degree of context is absent as readers are expected to be familiar with obscure references and inside jokes. Often, however, these photographs are accompanied by narrative text that supplements scenarios in the images and serves as a rich description of the hip entertainment provided. In fact, the text can be read like any other article, only that in this day of blurred lines between editorial and commercial speech it serves as a kind of lifestyle advertising. Such is the background for interpreting the advertising in this medium and for helping to gauge the particular forms of fetishism displayed.

The *Style* section is largely devoted to clothing fashion, especially women's, but its range extends beyond that. For example, some of these sections have been devoted to accessories, homes and designer furnishings, gadgets, cuisine, and even places such as the Hamptons. People of various types and ages are included in these sections, including a few sections that focus on men or children. The main focus, however, remains women's fashion with an emphasis on the types of models usually associated with fashion advertising. Much of the time, the thrust of fashion ads is overtly sexual. Still, the link of all the products and types is through style, a concept that serves the upscale target of the both the *New York Times* in general and the *Style* section of the *New York Times Magazine* in particular. Briefly, it should be noted that this inclusion of both products and people as style also reflects the broader scope of fetishization, discussed at the outset, which embodies all desire whether sexual or not as projected through thought and language. Thus, the sexuality in this section's images can be viewed as stylized fetishism in that whatever it embraces or includes is stylized in a way which plays with the high and low brow, the clean and the dirty, and the attractive and the raunchy.

For an example of one of the more sexually overt images, consider a photograph called "Pole Cats" for a Versace couture silk chiffon dress that purports to represent cardiostriptease (April 28, 2002). The image shows the fetishized model wearing the Versace dress while holding onto and apparently going around a striptease pole in order to lose weight. The headline reads: "The most delightful way to lose weight? Bump and grind." The accompanying narrative further supports her activity in the declaration that "participants learn the art of making an entrance, walking, turning, flexing, gyrating, flirting, posing . . . and of course, removing articles of clothing." There are a number of fetishes in this image, ranging from the striptease process to the pole and the model as striptease artist herself. The intertextual references to striptease itself are rather explicit although of course the actual strip and resulting nudity are not included. But, the function of this particular fetish, however, is not to enact but to suggest. Moreover, striptease is often viewed as sleazy (depending, of course, on the beholder), but here the essential fetishes are supplemented with an upscale ambiance, especially one palatable to women who might buy this dress. Most important from the advertising point of view is that the product, the Versace dress, is itself fetishized and charged with sexual energy. While the dress by itself—as well as the Versace name—is fetishized, it becomes more sexually charged with the linkage to striptease. Finally, it should be noted that I follow fetish convention and understanding in labeling this and the other examples as fetishization. To clarify, this means that I argue that when sexual content occurs in advertising and other media, it in fact is an act of fetishization by both producer and consumer (c.f. Lillie, 2002).

Now, let us consider some specific examples with pictorial illustrations focusing on the fetishization of people as displayed in the form of models. To exemplify the richness and panoply of the range of fetish possibilities, Table 15.1 provides some brief examples of fetishes in the *Style* section. More detailed examples are included in the following sections. These examples illustrate the specific ways fetishization of people in ads works: (1) the fetish of gender and gender roles, (2) the fetish of celebrity, and (3) the fetish of type.

Series 1: The Fetish of Gender and Gender Roles

I begin with, perhaps, the most fundamental fetish of all: gender. One series, "Blue Notes" (*New York Times Magazine*, July 21, 2002) played with

TABLE 15.1
Fetish Examples From *Style* Section of the *New York Times Magazine*

Fetish Category and Description	Quotes
Hair: Wide-eyed model with no clothing showing on her top staring at the reader is portrayed with several layers of "New Big Hair" with mention of Bumble & Bumble in text. (November 17, 2002)	"Ladies, start your teasing combs. Big hair is a big deal."
Women, age, time, and the movies: Older women and older times versus younger women as represented by actors in the film, *Eight Women*. Photos of famous older women such as Catherine Deneuve and Isabelle Huppert counterposed with younger models playing with age and time periods for various fashions. (September 1, 2002)	Women: "I was entranced by how perfect all of them looked, as if playing a woman was playing a part; the mask as reality." Younger woman playing different time: "This film was all about bosoms and lips and doe eyes straight out of the 50's." Older woman: "Oscar Wilde said the visible was more mysterious than the invisible, and I felt that here.... It's a relief to see women ... with their own teeth and hair."
Men and "The Boys of Soccer": Seven players on the U.S. World Cup Team are shown in various poses and featuring various clothes. (May 26, 2002)	"Meet seven hotshots of the U.S. World Cup team."
Broadway and the "Leading Lady": Rachel Weisz, actor, in various sex-imbued scenes from the life of a Broadway actress for various fashions. (February 17, 2002)	"Like fashion, the theater is ephemeral. Which is a good thing." Scenes: "The Rehearsal," "Taking Direction," "The Leading Man," "The Congratulations," and "The Stage Door."
Places: Dallas, Texas and various well-groomed women and men for fashions in scenes from "South Fork." (July 7, 2002)	"Move over South Fork: Dallas is back."
Fashion designers: Geoffrey Beene shown in a series with sexily posed model wearing his clothes; he discusses several topics including nudity in his work. (October 20, 2002)	"Clothes Made the Man." "Fashion is in a terrible state. An overdose of too much flesh... ["The greatest concubines"] knew that everything revealed with nothing concealed is a bore."
Clothing: Clothes are fetishized in various models' sexual poses as costumes inspired by Federico Fellini. (October 27, 2002).	"Costume Drama: The fall couture had all the frenzy, surrealism and artistry of the best Fellini flick."

gender by asking in the subheadline, "Who are we anyhow? That's what our clothes ask us each time we get dressed." The photographs take a "vs." perspective so that masculinelike portrayals with female models are juxtaposed with females in clear female garb. The male impersonators are often waiflike, with short hair and small or hidden breasts. The "feminine" females have long hair and are unambiguously "feminine." The theme is captured in a punning second headline and subheadline on the second and third pages of the spread:

> The wardrobe between the sexes: Masculine? Feminine? You decide. This fall, designers on both coasts of the Atlantic took up the subject of gender studies—starkly defining his-and-her looks for the woman who can't make up her mind.

The accompanying text reinforces the message for the clothing designer, Viktor & Rolf, in associating clothing not in a McLuhanesque manner as an extension of the skin but rather in terms of a projected extended self (c.f. Belk, 1988), albeit one constructed on an ongoing ad hoc basis (see as a contrast a McLuhanesque ad in Gould [2003] in which clothing is seen as "second skins"). In this respect, one produces and fetishizes oneself. In other words, one becomes the self-fetish through both the product and the image:

> When we look at something like an exploded paisley, say we chalk it up to ladies wear, or when we look at gang clothes, we feel the fear they inspire. What Viktor & Rolf offered was a scrim for the fantasies we feel each time we get dressed.... Are we trying to be manly men and womanly women when we costume ourselves as them? Who are we anyway? That is what our clothes ask us each day we put them on.

The text continues: "There is nothing to fear more than our own projections onto others, our own projections onto ourselves." This series attempts to explain itself, the featured clothing designer, and the reader in terms of what can be referred to as the interaction of postmodern cultural production (i.e., the creation and deconstruction of social roles, especially gender) and identity play such that the consumer is able to wear and shed identities as expressed metaphorically in the wearing and shedding of clothes.

Of the eight images, one is an exception in that it is not about contrasting masculine and feminine but about two feminine oppositional roles (see Fig. 15.1). In this photo, one conservatively dressed model is shown as a wide-eyed innocent holding a doll whereas the other woman is portrayed with half-opened eyes in a sexual gaze. She is also wearing a red silk dress with a wide-open Benjamin Cho top to reveal much of her full breasts in a provocative and enticing manner. One reading of this particular image in light of the other masculine–feminine ads is that conservative girl-like and manly roles are together in opposition to more adult feminine and sexually provocative roles. But, of course, as the text further notes, the people seeing this collection in a show (and implicitly the reader here) "took in whatever message they chose to see." In summary, this series plays off gender and related gender roles by provoking reactions to a number of

FIG. 15.1.   Fetish of gender and gender roles.

its permutations. Readers can focus on those gender displays that attract them.

Series 2: The Fetish of Celebrity

A second series (*New York Times Magazine*, February 24, 2002) featured film and television actress Rose McGowan. Throughout seven images, she is fetishized as prototypes of Hollywood actresses: taking a *Wrong Turn* as Dolores Del Rio; representing Clara Bow in *Call Her Savage*, 1932; Lana Turner, in *The Postman Always Rings Twice*, 1946; Ava Gardner in *Mogambo*, 1953; Jane Fonda in *Klute*, 1971; Sharon Stone in *Basic Instinct*, 1992; and Jane Russell in *The Outlaw*, 1943. The series represents two overlapping fetishes: McGowan herself and the fetish of each performer she represents.

Her fetishization is initiated in the teasing headline, "Goodness has nothing to do with it: A Hollywood bad girl reveals her inspirations." To support her bad girl image, quotes from Mae West are added in a section titled, "The Gospel According to Mae West." For example, one of the quotes reads, "Between two evils, I always pick the one I didn't try before." Then, McGowan's own qualities are explained in the accompanying text:

> McGowan's twinkle comes from her big-star comportment—not only does she have the curve and face of a 30's film star, but she talks like one too; her vanilla-icing complexion and shiny dark eyes complement her quick, funny patter, as she rattles off the facts like Rosalind Russell in "His Girl Friday."

In the first photo (see Fig. 15.2), McGowan takes her "wrong turn" as Delores Del Rio in a red dress and skirt from Sonia Rykiel, shoes from Stuart

FIG. 15.2. Fetish of celebrity.

Weitzman, and a top hat from Makins Hats, with her hat shown upside down on the ground as if she had flung it. As with the other images, the reader may or may not know Delores' identity because there is no description other than her name. If one reads the extensive accompanying text, one discovers that McGowan "just went for the way she looked." And, the way she looks here is as a stage performer showing off for the audience in red and black, which are well-established sexual dress colors. Celebrity is a major fetish category, and this series plays on that by showing celebrities who represent fetishes to people of different ages. Much as people react nostalgically to music from their own eras of interest, people have similar reactions to celebrities. By extension, McGowan becomes these celebrities while reinforcing her own celebrity fetish.

Series 3: The Fetish of Sexualized Lifestyle Type

Another series (*New York Times Magazine*, May 12, 2002) featured recording artist Alanis Morissette in five photos and extensive text (two columns on two different pages). Each photo is a fetish scene that reflects different sexualized lifestyles readers might be attracted to either personally or vicariously. The series promotes 11 different products and services, including the *New York Times* itself. This series' title reads, "Irony Maiden: Has the supposed former infatuation junkie finally kicked the habit?" Only people in "the know" would appreciate what this means. But, for those who are not in the know, the accompanying text describes this headline's meaning and Morissette's celebrity typing (p. 51):

> There has been a slew of sensitive female songbirds of late: quivering souls martyred by failed romances, stroking guitars in sexual effigy, looking to channel the pain into *Billboard's* Hot 100. They hurt, they pine, they blurt out whatever soothes the wounds or stokes the bathos. They're the anti-Barbies: Sheryl, Shania, Fiona, Jewel; musically accomplished and gorgeous to boot.

Yet, at the same time, the series displays Morissette in a number of fetish roles as represented in the five images. Similar to McGowan's pictorial, her hair, dress, stare, and behavioral roles change from page to page. In the first, she stares directly at the reader, but her left eye blinks as though she is flirting or sharing a secret with us. She is modeling necklaces from Christian Tse, and she is covered around her shoulders and torso while leaving her neck and chest bare (the picture is cut off before her breasts). This first introductory image occupies only a portion of the page while each remaining image occupies a full page. The second layout is a promotion for the *New York Times* itself, in the form of its Web site, with Morissette representing

Frida Kahlo and promoting a white polyester mesh top with macramé beading from Chloe, her necklace from Stephen Dweck, and two stores, Chloe and Sak's Fifth Avenue. The image relates Morissette to the medium where she is shown, thus promoting both, ">> Cyber-Chameleon >> Alanis Morissette changes with The Times. >> To see her morph to the beat click on nytimes.com magazine." Morissette is shown with butterflies, with one around her neck that is actually a bare-breasted woman, spreading her wings. Morissette's hair is up and she is gazing languidly at the camera.

The third image features Morissette in a partial full-body display going through what is described as "her Ed Ruscha stage." She is wearing a silver silk-satin ribbon dress by Benjamin Cho. Also, Morissette has a halo above her head as she stares off camera—a self-absorbed stare similar to the previous ad, but now off to the side rather than toward the reader. Unlike the other images, this one features her breasts as rounded and substantial. They are at the center of the image and presumably represent the dress at its best in terms of sexual allure. The emphasis on her chest can be thought of as making a statement about women's breasts, which are, perhaps, one of the most fetishized body parts. Not surprisingly, many of the images in the *Style* section focus on breasts in various guises and poses, revelation, and concealment. The fourth photograph features "Alanis as Mona Lisa (before getting the Marcel Duchamp treatment)." The image truly mimics the iconic Mona Lisa painting, but it is distinctly different. For example, Morissette is staring toward the camera with slightly more attention than the previous vignette while also referring to the enigmatic quality often attributed to the Mona Lisa. The image features the caftan she is wearing by Tom Ford for Yves Saint Laurent Rive Gauche, and she is embellished by more colorful flesh tones than the other photographs—the previous two are in black and white.

The final image features "Alanis with her knight in shining armor" (see Fig. 15.3). She is shown on the back of a Harley-Davidson holding onto the rider in knight's armor, who at a glance might also be a robot. This is the only image in which she appears with another person, though clearly the other "person" is a fetishized prop that contrasts the hardness of masculinity against the soft flesh of an otherwise not-so-soft Morissette. Here, Morissette displays much bare skin though it is her legs that are emphasized the most. Her ball skirt by Jean Paul Gautier (her corset is also from Gautier) is blown by the wind, revealing her legs as the motorcycle duo flies by. She is also modeling matching red boots by Hogan and a silver cuff bracelet by M & J Savitt. The butterfly theme recurs as a number of them trail behind, and she is shown looking back at them.

In these examples, lifestyle is sexualized in promotional culture as a mediator of life and lived experience. Take a lifestyle, add sex or draw on

FIG. 15.3. Fetish of sexualized lifestyle type.

its inherent sexuality, and a series such as this one emerges. Like its porno-graphic cousin, advertising is often a vicarious vehicle for transporting consumers to their idealized fantasy worlds, and the *Style* section follows this advertising lovemap formula. Simply follow the fetishized Morissette through her fantasy lifestyle mediascape and, by transference, you too can share in it by using the featured products.

DISCUSSION AND IMPLICATIONS

This chapter illustrates the process by which people and related objects are fetishized together in print media. The *Style* section in the Sunday *New York Times Magazine* provides rich examples, using types of fetishization widely available in advertising. The idea is that consumers are not sexually attracted to others without the simultaneous presence of objects, such as adornments like clothing, jewelry, and many other objects. Nor are they attracted to objects without people. There are many exceptions to this statement, such as when people sexually fetishize an object without requiring people to be a part of the attraction, though metonymic connections from past experience can still reflect a personal connection. But, more generally in the advertising lovemap, the joint presence of object and person form a fetish. A third element is the narrative that links the two. For example, in the *Style* section, substantial amounts of text accompany the images. These narratives reinforce the process of fetishizing lifestyles that readers both identify with and are attracted to, if only vicariously. What emerges is that almost anything about one's sexuality may be fetishized. Here, we considered three examples of fetish in terms of gender and gender roles, celebrity, and person–lifestyle types. In this regard, we further identify several aspects of fetishization, which may not only guide future research, but also may guide advertisers who apply sexuality in their creative strategies.

Fetish Segmentation

Fetish segmentation involves categorizing consumers by their interests and responses to particular fetish types. Such a strategy could be a useful tool when creating advertising, positioning products, and targeting consumers. Whereas these segments reflect lifestyles and psychographics as they have been applied in the past, articulating them as fetishes allows for a richer set of specific meanings to be constructed and applied. First, there must be consideration of the relationship between the fetish and consumer. What is it that the fetish means and what specifically does the consumer project into it? How is it that fetishes are constructed culturally and socially so that consumers come to have shared views of them? For example, a *Style* section reader represents an upscale profile although there are probably a number of additional subsegments within it.

Model and Brand Meaning

The interpretation of models in advertising, including celebrities, must be reformulated to consider how they are fetishized. Likewise, brand meaning is a major concern for advertising and concerns what brands mean to consumers. While such meanings are not necessarily fixed as proposed by poststructural theory, I would nonetheless suggest that long-standing fetishistic lovemaps are major components of them. Thus, as indicated earlier, it is instructive to conceptualize people and objects together in helping to form product and related brand meaning (McCracken, 1989). However, the present analysis problematizes these relationships and indicates a complex relationship between brand and the celebrity in meaning construction. In many cases, brands provide meaning to the celebrity as well as the other way around. As reflected in the examples in the *New York Times Magazine's Style* section, the fetishization of celebrity is often based in the fetishization of the brand. It is the union of brand and celebrity/model as total fetish that should be considered.

Fetishization and Integrated Marketing Communications

Last, fetishization has implications for implementing integrated marketing communications (IMC), especially when considered from its one-voice perspective. This perspective suggests speaking to the consumer with one voice or theme across promotional media. But, since the media also represent multiple sites of meaning, all with their own conventions and semiotic permutations, the advertiser must consider how fetishized sexual advertising plays out in different formats such as print and television. What is effective or accepted in one medium, such as the *Style* section, clearly would not work in prime-time television. These differences exist both in terms of message creation and media strategy. One-voice IMC has subtleties that need to be more finely tuned by both researchers and marketers before fetish promotion can be fully considered. As a cautionary note, nontargeted people may see images not meant for them. This caveat almost always applies to sexual advertising, where various ethical, legal, and taste considerations enter in. However, while general guidelines in terms of ethics and legality are factors for all sexual advertising (Gould, 1994), it should be emphasized that fetishization has a particular taste element. Thus, people who otherwise share demographic and psychographic tendencies may differ in their fetish predilections.

CONCLUSION

Although this chapter has focused on fetishization in its sexual aspect, it should be noted that fetishization reflects all desire projected through language, thought, and feeling. I once conducted a study (Gould, 1992–1993) that demonstrated how consumers "feel" commercials in different body parts from the genitals to the heart and the head (perhaps they were thinking about the commercial). These results inform my view of the fetish as reflecting different projective meanings and feelings, with the sexual response being a special case. For instance, I found that consumers reacted to rational commercials with feelings in their head (cognitive) and to commercials involving love in their hearts (affective). But, in sexually charged commercials, males responded to an attractive female in a sexually arousing situation by reporting feelings in their genitals, and females responded similarly when seeing attractive males. Considering examples discussed in this chapter, we see that promotional media link people and objects. Both simulate and enact the process of sexual fetishization, and in doing so foster both sexual desire and the desire to buy.

REFERENCES

Abraham, K. (1959). The man who loved corsets. In H. Greenwald (Ed.), *Great cases in psychoanalysis* (pp. 41–51). New York: Ballantine.

Balasubramanian, S. K. (1994). Beyond advertising and publicity: Hybrid messages and public policy issues. *Journal of Advertising, 23*, 29–46.

Baudrillard, J. (1983). *Simulations.* New York: Semiotext(e).

Belk, R. (1988). Possessions and the extended self. *Journal of Consumer Research, 15*, 139–168.

Elliott, S. (2003, February 24). Advertising: Stars of pornographic films are modeling in a campaign for Pony, the shoe company. *New York Times, 153*, C9.

Gould, S. J. (1991). Toward a theory of sexuality and consumption: Consumer lovemaps. In R. H. Holman & M. R. Solomon (Eds.), *Advances in consumer research,* Vol. 18 (pp. 381–383). Provo, UT: Association for Consumer Research.

Gould, S. J. (1992). A model of the scripting of consumer lovemaps: The consumer sexual behavior sequence. In J. Sherry & B. Sternthal (Eds.), *Advances in consumer research,* Vol. 19 (pp. 304–310). Provo, UT: Association for Consumer Research.

Gould, S. J. (1992–1993). Perceived affective symptoms: A new approach to affect patterning and response. *Imagination, Cognition and Personality, 12*, 249–271.

Gould, S. J. (1994). Sexuality and ethics in advertising: A research agenda and policy guideline perspective. *Journal of Advertising, 23*, 73–80.

Gould, S. J. (1995). Sexualized aspects of consumer behavior: An empirical investigation of consumer lovemaps. *Psychology & Marketing, 12*, 305–413.

Gould, S. J. (2003). Toward a theory of advertising lovemaps in marketing communications: Overdetermination, postmodern thought and the advertising hermeneutic circle. In T. Reichert and J. Lambiase (Eds.), *Sex in advertising* (pp. 151–170). Mahwah, NJ: Lawrence Erlbaum Associates.

Lacan, J. (1968). *The Language of the self.* Baltimore: Johns Hopkins University Press.

Lance, L. (this volume). Searching for love and sex: A review and analysis of mainstream and explicit personal ads. In T. Reichert & J. Lambiase (Eds.), *Sex in consumer culture: The erotic content of media and marketing.* Mahwah, NJ: Lawrence Erlbaum Associates.

Lillie, J. J. M. (2002). Sexuality and cyberporn: Towards a new agenda for research. *Sexuality & Culture, 6*, 25–47.

McCracken, G. (1989). Who is the celebrity endorser? Cultural foundations of the endorsement process. *Journal of Consumer Research, 16*, 310–321.

Money, J. (1984). Paraphilias: Phenomenology and classification. *American Journal of Psychotherapy, 38*, 164–179.

Money, J. (1986). *Lovemaps.* New York: Irvington Publications.

Mosher, D. L. (1988). Pornography defined: Sexual involvement theory, narrative context, and goodness-of-fit. *Journal of Psychology and Human Sexuality, 1*, 67–85.

Rubin, G., & Butler, J. (1994). Sexual traffic. *differences: A Journal of Feminist Cultural Studies, 6*, 62–99.

Schleifer, R. (1990). *Rhetoric and death: The language of modernism and postmodern discourse theory.* Urbana: University of Illinois Press.

Schleiner, A. M. (2001). Does Lara Croft wear fake polygons? Gender and gender-role subversion in computer adventure games. *Leonardo, 34*, 221–227.

Schroeder, J. E., & Borgerson, J. L. (2003). Dark desires: Fetishism, ontology, and representation in contemporary advertising. In T. Reichert and J. Lambiase (Eds.), *Sex in advertising* (pp. 65–87). Mahwah, NJ: Lawrence Erlbaum Associates.

Wise, T. N., & Kalyanam, R. C. (2000). Amputee fetishism and genital mutilation: Case report and literature view. *Journal of Sex & Marital Therapy, 26*, 339–344.

Zorach, R. (2001). Desiring things. *Art History, 24*, 195–213.

Chapter 16

Race and Gender in Advertising: A Look at Sexualized Images in Prime-Time Commercials

Dana E. Mastro

University of Arizona

Susannah R. Stern

University of San Diego

Without question, advertising serves as a driving force behind the media in the United States. In 2001 alone, approximately $234 billion was spent on advertising, primarily for television (Li, 2003). These advertisements aim to capture viewers' attention, raise awareness of available products, build brand loyalty, and, ultimately, encourage product purchase. One of the most popular features advertisers use to achieve these goals is to include sexual content in their ads. Attractive and seductive models, depictions of sexual relationships and desire, and even allusions to viewers' untapped sexual prowess are recurrent themes in contemporary advertisements. In fact, research indicates that sex appeals in television commercials and magazine ads are common and rising (Reichert et al., 1999). Yet, while numerous researchers have rigorously documented the pervasiveness of sex and sensuality across the media (e.g., Cope & Kunkel, 2002; Greenberg, Brown, & Buerkel-Rothfuss, 1993; Heintz-Knowles, 1996; Kunkel, Cope, & Colvin, 1996; Reichert & Lambiase, 2003), few studies have concentrated on variations in sexual depictions in advertising as a function of the race of characters. This is surprising, considering the fact that the rapidly growing size and economic strength of racial/ethnic minority populations in the United States (Selig Center for Economic Growth, 2002) have prompted advertisers to attend more than ever before to minority consumers (BWN, 2002). Consequently, it is imperative to better understand the manner in which minorities are portrayed, particularly in relation to the widespread sexual fare in advertising. The present chapter is focused on this endeavor.

Theories of media effects suggest that exposure to media images can impact social perceptions and behaviors as well as self-concept (Bandura, 1994, 2002; Gerbner et al., 2002). As such, awareness of the quality of these representations is critical. This may be markedly so for advertising messages as we encounter advertising more than any other form of media content (Harris, 1999; Lai, Tan, & Tharp, 1990). In light of this potential impact, we begin with a summary of the pertinent quantitative content analytic research that has investigated representations of race in magazine and television advertising, emphasizing studies that included measures of sex and gender. Next, we describe our own content analysis of prime-time television commercials that was conducted, in part, to document sexualized images of race. These findings add to the small amount of research examining both race and sex in advertising.

PORTRAYALS OF RACE/ETHNICITY IN ADVERTISING

Historically, depictions of racial/ethnic minorities in both print and television advertising have been infrequent and at times altogether nonexistent for some groups (Greenberg, Mastro, & Brand, 2002; Wilson & Gutierrez, 1995). The few quantitative content analyses that have been conducted indicate that when minorities have appeared in advertising, they were limited in number and narrow in scope, particularly in early advertisements (Wilson & Gutierrez, 1995). Rather than showing the diversity of cultures in the United States, advertising images of race/ethnicity often have supported the presumed values and norms of the dominant, mainstream culture (Coltrane & Messineo, 2000). This type of representation includes trivialized portrayals of minority races in large groups or as minor characters, as well as depictions that ridicule and subordinate minority groups (Wilkes & Valencia, 1989). Although some improvements have been documented over the past 50 years in terms of the frequency with which various racial/ethnic groups have been pictured, these advances occurred more often in television commercials than in magazine ads (Zinkhan, Qualls, & Biswas, 1990). Moreover, the rise in the rate of depictions has not always been indicative of progress with regard to the quality of these representations. The following review describes existing research documenting the frequency and quality of racial minority representations and notes examinations of sexual portrayals when available.

African Americans

Until relatively recently, images of African Americans in advertising were scarce and often unfavorable (Dates, 1993; Wilson & Gutierrez, 1995). In the first half of the 20th century, when African Americans were shown, they were often represented as servants and entertainers. Women in particular were frequently depicted as laborers or romanticized and eroticized as forbidden figures of desire (Mehaffy, 1997; Ruffins, 1998; Wilson & Gutierrez, 1995).

Despite growth in the frequency of African American images in the second half of the century, the nature of the portrayals remained unflattering (Wilson & Gutierrez, 1995). Frustrated, the National Association for the Advancement of Colored People launched a campaign in the 1960s and 1970s to improve and increase depictions (Dates, 1993; Wilson & Gutierrez, 1995). The group conducted a series of studies investigating representations of African Americans in advertising and reported its findings directly to the Federal Communications Commission, charging that although the number of depictions had improved, most African Americans remained in brief, low-status roles. Coupled with boycotts and protests organized by civil rights groups across the country, these efforts resulted in improvements in images of Blacks in advertising.

Notably, the number of African Americans in both magazine and television advertising rose in the period from the 1970s to the 1990s (Licata & Biswas, 1993; Plous and Neptune, 1997; Wilkes & Valencia, 1989; Wilson & Gutierrez, 1995), with commercial representation reaching 13.5% by 1974 (Dominick & Greenberg, 1970; Bush, Solomon, & Hair, 1977). Nonetheless, African Americans frequently remained confined to minor parts (Stern, 1999). When they were seen in central roles, they regularly appeared in advertisements for "vice" products (e.g., alcohol) or their sexual prowess was emphasized (Dates, 1993; Hacker, Collins, & Jacobson, 1987).

In terms of specific representations of sex and sexuality, researchers have found similarities across depictions of African Americans and Whites (Plous & Neptune, 1997; Snyder, Freeman, & Condray, 1995). In fact, gender appeared to play a greater role than race in differentiating characters in magazine ads. The bodies of both African American and White women received far greater exposure than did the bodies of their male counterparts. Women of both races also were more likely than men to be portrayed in sexual attire (Plous & Neptune, 1997) and these women's breast exposure increased significantly from the 1980s to the 1990s.

However, African American women were more often portrayed in provocative poses, in predatory scenes, and wearing animal prints than were White women, suggesting greater sexual activity and seduction on the part of these women. African American women were also less likely to be characterized as intellectual and ambitious (McLaughlin & Goulet, 1999), as evidenced by the lack of face-only images. In comparison, White women were nearly equally likely to be presented in either full body or face-only views (Jackson & Ervin, 1991). McLaughlin and Goulet (1999) studied images in popular White and African American magazines in 1996, and found that magazines targeted toward Whites more often showed characters exhibiting licensed withdrawal (removal of the character from the situation, indicating dependence), ritualized subordination (submissive behavior, either sexual or childlike), and feminine touch (representative of delicacy) than magazines targeted toward African Americans.

Racial depictions of sex and sexuality in television commercials have received almost no systematic attention by researchers, except from Coltrane and Messineo (2000), who documented that 15% of White models were portrayed as sex objects compared to 8% of African Americans. White women were more likely than White men to be shown in this manner. No comparable data are available on African Americans.

Altogether, relatively scant research has evaluated the intersection of African American imagery, sexuality, and advertisements. Without further inquiry, it is difficult to conclude that African Americans have received substantially different treatment with regard to how they are portrayed as sexual beings in comparison to Whites. It is clear, however, that African Americans have endured a long history of infrequent and unfavorable coverage, and that in some cases African American women tend to have been sexualized to a greater extent than White women.

Latinos

Little quantitative research has focused on depictions of Latinos in advertising over the decades. Certainly, this is largely a result of the fact that Latinos have been depicted so infrequently that many useful statistical analyses were precluded. Based on the research that is available, findings indicate that prior to the 1980s, images of Latino men typically centered on the dirty Mexican bandit or the lazy Mexican, while Latino women were primarily depicted in a sexualized manner (Wilson & Gutierrez, 1995). By the early 1970s, the growing economic power of the Latino community in the United States (alongside harsh criticism from activists and civic groups) compelled advertisers to take the Latino market more seriously. Changes have been only negligible, however.

In magazines, findings vary regarding the number of Latinos pictured in advertisements. Bowen and Schmid (1997), in their study of mass circulation magazines, reported that Latinos appeared in only 0.6% of ads in 1987 and 0.2% in 1992. Jackson and Ervin (1991) found no Latinos in their study of women's fashion magazines from the late 1980s. However, these rates fell below both the 1.5% reported by Czepiec and Kelly (1983) in their study of popular magazines from 1982 as well as the 4.7% found by Taylor and Bang (1997) and Taylor, Lee, and Stern (1995) in their look at ads from top-selling magazines from 1992–1993.

On television in the 1980s, Latinos appeared in commercials 5.8% of the time, with nearly 61% of these ads featuring only Latino men and 12% featuring only Latina women (Wilkes & Valencia, 1989). By the 1990s, Latinos were documented in 8.5% of television commercials, a rate below that of their real-world proportion of the population (Taylor & Stern, 1997). Coltrane and Messineo (2000) noted that when depicted, Latinos were seen as sex objects 17% of the time. Little more has been established about the qualities associated with either print or TV ads depicting Latinos, specifically those pertaining to sex.

Asian Americans

Much like early representations of African Americans and Latinos, initial portrayals of Asians and Asian Americans in advertising were often uncomplimentary, chiefly emphasizing unfavorable stereotypes (Wilson & Gutierrez, 1995). By the mid-1970s, several Asian American organizations came together to protest the continued negative portrayals in advertising, but for the most part, Asian Americans experienced very limited representation in advertising for the next few decades. Until the 1990s, in fact, Asians in advertising remained confined to a relatively small number of gendered roles, with men frequently relegated to roles as businessmen or martial artists and women often isolated to seductive and exotic characters such as China dolls, geishas, and Polynesian natives (Wilson & Gutierrez, 1995). By the 1990s, the sheer number of appearances had shown some improvement. In magazines ads, for instance, Taylor and Bang (1997) as well as Taylor, Lee, and Stern (1995) found that 4% of ads in top-selling magazines from 1992–1993 included Asian Americans. In commercials from the top 20 television programs in the early 1990s, Asian Americans comprised approximately 2% of representations and were portrayed as sex objects 6% of the time (Coltrane & Messineo, 2000). In the main, however, quantitative content analytic research is limited in its ability to describe the characteristics associated with Asians in advertising, as this group remains too infrequent in its appearances to permit extensive analyses.

Native Americans

Images of Native Americans have essentially been absent in both print ads and broadcast commercials (Wilson & Gutierrez, 1995). Research indicates that three primary portrayals of Native Americans appear in advertising (Merskin, 1998): the noble savage, the civilized savage, and the bloodthirsty savage (Green, 1993; Merskin, 1998). Unfortunately, representations of Native Americans are so extraordinarily infrequent that further discussion of the nature of these depictions, sexual or otherwise, is impossible.

Summary of Literature and Research Questions

Altogether, the information regarding racial representations in advertising is limited at best. The most obvious conclusions to be drawn from existing research are that minorities have been only marginally represented in advertising and while frequencies of depictions have increased, there still appears to be a relative lack of diverse imagery of minority races. Moreover, the intersection of racial representations and sexual content in advertising has been only peripherally addressed. Among the few studies investigating both race and sex in advertising, some gender differences have been detected. Historically, for example, minority women were typically portrayed as young, beautiful, and sexually seductive (Cortese, 1999). African American women in particular were depicted as alluring, animal-like, and primitive. Portrayals of Latinas and Asian American women generally included roles as sexually experienced and available (Coltrane & Messineo, 2000; Cortese, 1999; Wilson & Gutierrez, 1995). Native Americans have been and remain nearly invisible (Cortese, 1999; Wilson & Gutierrez, 1995). Documenting the qualities associated with advertising depictions of race becomes consequential when considering that theories of media effects suggest that exposure to media messages may have a measurable influence on the attitudes and behaviors of consumers.

To this end, the present study focused simply on a few key variables in a content analysis of prime-time television commercials from the 2001 season. Because little quantitative content analytic research has investigated these intersections, it is hoped that this examination of the ways in which sex and sensuality are associated with men and women from different racial/ethnic minority groups will lend insight into this imagery.

Two general research questions framed this content analysis:

RQ1: How will physical attributes related to beauty (body type and attractiveness) vary based on the race of characters in prime-time commercials?

RQ2: How will overt manifestations of sexuality (degree of dress, sexual gazing, self-gazing, and alluring behavior) vary based on the race of the characters in prime-time commercials?

METHOD

Sample

A 1-week sample of prime-time television commercials was compiled from a random sample of 3 weeks of programming from February 2001. The six major broadcast networks (ABC, CBS, NBC, FOX, UPN, and WB) were used in the creation of this sample. Prime-time was defined as all programming between 8 P.M. and 11 P.M. Eastern Standard Time on Monday through Saturday as well as programming from 7 P.M. to 11 P.M. EST on Sunday. Only national commercials (defined as ads marketing goods/services to a national audience) were included in the sample, resulting in 2,880 advertisements. Consistent with existing research, local ads, political promotions, and trailers for television shows, movies, and sports were excluded from the sample (Bartsch et al., 2000; Lovdal, 1989). Because one aim of the study was to document frequency of depictions, repeat commercials (those that were broadcast more than once within the sample) were included (Craig, 1992; Verna, 1975).

Units of Analysis and Variables

In order to assess the character-level attributes of the individual models appearing in the ads, the first three human characters with speaking parts were examined. Speaking parts were identified as singular, discernible voices or sounds emanating from a clearly identifiable character. Pilot testing of prime-time commercials revealed that these ads typically contained three or fewer speaking characters. Therefore, coding the first three characters provided a comprehensive picture of the characters in these commercials, while avoiding problems often associated with classifying primary or background characters in ads (e.g., Bartsch et al., 2000). This yielded 2,276 codable characters.

To provide a preliminary examination of the extent to which sexualized images exist in commercials and vary by race and sex, the following variables were measured. First, the *gender* of the character (male/female) and the *race* of the character (Asian American, African American, Latino, Native American, White, other) were identified. Next, the *age* of the character was evaluated based on five age levels: child (0–12 years), teen (13–20), young adult (21–35), middle-aged adult (36–65), and senior (over 65). To evaluate character attributes, the physical *attractiveness* of the model was measured on a 3-point scale from (1) very attractive to (3) not at all attractive (modified from Signorelli, McLeod, & Healy, 1994). This item was defined as the extent to which the character would be considered physically appealing to others, based on indicators such as facial symmetry and lack of blemishes. In addition, the *body type* of the character was appraised on a 3-point scale physically depicting both male and female body types from (1) thin to (3) overweight (modified from Stunkard, Sorensen, & Schulsinger, 1983).

In order to gauge the extent to which sexual imagery and behavior were prevalent in prime-time commercial ads, four additional variables were assessed. The *degree of dress* of the model was measured as an indicator of the suggestive/sexy nature of the character's attire (Fullerton &

Kendrick, 2000). Response options ranged from not at all suggestive (1) to very suggestive (3) on a 3-point scale. This item defined the characters' representation in revealing/skimpy/tight clothes or in a sensual state of (un)dress. The act of *sexual gazing* was evaluated using a dichotomous measure in order to assess whether or not the model gave/received sexual gazes (Coltrane & Messineo, 2000). Also rated as a dichotomous measure, *self-gazing* was appraised to ascertain if characters were involved in self-scrutiny (e.g., looking at one's body in the mirror) (Coltrane & Messineo, 2000). Last, a dichotomous measure of *alluring behavior* was included to indicate if the model took part in sexually tempting or provocative behavior (Coltrane & Messineo, 2000).

Reliabilities

Four undergraduate students served as coders, two male and two female. They were trained using television ads outside the actual sample until acceptable levels of intercoder reliability were obtained using Scott's pi for nominal level data (Potter & Levine-Donnerstein, 1999) and Rosenthal's effective reliability for ordinal and interval level data (Rosenthal, 1987). All reliabilities reported in the present study were recalculated on a subset of the actual sample. Scott's pi values of 1.0 were achieved for the variables sex, race, age, sexual gaze, self-gaze, and alluring behavior. Degree of dress and attractiveness each scored Rosenthal's reliability values of .92.

RESULTS

Analyses

Chi-squares were calculated to determine the extent to which variations in sexualized depictions emerged based on the race and sex of the character depicted.

Character-Level Findings

In total, 2,880 commercials were coded in this sample of prime-time TV. Within these, the race and gender of 2,276 speaking characters were identified (see Table 16.1). Overall, men outnumbered women by nearly a 3:2 margin. Whites, the most commonly depicted racial group (83.8%), were disproportionately overrepresented in comparison to the 2000 U.S. census figures (69.1%). In terms of gender representation, for every three White males shown, two White females were shown. African Americans, the next most commonly depicted race (12.3%), were proportionately depicted in comparison with their actual frequency in the United States (12.3%), with

TABLE 16.1

Representation of Gender and Race in Prime-Time Television Advertisements

Character Race	% Males	% Females	Total % of Sample	2000 U.S. Population
Black	53.4%	46.6%	12.3%	12.3%
	$n = 150$	$n = 131$	$n = 281$	
Asian	62.5%	37.5%	2.1%	3.6%
	$n = 30$	$n = 18$	$n = 48$	
Latino	50.0%	50.0%	1.0%	12.5%
	$n = 11$	$n = 11$	$n = 22$	
Native American	83.3%	16.7%	0.3%	0.9%
	$n = 5$	$n = 1$	$n = 6$	
White	60.0%	40.0%	83.8%	69.1%
	$n = 1,144$	$n = 763$	$n = 1,907$	
Other	91.7%	8.3%	0.5%	5.6%
	$n = 11$	$n = 1$	$n = 12$	
Column Totals	59.4%	40.6%	100%	104%
	$n = 1,351$	$n = 925$	$n = 2,276$	

Note. The U.S. Census (2000) provides demographic data based on the racial and ethnic makeup of the U.S. population, with some respondents choosing more than one race; therefore, totals exceed 100%.

males and females fairly evenly represented. Asian Americans were the next most frequently portrayed racial group (2.1%), followed by Latinos (1%). Both of these racial/ethnic groups were underrepresented compared with their real-life proportions (3.6% and 12.5%, respectively), especially Latinos, who currently comprise the largest racial/ethnic minority group in the United States. Asian American males outnumbered their female counterparts, but Latino males and females were equally likely to be depicted. Native Americans were all but invisible in this sample (0.3%), also falling below their percentage of the U.S. population (0.9%). When shown, they were far more likely to be male. People whose race did not fall into any of these categories comprised a total of 0.5% of the ads and were much more frequently male than female.

Looking descriptively at age, representations differed only slightly in terms of gender and race. Among males, African Americans, Asian Americans, and Whites appeared most commonly as young adults, whereas male Latinos were typically portrayed as teens and young adults. Native American males were identified as the youngest, typically appearing as teens. Among females, African Americans, Latinas, and Whites appeared most often as young adults. Asian American females and females categorized as "other race" comprised the youngest depictions in the sample, typically portrayed in an age range between teen and young adult.

The sole Native American woman appearing in the sample was identified as a middle-aged adult. (Hereafter, Native American and "other" race characters have been excluded due to their small sample size.).

Research Question 1: Depictions of Physical Beauty Based on Race

In order to determine how physical attributes related to beauty varied based on the race of characters in prime-time commercials, chi-square analyses were conducted. Significant differences in attractiveness were revealed based on the race of both female characters $\chi^2(4, N = 910) = 16.39$, $p < .01$ and male characters $\chi^2(4, N = 1316) = 12.06, p < .025$. Among the women, Asian Americans were identified as "very attractive" the majority of the time ($n = 14, 77.8\%$). The distribution was more equitable for African Americans and Whites, with African American women appearing as very attractive 48.1% of the time ($n = 63$) and White women shown as very attractive in 50% of appearances ($n = 456$). For the men, Asian Americans were most often identified as unattractive ($n = 14$, 46.7%), while African Americans ($n = 85$, 56.7%) and Whites ($n = 623$, 54.8%) were most frequently deemed moderately attractive. Due to insufficient representation on this variable, Latinos were not included in further analyses.

Chi-square tests examining the body type of the female characters based on race also revealed significant differences $\chi^2(6, N = 907) = 33.61$, $p < .01$. Although *most* African American females ($n = 72$, 55.8%), Asian females ($n = 12, 70.6\%$), and White females ($n = 464, 61.9\%$) were depicted as thin, *every* Latina ($n = 11$, 100.0%) appearing in the sample was identified as thin. Significant differences in male body type also emerged based on the race of the models $\chi^2(6, N = 1277) = 52.08, p < .01$. Both African American male characters ($n = 78$, 53.8%) and White male characters ($n = 770, 70.4\%$) were typically classified as average in weight. However, Asians ($n = 17$, 58.6%) and Latinos ($n = 6, 60.0\%$) were most commonly thin.

Research Question 2: Overt Manifestations of Sexuality Based on Race

Chi-square tests were again employed to identify variations in overt manifestations of sexuality based on the race of the prime-time commercial character. These assessments of sexualized imagery revealed significant differences by race for females in sexual gazing $\chi^2(3, N = 919) = 45.24$, $p < .01$ and alluring behavior $\chi^2(3, N = 920) = 55.24, p < .01$. For sexual gazing, the majority of African American ($n = 125$, 96.2%), Asian American ($n = 18$, 100%), and White women ($n = 687$, 90.4%) did not engage in sexual gazing. Conversely, Latinas ($n = 7, 63.6\%$) were most frequently found engaging in sexual gazing. The same pattern emerged for alluring behavior. Although the majority of African American ($n = 114$, 87%),

Asian American ($n = 18$, 100%), and White women ($n = 654$, 86.1%) were not involved in alluring behavior, nearly all Latinas ($n = 10$, 90.9%) engaged in such acts. Despite a significant chi-square measure for self-gazing $\chi^2(3, N = 918) = 24.17$, $p < .01$, differences on this variable were not meaningful based on the race of these female characters. The vast majority of models were not involved in self-gazing. Similarly, no differences by race emerged for women on degree of provocative dress $\chi^2(4, N = 912) = 2.10$, $p > .05$.

TABLE 16.2
Summary Findings Regarding Race in Prime-Time Television Advertisements

Race	Sexual Portrayal
Black	*Women*: With regard to physical beauty, most females were portrayed as thin (56%) and very attractive (48%). Overall, only 13% engaged in alluring behavior, and Black women were most commonly fairly conservatively dressed (48%).
	Men: Black males were most often portrayed as average in weight (54%) and moderately attractive (57%). Males did not participate in sexual gazing and almost never engaged in alluring behaviors (3%). Typically, Black males were fairly conservatively dressed (67%).
Asian	*Women*: The vast majority of Asian females were depicted as thin (71%) and very attractive (78%). They never engaged in sexual gazing or alluring behavior. Asian women were most commonly portrayed as conservatively clad (50%).
	Men: Asian men were most commonly shown as thin (59%) and unattractive (47%). None was involved in sexual gazing or alluring behaviors, and most were dressed fairly conservatively (83%).
Latino	*Women*: Every Latina in the sample was thin (100%), and almost as many were shown to behave alluringly (91%). A majority of characters were also shown to engage in sexual gazing (64%). The majority of Latina women were dressed fairly moderately (64%), although a full third were fairly suggestively clad (36%). No Latinas were dressed conservatively.
	Men: Typically portrayed as thin (60%), most Latino men were average in terms of their overall attractiveness (55%). Although Latino men were more likely than other males to exhibit sexual gazing (18%), no Latino men engaged in alluring behaviors, and the majority of men were fairly conservatively dressed (73%).
White	*Women*: The majority of females were portrayed as thin (62%) and very attractive (50%). White women were unlikely to behave alluringly (14%), and the majority of characters were either fairly conservatively dressed (54%) or moderately dressed (34%).
	Men: White males were typically shown as average weight (70%) and moderately attractive (55%). They rarely were depicted engaged in sexual gazing (0.5%) or alluring behavior (1.1%). Most were dressed fairly conservatively (71%).

Note. Due to insufficient representation, Native Americans and characters whose race differed from those coded were not included in assessments of character sexual portrayals.

Among the men, significant differences by race in terms of sexual behavior were found only for self-gazing $\chi^2(3, N = 1,325) = 57.83$, $p < .01$. While the majority of men were not depicted in acts of self-gazing (African American, $n = 150$, 100%; Asian American, $n = 30$, 100%; Latino, $n = 9$, 81.8%; and White, $n = 1,128$, 99.5%), Latino men were more likely than their counterparts to behave in this manner. No significant differences were found for degree of provocative dress $\chi^2(3, N = 1,318) = 3.64$, $p > .05$; sexual gazing $\chi^2(3, N = 1,326) = 6.21$, $p > .05$; or alluring behavior $\chi^2(3, N = 1,325) = 6.04$, $p > .05$.

CONCLUSIONS

Overall, these results indicate that in many regards the race of the character has little impact on manifestations of sex/sensuality in prime-time TV commercials. Suggestive dress and self-gazing were no more associated with one group of females than another. For men, depictions of provocative dress, alluring behavior, and self-gazing were equivalent across races. Nevertheless, the findings do reveal some notable distinctions in sexualized portrayals based on race, predominantly for Latinos.

Implications

While results from content analyses can provide only descriptive information regarding the depictions of race in advertising, theories of media effects make important contributions toward understanding the potential influence of exposure to such media images on consumers. In particular, Bandura's social cognitive theory and Gerbner's cultivation theory provide valuable insights into the potential impact of exposure on both individuals and society.

Social cognitive theory contends that viewers learn about the world, others, and themselves from both real-life models as well as media models (Bandura, 1994, 2002). Learning is particularly likely when models are attractive, rewarded (or not punished) for their attitudes and/or behaviors, and when consumers perceive similarities between themselves and the media characters (e.g., in terms of gender, age, race). Not only may consumers learn new behaviors, but they also may acquire knowledge about social values and rules of conduct. Exposure to behaviors depicted in the media has even been shown, under certain circumstances, to alter or introduce values as well as to influence opinions and attitudes (see Bandura, 2002, for a review). This may be particularly true of advertising content as the aim of these repetitive messages is, of course, persuasion. Great care is taken by advertisers to ensure that their ads are appropriately appealing and accurately targeted to interest the desired market.

Research provides some evidence for social learning from sexual media content with regard to body dissatisfaction and attitudes toward sex (Field et al., 1999; Greeson & Williams, 1986; Hofschire & Greenberg, 2001; Kalof, 1999; Stice & Shaw, 1994). Hofschire and Greenberg (2001) found that identification with thin models in the media and consumption of magazines and television were related to overall body dissatisfaction, belief in ideal body stereotypes (e.g., muscularity for males, thinness for females), and exercising and dieting. Correspondingly, findings from Stice and Shaw (1994) revealed that exposure to magazine images containing exceptionally thin female models resulted in greater depression, stress, guilt, shame, insecurity, and body dissatisfaction among women, compared with those who viewed average-sized models or no models at all. Similarly, scholars have found positive correlations between the frequency of reading women's magazines and increased prevalence of dieting or exercising to lose weight (Field et al., 1999). Attitudes about sex and its context have also been tied to social learning from the media. One experimental study found that teenagers who watched even a few music videos held more permissive attitudes about premarital sex than those who had no exposure (Greeson & Williams, 1986). Moreover, Kalof (1999) found that college women's acceptance of interpersonal violence was influenced by exposure to stereotypical images of gender and sexuality in music videos.

What does this mean for viewers exposed to the sexualized images of race/ethnicity found in the present study? Social cognitive theory would suggest that consumption of sexualized images of self (particularly when positively reinforced and repeated) may result in a belief that one's value or power comes from sexuality rather than other attributes. For Latino viewers, the potential for commercial images to guide real-world attitudes and behaviors would be most concerning. More than any other racial/ethnic group examined in this study, Latinos were associated with sexualized characteristics or engaged in sexual behaviors. Moreover, due to the scarcity of Latino depictions in advertising, they may receive added attention from individuals looking for images of self, thereby making the quality of these portrayals of even greater consequence. One possible message they (and all other consumers) may reap from television ads is that in order to be valued, they must fit idealized beauty standards of thinness and youthfulness. Moreover, Latinas, in particular, may learn that their value is based on emphasizing their sexuality. Considering their association with behaviors such as sexual gazing (as well as their underrepresentation), Latino males may learn similar messages about their ideal gender roles. From this theoretical framework, it would additionally be expected that these representations would impact non-Latino viewers. For instance, they might learn to organize their expectations about Latinos around perceptions of their sexual abilities and expertise (as emphasized in commercials), especially among viewers with little real-world contact to counterbalance these images.

Taking a more macro-level approach, cultivation theory proposes that television is a cultural storyteller, imparting messages about the way the world works through its patterned portrayals of people, events, and phenomena (Gerbner, Gross, Morgan, & Signorielli, 1994). Television's constant repetition of myths and ideologies results in a legitimization of the existing social order. Consequently, watching television over time can cultivate the impression, among heavy viewers, that the real world is very much like the world seen on TV. For example, studies have demonstrated that heavier television viewers are more likely to believe the world is violent and frightening, because they witness this on television (see Gerbner et al., 2002, for a review).

With regard to sexual content, research has shown that among adolescents, heavy television viewing is predictive of negative attitudes toward remaining a virgin (Courtright & Baran, 1980). Heavier exposure to sexual content on television also has been shown to be associated with earlier initiation of sexual intercourse (Brown & Newcomer, 1991; Peterson, Moore, & Furstenberg, 1991). Studies have additionally found that people who are heavy viewers of soap operas are more likely than nonviewers to overestimate the number of abortions, the incidence of sexually transmitted disease, and the occurrence of illegitimate children in the real world (Buerkel-Rothfuss & Mayes, 1981; Buerkel-Rothfuss & Strouse, 1993). Although no such study has tested this proposition, the cultivation hypothesis might predict that if racial minorities are thematically depicted in a sexualized manner in commercials, then heavy viewers might begin to associate sex with race outside of the television context.

Considering the implications based on these theoretical frameworks, one might expect that significant attention also has been paid to empirical tests of the influence of such imagery on viewers. On the contrary, only a handful of studies have addressed the effect of viewing sexual media content, and no studies have focused specifically on the effects of viewing sexualized images of racial minorities. Setting aside the limitations resulting from the small number of minority depictions in ads, at least part of the reason for this dearth of research is the perceived sensitivity of sex as a research topic (Brown & Stern, 2002; Reichert & Lambiase, 2003). Regrettably, societal discomfort with sexuality and its consequences often inhibits investigation of the relationship between sexual media consumption and sexual attitudes and behaviors. As an alternative, empirically describing and evaluating sexual media messages through content analyses such as this one provides a relatively innocuous means to consider such associations.

Limitations and Future Research

While this examination provides only an introductory glance at representations of sex across race and gender, the results do offer preliminary insights into this underexplored area of inquiry. Ultimately, however, quantitative content analysis may not be the ideal method for such assessments as the small number of minority representations prohibits many meaningful analyses. In future examinations, researchers may want to include textual analyses of this content as such assessments may provide the much needed in-depth evaluations that quantitative analyses are unable to provide (see Grimes, this volume). Additionally, detailed discussions of how such images are embedded within the context of individual commercials would shed light on the stories told about race and sexuality in television advertising.

Future studies might also expand the focus of this analysis to examine a larger array of media outlets, including those expressly targeted toward minority audiences (such as BET and Univision). Indeed, the current report's exclusive examination of broadcast networks paints only one piece of the larger picture of contemporary television advertising. On cable channels designed specifically for minority audiences, representations of minorities in advertisements are likely to be much more frequent as well as more diverse. Evaluating sexual imagery on these channels may offer greater insight into the kinds of information about sexuality that are offered to, and ultimately consumed by, audience members.

When considering issues such as the frequency of race portrayals, it is also important to recognize the implications associated with the inclusion of repeat commercials in the coding process. For example, one advertisement, shown multiple times or on multiple networks, could boost the frequency count of minority characters in the overall sample (despite a lack of distribution among advertisements) as well as skew assessments of content.

Finally, future research would wisely begin to examine how audiences process advertising messages featuring sexualized images of race and how they are affected by such content. Although content analyses are useful for documenting patterns in these portrayals, effects studies and audience research are necessary in order to understand the influence of exposure on the lives, behaviors, and attitudes of contemporary viewers.

REFERENCES

Bandura, A. (1994). Social cognitive theory of mass communication. In J. Bryant & D. Zillmann (Eds.), *Media effects* (pp. 61–90). Hillsdale, NJ: Lawrence Erlbaum Associates.

Bandura, A. (2002). Social cognitive theory of mass communication. In J. Bryant & D. Zillmann (Eds.), *Media effects: Advances in theory and research* (pp. 121–154). Mahwah, NJ: Lawrence Erlbaum Associates.

Bartsch, R., Burnetts, R., Diller, T., & Rankin-Williams, E. (2000). Gender representation in television commercials: Updating an update. *Sex Roles, 43,* 735–743.

Bowen, L., & Schmid, J. (1997). Minority presence and portrayal in mainstream magazine advertising: An update. *Journal of Mass Communication Quarterly, 74,* 134–146.

Brown, J. D., & Newcomer, S. (1991). Television viewing and adolescents' sexual behavior. *Journal of Homosexuality, 21*(1/2), 77–91.

Brown, J., & Stern, S. (2002). Sex and the media. In J. R. Schement (Ed.), *Encyclopedia of communication and information* (pp. 923–929). New York: Macmillan Reference.

Buerkel-Rothfuss, N. L., & Mayes, S. (1981). Soap opera viewing: The cultivation effect. *Journal of Communication, 31*(3), 108–115.

Buerkel-Rothfuss, N. L., & Strouse, J. S. (1993). Media exposure and perceptions of sexual behaviors: The cultivation hypothesis moves to the bedroom. In B. S. Greenberg, J. D. Brown, & N. Buerkel-Rothfuss (Eds.), *Media, sex, and the adolescent* (pp. 225–247). Cresskill, NJ: Hampton Press.

Bush, R., Solomon, P., & Hair, J., Jr. (1977). There are more Blacks in TV commercials. *Journal of Advertising Research, 17,* 21–25.

BWN (2002). *Business Women's Network, Chapter 71: Advertising/Marketing and Diversity.* Retrieved January 15, 2003, http://www.ewowfacts.com/.

Coltrane, S., & Messineo, M. (2000). The perpetuation of subtle prejudice: Race and gender imagery in 1990s television advertising. *Sex Roles, 42,* 363–389.

Cope, K. M., & Kunkel, D. (2002). Sex in teen programming. In J. Brown, J. Steele, & K. Walsh-Childers (Eds.), *Sexual teens, sexual media* (pp. 59–78). Mahwah, NJ: Lawrence Erlbaum Associates.

Cortese, A. (1999). *Provocateur: Images of women and minorities in advertising* (pp. 77–102). Oxford, England: Rowman & Littlefield.

Courtright, J., & Baran, S. (1980). The acquisition of sexual information by young people. *Journalism Quarterly, 57*(1), 107–114.

Craig, S. (1992). Women as home caregivers: Gender portrayals in OTC drug commercials. *Journal of Drug Education, 22,* 303–312.

Czepiec, H., & Kelly, J. (1983). Analyzing Hispanic roles in advertising: A portrait of an emerging subculture. *Current Issues and Research in Advertising, 6,* 219–240.

Dates, J. (1993). Advertising. In J. Dates & W. Barlow (Eds.), *Split image: African Americans in the mass media* (pp. 461–491). Washington, DC: Harvard University Press.

Dominick, J., & Greenberg, B. S. (1970). Three seasons of Blacks on television. *Journal of Advertising Research, 10,* 21–27.

Field, A., Cheung, L., Herzog, D., Gortmaker, S., & Colditz, G. (1999). Exposure to the mass media and weight concerns among girls. *Pediatrics, 103*(3), 361–365.

Fullerton, J., & Kendrick, A. (2000). Portrayal of men and women in U.S. Spanish-language television commercials. *Journalism & Mass Communication Quarterly, 77,* 128–142.

Gerbner, G., Gross, L., Morgan, M., & Signorielli, N. (1994). Growing up with television: The cultivation perspective. In J. Bryant and D. Zillman (Eds.), *Media effects* (pp. 17–41). Hillsdale, NJ: Lawrence Erlbaum Associates.

Gerbner, G., Gross, L., Morgan, M., Signorielli, N., & Shanahan, J. (2002). Growing up with television: Cultivation processes. In J. Bryant & D. Zillmann (Eds.), *Media effects: Advances in theory and research* (pp. 43–67). Mahwah, NJ: Lawrence Erlbaum Associates.

Green, M. (1993). Images of Native Americans in advertising: Some moral issues. *Journal of Business Ethics, 12,* 323–330.

Greenberg, B., Brown, J., & Buerkel-Rothfuss, N. (Eds.). (1993). *Media, sex, and the adolescent.* Creskill, NJ: Hampton Press.

Greenberg, B., Mastro, D., & Brand, J. (2002). Minorities and the mass media: Television into the 21st century. In J. Bryant & D. Zillmann (Eds.), *Media effects: Advances in theory and research* (pp. 333–351). Mahwah, NJ: Lawrence Erlbaum Associates.

Greeson, L. E., & Williams, R. A. (1986). Social implications of music videos for youth: An analysis of the content and effects of MTV. *Youth & Society, 18*(2), 177–189.

Harris, R. (1999). Advertising: Food (and everything else) for thought. In J. Harris (Ed.), *A cognitive psychology of mass communication* (pp. 71–95). Mahwah, NJ: Lawrence Erlbaum Associates.

Hacker, G., Collins, R., & Jacobson, M. (1987). *Marketing booze to Blacks.* Washington, DC: Center for Science in the Public Interest.

Heintz-Knowles, K. (1996). *Sexual activity on daytime soap operas: A content analysis of five weeks of television programming.* Menlo Park, CA: Kaiser Family Foundation.

Hofschire, L. J., & Greenberg, B. S. (2001). Media's impact on adolescents' body dissatisfaction. In J. D. Brown, J. R. Steele, & K. Walsh-Childers (Eds.) *Sexual teens, sexual media* (pp. 125–149). Mahwah, NJ: Lawrence Erlbaum Associates.

Jackson, L., & Ervin, K. (1991). The frequency and portrayal of Black females in fashion advertisements. *Journal of Black Psychology, 18,* 67–70.

Kalof, L. (1999). The effects of gender and music video imagery on sexual attitudes. *Journal of Social Psychology, 139*(3), 366–378.

Kunkel, D., Cope, K. M., & Colvin, C. (1996). *Sexual messages on family hour television: Content and context.* Menlo Park, CA: Kaiser Family Foundation.

Lai, H., Tan, Z., & Tharp, M. (1990). Receiver prejudice and model ethnicity: Impact on advertising effectiveness. *Journalism Quarterly, 67,* 794–803.

Li, H. (2003). *Advertising media.* Retrieved January 15, 2003, http://www.admedia.org/.

Licata, J., & Biswas, A. (1993). Representation, roles, and occupational status of Black models in television advertisements. *Journalism Quarterly, 70,* 868–882.

Lovdal, L. (1989). Sex role messages in television commercials: An update. *Sex Roles, 21,* 715–724.

McLaughlin, T., & Goulet, N. (1999). Gender advertisements in magazines aimed at African Americans: A comparison to their occurrence in magazines aimed at Caucasians. *Sex Roles, 40,* 61–71.

Mehaffy, M. (1997). Advertising race/raceing advertising: The feminine consumer(-nation), 1976–1900. *Signs, 23*, 131–174.

Merskin, D. (1998). Sending up signals: A survey of Native American media use and representation in the mass media. *Howard Journal of Communications, 9*, 333–345.

Peterson, J., Moore, K., & Furstenberg, F. (1991). Television viewing and early initiation of sexual intercourse. Is there a link? *Journal of Homosexuality, 21*(1/2), 93–118.

Plous, S., & Neptune, D. (1997). Racial and gender biases in magazine advertising. A content-analytic study. *Psychology of Women Quarterly, 21*, 627–644.

Potter, W. J., & Levine-Donnerstein, D. (1999). Rethinking validity and reliability in content analysis. *Journal of Applied Communication Research, 27*, 258–284.

Reichert, T., & Lambiase, J. (Eds.). (2003). *Sex in advertising: Perspectives on the erotic appeal.* Mahwah, NJ: Lawrence Erlbaum Associates.

Reichert, T., Lambiase, J., Morgan, S., Carstarphen, M., & Zavoina, S. (1999). Cheesecake and beefcake: No matter how you slice it, sexual explicitness in advertising continues to increase. *Journalism and Mass Communication Quarterly, 76*, 7–20.

Rosenthal, R. (1987). Sampling judges and encoders. In R. Rosenthal (Ed.), *Judgment studies: Design, analysis, and meta-analysis* (pp. 9–13). New York: Cambridge University Press.

Ruffins, F. (1998). Reflecting on ethnic imagery in the landscape of commerce, 1945–1975. In S. Strasser, C. McGovern, and M. Judt (Eds.), *Getting and spending: European and American consumer societies in the twentieth century* (pp. 372–406). Cambridge, England: Cambridge University Press.

Selig Center for Economic Growth (2002). *The multicultural economy 2002: Minority buying poser in the new century.* Retrieved January 15, 2003, http://www.selig.uga.edu/forecast/GBEC/GBEC022Q.pdf.

Signorielli, N., McLeod, D., & Healy, E. (1994). Gender stereotypes in MTV commercials: The beat goes on. *Journal of Broadcasting and Electronic Media, 38*, 91–102.

Snyder, R., Freeman, J., & Condray, S. (1995). Magazine readership profiles and depictions of African Americans in magazine advertisements. *Howard Journal of Communication, 6*, 1–11.

Stern, B. (1999). Gender and multicultural issues in advertising: Stages on the research highway. *Journal of Advertising, 28*, 1–9.

Stice, E., & Shaw, H. (1994). Adverse-effects of the media portrayed thin-ideal on women and linkages to bulimic symptomatology. *Journal of Social and Clinical Psychology, 13*(3), 288–308.

Stunkard, A., Sorensen, T., & Schulsinger, F. (1983). Use of the Danish adoption register for the study of obesity and thinness. In S. Kety (Ed.), *The genetics of neurological and psychiatric disorders* (pp. 115–120). New York: Raven Press.

Taylor, C., & Bang, H. (1997). Portrayals of Latinos in magazine advertising. *Journalism and Mass Communication Quarterly, 74*, 285–303.

Taylor, C., Lee, J., & Stern, B. (1995). Portrayals of African, Hispanic, and Asian Americans in magazine advertising. *American Behavioral Scientist, 38*, 608–621.

Taylor, C., & Stern, B. (1997). Asian-Americans: Television advertising and the "model minority" stereotype. *Journal of Advertising, 26*, 47–60.

Verna, M. (1975). The female image in children's TV commercials. *Journal of Broadcasting, 19*, 195–216.

Wilkes, R. E., & Valencia, H. (1989). Hispanics and Blacks in television commercials. *Journal of Advertising, 18*, 19–25.

Wilson, C., & Gutierrez, F. (1995). *Race, multiculturalism, and the mass media: From mass to class communication* (pp. 109–138). Thousand Oaks, CA: Sage.

Zinkhan, G., Qualls, W., & Biswas, A. (1990). The use of Blacks in magazine and television advertising: 1946–1986. *Journalism Quarterly, 67*, 547–553.

Chapter 17

"Getting a Bit of the Other":* Sexualized Stereotypes of Asian and Black Women in Planned Parenthood Advertising

Diane Susan Grimes
Syracuse University

Consider an advertisement showing a Black male and White male standing together and smiling. Now notice that the Black male is dressed in work clothes and hard hat while the White male is dressed as a manager. The advertisement appears to be progressive because it is racially inclusive. However, the superficial acknowledgment of difference is based on stereotypes rather than a range of possible roles for members of each racial group. In such stereotypical-but-progressive-appearing ads, we are encouraged to accept the assumption that White males are (and should be) managers and Black males are (and should be) workers. This appears normal, as the "natural order" of things. Therefore, appearances are deceiving because this "inclusive" advertisement does not support deep changes in power relations between different groups.

My goal in this chapter is to analyze the stereotypes about several race–gender groups as well as the relationships between these groups that are suggested in four advertisements for Planned Parenthood. Like the example above, analysis of the Planned Parenthood advertisements can demonstrate how problematic assumptions about various groups get continued and reinforced in subtle ways. The Planned Parenthood advertisements have serious consequences that go beyond perpetuating inaccurate stereotypes. For example, readers may feel members of certain groups are

---

*According to bell hooks (1992), "Getting a bit of the other" is a slang term for sexual intercourse.

dangerous sexual partners while others are not. Either of these assumptions could lead to problematic sexual behaviors. Or, readers who might benefit from the advertisements may ignore them because such readers do not feel the advertisements address them. This could also lead to problematic behaviors. These consequences will be fully explored in the following sections.

In short, I ask what stories these advertisements tell and what stereotypes they draw on to tell them. After a brief exploration of why it is important to attend to advertising and a discussion of method, I analyze the four advertisements by drawing on literature concerned with stereotypes of the relevant groups and relations between them. I conclude by considering possible negative consequences of the advertisements or those like them.

ADVERTISING MATTERS

The images that we see in advertising have consequences. O'Barr (1994) distinguished between "primary discourse," which are the ideas about the products or services that the advertisers straightforwardly portray, and "secondary discourse"—the ideas about society and culture suggested in advertising. In other words, the images show us who waits on whom, who likes to play basketball, who cares about the laundry, who is not too bright. Images are often presented in ways that both draw on and reinforce stereotypes because audiences will "understand" the image (Qualter, 1991). They have seen it before and know what it means (Baker, 1961).

For example, Danae Clark (1993) wrote about heterosexist and nonheterosexist "readings" of ambiguous fashion advertisements. If readers follow typical stereotypes, they will read a male and female together as a couple but two women lounging together as roommates or friends (Cortese, 1999). A nonheterosexist reading opens the possibility that the two women are lovers. Exploring the history and characteristics of relevant stereotypes allows us to read advertising in new ways. It allows us to question what we have been taught and begin to be aware of our assumptions and how we acquired them.

Awareness of assumptions is useful because stereotypical representations impact how various groups are perceived, their treatment, and the resources available to them. Group members may be marginalized—they may not be seen or heard; they may be thought of as unimportant. They may be "Othered," seen as fundamentally different from "ordinary" people and therefore deserving of different treatment. The Other is usually everything "we" are not, implying that "they" represent all the negative characteristics we wish we did not have (Miles, 1989; Takaki, 1990). Some othered groups may be seen as having positive qualities, but even positive stereotypes are problematic. Stereotypes always lump group members together without leaving room for the variation that is present in all groups.

O'Barr (1994) argued that secondary images of othered groups provide suggestions for relations between advertising's intended audience and those defined as outside that audience. These suggestions constitute a guide for relations between the self and others, between "us" and "them." The most frequently depicted qualities of such relationships are hierarchy, dominance, and subordination.

THEORETICAL APPROACH

The goal of this study is to identify and explicate stereotypes in four advertisements for Planned Parenthood and to explore how the examples might reinforce racial and gender status quos. I first saw these advertisements in 1994 in the school newspaper at my university. However, I did not believe they were part of a local campaign. This is because my university and the surrounding town are very White (at that time, the university was about 95% percent White and the town was 98% White) with high levels of racial tension. If audience analysis had been done for a local campaign, I do not think it would have resulted in these (superficially) racially inclusive ads. Several months later, I also saw one of the same advertisements in an out-of-state newspaper.

I chose the Planned Parenthood advertisements based on their heuristic value. Since much of my work deals with diversity (Grimes, 2002a; Grimes & Richard, 2003) and Whiteness (Grimes, 2001, 2002b), I make it a practice to scan my environment for interesting arguments and examples of everyday assumptions about difference. To explore these assumptions, "close reading" is useful because it allows for the examination of interpretations that arise out of a detailed engagement with a text. In poetry, such a reading might focus on features like "setting, imagery, key statements, the sound of the poetry, language use, [and] intertextuality" (Lye, 1997). In my work, I look for hidden assumptions that have to do with power and difference, and in this case, worth.

Because I examine what is hidden below the surface (Deetz & Kersten, 1983), a small corpus of texts (while drawing on a broader understanding of the issues) allows for a richer analysis. Clark's (1993) analysis of the ambiguous fashion advertisements mentioned above is a pertinent example. Analyses of a small body of (or even single) movies are not uncommon (e.g., Barlowe, 1998; Madison, 1999; Shome, 1996). Useful precedents may also be seen in close readings of brief passages of a discipline's core texts (Calás & Smircich, 1991) as well as of single organizational events (Rosen, 1985, 1988).

I would rather offer a perspective that allows readers to become aware of problematic texts in their everyday lives than to (a) make an argument about the creators' intentions or (b) to "prove" that a certain percentage of readers will read a text in the way I have described. Each of these points would be made particularly difficult because creators and readers may not be aware of the assumptions about difference they draw on and how those assumptions influence their reading of a text. In addition, each point would require a very different study and a different method.

ANALYSIS

Of the four advertisements for Planned Parenthood, three feature photographs of a male and female (the pairs are an Asian woman and White man, a Black woman and White man, and a White woman and Black man). The advertisements present information about Planned Parenthood's counseling, testing, treatment, and referral services for sexually transmitted diseases. In the fourth advertisement, a Black woman directly addresses the reader about her experiences with Planned Parenthood's gynecological services.

Because human beings are sense-makers, when we see images we create narratives about them. We do this by drawing on both the primary and secondary discourses of advertising. Narratives tend to have a moral quality—they are about right and wrong; they contain "do's" and "don'ts" (White, 1987). So, we might imagine a "boy meets girl" story about the male/female pairs we see in the Planned Parenthood advertisements. We might, if we read them as heterosexist texts, think of the pairs as potential sexual partners. The pairs are *potential* partners because they are photographed separately, not as a couple with their arms around each other, for instance. Their potential liaison is also suggested by the advertisements' topics—sexual activity and its consequences. Therefore, I argue the advertisements are moral narratives—about who should sleep with whom.

The analysis unfolds as follows: I describe the advertisements and the stereotypes of the various "Others" presented. I turn first to the two advertisements featuring women of color and White men. Next, I analyze the advertisements based on the stereotypes they draw on. Then, I discuss the last female/male pair (the Black man and White woman) and, finally, the advertisement featuring the Black woman. Although chronologically this last advertisement appeared first, I discuss it last as it offers a contrast and a potentially useful alternative to the three advertisements featuring the female/male pairs.

Lotus Blossom

The first advertisement offers the large headline: "ARE YOU SLEEPING WITH SOMEONE TO DIE FOR?" Beneath this headline and to the left is a photograph of a college-age Asian woman (see Fig. 17.1). She is shown from the chest up, her shirt unbuttoned to the bottom of the photograph,

Are you sleeping with someone to die for?

The person you're sleeping with could have a sexually transmitted disease. Even AIDS. If you're not up to date on how to protect yourself, you could be making a date with death.

It's not our intention to scare you. What we want to do is help. We sincerely care about you. We're sensitive, understanding and professional. We're also very affordable and everything is confidential.

You can talk to us about anything, and get straight answers. Our extensive range of services: safer sex education, testing and treatment of sexually transmitted diseases, plus HIV testing, counseling and referral, and more.

To be honest, abstinence is the only sure protection. But we're not going to tell you how to lead your life. We just want to offer you the best reproductive health care you can get.

Make the smart choice. Come to Planned Parenthood.

Evening Clinics Available!
For An Appointment, Call 743-4434
📁 Planned Parenthood®
103 Northwestern

FIG. 17.1. Lotus Blossom.

her long hair seductively arranged over one shoulder. Her gaze is direct, meeting that of the viewer. Her head is lifted and tilted sideways, exposing her neck in a classic pose of submission. Among all the photographs, hers is the only one in which her sexualization is depicted through her dress and pose. Beside her photograph are the words:

> The person you're sleeping with could have a sexually transmitted disease. Even AIDS. If you're not up to date on how to protect yourself, you could be making a date with death.

In the bottom right-hand corner is a photograph of a college-age White male. He is sitting on a stool; we see him from the knees up. His stance is reminiscent of a boxer's; he crouches forward, arms back, looking distrustfully at the camera. His dress is not sexualized and he looks younger and less "experienced" than his counterpart above. While the "Oriental temptress" looks like she is coming ever closer, the young man looks like he is ready to turn around and walk out of the back of the photograph. The words beside his photograph are:

> To be honest, abstinence is the only sure protection. But we're not going to tell you how to lead your life. We just want to offer you the best reproductive health care you can get.

The "boy meets girl" story suggested in this advertisement conjures up long-standing stereotypes of Asian women as exotic, sexualized Others (Gerster, 1995; Tajima, 1989).

One such stereotype, presented by Aki Uchida (1998), is the Oriental Woman. She (singular because she supposedly encompasses all Asian women, ignoring the many differences in any group of women) represents an image of Asian women as "created by the Western mind based on the Western experience of the Orient" (p. 161). The Oriental Woman's characteristics include "submissiveness, subservience, obedience, passivity and domesticity" (p. 162). She is an exotic "love interest for White men" (Tajima, 1989, p. 309).

Mainstream U.S. media focus on the Oriental Woman as "exotic and sexy" (Uchida, 1998, p. 162) based on her historical association in the United States with prostitution. The few Chinese women brought to the United States in the latter half of the 1800s were sold into prostitution to serve Chinese laborers. Allowed in the country only as temporary workers, these men were forbidden by custom and law from bringing their wives to the United States or marrying White women (Fujitomi & Wong, 1973). The association with prostitution also links the "subservient but devious" (Uchida, 1998, p. 164) Oriental Woman to "sexual corruption," "demoralizing and tainting the blood of White American youths" and "spreading diseases" (p. 163).

The Oriental Woman also had a well-known career in Asian countries during U.S. involvements there. Again, the focus was on sexuality, since Japanese and Korean women labored as bar girls, prostitutes, and geishas serving U.S. forces. Because this was usually the only context in which members of the military interacted with Asian women, upon return to the United States, these stereotypes were transferred to Asian and Asian American women here. In movies, the overseas Oriental Woman was paired with a White male who predictably returned home to his White woman, his Lotus Blossom (one personification of the Oriental Woman) having had the good sense to expire from a fatal illness (Tajima, 1989).

I would argue that the woman in the Planned Parenthood advertisement is none other than Lotus Blossom. She is sexy, exotic, submissive yet unsafe, associated with disease, dangerous to young White males. In the old movies, Lotus Blossom died from some exotic disease that did not affect her partner. In the present and future, that disease could be AIDS, suggesting a different ending than the half-happy one in the old movies. I spin out some of the implications of this argument after I describe the advertisement featuring the Black female and White male.

Brown Sugar

The next advertisement depicts a Black woman in the upper left-hand photograph slot (see Fig. 17.2). She is under a large headline that reads: "HOW OFTEN DO YOU HAVE KILLER SEX?" In this advertisement, the female and male models are more similar to each other; they are both

FIG. 17.2. Brown Sugar.

pictured at a similar distance from the camera and both are wearing rather baggy sweatshirts. The woman has her elbow resting on her knee and her chin on her hand. She is not smiling and her head is tilted slightly back, suggesting a disdainful attitude. Beside her photograph are the words:

> We're talking about killer sex in the true sense of the word. Sex without the right precautions. Sex that can turn you off... for good.

The White male in the lower right-hand photograph slot is shown slumped forward and to the left on his stool. His hair is parted in the middle, and he looks young, kind of goofy, unsure and perhaps embarrassed. Beside his picture are the words:

> These days, you've got to know all about safer sex. And we can help. We also provide testing and treatment of sexually transmitted diseases, plus HIV testing, counseling and referral, and much more.

Like Asian women, Black women are stereotypically associated with sexuality (Collins, 1990; Giddings, 1984; Pieterse, 1990). During slave times, all Black women were assumed to be sexually immoral by nature (hooks, 1981; Jacobs, 1987). In a chapter entitled "Selling Hot Pussy: Representations of Black Female Sexuality in the Cultural Marketplace," hooks (1992) pointed out that Black women are represented as "sexually available and licentious" (p. 65), as having a sexuality "synonymous with wild animalistic lust" (p. 67), and as "sexual savages" (p. 68). In other words, they are seen as primitive and wild (Cortese, 1999). Hooks argued that contemporary representations of Black female sexuality have not changed much from those of centuries ago. Some recent advertisements portray Black women as made up and dressed like wild animals, for example, tigers (Cortese, 1999). Hooks noted the fascination with "the exotic Other who promises to fulfill racial and sexual stereotypes, to satisfy longings" (p. 73).

Sexualized Black female Others can be seen in unexpected places. I noticed them in a fashion catalog in which almost all the models are White except in the beachwear section. The beachwear section features mostly models that readers are expected to understand as non-White. There are multiple iterations of page-filling close shots of non-White headless and legless bodies. In my undergraduate social psychology textbook, there are photographs accompanying each chapter's title page. The only photograph that includes a Black woman begins the chapter on sexual behavior. She is shown locked in passionate embrace with her almost nude lover. Many repetitions in multiple contexts reinforce this image while allowing us to be unaware of its influence.

This exotic Other is also dangerous in that Blacks are seen as diseased (Williams, 1997). In the popular imagination, Africa is the origin point of AIDS. Given the disdainful look of the model in the Planned Parenthood advertisement, hooks' (1992) further nuanced reading of the sexually available Black female is instructive. In discussing Tina Turner's image, she noted a coming together of sexuality and power. Of Turner she said:

> It is not that she is no longer represented as available; she is open only to those whom she chooses. Assuming the role of hunter, she is the sexualized woman who makes men and women her prey. . . . Rather than being a pleasure based eroticism, it is ruthless, violent; it is about women using sexual power to do violence to the male Other. (pp. 68–69)

This certainly fits well with the headline referring to death. Because of this, and because of the particular image of Black female sexuality represented, I contend this more nuanced stereotype is at play in the Black female/White male advertisement. These elements make Brown Sugar every bit as dangerous to unsuspecting White males as Lotus Blossom.

Having explored the stereotypes associated with the women in each of these advertisements, it is possible to analyze them more fully. A first consideration is audience.

"Keep Away From Those Girls"

An interesting question is who is being addressed in these two advertisements. It appears that in each an omnipotent narrator gives a warning to the White male about the dangerous yet exotic female Other. This reading is suggested by the proximity of the advice portions of the advertisements to the photographs of the White males. The warning sections of the advertisements, both headlines and text, are near the photographs of the female Others. This positioning is quite different from the advertisement (discussed below) in which the female model directly addresses the reader, both in the headline and text, and describes her own experiences.

It could be that these two advertisements are attempting to subvert common stereotypes, and indeed there are potentially progressive elements at play. There may be an assertion of sexual agency in the case of the women. The male models are not stereotypical powerful White males. The advertisements may be trying to get away from the image of "wild young guys" who cannot or will not control themselves by portraying males who look uncertain contrasted with females who appear more forward. Or, the advertisements may be portraying visually how young men feel rather than the confident appearance that they are obligated to project. The desire "to leave behind White 'innocence' and enter the world of 'experience" (p. 23) is noted by hooks (1992):

> It was commonly accepted that one "shopped" for sexual partners....To these young [White] males and their buddies, fucking was a way to confront the Other, as well as a way to make themselves over....As is often the case in this society, they were confident that non-White people had more life experience, were more worldly, sensual, and sexual because they were different. (p. 23)

"Precisely!" says the advertisements' narrator, "And boys, this is exactly the type of behavior I am cautioning you about." Both women of color and their attendant stereotypes also conjure up notions of prostitution that link with popular depictions of prostitutes continuing to "turn tricks" after contracting AIDS; both call for strong warning from the narrator.

The narrator has no advice for the female Others. The focus is on prevention, those "good and worthy people" who do not (yet) have sexually transmitted diseases are warned to stay away from the "killer sex" of those "bad and unworthy people" who already have sexually transmitted diseases. This message is why I contend the advertisements can be read as a warning to people like one type of model (the White males) while holding up people like the other (the exotic and sexualized female Others) as an example to be avoided. As Julie Burchill put it in her exploration of Black female/White male relationships in *Girls on Film*:

> Multiracial romance brought tears, traumas, and suicide. The message was clear: you intelligent White men suffer enough guilt because of what your grandaddy did—you want to suffer some more! Keep away from those girls....(as cited in hooks, 1992, p. 73)

In the case of the Planned Parenthood advertisements, suggesting that certain people are not worthy or are dangerous and already diseased could have negative consequences for the sponsoring organization's goals. If the goal is to persuade people to be responsible sexual partners and to be tested and treated if they have sexually transmitted diseases, excluding large groups of people from that goal, and indeed appearing to blame them for AIDS, is not helpful. This is why it is important to consider the stereotypes depicted in advertising and consider their possible consequences.

"Don't Have Sex With the Dark"

As I began to write this chapter, I saw the Planned Parenthood advertisements as problematic because of their depiction of sexualized female Others. I noticed there had not been a depiction of the "really taboo" mixed-race couple—the Black male and White female. Then, a new advertisement

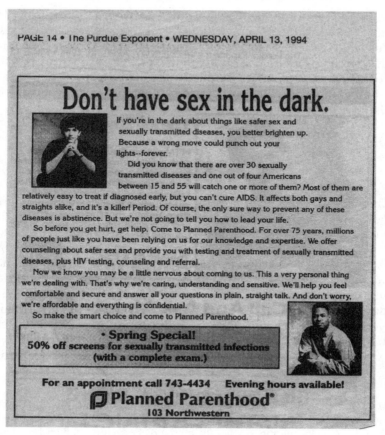

FIG. 17.3. "Don't have sex with the dark."

appeared (see Fig. 17.3). This one eschews the headline-question entirely, and begins with the advice "DON'T HAVE SEX IN THE DARK." The top left-hand slot, usually reserved for the exotic female Other, is taken over by a college-age White female. She is dressed all in black (the only one out of the seven photographs), sitting cross-legged, looking very symmetrical with her elbows on her knees and her hands clasped under her chin. She looks alert, with neither a "come-hither" look nor a fearful and uncertain look. She looks solid and grounded. She is not smiling. The advice continues immediately in the text rather than there being several sentences of information before the consequences—a "date with death," "turned off for good"—are brought up. The text reads:

> If you're in the dark about things like safer sex and sexually transmitted diseases, you better brighten up. Because a wrong move could punch out your lights—forever.

In the bottom right-hand corner sits a college-age Black male. He is leaning in toward the camera, with his arms casually crossed and resting on his leg. He seems (again, alone among all of the photographs) to be slightly smiling. The last two lines of the advertisement's text are next to the top of his photograph; however, one's attention is drawn to a highlighted and boxed announcement next to his photograph. In large, bold print it reads:

> * Spring Special! *
> 50% off screens for sexually transmitted infections
> (with a complete exam.)

The story that this advertisement tells can be understood by rewriting its headline to read "DON'T HAVE SEX *WITH* THE DARK." This directive is in parallel but more strident and authoritative than the advice the narrator addresses to the young White men. The advertisement suggests the stereotypical connection between Black men and violence. As hooks (1990) put it, "Representations of Black men in mass media usually depict them as more violent than other men" (p. 71). In a column of the same student newspaper that ran the Planned Parenthood advertisements, a university Director of Diversity and Multicultural Affairs related a story. In it, she is told (during an informal discussion of hate speech) that "Blacks are violent." This experience led her to reflect on the problems with this stereotype:

> There were no qualifiers such as "some" or "I perceive that," just "Blacks are violent".... This man, with the proverbial fell swoop, included everyone in the group, including me, my family, all the Black faculty, staff and students at [the University] and their families and millions of other innocent people. (Mason, 1994, p. 4)

In the Planned Parenthood advertisement, the connection between Black men and violence is made in the phrase "punch out your lights." While the other advertisements predict negative outcomes such as a "date with death" or "turned off for good," there is not the sense of one person intentionally doing physical violence to another. The juxtaposition of the "spring special" announcement with the photograph of the Black male model suggests that he is dangerous and to be avoided for another reason. We are reminded of representations of Blacks already mentioned that suggest that a high proportion of "them" have AIDS as well as allegations that AIDS began in Africa. Again, in this advertisement, certain groups are addressed and certain groups are blamed and seen as unworthy. Unworthy groups are not invited to benefit from Planned Parenthood's services, thus perpetuating possible negative consequences.

FIG. 17.4. "A woman's special medical concerns."

"A Woman's Special Medical Concerns"

Consider now the first advertisement of the four, the only one not directly concerned with sexually transmitted disease (see Fig. 17.4). It pictures a Black woman who looks to be in her early 30s. She looks like a middle-class professional dressed casually for the weekend. Her clothing and demeanor are not sexualized.

Her photograph is in the upper left-hand corner under a headline that quotes her as saying, "I went because they were affordable. I stayed because they're wonderful." The words directly to the right of her photograph read:

> I first went to Planned Parenthood because I really couldn't afford a gyne-
> cologist. I was young. And nervous. And didn't know what to expect. But
> now I can afford to go anywhere. And you know what? I still go to Planned
> Parenthood.

Her statements about being a poor (I think we are meant to assume) college student who is young, nervous, and unsure might apply to almost any young person going to Planned Parenthood for its various services. However, the depiction draws on stereotypes about Black females as well.

It is interesting that the Planned Parenthood advertisement itself mentions nothing about sexual practices. For all we know, the model could be a nun. But because the advertisement is for Planned Parenthood, there is an assumption of sexual activity. Because we are aware on some level of the stereotype of the sexualized Black Other, using a Black female model highlights that assumption.

The advertisement also draws on stereotypes of Black women as poor, as sexually active too young, as uneducated. The story that readers might tell themselves based on this advertisement is not a moral tale based on who should sleep with whom, but it is a moral tale nevertheless. The story might be a rags to riches narrative in which a young woman controlled her reproduction and was able to "make it." There is an undercurrent of this story in contemporary discussions about "welfare mothers," "babies having babies," and other issues which focus on individual choice as if there were no issues that need to be considered at a societal level (Williams, 1997).

However, I believe this advertisement has potentially progressive elements as well, although still at the level of individual decisions. On one level, because the model states that she can afford to go to any gynecologist, she subverts the assumption that all Black people are poor. She went to Planned Parenthood, where she was exposed to family planning, while quite young. This might subvert the Black-girl-having-a-baby-just-to-get-on-welfare stereotype.

I find this advertisement to be the least problematic of the four because it shows the model speaking directly to the audience about her experiences. This is more helpful than having an omnipotent narrator whose intent is to lecture, frighten, and divide groups from one another, as do the other three advertisements. Therefore, it offers a good starting place for potential alternatives. Because the narrator is a hidden character in the narrative, he offers a subtle way to support the stereotypes presented by the images. While it is useful to reach out to young White males, which seems to be the narrator's role in several of the advertisements, to address these White males (as well as the White female) through scapegoating people of color is not helpful. If what we learn from the narrator were to be presented straightforwardly as some individual's experience, we might reject it as idiosyncratic or dismiss the individual as prejudiced. But because the narrator is hidden, we do not notice. He creates the world of the advertisements and we accept that world.

DISCUSSION AND CONCLUSIONS

The three Planned Parenthood advertisements that feature female–male pairs use problematic images and narrative structure. For some groups, the advertisements are prevented from doing what they are supposed to do, which is to encourage young people to get tested and treated for sexually transmitted disease, especially AIDS. For the in-group, in this case White males and White females, the underlying message is that if they "keep away" from sexual partners who are different, they will be safe.

Young people from Australia had similar misconceptions about AIDS—they thought that dangerous Others (the more distant socially, the more dangerous) were to blame for AIDS (Pittam & Gallois, 2000). It is possible that the Planned Parenthood advertisements reinforce rather than challenge similar racist misconceptions in the United States. And, of course, the advertisements do not give in-group readers a realistic picture of their risks or the behaviors they should change since members of their own group could give them AIDS.

In addition, those young people in the Othered groups may understand that the advertisements blame them and do not offer assistance or advice. Viewers of televised AIDS public service announcements divide advertisements into those "for me" or "not for me" (Lee & Davie, 1997). Readers of the Planned Parenthood advertisements may do the same, with non-Whites concluding the advertisements are "not for me" and therefore paying less attention, remembering less, and being less likely to change their behavior. Each advertisement may also be just one more negative message to Othered groups that they are not worthy. If such groups internalize that message, they may be less likely to protect themselves and others.

However, there are possible alternatives. Both the marginalization of sexualized exotic Others and the othering of those "bad" people (of whatever gender/race) who might give "us" a disease must be avoided. Photographs of couples might be used so that there is not the impression that one person in the dyad is worthy and the (O)ther is not. Or, males and females could be addressed in separate advertisements. Shots of models representing a group of five or six same-sex friends might be more realistic because we learn so much, whether accurate or not, from our peers. If these groupings were racially inclusive, they (depending on how they were actually photographed) might get away from othering people of color.

The advertisements should consciously use nonblaming language and must include and address those who may have sexually transmitted diseases. While the emphasis on prevention is understandable, it does not make sense to "other" the people who are portrayed as having sexually transmitted diseases. People with sexually transmitted diseases are part of

the population Planned Parenthood purports to serve. Being attentive to
this population further enhances prevention.

Thinking about and challenging stereotypical images do not come "naturally" to anyone; it is hard work. Many of the stereotypes discussed here
have a long history (Miles, 1989; Pieterse, 1990). It is important to make
ourselves aware of the various ways they appear in the present and the consequences they can have. The Planned Parenthood advertisements portray
sexualized images of exotic Others, drawing on myths and stereotypes that
must be challenged. The subtle implication that some groups are not worthy also needs to be questioned. I have suggested a process through which
stereotypes get perpetuated and reinforced without the need to claim a
conscious conspiracy of unfairness. Critiques like the one made here could
be made of other images in other contexts, with the goal of awareness.

ACKNOWLEDGMENT

The author would like to thank Tony Lemelle and Kendall Phillips for help
in conceptualization and Travis Altman for research assistance.

REFERENCES

Baker, S. (1961). *Visual persuasion: The effect of pictures on the subconscious.* New York:
McGraw-Hill.

Barlowe, J. (1998). The "not-free" and "not-me": Constructions of Whiteness in
Rosewood and *Ghosts of Mississippi. Canadian Review of American Studies, 28,* 31–
46.

Calás, M., & Smircich, L. (1991). Voicing seduction to silence leadership. *Organization Studies, 12*(4), 567–601.

Clark, D. (1993). Commodity lesbianism. In H. Abelove, M. Barale, & D. Halperin
(Eds.), *The lesbian and gay studies reader* (pp. 186–201). New York: Routledge.

Collins, P. H. (1990). *Black feminist thought: Knowledge, consciousness and the politics
of empowerment.* New York: Routledge.

Cortese, A. (1999). *Provocateur: Images of women and minorities in advertising.* New
York: Rowman & Littlefield.

Deetz, S., & Kersten, A. (1983). Critical models of interpretive research. In
L. Putnam & M. Pacanowsky (Eds.), *Communication and organizations: An interpretive approach* (pp. 147–171). Beverly Hills, CA: Sage.

Fujitomi, I., & Wong, D. (1973). The new Asian-American woman. In S. Stanley and
N. Wagner (Eds.), *Asian-Americans: Psychological perspectives* (pp. 252–263). Ben
Lomond, CA: Science and Behavior Books.

Gerster, C. (1995). Grappling with media images: Three films by Asian-American
women [Electronic version]. *Feminist Collections: A Quarterly Women's Studies
Resources, 16,* 9.

Giddings, P. (1984). *When and where I enter: The impact of Black women on race and sex in America.* New York: Bantam.

Grimes, D. (2001). Putting our own house in order: Whiteness and organizational change. *Journal of Organizational Change Management, 14,* 132–149.

Grimes, D. (2002a). "I dream a world": Re-imagining change. *TAMARA: The Journal of Critical Postmodern Organization Science, 1*(4), 13–28.

Grimes, D. (2002b). Challenging the status quo? Whiteness in the diversity management literature. *Management Communication Quarterly, 15,* 381–409.

Grimes, D., & Richard, O. (2003). Could communication perspective impact organizations' experience with diversity? *Journal of Business Communication, 40,* 7–27.

hooks, b. (1981). *Ain't I a woman: Black women and feminism.* Boston: South End Press.

hooks, b. (1990). *Yearning: Race, gender, and cultural politics.* Boston: South End Press.

hooks, b. (1992). *Black looks: Race and representation.* Boston: South End Press.

Jacobs, H. (1987). *Incidents in the life of a slave girl: Written by herself.* Cambridge, MA: Harvard University Press.

Lee, J. S., & Davie, W. (1997). Audience recall of AIDS PSAs among U.S. and international college students. *Journalism & Mass Communication Quarterly, 74,* 7–22.

Lye, J. (1997). *Critical reading: A guide.* Retrieved February 28, 2000, from Brock University, English Department Web site: http://www.brocku.ca.English/jlye/criticalreading.html.

Madison, K. (1999). Legitimation crisis and containment: The "anti-racist-White-hero" film. *Critical Studies in Mass Communication, 16,* 399–416.

Mason, M. (1994, March 3). Stamping out stereotypes. *Purdue Exponent,* 4.

Miles, R. (1989). *Racism.* New York: Routledge.

O'Barr, W. (1994). *Culture and the ad: Exploring otherness in the world of advertising.* Boulder, CO: Westview.

Pieterse, J. (1990). *White on Black: Images of Africa and Blacks in Western popular culture.* New Haven, CT: Yale University Press.

Pittam, J., & Gallois, C. (2000). Malevolence, stigma, and social distance: Maximizing intergroup differences in HIV/AIDS discourse. *Journal of Applied Communication Research, 28,* 24–43.

Qualter, T. (1991). *Advertising and democracy in the mass age.* New York: St. Martin's Press.

Rosen, M. (1985). Breakfast at Spiro's: Dramaturgy and dominance. *Journal of Management, 11*(2), 31–48.

Rosen, M. (1988). You asked for it: Christmas at the bosses' expense. *Journal of Management Studies, 25,* 463–480.

Shome, R. (1996). Race and popular cinema: The rhetorical strategies of Whiteness in the City of Joy. *Communication Quarterly, 44,* 502–518.

Tajima, R. (1989). Lotus Blossoms don't bleed: Images of Asian women. In Asian Women United of California (Eds.) *Making waves: An anthology of writing by and about Asian American women* (pp. 308–317). Boston: Beacon Press.

Takaki, R. (1990). *Iron cages: Race and culture in 19th-Century America.* New York: Oxford University Press.

Uchida, A. (1998). The orientalization of Asian women in America. *Women's Studies International Forum, 21,* 161–174.

White, H. (1987). *The content of the form: Narrative discourse and historical representation.* Baltimore: Johns Hopkins University Press.

Williams, P. (1997). *Seeing a color-blind future: The paradox of race.* New York: Noonday Press.

Chapter 18

Homoeroticism in Advertising: Something for Everyone With Androgyny

Gary Soldow
Baruch College, The City University of New York

From the perspective of advertisers, the gay audience is not to be ignored. With at least 15 million self-identified gays in the United States, it is estimated that they represent more than $485 billion in combined buying power (Bean, 2003).[1] Although this buying power does not necessarily mean that gays are more affluent than the general public, gay men may have greater disposable income, in part because they are far less likely to have children. Moreover, gays are twice as likely to have graduated from college, have an income over $60,000, and, even more surprisingly, are twice as likely to have an income over $250,000. More specifically, Wilke (1997a) indicated that over 28% of gay households have incomes greater than $50,000 and 21% have incomes over $100,000. In addition, industry sources indicate that homosexuals are extraordinarily loyal to brands that advertise to them (Bean, 2003). Establishing the actual size of the gay population is difficult, but a recent estimate suggests that from between 4% and 10% of the overall population is gay (Wilke, 1997b). Even at 4%, the consumption potential is substantial from a marketing perspective.[2]

Therefore, one obvious conclusion is that advertisers should market to the gay audience. In fact, marketers do target gays but much of that communication is limited to ads in the gay media such as *Out, The Advocate, Instinct,* and cable television and radio programming directed to gays. Difficulties with relying on gay-specific media are that not all gays are exposed to them and those that are may resent being reached with fringe

---

[1] It should be noted that most information that describes the gay market in terms of buying power does not make a distinction between gay men and lesbians.

[2] Critics and queer theorists, however, believe these figures do not represent gays with AIDS or gay men of color (Kates, 1999).

media. Whereas these publications have gained respectability and are not pornographic (Hicks, 2003), "gays are growing weary of being courted in secret. They want to be marketed to out in the open" (Wallace, 2003, p. 2).

This chapter explores the ways that some marketers target gay audiences with advertising in mainstream media by tracing the history of the use of men's bodies to appeal simultaneously to homosexual and heterosexual audiences. In both contemporary and past media forms, these appeals have been constructed in such a way that sexuality resides in the eye of the beholder. In other words, sex is used in a way that is attractive to both heterosexuals and gays, without offending either group. These "dual" appeals are accomplished with a deliberate use of attractive and androgynous male models who are erotic by virtue of their youthfulness, physical beauty, and scantily clad bodies.

Homoeroticism is very much a part of advertising in current mainstream media. It is made palatable, however, precisely through the use of androgyny. In effect, the gay–straight dichotomy, as exemplified by images in the Abercrombie & Fitch catalog, is not easily defined and labeled. Whether this middle ground reflects reality or is, in fact, an artifact of advertising is difficult to determine, but as will be shown an androgynous zone does exist in advertising.

The chapter begins with a discussion of homoeroticism and the complex issues surrounding its interpretation. This is followed by several examples as seen through an historical perspective and the broader cultural context in which homoeroticism is operative. To further illustrate these points, the chapter concludes with an analysis of the Christmas 2002 edition of the Abercrombie & Fitch catalog. Throughout the chapter, the discussion addresses the underlying question: Is homoeroticism in advertising acceptable to audiences who would, presumably, respond unfavorably to its frequent use?

HOMOEROTICISM

Homoeroticism is a complex concept because the distinction between eroticism and homoeroticism is a fine one. This often blurred distinction is evident historically when human beauty, particularly male beauty, is depicted as perfection—from ancient Greece to Fascist Germany to the present. Presumably, beauty as conveyed by perfection should appeal to all audiences. More important, such beauty is often associated with male homosexuality.

Meaning in the Eye of the Beholder

In a broad sense, it has been suggested that the consumption of style is a central feature of life, with objects of acquisition laden with meaning.

Indeed, the association between concrete objects and meaning is precisely what occurs (or is hoped will occur) through advertising (Ewen, 1988). One indication of successful advertising is whether the intended meaning of the product is consistent with the meaning received by the consumer. However, "consumers do not passively accept marketing communications but may actively renegotiate the meaning subjectively and construct their own interpretations" (Brownlie, Saren, & Wensley, 1999, pp. 113–114). Thus, in the case of homoeroticism, it can be argued that the message and subsequent meaning received and constructed may or may not be what the advertiser intended. The deliberate use of androgynous images in advertising becomes a desirable practice because the ambiguity allows receivers to interpret meanings they are comfortable with.

Androgyny and Eroticism

By definition, androgyny entails ambiguity in terms of masculine versus feminine. An androgynous person is said to express both male and female traits, including nurturance, compassion, tenderness, sensitivity, aggressiveness, leadership, and competitiveness (Pyke, 1980). In other words, androgyny entails traditional female traits coexisting with and counterbalanced by traditional male traits. In terms of traditional conceptions of sexuality, these countervailing forces result in a form of vagueness such that neither maleness nor femaleness predominates. Much personality work by Bem (1974, 1975, 1977) established a scale that measures androgyny—the Bem Sex Role Inventory—as well as the constructs of masculinity and femininity.

Androgynous models appearing in ads naturally lend themselves to greater personal interpretation. And, the interpretation is where androgyny and eroticism can coexist. Erotic visuals do, in fact, leave something to the imagination. It can be argued that use of commercial eroticism is socially acceptable if its use is mild or primarily aesthetic (Slade, 2000). With erotic representations, we see partially clothed bodies or bodies with certain parts strategically hidden from view. In many instances, through extreme close-ups or peculiar camera angles, body parts become almost unrecognizable and, hence, abstractions of the part they represent. These suggestive representations are distinct from pornography, which explicitly depicts nude models and actual sexual behavior (Slade, 2000). On the other hand, homoeroticism in advertising consists of sexually suggestive same-sex images. Because of its vague nature, a narrow range of homoeroticism is palatable to many audiences, particularly given that "the words used to describe homoerotic expression in the United States are varied, confusing, contradictory, and often derogatory" (Schwartz, 2002).

For some mainstream advertisers who wish to appeal to multiple audiences, the task is to appeal to gays in such a way that they interpret meaningful and pleasing images, while nongays perceive the same images as meaningful and pleasing. In other words, the tactic is to provide erotic stimulation that is simultaneously pleasing to gays and nongays. Such advertising may involve eroticism with a vague suggestion of a romantic theme or embedding it in a narrative (Geer, Judice, & Jackson, 1994; Quackenbush, Strassberg, & Turner, 1995), both of which, as will be discussed, are often employed in Abercrombie & Fitch catalogs.

Obviously, if advertisers restrict themselves to media that are intended for and used primarily by gays (e.g., *Out, The Advocate*), there is little likelihood of crossover readership and the need for visual androgyny is unnecessary. Thus, advertisers can maintain two distinct message strategies if they try to reach gays through gay media and gays through nongay media. There is evidence that advertisers are increasingly localizing their messages when attempting to appeal to gays. For instance, advertising revenue in gay print media has risen 36% (Wilke, 1997b). These advertisers include United Airlines, Subaru, Chase Manhattan, and Lotus, to name a few.

For the reasons previously suggested, however, it may be more effective to reach gays through mainstream media. Indeed, there is much evidence that gays are important consumers of these media, and it would be unwise to neglect appealing to gays because of their relative affluence and buying power. In addition, gays are a desirable audience given their interest in the arts. Far from being a stereotype, a comparison of gays to the general population found that gays are more arts centered. For example, they are more likely to go to the theater (71% vs. 21%), attend a classical music concert (39% vs. 8%), and see a dance performance (29% vs. 7%; Wilke, 1997a). The affinity for the arts, fashion, and design contributes to opinion leadership in these areas. One obvious attempt to capitalize on these trends is the Bravo Channel's reality show, *Queer Eye for the Straight Guy*. The concept for this program consists of five gay men who make over a straight male's living space and personal appearance because of their assumed expertise in fashion, design, and style.

Several advertisers have recognized the potential for the gay audience, and the practice of placing ads directed to gays in mainstream media is increasingly common. Occasionally, these ads contain an overt, but subtle, gay theme. For example, IKEA, a Swedish home furnishings retailer, was one of the first companies to use such advertising. The 1994 commercial showed a male couple shopping together for a dining room table. It is important to note, however, that ads like this one rarely contain any homoerotic sexual tension.

Another example of a similar approach appears in Fig. 18.1. This ad for the Ron Chereskin clothing brand appeared in 2003 in the *New York Times*

FIG. 18.1. A Ron Chereskin clothing ad that appeared in the *New York Times Magazine,* September 2003.

Magazine. The headline reads, "R you ready to adopt a new lifestyle?" The visual is of two blond men whose legs are touching and who are holding three blond infants. Apart from the touching of the legs, there is nothing particularly erotic about this visual, but it is clear that the union represents a nontraditional family with children. Particularly interesting about this family, however, is the androgynous nature of the two men. A careful viewer of this ad is likely to assume that the two males are in a homosexual relationship. Given that all of the family members are arguably beautiful models (as opposed to handsome), a less careful viewer of the ad, particularly one with a heterosexist frame, may perceive the two grownups as a man and a woman.

Of course, many ads exist in which androgyny is not operative and homoeroticism is strikingly obvious. Consider one such ad for American Express (see Fig. 18.2) that appeared in *New York Magazine.* In this ad, two men are positioned so that the older one on the right is staring longingly at a younger man on the left. It may be obvious that the man on the left is the other's object of desire. In addition, the younger man is leaning against an object in such a way than his left arm is draped over his genitals as if to call attention to them. One could safely infer that the younger man is encouraging the other one to engage in a sexual encounter.

For the purposes herein, the Chereskin ad is of greater interest. First, it involves what was recently referred to as "gay vague" advertising (Hamilton, 2000) since "same-sex innuendo" exists in the ad. Second, the ad contains male models who are both attractive—or, perhaps, even beautiful—and

FIG. 18.2. This ad for American Express recently appeared in *New York Magazine*.

androgynous. Third, it approaches what are referred to in the following section as "crossover models."

THE COMPLEX ISSUES SURROUNDING THE USE OF HOMOEROTICISM

As previously mentioned, advertisers use "crossover" male models and celebrities to appeal to gays. Not only do women find them attractive, but their beauty and androgyny also make them attractive to gays as well. One such example of a "crossover" celebrity is the Puerto Rican pop singer and teen idol Ricky Martin (Griffiths, 1999). In addition to having a successful recording career, Martin was the spokesperson for Puerto Rican Tourism and Pepsi Cola advertising directed at Hispanics.

Not only is Martin young and attractive, but also he is rumored to be gay and to have a gay following (Griffiths, 1999). While it is an empirical question, we can assume that rumors about Martin's sexuality are primarily circulated among gays. From the perspective of heterosexual males, Martin is adored by women and, thus, presumably heterosexual. It can certainly be assumed, however, that the rumors of his homosexuality are known beyond gays, and questions arise about the perceived meaning of his endorsements. Specifically, what meanings did gays give to products or services endorsed and, equally important, what meanings did nongays give to those same products or services?

Moreover, we can ask if Martin is handsome, beautiful, sexy, or androgynous. For gays, other men can be beautiful "in the way one spoke of beautiful women in the 1920's as Ziegfeld Girls . . . frequently tanned, defying age and gravity . . . a living object d'art—fatless, shaved, oiled . . . incapable of standing without striking a pose, the faces crowning these bodies of [full self-awareness of] their . . . supremacy over the rest of the earth" (Giles, 1997, p. 11). Or, as Paglia (1994) suggested in discussing the origins of homosexuality, "the beautiful person is something to be admired and put on a pedestal" (p. 6). Perhaps the only real way to answer the question posed about Martin is to allow that he is all of the above. The singer is handsome and sexy to heterosexual women, beautiful and sexy to gay men, and, for heterosexual men, a magnet for women. In a sense, Martin becomes "something for everyone."

More broadly, one can ask whether homoerotic imagery is erotic only to gays, or do gay men and heterosexual women have a similar response to such imagery? That both groups respond positively to Ricky Martin suggests that both genders do respond similarly to homoeroticism as a stimulus (Griffiths, 1999), although for women, the response is one linked to heterosexual desire. In terms of the fluidity of gender, however, women do not generally engage in male gaze behavior and voyeurism (van Zoonen, 1994).

Gender Role Identity

The response to homoeroticism may also, in part, be mediated by gender role identity. For example, one study reported that women with traditional gender role identities had less positive attitudes toward homoeroticism than men and less positive attitudes than women who were classified as nontraditional (DeSouza, 1995). Similarly, Theodore (2000) found that males who perceived themselves to be most at variance with cultural expectations regarding masculinity while also believing that acting like a man was very important, were most likely to be homophobic.

Further complications in gender role identity occur when we consider a new group of men labeled *metrosexuals* (Simpson, 2002; also see Flocker, 2003). Metrosexuals are urban, heterosexual males who are often mistaken for being gay although they are not disturbed by the inaccurate assumption. Indeed, apart from their heterosexual orientation, metrosexuals easily fit the gay stereotype of being interested in and concerned about fashion, style, and grooming. As such, they are attractive to both heterosexual women and homosexual men and report not being threatened by their attractiveness to the latter.

Gay men, despite their objection to nongays' reliance on gay stereotypes (Conley, Calhoun, Evett, & Devine, 2001), themselves have stereotypes of gay men as effeminate, androgynous, or unmasculine. Consequently, their erotic preference for masculinity is a function of "contempt and hostility toward effeminacy and effeminate men" (Taywaditep, 2001). Thus, gay men and straight men can be said to have an equally positive attitude about masculinity and an equally negative attitude about femininity relative to men.

Nonetheless, the perception of what masculinity means is becoming increasingly complicated (see Stern, 2003). Consider, for example, body hair, which is typically associated with masculinity. A recent phenomenon, however, is the absence of body hair among professional athletes as well as among men in male-oriented reality television shows such as *Survivor* (Dumenco, 2003, pp. 26–27). Shaving body hair was, until recently, something that gay men were more likely to do than straight men. That trend appears to be reversing, however, with straight males now more likely to have shaved bodies in these mediated displays. Dumenco (2003) pointed out that "denuding oneself is literally a form of infantilization. While many men have naturally smooth or sparsely haired chests, a bald crotch is a retreat, of sorts, to dewy youthfulness.... In that sense ... straights are once again following the gay lead: Gay men have always been pioneers of youth worship (p. 26)." That is, hairlessness is associated with youth and innocence, two features that gay men try to maintain in order to make themselves attractive to other men.

Body hair and its absence are indicators of the fluid nature of masculinity as well as the homogenization of perceptions of masculinity among gay and heterosexual males. Heterosexual men can be said to be embracing a form of androgyny among themselves. In so doing, they may unwittingly be making themselves more attractive to gay men. Again, we see a movement toward a middle realm of masculinity and sexuality such that concrete labels cannot be easily employed.

At this point, we can conclude two things: First, homoeroticism can appeal to many segments across the spectrum of sexuality, and second, homoeroticism can be employed in advertising with minimum offense. As such, referring to this trend as homoerotic advertising does not accurately represent what is occurring. Indeed, a more accurate characterization might be *androgynous marketing* that entails a multifaceted eroticism that includes homoeroticism. One of the hallmarks of androgynous marketing is the deliberate use of beautiful male models in the sense previously discussed.

The use of androgynous male beauties becomes even more reasonable if we consider the historical use of male beauty in classical art and Nazi propaganda. As well, we can see that when men are in the company of other men, there is a risk of inferring homosexual activity unless there is also a surrounding context such as preparation for war or sports.

THE CULTURAL CONTEXT FOR HOMOEROTICISM

The use of male representation as aesthetic object has a long history. In Platonic Greece, "they fix[ed] in marble perfectly proportioned bodies, whose symmetry excludes any disequilibrium... these bodies look immortal, completely sovereign in nature... bodies not fleeing dangers... running with no other purpose than to display their inner mastery" (Lingis, 1996, p. 177). A similar depiction of male perfection was emphasized during the Nazi regime in Germany.

Similar to the Greeks, the Nazis were interested in displaying physical perfection (Sontag, 1980). Indeed, "their nudes look like pictures in physique magazines: pinups which are both sanctimoniously asexual and (in a technical sense) pornographic, for they have the perfection of a fantasy" (Sontag, 1980, p. 93). Physique magazines of the 1950s and 1960s that Sontag is referring to were intended for gay men. They were smaller in dimension than most magazines and displayed male models mostly or completely nude in various athletic poses with minimal prose. Given the relatively hidden nature of homosexuality at the time, the magazines appeared appropriate for bodybuilders, but they were intended to provide homoerotic entertainment.

One example of the Nazis' use of physical perfection through homoeroticism may be found in the work of Leni Riefenstahl, an associate of Hitler and a well-known filmmaker during the Nazi era (e.g., *Triumph of the Will*). Sontag suggested that Riefenstahl, in a more recent film, *The Last of the Nuba*, continued her earlier Nazi tradition by depicting one other dimension of fascism: "a society in which women are merely breeders and helpers, excluded from all ceremonial functions, and represent a threat to the integrity and strength of men" (p. 90). What is particularly interesting about Sontag's critique of Riefenstahl is that the Nazi ideal Riefenstahl depicted comes amazingly close to what we see today in terms of androgynous males in various advertising contexts:

> They flow from (and justify) a preoccupation with situations of control, submissive behavior, extravagant effort, and the endurance of pain; they endorse two seemingly opposite states, egomania and servitude.... The Fascist dramaturgy centers on the orgiastic transactions between mighty forces and their puppets, uniformly garbed and shown in ever swelling numbers. Its choreography alternates between ceaseless motion and a congealed static, "virile" posing. Fascist art glorifies surrender, it exalts mindlessness, it glamorizes death. (1980, p. 91)

Fascism, which eschewed and severely punished homosexuality, may be seen as glorifying it through dissemination of male images that were asexual and masculine, and, at least according to Sontag, were nonetheless "prurient... with an ideal eroticism" (p. 93).

Hence, the depiction of males in this asexual manner appealed to both heterosexual and homosexual men simultaneously without either group being aware of the other's response. Like today, homoeroticism was carefully fashioned to appeal to people of all sexual orientations in a nonthreatening manner, even when men are in the company of other men. However, a group of men, absent women, can be suggestive of homosexuality. Depending on the context, however, images of groups of men are ripe for homoerotic interpretation. This is precisely the interpretation that can occur in masculine sporting activities such as football.

Football and other sports allow for a metaphor of oppression, resistance, and surrender according to postmodern gay and queer theories. That is, "competitive sport fosters the emotional logic that is embedded in the will to power produced by the mythical union of an ever-expanding phallus and territorially enclosing anus—these work together in sport in the desire to conquer the space of the other" (Pronger, 1999, p. 373). Pronger further suggested that both male and female athletes are sexually attractive "as a byproduct of the sport, not inherent in the activity itself. Athletic training builds taut muscular bodies... competitive sport is popularly understood to confer orthodox masculinity on the men who engage in it, or are simply fans of it" (p. 374). Yet, it should be noted that athletes who are young and masculine have been a central feature of gay erotica for at least the last 50 years (Pronger, 1990). Male sports figures can be simultaneously attractive to gay males and heterosexual females—van Zoonen's dismissal of the female gaze notwithstanding—as well as to heterosexual males in a nonsexual way.

By definition, male sporting activity allows heterosexual men to "exclude women and girls from their all-male environments, permits them to play with each other's bodies, to surround themselves with naked men in the showers and locker rooms, to enjoy that all-male contact without suffering the vilification that usually comes from the open acknowledgment and pursuit of masculine erotic contact, the stigma of 'being homosexual'" (Pronger, 1999, p. 373). These activities mirror the depictions in a Riefenstahl film, with males cavorting and touching as they simultaneously prepared for war. Once again, we discover that male homosexuals and male heterosexuals may enjoy the same depictions. Perhaps this "thing" is that earlier-mentioned, unidentifiable middle ground that is not amenable to concrete labels.

In addition, the idealized images produced during the Nazi era and more recently as by-products of professional sports have much in common with gay erotica attributed to Tom of Finland. These drawings, prevalent in the 1950s and 1960s, present distinctly different images than photographs in physique magazines. Instead, Tom of Finland's drawings presented the gay macho look (see Fig. 18.3). Of note is the exaggerated muscularity, with depiction of the pectoral muscles reminiscent of female breasts. And, the man who seems to be the sexual aggressor is in uniform. From a postmodern perspective, specifically derived from Michel Foucault, it may be argued that Tom of Finland's drawings presented a "multiplicity of power and [an] ambivalent interaction of resistance and oppression" (Lahti, 1998,

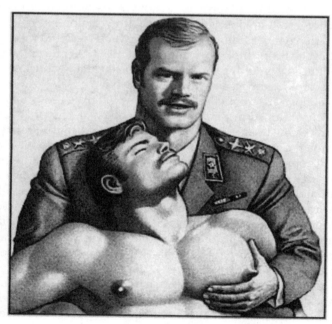

FIG. 18.3. A drawing from Tom of Finland.

p. 186). This resistance and oppression are a direct analog to anal penetration, as suggested by Pronger.

Overall, it is not being suggested here that most males are homosexual, but that many men can deal with and, perhaps, even appreciate homoerotic imagery that is emblematic of androgynous marketing—assuming that the context is appropriate and the homoerotic referents are subtle. In addition, responses to homoerotic imagery are further complicated because many acts of homosexual sex occur between people who do *not* identify themselves as gay (Herek, 2000).

THE ABERCROMBIE & FITCH CATALOG: THE ULTIMATE IN ANDROGYNOUS MARKETING

As an example of androgynous marketing, consider the Abercrombie & Fitch catalog. These catalogs have been reviled for several years by both family-centered and conservative groups as promoting sex among teenagers through pornography. Other people, however, have suggested that the images in the catalog are not pornographic: "In truth, . . . like much of [the photographer] Weber's work, the Abercrombie photos were too stylized—too improbable—to be much of a turn-on. They were not erotic so much as dreamy" (McGrath, 2004, p. 8). At the same time, it has been explicitly suggested that Weber is "synonymous with erotically charged depictions of good-looking young men . . . [the catalog has] pictures that might once have hung framed in the steamy underground meeting place for a Cult of the Beautiful Boy" (Muschamp, 1999). At one point, the company announced it would cease publication of its catalogs, but later decided to revise its look, keeping Weber as photographer.

These catalogs are compelling exemplars of androgynous marketing—homoeroticism framed in a context so as to be palatable for several audiences. Many of the images in the catalog consist of beautiful male models who are, for the most part, androgynous. These models, with a blond, northern European look, typically do not display any feminine characteristics, although no body hair is visible. Trim and well-proportioned, the models are not buffed-up, muscular men. As such, they are nonthreatening and attractive. Whereas they are frequently partially undressed, even suggestively so, their various stages of nakedness are not necessarily gratuitous. Merely, they are frolicking young boys who are touching each other to show camaraderie—behaviors reminiscent of those of young soldiers in Riefenstahl's *Triumph of the Will*.

The occasional presence of a woman in the catalog is also reminiscent of Riefenstahl's work because the catalogs do not depict a completely same-sex environment. These women are the equivalent of female cheerleaders at a college football game. Their presence removes homosexuality as a motive for the male interactions on the field, as queer theorists suggest. Nonetheless, homoeroticism lurks just beneath the surface.

In addition, the catalog presents a series of photographic vignettes or stories. Within these photo narratives, only the first names of the characters are used. The use of first names to depict the characters/models is suggestive of physique magazines from the 1950s and 1960s, in which nude men were posed to presumably deemphasize their sexuality, but with a posing strap to cover their genitals in order to remind the viewer that there was something there. In the catalogs, the stories do have an implied narrative with a hint of a romantic theme, perhaps because people are more responsive to eroticism with such a theme (Quackenbush et al., 1995).

The romantic hint notwithstanding, the stories are relatively plotless, usually involving two or more people and suggesting some minimal degree of tension in terms of two men competing for a single woman or possibly one man trying to win over another man. Pornographic films are equally plotless and have themes similar to those in the A&F catalog. Indeed, a distinction has been suggested between romantic films and pornographic films: The former "focus[es] on the establishment of personalized, exclusive relations—bonds of love," while the latter "focus[es] on anonymous desire" (Grodal, 2004, p. 26). The stories depicted in A&F catalogs appear to be closer to anonymous desire than to bonds of love.

It is interesting that, in the first third of the catalog, there are pictures of men and women together, primarily in a nonsexual manner. They are both frequently nude from the waist up, with no genitalia displayed. However, the men and the women are curiously similar in their seminude state. As previously mentioned, none of the men—or women for that matter—has any body hair. All the men and women are very beautiful, and all have a look of innocence. Even though the women have developed breasts, they also have a prepubescent look. The search for youth is certainly operative here.

Several images strongly suggest homoeroticism. For example, Fig. 18.4 displays a man with his hand circling his right nipple. His pose is emblematic of a female model and in this context is certainly suggestive of homoeroticism. Other photographs display males in ways similar to the physique magazines. In one, a male with long, blond-streaked hair is wrapped in Christmas ribbons, including one very large bow over his genitals. This Christmas "packaging" is provocative and resembles a pose more likely to be found in a magazine directed at homosexual males than a fashion retailer. In another photo, an attractive man is wearing only underwear with the words "Abercrombie & Fitch" stitched continually around the waistband, and with red reindeer over the remaining material. The result gives the underwear the appearance of children's clothing, thereby making the model far too innocent for any type of *sanctioned* desire.

FIG. 18.4. A homoerotic image in the Abercrombie & Fitch catalog.

The strongest hint of sexual activity appears in a photograph of a male model with his genitals covered by a nub on the tree branch that is strategically positioned where his penis would be. The result is a beautiful boy with an erection, but the erection is not really a part of him. Figure 18.5 shows two male models fully clothed, playing together on a bench. They almost appear to be wrestling, but Travis (on the left) really appears to be hugging Leif (on the right) since Travis has one arm around Leif's neck while also gently grasping his wrist. Leif's hand is touching Travis's knee. While this positioning has the appearance of sexual foreplay, the first order of meaning allows them to be touching since they are—at least minimally— engaged in the male sport of wrestling. Their facial expressions, however, suggest pure enjoyment and happiness, even ecstasy; no suggestion of competitiveness or aggression exists.

FIG. 18.5. An instance of playful wrestling?

DISCUSSION AND CONCLUSION

In fairness to Abercrombie & Fitch, even perhaps to Riefenstahl, it could be argued that what is really being presented is a world where sexuality and sexual orientation are fluid. While it seems that the majority of people identify themselves as either heterosexual or homosexual, their behaviors with respect to masculinity and femininity more likely occur in some middle ground of a broad continuum. As a result, their responses to erotic stimulation most likely occur in a similar middle ground.

It is clear that advertisers have for some time utilized erotic stimulation to woo consumers. And, it is also clear that homoeroticism, as a form of androgynous marketing, also is used to generate a response. Whether advertisers deliberately seek to utilize homoerotic appeals is likely a proprietary issue and, hence, not easily determined. What remains no mystery is that androgynous marketing is highlighted by the use of extremely attractive, beautiful models that is in keeping with the use of beautiful specimens of humanity from the beginning of Western civilization. As well, there is a great deal of evidence that there is something universal in what is considered to be beautiful.

However, once we rely on beautiful people as models, we find that the distinction between masculinity and femininity becomes very unclear. As well, the distinction between men and women becomes somewhat blurred. Thus, the advertiser is jumbling sexuality into an androgyny that allows one to interpret whatever meaning one chooses. These meanings will likely reflect the sexual preferences of the audience member. It can be inferred, then, that advertisers are either deliberately or unwittingly not segmenting their audiences in terms of sexuality and the audience's responses to eroticism.

Several additional issues emerge from this chapter. For one, people involved in creating advertising are part of the same culture that appears to respond positively to androgynous marketing. Thus, it may be that this advertising merely reflects what exists rather than a deliberate attempt to manipulate cultural norms. Of course, this notion is related to the central argument involving advertising as a reflection or a creation of society.

Still, there is that inclination to perceive beautiful men together as homosexual. This appears not to be the case when beautiful women are pictured together. Does the former change if a few women are included such that they are tokens or simple breeders, as was the case for the Nazis? Such depictions, of course, minimize women since it is a gross distortion of their actual societal roles. At the same time, if men are portrayed as sexual objects, they are also reduced to being sexual objects. If so, the case is further complicated as it has been argued that those being gazed upon as sexual objects are not diminished because they have power relative to the gazer (Paglia, 1998).

Perhaps the most important point to recognize is that, to the extent that advertising reflects reality, we may indeed be approaching a middle ground with respect to homosexual-heterosexual and masculine-feminine dichotomies. Accordingly, these labels may be increasingly less meaningful and correspond to an even greater acceptance of homosexuality. This movement toward the middle ground is consistent with what is happening with respect to racial labels. In light of the increasing number and variety of interracial marriages, our traditional labels for racial classification are also no longer reflective of reality. Indeed, we may be approaching ethnic neutrality wherein "ambiguity is chic" (LaFerla, 2003). A similar phenomenon may be occurring with respect to sexuality, a phenomenon that is reflected in androgynous marketing.

REFERENCES

Bean, L. (2003, September 2). Gay, lesbian buying power as gay rights issues take center stage. *DiversityInc.com*. Retrieved December 20, 2003, from http://www.diversityinc.com/ members/5528.cfm, p. 1.

Bem, S. L. (1974). The measurement of psychological androgyny. *Journal of Consulting and Clinical Psychology, 42*, 155–162.

Bem, S. L. (1975). Sex role adaptability: One consequence of psychological androgyny. *Journal of Personality and Social Psychology, 31*, 634–643.

Bem, S. L. (1977). On the utility of alternative procedures for assessing psychological androgyny. *Journal of Consulting and Clinical Psychology, 45*, 196–205.

Brownlie, D., Saren, M., & Wensley, R. (1999). *Rethinking marketing: Toward critical marketing accounting.* London: Sage.

Conley, T. D., Calhoun, C., Evett, S. R., & Devine, P. G. (2001). Mistakes that heterosexual people make when trying to appear non-prejudiced: The view from LGB people. *Journal of Homosexuality, 42*(2), 21–43.

DeSouza, R. (1995). Responses toward sexual stimuli in Brazil as a function of one's gender role identity and sex. *Revista Interamericana de Psicologia, 29*(1), 13–21.

Dumenco, S. (2003, September 29). Smooth operators. *New York Magazine,* 26–27.

Ewen, S. (1988). *All consuming images: The politics of style in contemporary culture.* New York: Basic Books.

Flocker, M. (2003). *The metrosexual guide to style.* Cambridge, MA: Da Capo Press.

Geer, J. H., Judice, S., & Jackson, S. (1994). Reading times for erotic material. *Journal of General Psychology, 121*(4), 345–352.

Giles, P. (1997). Better dead than ugly. *Harvard Gay and Lesbian Review, 4*(3), 11–16.

Griffiths, J. (1999, July 6). Ricky Martin cross appeal. Advocate.com. Retrieved December 20, 2003, from http://www.advocate.com/html/stories/0799A/0799_Martin_Michael.asp, p. 1.

Grodal, T. (2004). Love and desire in the cinema. *Cinema Journal, 43*(2), 26–47.

Hamilton, W. L. (2000, July 20). When intentions fall between the lines. *New York Times, 149*, F1–4.

Heer, J. (2001). POW! WHAM! PERMISSION DENIED. *Lingua Franca: The Review of Academic Life, 11*(2), 21–23.

Herek, G. M. (2000). Homosexuality. In A. E. Kazdin (Ed.), *Encyclopedia of psychology* (pp. 149–153). Washington, DC: American Psychological Association and Oxford University Press.

Hicks, G. R. (2003). Media at the margins: Homoerotic appeals to the gay and lesbian community. In T. Reichert and J. Lambiase (Eds.), *Sex in advertising: Perspectives on the erotic appeal* (pp. 229–246). Mahwah, NJ: Lawrence Erlbaum Associates.

Kates, S. (1999). Making the ad perfectly queer: Marketing "normality" to the gay men's community. *Journal of Advertising, 28*(1), 25–37.

LaFerla, R. (2003, December 28). Generation E.A.: Ethnically ambiguous. *New York Times,* sec. 9, p. 1.

Lahti, M. (1998). Dressing up in power: Tom of Finland and gay male body politics. *Journal of Homosexuality, 35*(3–4), 185–205.

Lingis, A. (1996). Beauty and lust. *Journal of Phenomenological Psychology, 27*(2), 174–193.

McGrath, C. (2004, January 4). Arrested developments: The way we live now. *New York Times,* sec. 6, p. 7.

Muschamp, H. (1999, November 14). Beefcake for the masses. *New York Times,* sec. 6, p. 36.

Paglia, C. (1994). Where gay boys come from. *Harvard Gay and Lesbian Review, 1*(2), 4–9.

Paglia, C. (1998, October 7). Enough with the male gaze. *Ask Camille,* Salon.com. Retrieved December 20, 2003, from http://archive.salon.com/it/col.pag1/1998/10/07/pag1.html, p. 1.

Pasko, L. (2002). Naked power: The practice of stripping as a confidence game. *Sexualities, 5*(1), 49–66.

Pronger, B. (1990). *The arena of masculinity: Sports, homosexuality and the meaning of sex.* New York: St. Martin's Press.

Pronger, B. (1999). Outta my endzone.*Journal of Sport and Social Issues, 23*(4), 373–390.

Pyke, S. W. (1980). Androgynous therapy. *Canada's Mental Health, 28*(1), 6–10.

Quackenbush, D. M., Strassberg, D. S., & Turner, C. W. (1995). Gender effects of romantic themes in erotica. *Archives of Sexual Behavior, 24*(1), 21–35.

Schwartz, M. E. (2002). Of uranians, homosexuals, queers and straight-acting men: Examining concepts of homoerotic expression among self-identified gay men using a grounded theory approach. *Dissertation Abstracts International: Section B: The Sciences and Engineering, 62*(11-B), 5433.

Simpson, M. (2002, July 22). Meet the metrosexual. Salon.com. Retrieved December 20, 2003, from http://salon.com/ent/feature/2002/07/22/metrosexual, p. 1.

Slade, J. W. (2000). *Pornography in America.* New York: ABC-Clio.

Sontag, S. (1980). Fascinating Fascism. In S. Sontag, *Under the sign of Saturn: Essays* (pp. 73–105). New York: Farrar, Straus & Giroux.

Stern, B. B. (2003). Masculinsim(s) and the male image: What does it mean to be a man? In T. Reichert and J. Lambiase (Eds.), *Sex in advertising: Perspectives on the erotic appeal* (pp. 215–228). Mahwah, NJ: Lawrence Erlbaum Associates.

Taywaditep, K. J. (2001). Marginalization among the marginalized: Gay men's anti-effeminacy attitudes. *Journal of Homosexuality, 42*(1), 1–28.

Theodore, P. S. (2000). Heterosexual masculinity and homophopia: A reaction to the self? *Journal of Homosexuality, 40*(2), 31–48.

van Zoonen, L. (1994). *Feminist media studies.* London: Sage.

Wallace, R. (2003, September 16). Does spending power buy cultural acceptance? Foxnews.com. Retrieved December 20, 2003, from http://www.foxnews.com/story/0,2933,97293,00. html, p. 2.

Wilke, M. (1997a, February 3). Data show affluence of gay market. *Advertising Age, 68,* 58.

Wilke, M. (1997b, October 6). Gay print media ad revenue up 36%. *Advertising Age, 68,* 26.

Chapter 19

Searching for Love and Sex: A Review and Analysis of Mainstream and Explicit Personal Ads

Larry Lance

University of North Carolina, Charlotte

Good looking, very interesting W/F, youngish 50, 5'8", 145 lbs., reddish-brown hair, big, brown eyes. Over educated, but don't take myself too seriously. Like to walk, travel, read, converse, laugh; enjoy classical and mountain music. Good values. Ready to meet humorous, honest, financially stable guy for romance.

Truly handsome, celebrity looks, 40, SWM, sophisticated, tall muscular, well-endowed, experienced, exceptional lover, passionate, clean, d&d free, seeks ... gorgeous voluptuous (not over-weight), very sexy uninhibited d&d free, baggage-free female, 25–45, who loves to wear sexy clothes, i.e. short skirts, high heels, who truly loves sex and other pleasures of life, i.e. fine dining, travel, stimulating conversation, to enjoy great times with their ultimate partner.

White male versatile seeking versatile cpls and single girls for oral sex and intercourse. Black couple OK.

Today, thousands of magazines, newspapers, Web sites, and chat rooms in societies around the world include a section where advertisers solicit responses from potential partners. Those who advertise and those who respond range from heterosexual to gay, from single to married, from teenagers to the elderly, and from those looking for marriage to those looking for casual sex or something more exotic. However, the most popular ads are prepared by heterosexual singles who claim to be in search of marriage-oriented relationships.

Personal ads in general, as well as those listed above and throughout this chapter, provide a convenient means for people to find and initiate romantic interactions, social affairs, and commitment-free sexual encounters. Furthermore, the Internet offers a convenient and readily accessible medium for personal ads. In an increasingly overscheduled and disconnected culture, people have limited opportunities for traditional courtship initiation: meeting face-to-face or being introduced by friends (or parents). In addition, personal ads provide individuals with the chance to prescreen prospective dates or sex partners while avoiding the awkwardness of face-to-face rejections (Woll & Young, 1989).

From a research perspective, this form of advertising offers a unique information source on female and male preferences as well as a view of an extremely public approach to interpersonal marketing (Deaux & Hanna, 1984; Harrison & Saeed, 1977). As a way of matchmaking, personal ads provide clues about what both the seeker and the sought-after value in regard to physical and personality characteristics. The chance that certain traits such as physical attractiveness, financial resources, commitment, social skills, or sexual techniques will be mentioned typically depends on an advertiser's gender (Bereczkei, Voros, Gal, & Bernath, 1997; Greenless & McGrew, 1994; Pawlowski & Dunbar, 1999; Pawlowski & Koziel, 2002; Wiederman, 1993). For the purposes of this chapter, advertiser refers to individuals who place personal ads.

For example, heterosexual males consistently mention attractiveness, beauty, and youth while females seek financial security. This difference is often referred to as the marriage gradient, which will be discussed in greater detail in the following section. The preference contrast between men and women is illustrated in two personals at the beginning of this chapter in which a "good-looking" female is ready to meet a "financially stable" man and a "sophisticated" man is seeking a "voluptuous (not overweight)" female who loves to wear sexy clothes. These personal ads reflect traditional gender-appropriate characteristics, men as success objects and women as sex objects (Davis, 1990; Montini & Ovrebro, 1990; Smith, Waldorf, & Trembath, 1990; Willis & Carlson, 1993). Whereas most personal ads suggest companionship and long-term commitment as goals, some ads focus exclusively on sexual relations. Not to be mistaken for mainstream personals, sexual preferences are often explicitly stated as the personal in which the male seeking "versatile cpls and single girls" demonstrates.

The following discussion reviews theory and research regarding mainstream personal ads placed by men and women in search of interpersonal relationships that could lead to love and long-term commitment. The second half of this chapter describes a formative analysis of sexually explicit personal ads placed by individuals in search of intimate sexual encounters.

THEORETICAL ORIENTATIONS

Evolutionary Orientation

Several theoretical orientations have been employed to explain the causes and variation in human sexual behavior, mating, and courtship (see Table 19.1). Two that are particularly relevant are the evolutionary and sociological orientations. Researchers who employ an evolutionary perspective propose two fundamental questions about the source of sexual behavior. One question pertains to how specific sexual behaviors come to exist. This question takes into account the genetic, biological, or psychological courses of given sexual behaviors. The second question seeks to discern why certain sexual behaviors exist. Overall, the assumption underlying the evolutionary orientation is that sexual behaviors exist and are maintained because they result in reproduction. Based on this perspective,

TABLE 19.1
Summary of Theoretical Orientations in Understanding Human Sexuality

Theoretical Orientation	Major Points
Evolutionary Orientation	Traces causes of contemporary sexual behavior back to distant ancestors.
	Maintains that sexual behaviors exist since they provided the cause of reproductive success in the past.
	Characteristics of contemporary females and males, along with courtship patterns, evolved since they led to reproductive success of their ancestors.
Psychoanalytic Orientation	A study of the history of the person instead of the history of our species.
	Places emphasis on early experience as a determinant of adult sexuality and personality.
Learning Orientation	Assumes most sexual behavior is learned.
	Applies principles of learning to the conditioning, maintenance, and elimination of sexual behaviors.
	Increases, reduces, or eliminates, the performance of sexual behaviors by manipulating the reinforcements for those particular behaviors.
Sociological Orientation	Attempts to explain how social institutions influence our sexual behavior.
	The power structure of society determines how male and female gender roles are defined.
	Sexual interaction is the result of scripts that are learned so completely that generally we are not aware of them.

contemporary sexual behavior can be traced back to reproductive behaviors believed to be present in early hunting and gathering societies.

Gender has emerged as a significant variation in human sexual behavior. An example would be the difference between females and males with respect to attitudes toward casual sex. In contrast to females, males have maintained considerably more permissive attitudes toward sexual intercourse between people in casual encounters. This finding is congruent with evolutionary-based predictions such that single mothers are less capable of providing for their offspring than are females who conceive within a committed relationship. On the other hand, the survival of men's genes is less at risk in the absence of romantic commitment. What males sacrifice in the survival of their offspring would be compensated by the larger number of offspring sired.

Taking into account the self-reported roles of men and women, one psychological researcher (McCormick, 1979, 1994) studied contemporary sexual behavior among college students. In this research, males reported employing more strategies to initiate sexual behavior than did females. On the other hand, females reported the implementation of more strategies to avoid or limit sexual behavior than did males.

Sociological Orientation

In contrast to those who adhere to the evolutionary or psychoanalytic orientations (see Table 19.1), most sociologists who study sexuality maintain that human sexual behavior is more easily understood by examining the socialization processes, cultural beliefs, and norms than by post hoc biological explanations or individual learning experiences. This perspective, referred to as the sociological orientation, is similar to the perspective taken by social learning theorists. However, while learning theorists emphasize socialization and conditionality of the individual, the broader perspective shared by sociologists considers the relationship between values and norms shared by members of a society to fully understand sexual interactions.

From the standpoint of social stability, groups seek to define proper behavior for a specific situation. Members of a society are provided with a set of social guidelines, or scripts, that can be adopted or altered to suit their purposes (Simon & Gagnon, 1986). Based on script theory, very little sexual interaction is spontaneous. Members of a culture share learned patterns that facilitate sexual interaction. Script theory suggests that scripts guide sexual behavior by providing participants with a program that names the actors and plots the sequence of events. At a dance, for example, when a male wishes to dance with a female, he will walk over to her and politely ask her to dance rather than yell across the floor or grab her by the arm.

EMPIRICAL STUDIES OF PERSONAL ADS DIRECTED TOWARD COURTSHIP

When searching for a partner through the personals, what characteristics are important for mate attraction? With little doubt, previous interpersonal studies have established that physical attractiveness is a highly valued attribute (Patzer, 1985; Hatfield & Sprecher, 1986; Woll, 1986). For example, the results of a "computer dance" study revealed that attractiveness was the only factor that determined if respondents liked their dates, wanted to date the person again, or would actually ask the person for another date (Hatfield, Aronson, Abrahams, & Rottmann, 1966). Another study reported that attractiveness had an ongoing influence on liking another person (Mathes, 1975).

Whereas physical attractiveness is valued by members of both sexes, previous research suggests that physical attractiveness is valued more in a partner by men than women. Women, on the other hand, are more likely to value financial security in partners. Requests and offers described in personal ads appear to coincide with the roles that males and females generally convey in dating. For example, in personal ads men have been found to request attractiveness in a partner and offer financial security while women tend to offer attractiveness and request a partner who is financially secure (Buss et al., 1990; Cameron, Oskamp, & Sparks, 1977; Deaux & Hanna, 1984, Hirschman, 1987; Koestner & Wheeler, 1988; Smith, Waldorf, & Trembath, 1990).

The emphasis on females seeking males who offer financial security, and males seeking females who offer attractiveness, is known as the "marriage gradient" (Willis & Carlson, 1993). Studies that examine the marriage gradient also emphasize trade-offs. For example, research indicates that individuals commodify personal characteristics such as occupation, education, attractiveness, age, personality, and wealth. As mentioned, males are more likely to offer financial security in exchange for attractiveness (Cicerello & Sheehan, 1995; Davis, 1990; Goode, 1996b; South, 1991; Wiederman, 1993). While some individuals make absolute requests such as age or attractiveness requirements, others consider a package of characteristics with the idea that less desirable characteristics are balanced by desirable characteristics.

Support for the gradient has been found in several studies. For example, males placing personal ads in a Canadian newspaper were most interested in females who were physically attractive and younger (Zhon & Abdullah, 1995). Females placing personal ads were most interested in older males with established careers. Based on the concept of trade-offs, research indicates that males emphasize physical attractiveness when searching for a mate more than do females. An analysis of a video-dating service indicated

TABLE 19.2

Most Commonly Mentioned Characteristics Sought in Potential Partners in Personal Ads in American Newspapers and Magazines

Sample		
Metropolitan Newspaper	Leisure Magazine	Singles Magazine
	Males Seek in Women	
Personality	Personality	Personality
Good looks	Good looks	Good looks
Slim & trim	Professional/College Degree	Non-smoker
Professional/College Degree	Slim & Trim	
Non-smoker		
	Females Seek in Men	
Personality	Personality	Personality
Professional/College Degree	Financially secure	Non-smoker
Good looks	Professional/College Degree	Professional/College Degree
Non-smoker	Good looks	Good looks
Tall, slim, & trim	Must like children	Spiritual

Note. Based on U.S. sample from Lance's (1998) content analysis. Characteristics ranked in order from most mentioned to least mentioned.

that attractive females were more apt to be asked for dates (Stock, 1996). Another study found that males were more likely to respond to personal ads placed by attractive females of lower socioeconomic status than to ads placed by average-looking female professionals (Goode, 1996b).

A recent content analysis of personal ads suggests some variation on the marriage gradient (Lance, 1998). The findings indicate that personality traits such as a sense of humor, kindness, honesty, and intelligence were very important traits listed by both women and men when seeking a future partner (see Table 19.2). Overall, females and males both listed personality characteristics more often than either physical attractiveness or financial security. One possible reason for the pattern of findings is that females have become more professionally oriented, which could result in a reduction in the perceived need for a mate who provides financial security. Another factor may be the increase in the age people get married, which might amplify the value of personality and decrease the value of outward appearance. Also, since females and males are living longer now than in the past, good looks gradually decline with advanced aging while personality traits remain relatively constant. Another intriguing finding was an apparent emphasis on smoking habits of potential partners (Lance, 1998). Both men and women listed nonsmoking as one of the top-five desired characteristics in a potential partner. Concern with smoking may be the result of public acknowledgment of the hazards of smoking.

Gay Personals

Analyses of gay male personal ads reveal that descriptions of one's own body and physical characteristics are most prevalent as well as the advertiser's age (Bartholome, Tewksbury, & Bruzzone, 2000). Similarly, another analysis found physical attractiveness to be regarded as a high priority in potential partners (Hatala & Predhodka, 1996). The content of gay personal ads frequently included height, weight, hair length and/or color, eye color, and the possession or absence of facial and body hair (see Soldow, this volume). Personal ads placed by gay males also included specific descriptions of male genitalia and sexual activity (Bartholome et al., 2000). Overall, personal ads by gay males appear to be more sexualized than personal ads of females or heterosexual males. When considering statements of desired sexual behaviors by gay males, oral sex was most frequently mentioned.

Besides physical characteristics and sexual content, the HIV status of males seeking males in personal ads was often mentioned. One study analyzing personal ads of gay males between 1986 and 1993 found a sixfold increase in the reporting of HIV status (Hamers, Bueller, & Peterman, 1997). In comparison, only about 10% of personal ads placed by gay males between 1985 and 1996 referred to safe-sex issues (Smith, 2000). In addition, Smith found no association between the personal characteristics of gay men with ads that do and do not mention safe sex. A study assessing gay male Internet ads and traditional personal ads found ads on the Internet to be more sexually explicit and little evidence of a connection between preferences for unprotected sex and an active quest for HIV infection (Tewksbury, 2003).

Race and Personals

Regarding sexual orientation and race, a recent study examined 2,400 Internet personal ads placed by males (Phua & Kaufman, 2003). Considering the advertiser's desire for a partner of a specific race and the influence of the advertiser's race and sexual orientation, Phua and Kaufman found that Black, Hispanic, and Asian men are more inclined than White men to indicate a race preference. Furthermore, gay males were more inclined to mention race than straight males. However, gay Black and Hispanic males were less apt to have a race preference. Phua and Kaufman concluded that race is an important factor in male mate selection.

Because White males are less likely to mention a race preference than are minorities, it appears that minority males are more sensitive to race than White males, perhaps as a result of their experience as minorities. Furthermore, Phua and Kaufman (2003) suggested that minorities' racial preferences reflect racial hierarchy. Most males who place personal ads prefer their own race or Whites, and least prefer Blacks, regardless of sexual orientation, although some exceptions existed.

EXPLICIT PERSONAL ADS: AN INFORMAL ANALYSIS

It has been established that people are increasingly turning to personal ads when searching for romance and long-term commitments. The same can be said of people seeking short-term sexual encounters. People obviously continue to rely on traditional means of meeting people for casual sex (e.g., singles bars and nightclubs). However, individuals have the option of placing or responding to personal ads in specialized magazines designed to facilitate sexual encounters. These magazines are referred to by various names such as "contact magazines," "swingers magazines," and "couples magazines." Unlike publications that feature mainstream personals, these magazines are relatively expensive, costing up to $10 an issue, and are found in adult bookstores arranged under titles such as "swingers" and "bondage."

Surprisingly, contact magazines are not a recent phenomenon. As far back as the 18th century, addresses of "easy women" were available in Britain. In the 1800s, mainstream newspapers and magazines in Britain published thinly disguised ads for sex as well as "ladies directories." In some cases, these directories contained listings for prostitutes, often detailing names, addresses, prices, and specialties. Eventually, these directories were printed separately and often had a pocket in the back to hold condoms.

Contemporary contact magazines in the United States emerged as a result of increased societal permissiveness. They first appeared in the mid-1950s, with the publication of a swingers' paper titled *La Plume*. Currently, *Screw* is the most popularly explicit contact magazine in the United States. In Britain, *Lovely* and *His and Hers* are popular equivalents to *Screw*. Containing some legal risk, the circulation of contact magazines is generally restricted to subscribers.

Overall, the circulation of these magazines is relatively small, as most people in Western societies disapprove of extramarital relationships in any form (Wiederman, 1997). Despite their disapproval, a recent investigation revealed that approximately 25% of males and 16% of females reported having extramarital affairs (Laumann, Gagnon, Michael, & Michaels, 1994). Similarly, a sample of the U.S. populace indicated that 21% of males and 13% of females reported having extramarital affairs (Smith, 1991). Swinging, on the other hand, is less common than extramarital sex involving deception. Swinging involves couples who engage in recreational sex with relative strangers (other couples or singles) with whom no future involvement is anticipated—except, perhaps, future sexual activity. Swinging also can involve mate exchange or mate swapping, in which two or more couples switch partners for purposes of sexual or emotional intercourse.

The Magazines

For this informal investigation, two contact magazines were selected from the "swingers" shelf at an adult bookstore located in the southeastern United States. The magazines, priced at $5 and $6, were selected from approximately 15 contact magazines individually sealed in plastic. According to the publications, both contained personal ads that provide a relatively discreet means of introduction and communication for active, fun-loving people who share mutual desires. Also according to the magazines, personal ads can help people expand their circle of friends to include warm, congenial people who can provide a new world of pleasurable activities.

As with most publications that feature mainstream personals, both magazines charged a fee for placing an ad. One magazine charged 20 cents a word per issue. Only single men were required to pay for their ads; including a $5 photo charge. In the other magazine, the charge for single males was $3. Ads were free for single women and couples who sent photos. One of the magazines contained 173 pages of ads, the other 62.

In addition, the two magazines differed in the way that interested readers responded to ads. In one magazine, advertisers were assigned code numbers that represented the only way they could be identified for contacts. In this case, a person answering an ad would send a letter to the magazine. The fee to contact someone was $2 for subscribers. The other magazine operated a similar system, except that advertisers could include phone numbers in their ads for more immediate and personal responses.

In spite of the purpose of these magazines, one placed certain restrictions on ads. For example, the editor refused to publish any ad that referred to animal training, bondage and discipline, or sadomasochism. In addition, photos could not contain images of bondage, animals, penetration, intercourse, masturbation, or a penis. The second magazine contained no such restrictions. The difference may be because the first magazine is available by subscription while the second is available only over the counter. Federal regulations on mailed material are more restrictive than material available only in an adult retail shop.

The Advertisers

A look at the social and demographic characteristics of advertisers revealed some interesting findings (see Table 19.3 for exemplars of common ads). In

TABLE 19.3

Personal Ads in Sexually Explicit Contact Magazines

Prototypical personal ads:
1. Interested in White couples to watch and be watched. Some photos and movies if all agree. She 34, 5'5", 125, 36-26-36. He 6'4", 240, 34.
2. White couple, 36, both in very good shape. Love beach, nudism, all sex except S/M, B&D.
3. White couple, mid 30's, very attractive. She 5'2", 110, 34-25-35; he 6', 200. Would like to meet broad minded couples.
4. Attractive Cauc. Couple, early 30's seek other Cauc. cpls., females. Wife Bi and safe, husband well built. No S/M, B&D or drugs.

Examples of preference variations in personal ads:
5. Attractive couple seeks other swinging couples and single males and females for fun and games. No far-outs or B&D. Enjoy French. He 36, 6' 185 and well endowed. She 35, 5'5", 130, 36-25-35.
6. Attractive young submissive, 24 female seeking dominant male master who wants a willing sex slave.
7. Cauc. Male, 35, 5'11", 150 nice looking seeks married ladies, also cpls. for 3-somes.
8. Couple, AC-DC, looking for well endowed males to give French and Greek lessons to us. Age and color second to size.

both magazines, for instance, Caucasian was the most prevalent race for those who placed ads. Regarding age, it appeared that the most prevalent group was people in their 30s, with people in their 20s and 40s a distant second. In addition, ads were most commonly placed by couples, followed by ads placed by men. As the examples in Table 19.3 demonstrate, these couples generally sought other couples, although some sought bisexual males or females.

In many cases, ads were accompanied by photographs. These images primarily featured women and men in various stages of undress. Some photos showed women with garter belts and fishnet hose, and some showed men and women in bathing suits, but most photos showed men and women fully unclothed. Only a few images consisted of face-only shots. Most photos showed bodies posed in a variety of positions.

Ads placed in these contact magazines represented a wide range of interests. The first example in Table 19.3 is a couple in their 30s seeking other couples for swinging, exchanging partners, or single males and females for threesome sexual activities. This couple does not want bondage (restraint in all of its forms) or discipline (disciplinary actions ranging from mild spankings to painful beatings). This couple does, however, enjoy French sex (oral–genital activities). The second example in the bottom half of Table 19.3 was placed by an "attractive" young female looking for a male for bondage and discipline. The last example was placed by an AC–DC couple (bisexuals or individuals who have sex with either gender) who is looking for well-endowed males for French or Greek sex (anal intercourse). As the couple indicates, both age and race of the male are secondary to penis size.

Last, perhaps because contact magazines can be regionalized, most ads were placed by people on the East Coast. For example, over 41.5 pages of personals were placed by people in New York, New Jersey, and Pennsylvania. People in Florida had a presence in both magazines with over 18.5 total pages. The prevalence of Floridian ads may be the result of the state's attraction as a vacation destination. A reading of the Florida ads suggests they are aware that visitors may want to meet like-minded others when in the area.

A Swingers Club

In an attempt to discern the relative popularity of swinging in one southeastern metropolitan area, the author contacted the director of the Social Swing Club. According to this person, the club has been in existence locally for 7 years and boasts over 250 members from six states. Meetings consist of private parties held in ballrooms of big hotels on Saturday nights. Averaging 40 to 50 people, the meetings usually last until 1 or 2 o'clock in the morning. A primary purpose of these parties is for members to meet and socialize. If a couple becomes sexually interested in another couple they met at the party, arrangements are made to meet at a mutually agreed-upon time.

Ads for membership in the swinging club are placed in the local newspaper, which attracts about 5,000 responses annually. Only a few applicants are successfully admitted as relatively stringent membership requirements exist. For example, members cannot be over- or underweight. Business and professional types at least 18 years old, but generally not over 40, are preferred. An age estimate suggests that men average about 32 years old and women about 27.

Asked about the sexually explicit swinging magazines, the director was dismissive. In his opinion, contact magazines cheapen the swinging lifestyle. He maintained that the majority of people pictured in the ads are unattractive and that a large proportion of the females who advertise are prostitutes. In contrast to ads in the swingers magazines, the director asserted that members of his swinging club are both higher class and more physically attractive. In addition, the director indicated that his members typically have very strong marriages but prefer some added excitement in their lives. They prefer swinging together to affairs or open marriages. Last, the director maintained that couples who choose to swing have such stable marriages that the experience tends to strengthen instead of weaken their relationships.

SUMMARY

As text-based relational conduits, personal ads are a rich source of archival data. Over the past 25 years, researchers have mined this data with content analyses to investigate what people are willing to disclose about themselves and what characteristics they value in others. Findings from early research demonstrated that people tend to make requests congruent with the marriage gradient and gender-role stereotypes. To illustrate, females are more apt to express interest in the financial security and resources of a prospective male while males are more inclined to search for attractive partners with whom they can engage in sex. More recent research has expanded to compare the ad specifications of heterosexuals and homosexuals (Gonzales & Meyers, 1993). A general conclusion from this research is that gender appears to have a larger influence on ad specifications than sexual orientation (Hatala & Prehodka, 1996).

In addition to mainstream personal ads, individuals also use ads to search for willing sex partners. In contrast to relationship personals, sex ads almost always indicate physical characteristics desired by both parties. Generally, contact magazines appear to be a way for people to seek short-term sexual partners. It is doubtful that people in relatively stable relationships who seriously consider swinging would advertise in these magazines. On the other hand, swinging clubs may represent a more reliable means of meeting those with similar interests.

REFERENCES

Bartholome, A., Tewksbury, R., & Bruzzone (2000). I want a man: Patterns of attraction in all-male personal ads. *Journal of Men's Studies, 8*(3), 309–321.

Bereczkei, T., Voros, S., Gal, A., & Bernath, L. (1997). Resources, attractiveness, family commitment; reproductive decisions in human mate choice. *Ethnology, 103*, 681–699.

Bolig, R., Stein, P. J., & McHenry, P. C. (1984). The self-advertisement approach. *Family Relations, 33*(4), 587–592.

Buss, D. M., Abbott, M., Angleitner, A., Asherian, A., Biaggio, A., Blancovillasenor, A., Bruchonschweitzer, M., Chu, H. Y., Czapinski, J., Deraad, B., Ekehammar, B., Ellohamy, N., Fioravanti, M., Georgas, J., Gjerde, P., Guttman, R., Hazan, F., Iwawaki, S., Janakiramaiah, N., Khosroshani, F., Kreitler, S., Lachenicht, L., Lee, M., Lik, K., Little, B., Mika, S., Moadelshahid, M., Moane, G., Montero, M., Mundycastle, A. C., Niit, T., Nsenduluka, E., Pienkowski, R., Pirttilabackman, A. M., Deleon, J. P., Rousseau, J., Runco, M. A., Safir, M. P., Samuels, C., Sanitioso, R., Serpell, R., Smid, N., Spencer, C., Tadinac, M., Todorova, E. N., Troland, K., Vandenbrande, L., Vanheck, G., Vanlangenhove, L., & Yang, K. S. (1990).

International preferences in selecting mates: A study of 37 cultures. *Journal of Cross Cultural Psychology, 21,* 5–47.

Cameron, C., Oskamp, S., & Sparks, W. (1977). Courtship American style: Newspaper ads. *Family Coordinator, 26,* 27–30.

Cicerello, A., & Sheehan, E. (1995). Personal advertisements: A content analysis. *Journal of Social Behavior and Personality, 10,* 751–756.

Davis, S. (1990). Men as success objects and women as sex objects: A study of personal advertisements. *Sex Roles, 23,* 43–50.

Deaux, K., & Hanna, R. (1984). Courtship in the personals column: The influence of gender and sexual orientation. *Sex Roles, 11,* 363–375.

Gonzales, M. H., & Meyers, S. A. (1993). Your mother would like me: Self-presentation in the personal ads of heterosexual and homosexual men and women. *Personality and Social Psychology Bulletin, 19,* 131–142.

Goode, E. (1996a). The ethics of deception in social research: A case study. *Qualitative Sociology, 19,* 11–33.

Goode, E. (1996b). Gender and courtship entitlement: Responses to personal ads. *Sex Roles, 34,* 141–170.

Goode, E. (1998). Photographs as sexual advertisements: Responses to personal ads. *Sociological Focus, 31*(4), 373–389.

Greenless, I., & McGrew, W. (1994). Sex and age differences in preferences and tactics of mate attraction: Analysis of published advertisements. *Ethology and Sociology, 15,* 59–72.

Hamers, F., Bueller, H., & Peterman, T. (1997). Communication of HIV serostatus between potential sex partners in personal ads. *AIDS Education and Prevention, 9*(1), 42–48.

Harrison, A. A., & Saeed, L. (1977). Let's make a deal: An analysis of revelative and stipulations in lonely hearts advertisements. *Journal of Personality and Social Psychology, 35,* 257–264.

Hatala, M. N., & Prehodka, J. (1996). A content analysis of gay male and lesbian personal advertisements. *Psychological Reports, 78,* 371–374.

Hatfield, E., Aronson, V., Abrahams, D., & Rottmann, L. (1966). Importance of physical attractiveness in dating behavior. *Journal of Personality and Social Psychology, 4,* 508–516.

Hatfield, E., & Sprecher, S. (1986). Mirror, mirror...the importance of looks in everyday life. Albany: State University of New York Press.

Hirschman, E. C. (1987). People as products: Analysis of a complex marketing exchange. *Journal of Marketing, 51,* 98–108.

Koestner, R., & Wheeler, L. (1988). Self-presentation in personal advertisements: The influence of implicit notions of attraction and role expectations. *Journal of Personal Relationships, 5,* 149–160.

Lance, L. (1998). Gender differences in heterosexual dating: A content analysis of personal ads. *Journal of Men's Studies, 6,* 297–305.

Laumann, E. O., Gagnon, J. H., Michael, R. T., & Michaels, S. (1994). *The social organization of sexuality: Sexual practices in the United States.* Chicago: University of Chicago Press.

Lynn, M., & Bolig, R. (1985). Personal advertisements: Sources of data about relationships. *Journal of Social and Personal Relationships, 2*, 377–383.

Mathes, E. W. (1975). The effects of physical attractiveness and anxiety on heterosexual attraction over a series of five encounters. *Journal of Marriage and the Family, 37*, 769–773.

McCormick, N. (1979). Come-ons and put-offs: Unmarried students' strategies for having and avoiding sexual intercourse. *Psychology of Women Quarterly, 4*, 194–211.

McCormick, N. (1994). *Sexual salvation*. Westport, CT: Greenwood.

Montini, T., & Ovrebo, B. (1990). Personal relationship ads: An informal balancing act. *Sociological Perspectives, 33*, 327–339.

Patzer, G. L. (1985). *The physical attractiveness phenomena*. New York: Plenum.

Pawlowski, B., & Dunbar, R. (1999). Withholding age as putative deception in mate search tactics. *Evolution and Human Behavior, 20*, 53–69.

Pawlowski, B., & Koziel, S. (2002). The impact of traits offered in personal advertisements on response rates. *Evolution and Human Behavior, 23*, 139–149.

Phua, V., & Kaufman, G. (2003). The crossroads and sexuality: Date selection among men in Internet "personal" ads. *Journal of Family Issues, 24*(8), 981–994.

Sergios, P., & Cody, J. (1985). Physical attractiveness and social assertiveness skill in male homosexual dating behavior and partner selection. *Journal of Social Psychology, 125*, 505–514.

Simon, W., & Gagnon, J. H. (1986). Sexual scripts: Permanence and change. *Archives of Sexual Behavior, 15*(2), 97–120.

Smith, A. (2000). Safety in gay men's personal ads, 1985–1996. *Journal of Homosexuality, 39*(1), 43–48.

Smith, J., Waldorf, V., & Trembath, D. (1990). "Single white male looking for thin, very attractive . . ." *Sex Roles, 23*, 675–685.

Smith, T. (1991). Adult sexual behavior in 1989: Number of partners, frequency of intercourse, and risk of AIDS. *Family Planning Perspectives, 23*, 102–107.

Soldow, G. (this volume). Homoeroticism in advertising: Something for everyone with androgyny. In T. Reichert & J. Lambiase (Eds.), *Sex in consumer culture: The erotic content of media and marketing*. Mahwah, NJ: Lawrence Erlbaum Associates.

South, S. (1991). Sociodemographic differentials in mate selection preferences. *Journal of Marriage and the Family, 53*, 928–940.

Stock, S. (1996). The effect of physical attractiveness on video dating outcomes. *Sociological Focus, 29*, 83–85.

Tewksbury, R. (2003). Bareback sex and the quest for HIV: Assessing the relationship in Internet personal advertisements of men who have sex with men. *Deviant Behavior, 24*, 467–482.

Waynforth, D., & Dunbar, R. (1995). Conditional mate choice strategies in humans: Evidence from "lonely hearts" advertisements. *Behavior, 132*, 755–779.

Wiederman, M. W. (1993). Demographic and sexual characteristics of nonresponders to sexual experience items in a national survey. *Journal of Sex Research, 30*, 27–35.

Wiederman, M. W. (1997). Pretending orgasm during sexual intercourse: Correlates in a sample of young adult women. *Journal of Sex and Marital Therapy, 23,* 131–139.

Willis, F., & Carlson, J. R. (1993). Singles ads. *Sex roles, 29,* 387–404.

Woll, S. (1986). So many to choose from: Decision strategies in videodating. *Journal of Social and Personal Relationships, 3,* 43–52.

Woll, S., & Young, P. (1989). Looking for Mr. or Ms. right: Self-presentation in videodating. *Journal of Marriage and the Family, 51,* 483–488.

Zhon, N., & Abdullah, Z. (1995). Canadian matchmaker advertisements: The more things change, the more they remain the same. *International Journal of Advertising, 14,* 334–348.

Author Index

Laumann, E. O., 344, *349*
Lavine, H., 108, *121*
Lee, J., 111, *122*, 284, 285, *298*
Lee, J. S., 315, *317*
Lee, M., 341, *348*
Lee, S., 161, *176*
Leidner, R., 248, *260*
Leslie, L., 33, *48*
Levine-Donnerstein, D., 19, *29*, 288, *298*
Levinson, J. C., 248, *261*
Lewis, L. A., 34, 39, 45, *49*
Li, H., 281, *297*
Licata, J., 283, *297*
Lik, K., 341, *348*
Lillie, J. J. M., 264, 265, 269, *279*
Lin, C. A., 26, *29*, 127, 129, 134, *138*, *139*, 142, 152, *156*
Lingis, A., 327, *335*
Linsangan, R., 16, *29*, 57, *63*, 129, *138*
Linz, D., 59, *64*, 111, *120*
Lipman, J., 166, *176*
Lippert, B., 184, *197*
Lippke, R. L., 221, *240*
Lister, M., *240*
Little, B., 341, *348*
Lockeretz, S. W., 110, *120*
Loeb, M., 70, *85*
Long, E. C. J., 35, 38, *50*
Longmore, M. A., *261*
Longo, L., 246, 247, *260*
Lottes, I., 59, *62*
Lovdal, L. T., 127, *139*, 287, *297*
Lowry, D. T., 16, *30*, 111, *122*, 126, *139*
Lull, J., 37, *50*
Lundren, S. R., 247, *260*
Lye, J., 303, *317*
Lynn, M., *350*

M

MacIan, P., 27, *29*
MacInnis, D. J., 179, 181, 184, *197*
Madison, K., 303, *317*
Makhijani, M. G., 247, *260*
Malamuth, N., 52, *64*
Malkin, A. R., 69, 72, 74, 79, *85*
Maly, K. R., 34, *50*
Marcus, D. K., 247, *261*
Marin, B., 108, *121*
Marin, G., 108, *121*
Marshall, G., 224, 225, *241*

Marshall, J. C., 248, *261*
Martzke, R., 96, *104*
Mason, M., 312, *317*
Mastro, D. E., 111, *121*, *122*, 282, *297*
Mathes, E. W., 341, *350*
Mayes, S., 294, *296*
Mayo, C. M. 110, *122*
McArthur, L. Z., 113, *121*, 127, *139*
McCarthy, M., 167, 169, 174, *176*
McCauley, E. A., 223, *240*
McCormick, N., 340, *350*
McCracken, G., 181, *197*, 277, *279*
McDonagh, P., 181, 195, *197*, 236, 237, *239*
McDonald, H., 207, *216*
McElroy, J. C., 247, 259, *261*
McElroy, W., 201, *216*
McGrath, C., 330, *335*
McGrew, W., 338, *349*
McHenry, P. C., *348*
McKee, K. B., 33, *49*
McKelvey, K., 163, 165, *176*
McLaughlin, T., 283, *297*
McLeod, D., 26, *30*, 35, 36, *50*, 69, *86*, 110, *122*, 287, *298*
McNair, B., 34, *49*, 201, *216*
Medoff, N. J., 143, *156*
Mehaffy, M., 283, *298*
Merskin, D., 285, *298*
Messaris, P., 181, *197*
Messineo, M., 26, *29*, 282, 284, 285, 286, 288, *296*
Metts, S., 248, 259, *261*
Meyer, T., 111, *120*
Meyers, S. A., 348, *349*
Michael, R. T., 344, *349*
Michaels, S., 344, *349*
Mika, S., 341, *348*
Miklitsch, R., 222, *241*
Miles, R., 302, 316, *317*
Miller, B., 248, *261*
Miller, R. S., 247, *261*
Mirzoeff, N., 220, 229, *241*
Mnookin, S., 70, *85*
Moadelshahid, M., 341, *348*
Moane, G., 341, *348*
Money, J., 265, 267, *279*
Montero, M., 341, *348*
Montini, T., 338, *350*
Moore, K., 294, *298*
Morgan, M., 282, 294, *297*

Subject Index